LATELY I'VE BEEN THINKING

LATELY I'VE BEEN THINKING

Powerful ¶ Posts for an Awesome Life

By SONDRA RAY

Immortal Ray Productions

Nashville   Washington D.C.

OTHER BOOKS BY SONDRA RAY

- ❖ Rebirthing in the New Age
- ❖ I Deserve Love
- ❖ Loving Relationships I
- ❖ The Only Diet There Is
- ❖ Celebration of Breath
- ❖ Ideal Birth
- ❖ Drinking the Divine
- ❖ Pure Joy
- ❖ Inner Communion
- ❖ How To Be Chic, Fabulous, and Live Forever
- ❖ Interlude With the Gods
- ❖ Loving Relationships II
- ❖ Essays on Creating Sacred Relationships
- ❖ Healing and Holiness
- ❖ Pele's Wish
- ❖ Relationships Treasury
- ❖ Rock Your World with the Divine Mother
- ❖ Liberation Breathing: The Divine Mother's Gift
- ❖ Spiritual intimacy: What You Really Want with a Mate
- ❖ Babaji: My Miraculous Meetings with a Maha Avatar
- ❖ Physical Immortality: How to Overcome Death

Books by Markus Ray

- ❖ Liberation Breathing: The Divine Mother's Gift
- ❖ Odes to the Divine Mother
- ❖ Miracles with My Master, Tara Singh
- ❖ Babaji: My Miraculous Meetings With A Maha Avatar
- ❖ The Master is Beautiful
- ❖ Little Ganesh Book
- ❖ A Painter's Life (in progress)

IMMORTAL RAY PRODUCTIONS
301 TINGEY STREET, SE
WASHINGTON DC, 20003

Immortal Ray Productions
Nashville   Washington D.C.

Library of Congress Cataloging in Publication Data

Ray, Sondra; Lately I've Been Thinking

I. Relationships. 2. Self-Mastery. 3. Life Wisdom

Cover Design: Markus Ray
Cover Image: Judy Totton Photography of London
Back Cover Image: Judy Totton Photography of London.

ISBN 13: Paperback 978-1-950684-99-1
ISBN 13: E-Book 978-1-950684-98-4

DEDICATION

I dedicate this book to my husband, Markus Ray, who convinced me to start writing Facebook posts, and who helped prepare this book for publication. He is alive with the light of God and is a blessing wherever he goes. It is wonderful to live with an enlightened man who is also a poet, artist, and teacher of *A Course in Miracles*. I only see what is glorious about him. A fantastic change has come over me because of him.

"Every loving thought is true.
Everything else is an appeal for
healing and help."

—Jesus of A Course in Miracles—

Table of Contents

FOREWORD

The insights in this book will turn your world around.

Lately I've Been Thinking is an easy read that is best taken in small doses, which goes along with the journal/daily guide format of the book. The insights are so rich, it pays to read a bit, ponder it, take it in and digest before moving to the next section.

Having said that, the book is so entertaining that it's hard to put down, a rarity for a self-help tome.

This writing does what I rarely see done containing a perfect mix of wisdom, personal anecdotes, illustrative stories and travelogue.

I first heard of Sondra and Markus Ray many years ago. These renowned teachers were always lavishly praised and highly recommended to me. Their reviews on Amazon support that reputation. As do their many testimonials from students, readers and clients. Not to mention their huge following.

My own students would mention that Sondra and Markus recommended my bestselling books as a supplement to their own work, so I went on a search to find out more about their work.

What I found was most inspiring. This couple are teachers who live their mission of lifting the planet. They embody the dream that I so often talk about in my work. They tirelessly travel the world to speak, and I have never seen more prolific writers.

Finally meeting Sondra and Markus did not disappoint. They are even more vibrant, personable and wise (if that is possible) in person. It became instantly clear these two are soulmates on a soul journey.

.

As you dive into *Lately I've Been Thinking*, you are in for a treat.

This book contains pearls of wisdom that are unexpected and precious in their profundity.

My own work is very closely aligned with the work of this couple.

One thing I teach about soulmates is that they have a higher path together. They fit like a glove, recognize the deep connection between them and usually have a significant soul purpose as a couple. Their love transcends time and space. It is lasting and inspires them to greater heights.

Sondra & Markus are a textbook case of this.

You may know that Sondra and Markus travel the globe teaching workshops, speaking and spreading light. This book is their ponderings from the road over a period of many months.

The book is a delightful blend of wisdom, personal anecdotes, experiences on the journey of teaching and glimpses into something unusual and sought-after, a functional relationship.

To read this book is to know and love Sondra and Markus, to appreciate their special gifts as teachers.

You gain profound insight into relationship, family, love, health, healing, life purpose and much more.

You will gain effective techniques to heal, to create what you want and to grow into more love & connection.

An abundance of case studies, illustrative stories to show how these techniques look applied, make this book a rich resource for transformation. What I find especially helpful is how Sondra & Markus trace the effect our birth families have on our lives and how we can overcome past wounds and programming.

Dear to my heart and so in alignment with my own work is the wisdom Sondra and Markus share so freely on how to enrich your relationship, use the Universe as your dating service, overcoming loneliness & how to be an enlightened couple.

They have done a service to share themselves in such a heartfelt way.

I invite you to dive in and savor this sacred book. You'll be glad you did, and your life will be enriched immeasurably.

Every blessing as you embark upon this incredible journey with Sondra and Markus!

Much love & blessings to you,

Kathryn Alice

Author of the bestseller, **Love Will Find You**

PREFACE

As a writer, I feel I have a sacred obligation to help produce enlightenment. A few years ago, I started writing posts on my Facebook for people to enjoy. I wanted these passages to help bring happiness to people—peace, wisdom, etc. I wanted people to experience a touch of enlightenment quickly with a paragraph or two. I wanted people to have enlightenment in their daily life. This was also fun for me to see what I could come up with. Sometimes I would share what I learned in my travels around the world. Sometimes I would share a quote that I felt was important. Sometimes I would share what I learned in my special field—relationships technology. Sometimes I would talk about health and longevity. But it was always something I myself found interesting, even if nobody else read it. I was happy that people wrote me a lot of comments about it all. I almost never got any negative comments. Then the readers started begging me to put them all in a book. So that is how this book came about.

There are many different definitions of enlightenment. Leonard Orr, the founder of Rebirthing, used to define enlightenment as "the certain knowledge of the absolute truth" (i.e. knowing and remembering that your thoughts always create your results). *A Course in Miracles* defines enlightenment as replacing the ego's thought system with the Holy Spirit's thought system. (The ego is a false self we made up which is based on separation from our Creator of essential Peace, Love and Joy; the result being guilt, separation, fear, pain, struggle, misery, suffering, anger, depression, sickness and death.) The ego is a collection of all your negative thinking that keeps you from remembering you are one with God.

Enlightenment is this very remembering—this reunification with our Love, Peace and Joy, which *you really are*. (The Holy Spirit's Reality is also yours—union, life, love, joy, harmony, peace, health, and bliss.) To make this Divine Connection your mind must be quiet and clear. We need to constantly keep the mind and body clear. Well, you might say enlightenment is the key to everything.

Being enlightened has to do with taking responsibility for all the results in your life—all the time. The source of all our experience is the mind. We rule and direct our minds and consequently, we must change our thoughts to restore our mind to its full potential—and to get different results. I hope and pray that this book inspires you and works toward the goal of healing and perfecting yourself. Since we are here to develop self-mastery, I offer this book to you for that reason.

Your ability to feel JOY is a gauge of your enlightenment. Are you a seeker—somebody open to enlightenment? Do You bring your enlightenment to the world? Or are you just surviving with some interesting hobbies? Are you here to realize your inner Divinity? Can you touch the miracle of being alive? I wrote these passages to empower myself and you, my readers, to have an awesome life. Each passage changed me for the better, and I hope will change you. Write to me about your miracles and your victories, and your stories of how these passages changed your life. Please write to me any of your comments and questions. I love hearing from you. Contact@SondraRay.com

ACKNOWLEDGEMENTS

On our travels around the world there are many who aid us in our mission to bring enlightenment to the people. They are too numerous to mention here. But there are a few who are dear to me, who have taken steps to aid others in their process of spiritual awakening. These are the certified *Liberation Breathing Practitioners* who serve their communities and aid us in producing the Loving Relationships Trainings around the world. They are Tove Jensen of Denmark; Pille Tali of Estonia; Lucy Pattinson of the United Kingdom; Silke Modersohn of Tenerife, Spain; Krzysztof Pesla of Poland; and Monique van der Toorn of Holland. In addition, I include Barbara Milbourn, who edited this manuscript with an astute skill and professionalism, and Judy Totton, who took the fabulous photos for the cover and frontispiece. I am grateful for countless others too. You know who you are. We could not do our work without you. You are friends, organizers, colleagues, teachers, and students who take the high road, think the high thoughts, and live the awesome life in the grasp of the Divine. I am indebted to you for your service to humanity, and for placing Truth, Simplicity and Love at the top of your principles for living. I bow to you, who are always on my mind, when lately I've been thinking.

Love,

Sondra Ray

INTRODUCTION

I married Sondra Ray on April 4th, 2009 in Herakhan, India, encircling the holy fire of the Divine Mother. We had the blessings of Babaji and all of His lineage behind us. Having recently passed the milestone of our tenth anniversary, I am honored even more than I was just over a decade ago, to call this remarkable woman *my wife*. Others have called her a pioneer, a dynamo, a seer and a sage, a voice for Babaji in the West, as well as a warrior Goddess. She is all of those, and more. And over thirty years ago, when we first met at a Loving Relationships Training in Philadelphia, I knew even then my life would never be the same—after her *meteoric* entry into my world. Now I find myself searching for a greater gratitude in line with my good fortune to spend my days with Sondra Ray. Every day—365 a year—as a matter of fact. It never grows old being with her. The newness of our daily life together astounds me. Even when it seems we are doing the same thing—it is never the same thing. Wonder abounds. Creativity is always on the crest of our daily actions.

I am a painter, you probably know. I find myself comforted by the saying of *no words*. In fact, as a boy, I loved seeing the "Wordless Workshop" cartoons in my dad's Popular Science magazines, which showed me how to make little home projects with only a few clear line drawings. *No words!* Sometimes I felt being silent was better than talking. Even better, working with my hands and making stuff. Drawing and painting formed my high road of creativity. I went to art school for college, then graduate school for a

Master of Fine Arts degree in painting, drawing, and sculpture. That was in Philadelphia.

Not long after that, in the mid-1980s, I met Sondra Ray. I don't say *meteoric* lightly. Her entry was dazzling. My world was shaken up. I went to India with her for the first time in 1987. It might as well have been *the moon* it was that much of a leap of faith for me to venture that far from home. But guess what, that trip was taking me to my real Home. I was lost in a sea of littleness before that India Quest of 1987. After being in Herakhan, Babaji's ashram, participating in the Divine Mother Festival, I was placed in an ocean of devotion to my own grandeur, to the better part of me. Littleness no longer existed in my reality. I was launched on a life-long Quest to be my true and God-created Self.

A Course in Miracles, which Sondra introduced me to in 1985, also stood large in my colonnade of spiritual pillars. As life would have it, after 1989 when I met Tara Singh, who was to be my teacher of *A Course in Miracles* for 17 years, I lost track of Sondra Ray. I did not see her again until nearly twenty years later. I had to be cooked and boiled down by an authentic master teacher in order to get close to a woman like that again. Tara Singh prepared me well. My ego was blasted again and again, through his compassionate but tough lessons. He was the Light in my life which dispelled my darkness—even the darkness I never even knew I had. He prepared me for a new life, one of holy service. And then he left. His job was done.

In 2008 my reunification with Sondra Ray took place. I left Philadelphia in the Spring, with two suitcases in hand, leaving everything else behind that was unessential—including a 30-marriage that had been dead for ten years already. Death did do us part, and a resurrection was about to take place. I headed for the *meteor* I knew had ignited my life on fire over twenty years before. I headed toward India again, amidst the unquenchable burning light of Sondra Ray.

Sondra and I travelled around the world for our first year together, hailing out of Los Angeles. And we have never stopped since. We married a year later, with the clear intention of our world-wide mission in mind. I think I have been around the world eleven times since then. Like I said, life is always new when you *spend your day with Sondra Ray.*

Lately I've Been Thinking is a taste of this newness. You can spend your day with Sondra Ray and see what I mean. And you don't need to spend that much time doing it either—a few moments only to read one passage—to have those moments return to you in a holy encounter throughout your day. Blanket your mind with bliss from one of her *passages* or give yourself something to think about regarding your greater purpose here. Why would you not want to do that, if you could? Ponder the importance of your Godly Self? These passages will surely empower you and formulate a backdrop for your awesome life. You have to do your part, but with these tidbits of wisdom you will be led lovingly along a meandering road to remarkable freedom.

In 1985 I had studied yoga already for a few years. In that period I had learned a Sanskrit phrase, *Jivan Mukta,* which means a free soul—one who is free in this life. When I met Sondra Ray, I said to myself, here is a *Jivan Mukta,* a free soul. I never forgot that. So, when she reappeared in my life in 2008, there was no question in my mind destiny was bringing us together again for a lofty purpose. My own *Liberation* was being given a new set of parameters. And I would be plummeted by the Lord toward my true destiny.

BABAJI, JESUS of *A Course in Miracles,* and the DIVINE MOTHER we call the "Dream Team" in our house. These pages are imbued with their blessings. Sondra's couple of years of Facebook posts—**Powerful ℥ Posts for an Awesome Life**—will give you a glimpse of a *Jivan Mukta,* one you can hold in your hands and commune with in the short meditations of your morning, or on your lunch break, or after the dishes are done at night. This book is a real time dispensary of timeless questions and answers. Where would you go for a Q&A about life itself? Your life, in all its grandeur. Well, here it is—a roadmap to your higher Self though Sondra's encounters with daily living.

Lately I've Been Thinking is just that. It is a roadmap that meanders through the issues of your life, our issues, everyone's issues, even Sondra Ray's issues. Step into that world in which you meet Sondra Ray in all her authenticity, all of her vulnerability, all of her self-honesty we have grown to love about her over the years. This book is as fresh as **I Deserve Love** she wrote as a pioneering Rebirther in 1976. Like I said, it is on the crest of a creative act, on every page. Go to that high ground and take it into your life. You will end up more free, your life more awesome than before, and on the road to being a *Jivan Mukta* yourself. It is not far away. It is in the stillness of your heart—between the in and out of your own Divine Breath. May holding and reading this book help you achieve *the perfect happiness God wills for you*, in this life, NOW, without delay.

Love,

Markus Ray

Washington DC
July 2, 2019

LATELY I'VE BEEN THINKING

November 16, 2015

❡ GETTING THROUGH FEAR
I read in a book by a guru once that when you go through the changes of enlightenment you need a technique for handling fear. I was glad I have *Liberation Breathing / Breathwork* for that. What else can you be liberated from? So many things! Breathwork can liberate you from pain, negative thoughts, tension, symptoms and disease, anger, guilt, sadness, the effects of traumatic incidents, blocks to abundance, addictions, negative patterns in relationships, birth trauma, parental disapproval, unconscious death urge, the past (including past lives), false religious theology and dogma, depression, and the ego. You can even be liberated from death itself! You can also use the breath to stabilize yourself, have more energy, enhance the immune system, create beneficial brain waves, travel to the interior of your being, acquire transcendent knowledge and information, and seek higher consciousness! Clients tell us about miraculous transformations all the time. They get through their fears and go for what they really want out of life. (From our book *Liberation Breathing: The Divine Mother's Gift*) It is a real spiritual purification!

November 17, 2015

❡ PROTECTION
Wouldn't you like to feel that in these troubling times? Babaji taught that the simplest and most powerful method for bringing peace and protection is through the singing or saying of the Lord's name. He said:

> *"This is the Maha Mantra (ultimate mantra:) OM NAMAH SHIVAY—the great mantra given by the Lord to humanity. Everyone should repeat it. It can be given to anyone and everything can be achieved by it. The power of this mantra is infinite. It is more powerful than the atom bomb!"*

1

♪ "Om Namah Shivay" means "I take refuge in God. I surrender to Shiva, the part of God that destroys my ignorance." It also means Infinite Being, Infinite Spirit, and Infinite Manifestation.

♪ He said it is the highest thought in the Universe. It can wipe out your negativity (ego) and fortify you at the same time! Chanting it not only gives you protection, but helps you manifest what you want. The mantra is like nectar nourishing you. It is like plugging yourself into the Source. It charges you up! It is one of the best forms of devotion there is. It purifies your heart. You can also use it to cure disease. There are CDs you can order on line if you want to sing along. Mainly you should get a set of mala beads with 108 beads and do one round every day. For stronger protection, do ten rounds. Take my word for it. Try it.

November 18, 2015

♪ MORE PROTECTION

Another very important thing for protection is to strengthen your life urge. *A Course in Miracles* says, "Death is a result of a thought called the ego, just as surely as life is a thought called God." Clearing your ego is the job we all have here on earth. That is, if we want to be enlightened. Clearing out the unconscious death urge is the place to start, not end. Death is the stronghold of all fears anyway. If I processed you down on all your fears, the bottom one would be death. What if you cleared your death urge out of your mind with *Liberation Breathing*? You would become very strong and not susceptible to dangerous things. You would not be standing where the danger was. If you stay on the path of ascension through making the breathwork a life-long spiritual path, you will keep on getting more and more light in your body and raising your frequency. The purpose of achieving ascension and physical immortality is to stay alive so that you can be strong to do a mission of Divine Service that the Masters ask you to do. This is the highest thing. You will be protected doing this. Besides, Babaji says the formula for happiness is TRUTH, SIMPLICITY, LOVE, and SERVICE to mankind. Your mission could start any minute.

❡ If you stay on the path of ascension, you will have more health, more strength, more energy, more fun, more joy, more potential for regeneration— and you can ultimately become ageless. This topic is so grand and so broad that I would need days to explain it all. It is best that you study it yourself. Start by reading all about it in our book *Liberation Breathing: The Divine Mother's Gift.* After that, you can get a whole list of books on the subject if you really want to get into it. They are listed in the back of this book. Try reading only books on that subject for a whole year. You will become a very different person. You will achieve full realization of who you really are! What better thing could you do for yourself while the world is going crazy?
Love, Sondra

November 19, 2015

❡ PHYSICAL IMMORTALITY
Here is a quote about physical immortality from an Indian Master:

> *"The body is not only a ladder that can lead to the realm of immortality, but also an excellent instrument for expressing the glory of immortality in life and society. It is capable of being thoroughly penetrated by the light of the Spirit. It is capable of being transformed into what has been called the diamond body. As a result of such transformation, the body does not appear any more to be a burden upon the liberated self. It shines as the spirit made flesh. It functions as a very effective instrument for creative action and realization of higher values in the world. It is purged of all inner tension and conflict. It is liberated from the anxiety of repressed wishes. It is also liberated from the dangerous grip of the death impulse, born of self-repression. Mystics who look upon the body as a burden, suffer from the anxiety of self-repression and the allurement of the death wish.*
> *❡ With the diamond body, the total being of an*

individual becomes strong and steady, whole and healthy. There is a free flow of psychic energy. It is increasingly channeled into ways of meaningful self-expression. Under the guidance of the indwelling light of the eternal, it produces increasing manifestation of spirit in matter." (Harida Chandhuri)

❡ Say *Yes!* to giving up the death urge now. You can also read my book, *How to be Chic, Fabulous and Live Forever* and my upcoming book, *Physical Immortality: How to Overcome Death.*
Love, Sondra

November 20, 2015

❡ MANA
In these troubling times, it is very important to develop your *mana.* Mana is the *life force*, or spiritual power that the Hawaiians believe inhabits all things and creatures. It comes streaming in from another Universe and is also absorbed from the environment by eating and breathing. The kahunas said that the most effective way to gather mana is to do deep breathing! So here is another reason to do *Liberation Breathing / Rebirthing!* Chanting also generates tremendous mana, which is why Babaji keeps insisting we chant the mantra. Mana can be directed to flow outward for the purpose of healing. It can also be directed to our own goals and projects. Mana is stored by the body and manifests as vigor! The goal the kahunas had was to acquire and guard one's personal mana. It was believed that the amount of one's mana determined one's success and luck. Mana is considered to be an inherent quality of command and leadership. The blocks to having mana are anger, resentment, guilt, fear, anxiety, and negativity. Hanging out with the wrong people can dilute your mana. Hanging out with lofty people will obviously build it. Now you know why we go to India every year to be with the yogis and masters. In your spiritual life, this is called "The Principle of Right Association." So, associate with people who force you to "adapt upward." Mana will give you a reservoir of

strength. It will give you a personal magnetism. It will make you a high- impact personality. It will give you charisma. For sure it is the genius and inspiration of a king. No leader wants his mana diluted. That is why they are careful who they hang out with. Are you taking responsibility to develop your mana? From my book *Pele's Wish*.
Love, Sondra

November 21, 2015

❡ A SOLID RELATIONSHIP
I wish for you all to have a solid holy relationship to comfort you during these times. First, you have to be clear on your relationship to the Divine. I teach more and more now what the Holy Relationship is in the Loving Relationships Training (The LRT®). We need to learn that, as we had no models for that. On Saturday, I try to undo the special hate relationship and the special love relationship so that on Sunday I can teach the new paradigm = the Holy Relationship. I am looking forward to teaching the LRT in Santa Fe and Sedona in January and here in Nashville in February (Valentine's weekend) in case you want to come. What is the difference between the special love relationship and the special hate relationship? Do you know? It is all in the ACIM Text. Both of these are of the ego and both of these are treacherous.
❡ The special love relationship starts with the belief that there is something lacking in us that can never be filled. One says, "I can no longer tolerate how unworthy I feel—I will find the answer outside." Or one says, "There are certain special needs I have that cannot be met within myself or by God and I cannot find happiness without them: But YOU, a special person with special characteristics, can meet my needs." Those who we perceive "fill these needs," we love. It is the ego's version of a marriage made in Heaven. "As long as you, my special love, continue to meet my needs, I will love you. But if you don't continue, I won't love you." This means the person has placed hope for salvation on this one special person. It is co-dependent. Dependency breeds contempt. We feel guilt for using the

other to fill our shaky identity. "Guilt demands punishment."
You will hurt yourself in this relationship.

ℑ In the special hate relationship, the responsibility for one's
misery is shifted to the other. "It is YOU who has done this
terrible thing to me." There is an "if only" orientation. The
ego's plan for salvation here is centered on holding
grievances. This anger involves projection and separation.
Projection, while seeming to deliver us from guilt, in reality
reinforces it. There is a lot of attack (anger) in this
relationship. This brings more guilt. And you know guilt
always demands punishment. This relationship will always
hurt you.

ℑ We build defenses against our mate who is attacking us.
But defenses attract more attack. In the special hate
relationship, the hated person's past mistakes are used to
build a case against him.

ℑ In other words, in the special love relationship, you make
your mate your savior, your idol. In the special hate
relationship, you make your mate your enemy. None of this
is any fun. It is brutal. So, this is why I keep on teaching the
Loving Relationships Training, which I am always updating.
We all need it to get out of the family mind and get into the
Holy Spirit's mind. We need it to have a solid relationship to
LIFE!
Love, Sondra

November 22, 2015

ℑ PRIVATE AUDIENCE
When Markus and I had our last private audience with
Muniraj in India, he told us that a lot of people would be
getting sick and he insisted we do healing seminars and
relationships seminars, as people would have trouble in the
latter, also. Since these are my two favorite subjects, I was
glad I was already on the right track. I wrote a whole book
called *Healing and Holiness* which is very thorough. Here is
just one page:

❖ The mind rules the body.

❖ The body is at the effect of the mind.

❖ Negative thoughts produce all negative results in the body.

❖ Anything can be cured (ACIM). To God all things are possible.

❖ We will give up pain and sickness when we see no more value in it.

❖ The real physician is the mind of the patient and the outcome is what the patient decided. Disease is often anger taken out on the body.

❖ Resentment, anger, hate, condemnation, and desire to get even tear down the body.

❖ When there is a health problem, there is a forgiveness problem.

❖ Sickness is guilt projected onto the body.

❖ All healing is essentially the release from fear.

❖ You are not a victim. There are no victims. Life presents to you what your thoughts are; conscious and unconscious.

❖ Sickness is idolatry because it is the belief that power can be taken from you. It is deciding against God.

❖ Healing reflects our joint will with the Holy Spirit. The Holy Spirit cannot help without your invitation. Only you can deprive yourself of anything.

❖ Nothing will be beyond our healing power because nothing will be denied your simple request.

Love, Sondra

November 23, 2015

❡ YOUR PURPOSE HERE

So often I see couples who each have different priorities; thus they are not aligned and they get stuck. I ask them, "Have you ever sat down together and discussed the purpose of life?" Of course, they have not.

❡ I know of a famous movie star whose mother told him that the purpose of life was INTENSE JOY! Imagine having a mother like that. *Pure Joy* is one of the highest expressions of God— so that is really spiritual. My gurus in India say it this way: "The purpose of life is to immerse yourself in the Supreme." In other words, we are here to recognize ourselves and others as part of the Supreme God. Knowing who you really are leads to intense joy.

❡ Another purpose is to learn. Our world is a school. People are in various grades depending on past lives, etc. Learning includes changing and expanding.

❡ Another purpose is to clear your karma. Interesting books on past lives that will blow your mind are: *You Were Born Again to Be Together* (by Dick Sutphen) and *Other Lives and Other Selves* (by Dr. Roger Woolger) Ram Dass once said, "You are here to take the curriculum." You can use your "case" as we say in Breathwork (or your issues) as a stepping stone for inner awakening.

❡ A very important purpose in life is to SERVE HUMANITY. In India they call this Karma Yoga. It is considered the first and foremost duty of a mature soul. And don't forget, you both need to know that the purpose includes becoming enlightened (dissolution of the ego). This is a step–by–step process of giving up separation and limitation, which leads to our becoming Divine Masters.

❡ If both parties in the couple know this, they will make it a priority to work on themselves and that is my whole point here. Unfortunately, too often I hear that one person in the relationship won't work on him or herself.

❡ A relationship should have as its purpose to enhance all of the above. Both partners must share in this intention or they are missing the boat. Otherwise you will just have to keep dying and reincarnating until you wake up in one life and *get it.* When are you going to get it?

❡ Wake up now! *A Course in Miracles* and Liberation Breathing will help greatly with all this. That is why we are starting an on-line course to help people learn ACIM and it will include Liberation Breathing. The more I did breathwork, the more I could understand ACIM. The program is called "Miracles for You—1Year Support Network for Serious

Study of *A Course in Miracles.*" You can register on my
website here: *bit.ly/Miracles4You*

November 24, 2015

❡ THE GLORY OF IMMORTALITY
I have seen so many relationships in which each person is
constantly dealing with the suppression of fear such as,
"When is this person going to leave or die?" Also, a typical
couple usually projects the unconscious death urge onto the
relationship. Then the tendency is to kill off the relationship
in insidious ways.
❡ Instead of getting old together and dying—imagine the
opposite! What if both could become ageless and live as
long as each wanted? Two people become the immortal
couple! An immortal is a soul who has already taken on
enough male and female incarnations that the birth/death
cycle can now be transcended. You stay here and commit
to a life of Service to the Divine. And—it is fun! (You want to
stay here, not check out.)
❡ What this does for a relationship is simply marvelous. The
relationship takes on a whole new vibration of sheer vitality.
The sacredness increases because life and God go
together. More life equals more holiness! There is a sense
of well-being that pervades the underlying structure of the
relationship.
❡ But many people cannot stand the idea because it is too
exciting. They are addicted to pain, struggle, and death.
Some people hate their lives—they do not understand that
one reason their lives do not work is BECAUSE they have
not cleared their death urge.
❡ When a couple strives for the expression of the Divine,
they each become strong and healthy; there is a miraculous
and free flow of psychic energy. They express together the
glory of immortality into their life and society and function as
effective instruments for creative action and realization of
higher values in the world. They truly are here to make a
contribution.
Love, Sondra

November 25, 2015

❧ HAPPY THANKSGIVING

"Oh, Divine Mother, Thou Who is giver of Life Force on all planes. It is due to You that we are able to release our sorrows. It is due to You that we shall find happiness. It is due to Your transcendent nature and all-pervading light that You are worthy of being worshiped and adored. We call upon You to ignite us with illumination. You are the personification of intelligence that creates matter. Everything we possess is a gift from You! All the universes, all our relationships and our bodies—the entire quantum field of Creation is Your Heart. I seek You in my own heart, where You abide."
Love, Sondra

November 27, 2015

❧ NOTHING HIGHER

In India they say there is nothing higher than worship of the Divine Mother. They also say only she gives the boon of physical immortality. The Divine Mother is like the original spark of creation. She is the feminine aspect of God. The Virgin Mary is just one aspect of the Divine Mother. We are talking about the power of the atom here. By repeating the names of the Divine Mother, one can link up with the qualities of that Force. These are all listed in our new book on Babaji which is at the publisher's now. There are 108 names: Here is a sample:

> OM, I Bow to Her:
> ❖ Who is Divine Energy.
> ❖ Who Removes the Troubles of the Universe.
> ❖ Who Showers the Nectar of Grace.
> ❖ Who Removes All Pain.
> ❖ Who is Beyond All Things.
> ❖ Who is the Goddess of Perfection.
> ❖ Who is the Power of the Beginning.
> ❖ Whose Body is the Universe.

❖ Who is Divine Sound and Light.
❖ Who Gives Nourishment and Plenty.

❡ Every Spring we go to Navaratri (Divine Mother Festival) at Babaji's ashram, which we call the **India Quest**. People come from all over the world. It is the best time to go to India as you get the power of that festival. Babaji told me that in *one day* there you can make so much spiritual progress it would take you 12 years to advance that much in the outside world. That is how deep it is because of that location, the temples that are there, the astrological configuration of that time, the ancient ceremonies done for nine straight days, and the yogis you mingle with. Are you ready to change your whole life?
Join us on the India Quest.

Love, Sondra

November 28, 2015

❡ SPOTLIGHT
Markus and I saw a great movie worthy of an Oscar: SPOTLIGHT. I recommend it! I wonder what Catholics are thinking who see that.
❡ Ammachi says one of the three shadows we have to work out is the "religious shadow"—in other words, religious dogma. (She also said we have to work out the personal shadow and the family shadow.)
❡ Imagine belonging to a spiritual community where a group of fabulous people were helping each other work out these shadows—a community where all were working on enlightened ideas together and helping each other become healed, happy, and whole. And I am not talking about a cult. Quite the opposite. In my book *Pure Joy,* I wrote a whole chapter on the difference between a cult and a true spiritual family. That chapter came through me in 15 minutes.
❡ I am always trying to create communities wherever I go where people empower each other to become all that they can be; a community where they feel safe to share the problems they are having in their relationships and in life and actually get help with them. When you are trying to

break out of the family mind and cultural traditions, you need that. Otherwise you will feel alone in your attempt to get enlightened. Imagine being able to hang out with totally alive, safe, peaceful, innocent people living in the present who are experiencing their own magnificence—those who are working toward becoming super beings. We lovingly call this family the *OHANA*, which in Hawaiian means, "A chosen family who breathes together." If you do not have this around you, we could come and help you create that. All you have to do is gather your friends together and we will come, if you invite us.

Love, Sondra

November 29, 2015

❡ THE NEW PARADIGM
In the new paradigm a sensitive and enlightened partner helps his or her mate look at how he or she creates situations—WITHOUT making them feel guilty. Together they figure out how to turn the situation into a win. After they have done self-analysis to discover the consciousness factor that caused the situation, they clear it using spiritual practices to become more aware.

❖ "I got a parking ticket" (How did I create that?)
❖ "The boss really disapproved of me today"
(How did I create that?)
❖ "I lost everything in the computer today."
(How did I create that?)
❖ "Somebody stole the tape deck out of the car today."
(How did I create that?)

❡ Everything that happens to you is a computer printout of your mind. Everything is a mirror. Life presents to you what your thoughts are. When you take responsibility like this for all of your results, you can see the emerging patterns. All of life becomes like a Rorschach test. Maybe you know this; but maybe you have never made it a game in your relationship. Couples can have fun going out into the world

12

to see what they will create that day.

❡ The trick is to keep seeing it as a game and not something to make yourself wrong about or make your mate wrong about. You can figure out how you make up anything unpleasant by simply saying, "The negative thought I had that made me attract THAT was_____," and fill in the blank. By changing the thoughts and breathing them out through Liberation Breathing you won't have to repeat the thing you did not like. It is good to have this affirmation as well, in case things go off: "Even though I made a mistake, I still completely love and accept myself."

Love, Sondra

November 30, 2015

❡ ARE YOU READY TO JOIN?

I read an article called "Loneliness Is Bad for You." It stated that loneliness is linked with high blood pressure, inflammation, and a weakened immune system. Studies prove that loneliness triggers cellular changes making you very susceptible to viral infection. It is like a "hostile environment" leading to flight or fight syndrome. I thought of all the lonely people in the world and what could be done about it. I know some people who like to be alone, they say. I wonder if they are kidding themselves. Maybe some people are just resigned to it. I think some people don't know how to get over being lonely. They may want a relationship but are either afraid of it or don't know how to create one. If you are lonely there are a few things you can do. You don't have to remain alone. You CAN create a relationship if you are ready to join.

> ❖ *God will bring you one if you use the "cosmic dating service" which produces better results than dating on line (although that is working for some). See our book* **Spiritual Intimacy** *in which I describe how I attracted Markus into my life in chapter 21!*
> ❖ *The other choice is you can enjoy being alone. Before I married Markus, I was alone for years—but I never ever felt lonely. People did not believe me;*

13

but the reason I never felt lonely is I had Babaji as the center of my life. A spiritual master is one answer when there are periods in which you are alone.

❖ *After many years I made the DECISION very, very consciously that I wanted to experience a holy relationship in this incarnation. I asked Babaji for that. I did have to work on myself to get open enough to let it in. I had to allow it, as Esther Hicks says.*

❖ *ASK AND IT IS GIVEN, but you have to ALLOW it. I had to work on myself as I was very used to being overly independent. Anyway, you can overcome loneliness one way or another. It is not good for your health to stay in that state. If you need help in this area, contact me for a* Liberation Breathing session by Skype.

Love, Sondra

December 1, 2015

❡ HOW TO PROCESS YOURSELF
Enlightened couples have problems like everyone else; however, the way they solve them is completely different. They use self-realization techniques which are very effective. They deliberately break old destructive habits of arguing. But when one in the couple is willing to practice self-analysis and the other is not—the combination rarely works. The spiritual master Yogananda always said that self-analysis is the key to mastery of life. He also said that without self-analysis, man leads a robot-like life. Here is what he says exactly: "People who never process themselves are like mechanical products of the factory of their environment. They are preoccupied with breakfast, lunch and dinner, working and sleeping, and being entertained. They don't know what or why they are seeking, nor why they never realize complete happiness." And he is not talking about going to an analyst. He is talking about looking within yourself; perfecting yourself.

❡ The Bible says, "Be ye perfect even as God is perfect." That is an assignment. The only way to have a perfect relationship is if both people are willing to experience their perfection. To experience your own perfection, you must release the ego's thought system. And in a relationship, you both have to be committed to this. How do you do it? Read ACIM and do Liberation Breathing, chanting mantras, and clearing processes.

❡ If there is a resistance to self-analysis, find out why. It is not hard. It is even fun. Here are the three steps:

1. My negative thoughts that created this situation were _____.
2. The desired outcome for this situation is _____.
3. The new thought (affirmation) I need to think in order to achieve this desired result is _____.

Then do chanting, breathing, or whatever helps. You CAN have a sacred relationship that stays healthy!
Love, Sondra

December 2, 2015

❡ MYSTICAL PURPOSE
In the New Paradigm, we must have a mystical purpose that transcends the personal needs of the two people in a relationship. Not only does this require a partner who is willing to work with you on forming a triangle with the Source, but it also means having a spiritual mission together. The mission could be a joint career like Markus and I have; or if the careers are different, the couple should decide what kind of service they could offer the world together; apart from their careers.

❡ When people are deeply in love, they feel a natural concern for the state of the world and they want to do something about it. If love has waned and the relationship is stale, it might just be because the couple never acted on that sense of purpose. It is never too late to infuse your relationship with this gift of giving. It is not only a gift to the world; but it is a gift to the relationship because it gives the relationship a deep meaning.

ℐ I have studied successful relationships of partners who were equally powerful. They prevent competition by first sharing their commitment to public service. It is very important to focus your relationship on something greater than yourselves. Some famous people say, "Every several years every able body should do three months of public service." If you are single you might meet the person of your dreams. Doing it—you will attract a spiritual, giving person who can handle a holy relationship.

ℐ Missions are satisfying. In my case, finding mine felt like the beginning of my true life. Joining the Peace Corps, I call my boot camp for world service which I have been doing ever since. Try for something that is a stretch!
Big stretches make you expand; and at the same time, they heal you.

ℐ Remember that Babaji said the formula for happiness is this: *Truth / Simplicity / Love / and Service to Mankind*. If you don't have any ideas, read Bill Clinton's book *Giving*. There are so many ideas in the back of it.
Love, Sondra

December 3, 2015

ℐ LOOKING AT ANGER
Today, after another mass shooting, we have to look at ANGER. Here is what some gurus have said on the subject:

> ❖ Guru Mai. *"It is said that if you are a true ascetic, you are completely devoid of anger. If there is any trace of anger in you, you are called a scoundrel..."*
> A great being will go to any extent to remove the fire of anger. The greatness of a holy person is that he can drop something once he realizes he has it.
> ❖ Dalai Lama: *"We lose control of our mind through hatred and anger. If your minds are dominated by anger, we will lose the best part of human intelligence—wisdom. Anger is one of the most serious problems facing the world today."*

❖ Ammachi: *"Anger and impatience will always cause problems. Anger makes you weak in every cell of your body."*

Suppose you have a weakness of getting angry easily. Once you become normal again, go and sit in the family shrine room or in solitude and regret and repent your own anger and sincerely pray to your beloved deity, seeking help to get rid of it. Try to make your own mind aware of the bad outcome of anger. When you are angry at someone, you lose all your mental balance. Your discriminative power completely stops functioning. You say whatever comes into your mind and act accordingly. You may even utter crude words. By acting and thinking with anger you lose a lot of good energy. Become aware that these negative feelings will only pave the way for your own destruction.

☙ Tomorrow I will discuss how to handle anger and get rid of it forever.

Love, Sondra

December 4, 2015

☙ MORE ON ANGER

A Course in Miracles says, "Anger is never justified." (ACIM, Text; chap..30, sec. VI)

> *"All attack [anger] is self-attack. It cannot be anything else. Arising from your own decision not to be what you are, it is an attack on your identification. Attack is thus the way in which your identification is lost, because when you attack, you must have forgotten what you are. And if your reality is God's, when you attack you are not remembering Him. This is not because He is gone, but because you are actively choosing not to remember Him. If you realized the complete havoc this makes of your peace of mind you could not make such an insane decision."* (ACIM, Text; chap.10, sec. II)

So, what do you do about your anger then? Forgiveness dissolves anger. You have not forgiven everyone if you are angry. But let's say anger comes up in your relationship. Here is what Babaji says to do.

❖ You don't stuff it, that hurts your body.
❖ You don't dump it on another (like your mate), that hurts them.
❖ You CHANGE THE THOUGHT that causes the anger. (Emotions are spearheaded by thoughts.)
❖ You breathe out the "charge."

This is very effective by the way. You have to learn to say:

❖ "I am feeling activated" (This is saying I am not stuffing the fact that I am charged—but I am not going to yell either.)
❖ "The thought that is making me activated is_____."
❖ Then you change that thought to the opposite.
❖ Then you breathe. If you cannot get a breathwork session, you can run around the block 5 times or take a very cold shower.

This way you are not hurting anyone. If you dump your anger on someone you are going to have guilt. Guilt demands punishment. Then you are going to create punishing yourself and then things will go from bad to worse.

ჟ Try what Babaji recommends. It works. It is a discipline. Love, Sondra

December 5, 2015

ჟ THE CONSEQUENCES OF ANGER
The consequences of anger medically raises your blood pressure, lowers your immune system, constricts blood vessels, disturbs digestion, and leads to many diseases. Spiritually, anger shuts out the mind of God, puts you in a

18

low frequency, undoes all the spiritual progress you made before. "Anger makes you weak in every cell of your body," says our female Spiritual Master AMMACHI. It forms a groove in the brain that re-fires and makes you angrier. Relationship-wise, anger pushes people away, i.e. it provokes separation, destroys relationships, and is hurtful to others.

❡ If you are addicted to anger, you have to find out what your fear of giving it up forever is. Say this: "My fear of giving up anger and conflict forever is_____." See what comes up. You have to see these false "benefits" and let them go.   Love, Sondra

December 6, 2015

❡ ATTACK AND BLAME
There are two very important verses in the *Text* of *A Course in Miracles* that are in keeping with the theme I have been writing about lately: *"You will attack what does not satisfy, and thus you will not see you made it up."* (This means you will get mad at what you don't like rather than taking responsibility for making it up.) I see people doing this all the time.

❡ The other verse is even deeper and goes like this: *"Beware of the temptation to perceive yourself unfairly treated."* This means that when people do things to you that you think are unfair, you will tend to feel justified in your anger. You will react with anger instead of seeing that you attracted them doing that! It is very tempting, in other words, to blame. But this is not right. Blame is off the track. In other words, everything that happens to you, you called for it. You did not necessarily call for it consciously—probably unconsciously—that is why it is so important to know your unconscious thoughts that may even be preverbal, before you could speak. That is exactly what we go after in a **Liberation Breathing session.** If you really want to be enlightened, you will meditate on these two verses and apply them. It is applying them that matters, really.

Love, Sondra

December 7, 2015

♫ PARTENTAL BLAME

I am forever seeing clients and others blaming their parents for their problems in life. Many people feel they were born in the wrong family, or if they had only had different parents, their lives would be so much better.

♫ It is easy to blame one's parents and maybe it not so easy to take responsibility for choosing those parents. But that is exactly the point. You CHOSE those parents with your guides before coming here, so blame is off the track. You have to look at why you chose them. Either you had past life karma to work out with them OR you had big lessons they were going to provide you with, or both. Once you stop blaming them and see that you chose them, your life will start to clear up. Blame will never work.

♫ So one of the things you can do is say this:

"My good purpose for choosing that mother was_____."
"My good purpose for choosing that father was_____."

Make sure you don't say, "I don't know," for an answer. The right answer IS within you—so let go of the thought, "I don't know." You can get around that by saying, "If I did know why, the reason would be_____." Once you know the reason and take responsibility for choosing your parents, it is much easier to forgive. When you completely forgive your parents; it makes a HUGE difference in your relationships with mates and bosses and others. Trust me. Love, Sondra

December 8, 2015

♫ FAMILY FEELINGS

Since it is time for the holidays, it is time to think about how one feels about family. Going home can be traumatic if you have not forgiven everyone. Did you know that anything unresolved with your family will come up in your love relationships? How do we resolve all this then?

♫ First one should take my "forgiveness test." It goes something like this: zero is no forgiveness; ten is total complete forgiveness; five is half.

What number then do you get on:
- ❖ Your mother (?)
- ❖ Your father (?)
- ❖ Step parents (?)
- ❖ Siblings (?)
- ❖ Your Ex (?)
- ❖ Yourself (?)

Take the test even if your parents have passed over, as they are still very alive in your mind.

✄ If you got low scores you have work to do and going home won't be much fun. If you are not at 10 on all those answers, you are still angry. Anger is a defense and defenses attract attack.

✄ Forgiveness is a DECISION. It is not that one cannot forgive, it is more a stubborn refusal to do so. Remember our parents did not have the tools or help we have today to clear themselves. The best gift you could give someone is total forgiveness in your heart. Have a good holiday. We leave for the Bali Quest tomorrow for a spiritual retreat. We go every year from December 3-13. Why don't you join us! See our QUESTS HERE: *https://sondraray.com/quests/* Love, Sondra

December 9, 2015

✄ A PRAYER TO RELEASE ANGER
Completion on Anger Prayer by Yogananda:

May I abandon the Anger Habit.
O Eternal Tranquility!
Save me from attacks of fury fever
that shock my nerves and inflame my brain.
May I abandon the Anger Habit
that brings unhappiness to me and my companions.
Let me not indulge in fits of selfish vexation
that alienate from me the affection of my loved ones.
May I never invigorate my resentments

by attentively refueling their fires.
O Queen of Quietude!
Whenever I am rage full, place Thou before me a chastising
mirror in which to see myself made ugly by passion.
Let me not appear disfigured before others,
my face wrath-wrecked.
I would solve the difficulties of life through
thoughts and acts of love, not of hate.
Bless me, that I heal anger hurts in myself
with the salve of self-respect,
and anger hurts in others with the balsam of kindness.
May I realize, O SPIRIT,
that even my worst enemy is still my brother,
and that, even as Thou lovest me, Thou lovest him.

Love, Sondra

December 12, 2015

♫ LOVE FROM BALI
Love from Bali—I cannot guarantee the internet connection
here daily. I would love to write though. This is Heaven here
really: Bali is commonly called *The Island of the Gods.*
There are 10,000 temples on this island, and they use them
all. Every family relates to 7 different temples. You begin
with a temple in your home and you build the home around
it. Every morning every single family sits down together and
makes offerings of weaving baskets with incense and
flowers placed in them. They take these offerings to work,
where they have altars. Can you imagine if everyone in your
country did that daily? People are so sweet—I have never
seen anything like it. They are angels.
♫ The practice of keeping newborns next to the body of the
parents for months makes such a difference. Then when
they put the baby down, they have a religious ceremony.
People feel very secure whether they have much or not. It is
like a dream to constantly smell the combination of exotic
fruits, incense, exotic flowers and clove cigarettes in the air!
We have 15 people coming for a spiritual retreat. But we are
not going to be tourists. We are here to surrender to the

Divine Mother and to ascend.

❡ I have never seen my husband as happy as he is here. I want to share this energy with you. I hope I can honestly give you an experience of it all from where you are.

Love, Sondra

December 13, 2015

❡ WITH THE BALINESE

Yesterday we saw something so real, so authentic, so holy, so pure, so ancient that I will never be the same. Our driver (who is so impeccable, so divine that we consider him our guru) invited us to his home—a real Balinese compound where all the relatives live together in splendor, Balinese style.

There was a rare ceremony going on and he must have known we needed to see it. It was the day where everyone did ceremonies and prayers for metal things—like cars and motorcycles.

❡ The cars and motorcycles were all decorated as they put an altar on every car and motorcycle. There was a large altar in the courtyard with elaborate decorations on it. The local priest sat in front of that altar and did ancient prayers for literally two hours! About six women in the family participated in the ceremony, all to the Divine Mother of course. They were all dressed in their finest and most beautiful attire! I wondered what the priest was saying—probably asking for protection and well-working transportation.

❡ They offered flowers and water and incense to the altars on the motorcycles and cars. There were about 12 motorcycles as that is the common transportation here. We sat there mesmerized. To them it was the most natural thing—to us it was being on another dimension watching a movie. One woman gracefully waved a flower in front of all the vehicles. So beautifully did her hand wave that you went in a trance. After this lengthy puja, we then were fed with the fruit from the altar and Balinese rice and chicken.

❡ I felt very privileged to be invited to this holy ceremony. It gave me once again, such respect for these holy people. It

seemed like they could never ever have a problem, living like this. The little children took part also. More later.
Love, Sondra

December 13, 2015

♫ TAKING RESPONSIBILITY—BALI STYLE
Back when a club in Bali was bombed by terrorists, I cried when I heard it. It felt like they attacked innocence. But the Balinese people did not blame, they took responsibility and the priests questioned how they could have attracted that. They reviewed everything and found that awhile back they had failed to do one ceremony due to lack of funds. They realized the cost of that mistake and then they had to go back to a 1,000-year-old ceremony to correct their mistake!
♫ Amazing. They had no blame, no counter-attack, no anger. Where would you find such a story?
♫ Our group has now arrived, and we have people from Sweden, Denmark, Estonia, Poland, England, and USA. They are all thrilled to be here and so we start the Divine Mother Training today. We will have paired Liberation Breathing Sessions every single day, and outings every other day so I know everyone will go very deep.
Love, Sondra

December 14, 2015

♫ FIRE CEREMONY
Today is the day of the great Fire Ceremony. This was given by Babaji for Bali. A very amazing Balinese woman named Swasty was given the blessing of Babaji appearing to her telling her to build a fire pit in her back yard. He showed her exactly where to put it. But she protested that she did not have the funds to do it. He told her not to worry about that. Two days later people showed up out of the blue with the money and materials and it was done!
♫ He explained everything as to how to proceed. It is a very elaborate ceremony where the fire pit is painted fresh each time and decorated with flowers—people sit around the fire

pit with a plate of offerings in front of them. It takes quite a long time to prepare all the offerings of fruit, flowers, incense. and grains. The mantras that are read during this ceremony are very ancient and difficult to learn. Every time "SWAHA" is said, we make an offering to the fire. It is a giving back to the Divine Mother for all the blessings we have had, and hence it is a Thanksgiving. You are also allowed to ask the Mother (the fire is considered the mouth of the Mother) to help you release something at the same time. You can release a block, an illness or pattern. It has never failed me—always works. You feel totally cleansed after this ceremony. It is long, like all the ceremonies in Bali, and therefore very, very complete. It is very beautiful and changes your vibrations.

¶ After all that, there is a feast they have prepared for us of Balinese delicacies. It is wonderful to be with the whole family again, children, fathers, cousins, all relatives. The group was enthralled to be able to be present.

Love, Sondra

December 16, 2015

¶ THE ARTS IN BALI

Another thing that is very neat in Bali is the fact that each village is known for mastering a different art. In one they master the art of batik. In another, the art of wood carving. In another the art of stone carving. In another, the art of basket weaving. In another the art of making silver jewelry. In another the art of painting. So that makes it very, very interesting to see and to buy!

¶ I always tell students to be dropped off and picked up at our favorite hangout, The Lotus Café. (See Markus' video on Bali here: *bit.ly/BaliMovie.*) It is so wonderful to have a beverage while looking over the large lotus blossoms and then you can see in the background the entrance to an amazing temple through the gorgeous carved wood doors. By starting and ending shopping expeditions there, nobody gets lost.

Also, every single day our group is doing paired *Liberation Breathing Sessions.*

ℐ They love this because not only do they get to breathe to become clearer, they also learn to facilitate others in the process. Wonderful! Tomorrow we go to the Immortal Springs.
Love, Sondra

December 17, 2015

ℐ THE IMMORTAL SPRINGS
Today is the day for the Immortal Springs, *Tirta Empul.* It is one of the most powerful cleansing spots on the planet. It is where the ley lines are cleansed. We get in with our clothes on (along with the Balinese people). We bow 13 times at each of the 13 fountains where the cold water rushes over you to cleanse you. The only tricky part is when you change into dry clothes, there really aren't any private dressing rooms. But that is nothing as we can hold up sarongs in the unisex locker area for each other. After going in and changing to temple clothes we go to the main temple compound and sit on the ground behind the priest who is doing elaborate pujas to the main altar. Our driver is kind enough to bring the correct elaborate offerings for our group. This place is so holy that they actually have some government offices right nearby.

ℐ While people are bowing, we tell the group to watch their thoughts so that they become aware of any guidance and directions for the coming year. It is one of the reasons we love to come here every single year, as it is the only other place where we feel we get such direct guidance—as in Babaji's cave in India.

ℐ Yesterday I taught the group the knowledge of Physical Immortality and they had such profound *Liberation Breathing Sessions*, clearing their death programming that I really feel they are ready for this experience.
Love, Sondra

December 18, 2015

ℐ LEGONG DANCE

LATELY I'VE BEEN THINKING

Today is the day of the wonderful Legong dance. This is danced by children who start at age 4; and by age 14 they must retire from this dance because they are *too old*! They are dressed beautifully, and they are so innocent and sensuous that Markus even wrote the following poem after seeing it the first time.

THIS TINY TOWER OF PERFECTION

*So young to be a master, at her level, even all
the movements perfected in that small body before
us, just a few feet away, the best of Balinese
dancing.
The subtle shift of eyes and tender torso in a pose
so graceful and serene my heart opened like a
flower in homage to this tiny tower of perfection and
poise.
The costumes and the makeup so impeccably done
with colors bright and brilliant against the darkened
background of night.
Down the long colonnade the dancer came forth
from the black unknown, past the orchestra of men
who played heavenly music on instruments of local
origin; then the gongs provided base notes, and the
little dancer began to weave her magic, at first
alone, then joined by two others of her stature and
prowess, completing the trio of small Goddesses of
origins divine.
As the music brought us higher still, these
mesmerizing angels danced their way ever upward
to the heavens, taking us with them toward
Beauty's own beatitudes, and toward the ever-
widening circle of our appreciation. Immortality is on
the verge of paying homage to them, these
dedicated saints of the dance, these young girls
who ever captivate my soul to thee, Divine Mother
of the three, who weave their motion's magic
around the holy core of my male's most tender
aspirations.
To these I bow for this great gift to come my way so
easily, to my consort and me, in this form of
dancing Balinese, so masterful and free, the*

27

*youngest tiny towers three who danced a universe
around my love and me.*

By Markus Ray, from *Odes to The Divine Mother*
Love, Sondra

December 19, 2015

ॐ ELEPHANT CAVE
Today we visit the Elephant Cave or *Goa Gajah*, going back
to before the 8th century with Buddhist and Hindu
influences. The cave entrance shows a giant face with a
wide-open mouth at the door. It looks almost like a demon's
mouth, suggesting that people are entering an underworld.
Indentations in the walls show where meditating priests
once sat. There is a statue of Ganesh, the Elephant God,
who removes obstacles. It is a mysterious place with
ancient bathing pools outside amid the rice paddies. There
are stone Divine Mother statues which are amazing,
standing over the pools.
ॐ Before going in the cave, I will teach a class on spiritual
healing. The steps to spiritual healing are these:

1. Find the cause of the condition (which is always
   a negative thought).
2. Confession of the thoughts to a higher power.
3. Spiritual purification techniques to release the
   thoughts (such as visiting sacred sites).

A simple truth process will reveal the thoughts. One has to
know that the body is at the effect of the mind and the mind
rules the body. The physician is the mind of the patient
himself. You also need to know that all pain in the body is
the effort involved in clinging to a negative thought. That is
also true for all symptoms and therefore all disease. But, of
course, all healing is temporary until you heal the death
urge, as you will soon create another way to kill yourself if
you don't handle that.
ॐ Well, it's great we are all going into the Elephant cave
today, because Ganesh is the *remover of obstacles*. And

everybody has some kind of thing they want to get over or remove. We are all in good hands with Ganesh. JAI!
Love, Sondra

December 20, 2015

℥ IN THE HOT SPRINGS
Today is the day we go to the hot springs at Lake Batur. Mt. Batur is a large volcano which is still active. The hot springs near there are considered to be a gift from God. We will do wet *Liberation Breathing Sessions* there. This is exciting for the students as many of them have never tried a wet session. For this everyone has a buddy to support the person breathing. The person breathing is rolled up in the fetal position or stretched out straight under water, and breathing through a snorkel.
℥ It is not like snorkeling in the ocean, because one is doing the *rebirthing breath* in a circular smooth rhythm with no pause at the top and no pause at the bottom. This accumulates the energy in the body because the person is not moving and using up the energy such as in jogging. The water helps the person have memories of the womb. Wet Liberation Breathing is very powerful, and everyone loves it. We are doing this purification today to prepare ourselves for the grand Divine Mother temple on top of the mountain tomorrow. Everyone is thrilled to be here because they are changing so deeply while having fun at the same time. People say our villa is exquisite and the place one could have a honeymoon. More later.

Love, Sondra

December 21, 2015

℥ DIVINE MOTHER TEMPLE
Today is the highlight as we visit the *Besakih Mother Temple*. It is absolutely magnificent. It is the most important, largest, and holiest of temples. It is considered to be a special pilgrimage to make it there; and it is known to create

"cosmic balance." It dates from prehistoric times. It is built on seven levels terraced up on the slopes and leads a spiritual person upwards. There is a complex of 23 different temples combined. It goes up the slopes of Mt. Agung.

❡ In 1963 there was an eruption that killed many people and the lava came around it, up to a few meters away. The people consider the saving of the temple to be a miraculous event. Seventy festivals are held there yearly.

❡ We have a special priest/guide who knows all the protocol, who our driver Agung found for us. Usually we are lucky and we are taken to the top tier where tourists are not allowed. When we first came to Besakih, this guide recognized who I at once, and told me I was allowed to go to the top—which was a real honor. He has let us go every time as a group since, so we certainly hope to find him.

❡ Our plans are to read the Divine Mother names once up there, and several people in our group plan to take the IMMORTALITY VOW. We do this vow up at the very top, something we usually do in India under the immortal tree. But this year the group insisted that we let them do it here. It will be quite a day.

Love, Sondra

December 22, 2015

❡ IMMORTALITY VOW

We were so lucky that it did not rain when we went up the mountain and to the outdoor temples. Our favorite priest came to meet us and took my hand and led me and the group up to the top. There are seven levels. At the third level, we all read the 108 Divine Mother names and had a blessing. Tourists cannot go to the fifth, sixth, and seventh levels. But he knows we are not tourists. We are serious spiritual seekers. At the top level one is very surprised to find that there is NOTHING. All you get is SPACE. There is just a small grove of bamboo and a simple stone altar. It is so revealing of who the Balinese people really are. They know to worship space; the cosmos itself.

꿋 It was there that eight people in our group took the immortality vow and they did it in their native tongue. What I told them to say was this: "I dedicate my true will to ascension and the attainment of physical immortality," (meaning you stay here to serve humanity). Then they each read 10 reasons why they love life. It was very moving, to say the least.

꿋 After this we went to a beautiful restaurant to celebrate. There was an incredible view of the tiered rice paddies. I had prayed to Babaji like mad for good weather and we got it. But when we got to the restaurant and were well protected, there was a downpour, as often happens in Bali this time of year. It kept pouring rain, more rain than you can imagine. Like a monsoon. This went on for a whole hour! I was so happy that it did not happen when we were at the temple, which is all outdoors—people were stunned at the power of the experience which is often the all-time highlight for a soul.

Love, Sondra

December 23, 2015

꿋 THE CHRISTMAS STAR

It is two days before Christmas, and I read this in *A Course in Miracles:*

> "The sign of Christmas is a star, a light in the darkness. See it not outside yourself, but shining in the Heaven within, and accept it as the sign the time of Christ has come. He comes demanding nothing. No sacrifice of any kind, of anyone is asked by Him. In His Presence the whole idea of sacrifice loses all meaning. For He is Host to God. And you need but invite Him in Who is there already, by recognizing that His Host is One and no thought alien to His Oneness can abide with Him there. Love must be total to give Him welcome, for the Presence of Holiness creates the holiness that surrounds it. No fear can touch the Host Who cradles God in the time of Christ, for the Host is as

31

holy as the perfect Innocence which He protects."
— *(A Course In Miracles,* Text; chap. 15, sec. xi*)*

Love, Sondra

December 25, 2015

❡ CHRISTMAS DAY
Today is Christmas Day, and the weather is glorious here in Bali. Sun is shining. Our group has left, and we are relaxing in our wonderful villa. Here is what Jesus says today from His *A Course in Miracles:*

> *"Let no despair darken the joy of Christmas, for the time of Christ is meaningless apart from joy. Let us join in peace by demanding no sacrifice of anyone, for so you offer me the love I offer you. What can be more joyous than to perceive we are deprived of nothing? Such is the message of the time of Christ, which I give you that you may give it and return it to the Father, who gave it to me. For in the time of Christ, communication is restored, and He joins us in celebration of His Son's creation. By your welcome does He welcome you into Himself." — (A Course In Miracles,* Text, chap. 15, sec. xi*)*

Love, Sondra

December 26, 2015

❡ LAST DAY IN BALI
Every year we go to our true Balinese spiritual healer for a check-up. Balinese healers know they receive their gift from the Spirit. They are similar to a priest, so one must go with respect, reverence, and humility. They are so connected to service that they never turn anyone away. Your experience is very public because other clients are waiting and watching. We were so lucky this day as we were second in line! Our healer pokes you with very sharp sticks inside the

toes.

He will say that this one spot is lungs, this spot is liver, this spot is so and so. Sometimes his pokes are excruciatingly painful. But afterward you feel great, like a dark energy has been lifted.

⚘ Usually I just breathe through it all. On this occasion I was sure he was doing an exorcism on me. I was overcome with something in the family mind and it took me over—and then I let out a huge scream (something I would never do but something I could not control). I had wanted my DNA changed and that is what it felt like. I was so grateful—to put it mildly.

⚘ I know this is the Island of the Gods—as the Gods hang out here and your driver is a God and the people cleaning your room are angels and Markus keeps telling me I better see that.

⚘ We had a wonderful Christmas dinner at a spa run by two Americans, Lela and Randall. Taksu *is* the name of the spa. They created it from scratch. It is stunning. I recommend it. Now I have to pack.

Love, Sondra

December 27, 2015

⚘ THE MAGIC OF GRATITUDE
Arrived home. I am so, so grateful! Do you really understand the magic of gratitude? I certainly recommend two books about this. *The Magic* by Rhonda Byrne and *The Path of Wealth* by May McCarthy. Sure, you know it is a good idea, but these books teach you special things about the subject. I absolutely guarantee they will change your life in a miraculous way.

⚘ The Bible says whoever has gratitude will be given more and he or she will have abundance. Whoever does not have gratitude, even what he or she has will be taken away. Muhammad said that gratitude for the abundance you have received is the best insurance that the abundance will continue.

⚘ Buddha said that you have no cause for anything but

gratitude and joy. Lao Tzu said that if you rejoice in the way things are, the whole world will belong to you. Krishna said that whatever he is offered he accepts with JOY. King David spoke of giving thanks to the whole world. Jesus said *thank you* BEFORE he performed miracles.

❡ Einstein practiced gratitude every single day of his life. When he spoke of his achievements, he spoke only of giving thanks to others.

❡ Rhonda Byrne says any areas that are not wonderful are due to lack of gratitude. We know all this, but we have to impregnate our cells with it. That is why the exercises in the books I mentioned are so important. You need to have a gratitude journal. Trust me.

Love, Sondra

December 28, 2015

❡ EFFICIENT ACTION

Thinking about the New Year coming. It might be a great resolution to learn EFFICIENT ACTION. It is a principle of prosperity consciousness I learned from Wallace Wattles. The idea is to do every little thing well and complete and efficiently. No matter what it is you are doing, do it excellently and well—and that is a success then. If you do something half-heartedly, that is a little failure. PEOPLE FAIL BY ACCUMULATIONS OF INEFFICIENT ACTIONS. Do you complete every task in the absolute best way possible? Is every little thing you do, done perfectly?

❡ Not only do you build a success consciousness when you do every little thing well, it also feels good to carry out efficient action. It feels really good to change a situation that is not so desirable into one that is very desirable.

❡ It helps me a lot to have an altar in every room. (Something I started to do after my first trip to Bali in the '80s. These pretty altars remind me to make everything beautiful for God and to do everything efficiently for God.)

Love, Sondra

LATELY I'VE BEEN THINKING

December 29, 2015

ॐ A MESSAGE FROM BABAJI
From the Teachings of Babaji:

> *"In the world today, fire is bursting out on one side while nectar flows on the other. You must decide if you chose fire or nectar. While the flames of fire are spreading, it is up to us to save ourselves and others. We must be ALERT. At this moment people are jumping into the fire because of their ignorance. We must save these people, and we can do so only if we have great courage. We should give this courage to others as nothing can be done without it. Courage is the most important thing."*

ॐ Sri Babaji has told us many times to WAKE UP. Wake up yourselves and others. Control your mind and have a firm determination.

> *"Whoever comes here to Herakhan must vow to save himself and the world. Wherever you go, be prepared to save people. Be firm like a rock, deep and serious like the sea. Think of the earth as Mother. This is one earth. Don't be divided by thinking of yourselves as belonging to different countries. We belong to one earth. Proceed with this in mind. Be not afraid of water, fire or great storms—face them bravely. I am preparing you for the great Revolution. When the time comes you will all know."*

Sri Babaji, circa 1982

December 30, 2015

ॐ A VERY DEEP POEM BY RUMI

> *RESURRECTION DAY*
> *On Resurrection Day God will say,*

"What did you do with the strength
and the energy that your food gave
you on earth? How did you use your
eyes? What did you make with your
five senses while they were dimming
and playing out? I gave you hands
and feet as tools for preparing the
ground for planting. Did you, in the
health I gave you, do the plowing?"
You will not be able to stand
when you hear those questions.
You will bend double with shame
and finally acknowledge the glory.
God will then say,
"Lift your head,
and answer these questions."
Your head will rise a little
and then slump again.
"Look at me! Tell me what you've done."
You try, but you fall back
flat as a snake. "I want every detail!
Tell me!"
Eventually you'll be able to get
into a sitting position.
"Be plain and clear.
I have given you such gifts. What did you
do with them?"
Then you will turn to the right, looking to
the prophets for help, as though to say,
I AM STUCK IN THE MUD OF MY LIFE.
HELP ME OUT OF THIS!
And they will answer,
those kings,
"The time for helping is past.
The plow stands there in the field
You should have used it."
Then you will turn to the left,
where your family is, and they will say,
"Don't look at us! This conversation
is between you and your Creator!"
Then you will pray the prayer
That is the essence of every true ritual: "GOD

I HAVE NO HOPE. I AM TORN TO SHREDS.
YOU ARE MY FIRST AND MY LAST
AND ONLY REFUGE."
Don't do daily prayers like a bird
pecking its head up and down.
Prayer is an egg.
Hatch out the total
Helplessness inside.

By Rumi from *One Handed Basket Weaving* - Coleman Barks

December 31, 2015

♪ HAPPY NEW YEAR
Here is what *A Course in Miracles* has to say about this time:

> *"This is the time in which a new year will soon be born from the time of Christ. I (Jesus) have perfect faith in you to do all that you would accomplish. Nothing will be lacking, and you will make complete and not destroy. Say, then to your brother:*
>
> *'I give you to the Holy Spirit as part of myself I know that you will be released, unless I want to use you to imprison myself.*
> *In the name of my freedom I choose your release, Because I recognize that we will be released together.'*
>
> *So, will the year begin in joy and freedom. There is much to do, and we have been long delayed. Accept the holy instant as this year is born, and take your place, so long left unfulfilled, in the Great Awakening. Make this year different by making it all the same. And let all your relationships be made holy for you. This is our will. Amen."* (ACIM, Chap. 15, sec. XI)

P.S. I had to ask Markus the meaning of the line "Make this year different by making it all the same." He said that before this year we lived in a world of duality. But now, we can let that be dissolved. Make it all the same means, continue the joy all the time instead of going up and down from misery to joy. Live in the same joy all of the time all of the year.
Love, Sondra

January 1, 2016

🎵 NEW YEAR'S DAY
Happy New Year to all of you! Here is what I recommend for this coming year: If you are making a resolution, why not make it so that you would be willing to do spiritual practices every morning. Some suggestions:

> ❖ Om Namah Shivaya or other mantras 108 times on mala beads. (This can be combined with a walk outside.)
> ❖ The *Course in Miracles* Lessons—Start today on lesson one and do the whole year. If you have already done them, start over. Deeper the next time.
> ❖ Write in gratitude journal.
> ❖ Forgiveness and prosperity prayers.
> ❖ Read the Divine Mother Names out loud.
> (Always take a shower FIRST and do not go to the computer until after the above.)
> ❖ Align with your guru if you are lucky enough to have one. We recommend Babaji, Jesus, and Ammachi = The Dream Team
> ❖ Forgive everyone completely, especially parents and siblings, and YOURSELF!
> ❖ Show your appreciation to people.
> ❖ Listen to *Buddha Bar* music, (especially while making love). There are over a dozen different ones you can order on Amazon!
> ❖ For exquisite joy make a habit of listening to Indian Classical music such as: Hariprasad

Chaurasia— Classical Indian flute; Ali Akbar
Kahn—Classical Indian Sarod; Shiv Kumar
Sharma—Classical Indian Santoor. If you do this
frequently as meditation, you will be tapped into
bliss and infinite intelligence.

❖ Seriously consider making the pilgrimage to
Babaji's ashram with us in the Spring. Dates vary
every year, like Easter. You will be a changed
person after India, I promise. Go here to get more
information: **India Quest**

Love, Sondra

January 2, 2016

❡ DALE CARNEGIE
Today I want to share some notes I took from readings by
Dale Carnegie long ago:

❖ You have to have a general fondness for people.
❖ Any thought that is expressed ORALLY and
continuously repeated from day to day will be taken
over by the subconscious and carried out to its
logical conclusion.
❖ Successful men are known always as men of
action.
❖ A mere wish appears to make no impression on
the subconscious, but a deep burning desire is
picked up by the subconscious and acted upon.
❖ There is nothing that will take the place of HIGH
AIM.
❖ A successful man is always engaged in work he
LOVES to perform.
❖ The acquisition of money is not serious business:
it is a GAME you play with yourself.
❖ Inside the energy of abundance there is no
struggle.
❖ The negative pillaging of your self-confidence
gives off telltale signs that others pick up

immediately. People won't part with their money unless they feel safe.

❖ Eliminate any energy DRAG in your life so that positive things will resonate to you faster.

❖ You have to be proud to serve and do a good job. You need no acknowledgement for you have granted that to yourself.

❖ Become good at getting strong people around you.

❖ In hard times, mediocrity will be taken out at the knees, but excellence always survives.

Love, Sondra

January 3, 2016

❡ THE SCALE OF ENLIGHTENMENT
In the book *Power Vs. Force,* David Hawkins discusses levels of enlightenment, according to a scale of 1,000 points. He says that

❖ 1,000 is an Arch Angel.
❖ 900 is an Avatar.
❖ 700 is Enlightenment.
❖ 500 is Unconditional love.

❡ We should at least be at 500! BUT the shocker is that 78% of the people in the world only calibrate at 200 (or below). Now, that is really bad. No wonder things are in such a mess out there! He also says we were born with a score based on our evolution in past lives which would be due to how enlightened we got before, and how much service we did. Someone like Ammachi, the Hugging Saint, was born at around 900 from the get-go. The problem is that most people only go up a mere 5 points per lifetime. So that would take about sixty lifetimes to get to 500 from 200. This is very, very slow. Well, when you do spiritual practices as I mentioned on New Year's day, you can, of course, go up the scale faster—especially if you study *A Course in Miracles.*

❡ And especially if you do *Liberation Breathing / Rebirthing*. You can see why I have dedicated my life to teaching these things. You can see why I keep recommending them. So then, ask yourself how serious are you about becoming a master? Are you moving up the scale or are you wasting another incarnation?
Love, Sondra

January 4, 2016

❡ MORE ON LEVELS
I found some more information on levels of enlightenment that is very interesting; but I cannot remember where I took these notes from.

I. THE ASPIRANT LEVEL
❖ Does establish programs to help less fortunate.
❖ Does create order of law.
❖ Does help humanity in spiritual evolution.
❖ Will fight for causes, but is ruled by emotions.
❖ Is easily seduced.
❖ Loves drama.
❖ Enjoys sense of pleasure.
❖ Purpose is usually marriage and children.
❖ Motivated by reward and punishment.

2. THE DISCIPLE LEVEL
❖ Is disillusioned by traditional religion.
❖ Is seeking answers.
❖ In the human potential movement.
❖ Finds a guru or workshops.
❖ Still highly judgmental.
❖ Usually in New Age Movement.
❖ Zealots.
❖ Feels chosen.
❖ On a mission.
❖ Dealing with past lives and karma.
❖ Develops physically.

3. THE INITIATE LEVEL

❖ One of total service.

❖ Extreme sacrifices are made.

❖ Makes promises they must keep.

❖ Big responsibilities are taken on.

❖ Everything changes: point of no return.

❖ Enlightened—all answers are within.

❖ Spirituality is one's whole nature.

❖ Everything has a deliberate purpose.

❖ Has tolerance and understanding.

❖ Is awake.

❖ Has meetings with Immortals.

❖ Entire life is dedicated to betterment of humanity.

ℐ P.S. My personal comment on this: I hope I am in the Initiate Level. I still relate to a guru (Babaji), however— precisely BECAUSE OF HIM, I am at the level I am at. So, I feel I relate to Him more in a constant state of gratitude. I would never cut off from Him because of that.

ℐ Do not judge yourself at whatever level you are at. Just notice there is always more. Until we are really like Babaji and Jesus and the Divine Mother, such as Ammachi, we still have something to clear and higher to go; myself included. Love, Sondra

January 5, 2016

ℐ ABOUT ASCENSION
I love to write about Ascension. Maybe everything I write is contributing to that. We know that the entire planet is making the shift. All of humanity is on the path of ascension whether they know it or not. However, there is a VAST DIFFERENCE between those consciously on the path of ascension and those who are not conscious of it. Those who are consciously on it are functioning at a very different frequency. The rate you are vibrating will determine the space you move into.

ℐ Ascension grants means of releasing yourself from the wheel of karma. Ascending through feeling is the right brain (feminine). The ascension may happen gradually. The more highly evolved we become the less tolerant are our vibrations of any negative energy. Aging and decay are due to being a prisoner to the law of gravity. Death is unnecessary. If we overcome it, we have rendered a huge service to mankind. Ascension is the ultimate goal of spiritual growth!

> *THE ONLY THING WORTH STRIVING FOR IS CLARITY. THAT IS THE BEST THING YOU COULD OFFER TO OTHERS.*

¶ If we become plugged in for the light to radiate through the heart, we gently can change people. Jesus and Babaji need our willingness to become Their messengers of love. Only through us can they complete their work.

¶ The #1 priority is SERVICE. All our concerns with illness, money, safety, special relationships are but ego attempts to distract us from the work we are to do. Say this to the Masters: "See in your great wisdom that I do the perfect thing that you require. See that Your wisdom directs me in every day in every way. See that I serve in my fullest capacity. Mighty, I AM Presence, take complete possession of my being and world now. Prepare me and see that I make my Ascension as soon as and as certainly as possible!"

¶ Upon awakening give thanks you are one day nearer to your ascension. The Masters ask you to commit UP FRONT. WE cannot become masters if we resist life. Say this to yourself: "My most negative thought about life is_____," and then change it. Spiritual power is a result of living a balanced life. Living a balanced life is a result of changing your mindset to be free, flowing, and happy.

¶ If you let yourself become a Master you are permeated with the God-like qualities of love, devotion, gentleness, compassion and joy. You have to live in a state of love, praise, and gratitude. Love requires that no fear be present. Take this test now: "I choose to hold on to my fear of _____, rather than to ascend." Tell the truth to yourself and process it. The Masters suggest that you discard events and situations and persons that throw you back into a state of heaviness. It may mean a complete transformation of lifestyle.   Love, Sondra

January 6, 2015

❡ SRI SHASTRIJI

Nobody spent more time with Babaji alone than his high priest Vishnu Dutt Shastriji. Once a yogi asked Shastriji what was he doing all the time when he was alone with Babaji? Shastriji said, "Mostly reading prayers." Then the yogi asked, "What was Babaji doing?" Shastriji replied, "Listening to my prayers, of course!" The yogi inquired further, "Every day listening to your prayers?" Then Shastriji looked at the yogi in surprise and commented: "Of course, who do you think listens to your prayers?"

❡ The REAL sound of prayer is always the sound of Thanksgiving and love. Prayer is putting ourselves in tune with the Infinite Spiritual and Cosmic energies so as to draw upon all the Source of energy, harmony, and knowledge. Approach God, not as a beggar, but as a son. "I am your child. Thou art my Father. Thou and I are One." Pray until you feel joy manifest and then you will know that God has tuned into your prayer broadcast. Then say: "Lord this is my need. I am willing to work for it. Please guide me and help me to have the right thoughts and do the right things to bring about success. Instead of asking for specific things, ask for the KINGDOM. When we possess that, all else will be added.

Every moment of our life should be a prayer. Then you get peace and you shall be permanently receptive to all the higher powers.

❡ P.S. If you pray out of desperate need, that always involves a feeling of weakness and inadequacy. It could not be made by a Son of God who knows who he is. You must pray believing in the possibility of what you are praying for. When you persist, refusing to accept failure, the object of will must materialize. If it does not you are sabotaging it all with your subconscious and you should have a Liberation Breathing session to find out what your block is and to let it go.   Love, Sondra

January 7, 2016

❡ WASTING YOUR LIFE
I had a student in Europe who had a core belief
(subconscious) that was "I am not adequate." We call this in
Rebirthing a personal lie. He was addicted to this thought.
The way I process addictions is to find out what the fear is
of giving it up. When I asked him what the fear of giving up
that thought forever was, he said, "It would mean that I have
wasted my whole life!" That answer was both interesting
and profound. The group laughed; but my student was
serious. I reminded the group that we had all wasted our
time indulging in our negative thoughts, especially our core
belief (which is our personal lie).
❡ It made me look at how I had wasted time in my life. I
used to obsess about food for years, for example. Some
people waste a lot of time with worrying for example. Others
actually have catastrophic thinking.
❡ All negative thoughts are a waste of time really. Try
looking at just the last hour. Did you waste any minutes in
indulging in negative thoughts? Or were you in the flow of
you own joy and creativity?
❡ I remember a friend I was trying to get to Babaji and India
for many years. She always had some excuse why she
could not go. I never gave up on her though. It took me
twelve whole years to get her there! When she finally got
there and felt how strong and beautiful the energy was, she
actually had to lie down frequently while unpacking her
bags. She finally got what it was all about and why I had
wanted her to have this marvelous experience. She looked
at me and said, "Sondra, I have wasted my whole life until
this moment." Think about it.

Love, Sondra

January 8, 2016

❡ EMOTIONAL INCEST
A recent client had the following presenting complaint: He was only attracted to married women or women who were already in relationships. He had been involved in many relationships with married women. This was an immediate clue to me that he was stuck in what we call the "emotional incest pattern." His case was easy for me to unravel; but there was an interesting twist to it. He thought that there had been no big problems between his parents' relationship until it all surfaced after his mother died. His father found her diary in the attic and read it to him. His mother had written about an affair she had when he was about 8 years old. After finding this out, he had a memory of his mother taking him along with her and leaving him alone in a room while she was gone a few hours. Although he had no conscious memory of this before her death, he had obviously absorbed this and somehow knew what was going on at age eight, although it was suppressed.
❡ The result was that he would be totally bored with women who were available. He was very attracted to women who were taken as they were then having an affair with him just like his mother had had affairs. It is tricky to actually let go of an incest pattern as it is all so taboo and buried, and yet tantalizing at the same time. You cannot begin to let it go until you face it and see that you are not winning with this. Fortunately, he was a very good breather. Although it seems odd to pray about sexual and incest issues, usually you have to call in a higher power to get around it.

Love, Sondra

January 9, 2016

❡ ON THE SUBJECT OF MONEY
God does not give us money and houses, etc. God gives us DIVINE SUBSTANCE. This substance is available to all! This substance is like creative energy which flows through the mind of man and we mold it with our thoughts and

therefore it externalizes itself as a mirror of our thoughts. You have to know the substance is there and you have to have a RELATIONSHIP with it. That relationship can be summed up in one word: GRATITUDE! You have to mold it with your prosperity thoughts and give up all poverty thoughts. It makes no sense for enlightened beings to have poverty consciousness. Poverty is of the ego. Remember this: Only you can deprive yourself of anything. Here is an excellent prayer to do daily—

> "God : Enrich my life so that I can enrich the lives of others. Oh that You would bless me indeed and enlarge my territory, that Your hand would be with me, and that You would keep me from evil, that I may not cause pain." 1st Chronicles 4: 9-10

♫ You can also order the little *Abundance Book* by John Price. He has a 40-day plan in there that is marvelous. It is easy, too. You say out loud statements such as this—

> "God is lavish, unfailing abundance, the rich omnipresent substance of the Universe. This all-providing Source of Infinite prosperity is individualized as me, the Reality of me."

♫ Stick with it!

Love, Sondra

January 10, 2016

♫ MORE ABOUT MONEY
More on the subject of money. I took a lot of seminars and read a lot of books on money, but they did not really help until I cracked my own money case. That means I had to do introspection and find out what was my own personal wiring on the subject. What were my family patterns and what was my karma on money, and what were my thought patterns? Then I had to change all that and breathe it out with Liberation Breathing. Now I am down to using the process

in *The Path of Wealth* by May McCarthy, which I already wrote about. I can get the maximum value from that because I worked on my own case before.

❡ When a couple comes together, the money case of one can affect the relationship—for example, what if one in the couple has a "money rejection complex"? That could ruin things for both. Each partner should know thoroughly the financial habits of their own and their mate's family. Mates should help each other overcome this programming rather than be into blame.

❡ Some people even think money is sinful, and one is not spiritual if one has a lot of money. I already talked about this yesterday, showing how money DOES have a spiritual basis coming from Divine Substance. You must cease to believe that money is your support, your security, or your safety. Money isn't— God is! Transform your consciousness from one of effects (materialism) to one of cause (spirituality).

❡ Of course, you need to change your most negative thought about money and breathe it out. Also say to yourself, "What blocks me from receiving money or abundance is_____."

Change that thought and breathe it out!

Love, Sondra

January 11, 2016

❡ ON RELATIONSHIPS

"When two people resonate at the same frequency, it does not matter what they do. It feels good and it is fun. In this relationship the couple is more interested in the vibration of God than their problems. Problems become opportunities. They rise above the system of obstacles. There is a feeling of cherishing going on. They are cheerleaders for each other's evolution. The frequency of chemistry can truly be felt when one is combining the wonderful energy of sexuality and friendship, with the desire to use healing energy toward each other. In this combined frequency, the couple can heal each other, whereas in the old paradigm, couples could destroy each other. A couple should cultivate their capacity to ENJOY. There needs to be the intention of feeling good! Keep asking:

> ❖ Are we ascending the ladder of holiness this week or are we descending?
> ❖ Is what we are doing life-enhancing or life-depreciating?

❡ If what you are doing is descending the ladder of holiness, or is life depreciating, you are going to be feeling bad. If what you are doing is ascending the ladder of holiness and is life enhancing, you are going to be feeling good! The relationship viewed from the soul level (holy relationship) is very different from those viewed at the personality level (unholy relationship).

❡ A relationship that is with a soul mate has a lot of passion naturally. One that is not may have a lot of drama to get a rush. How will you ever get out of your karma that way? Your karma can bury you." From *Spiritual Intimacy: What You Really Want With A Mate*

Love, Sondra

January 12, 2016

❡ THE TROUBLE WITH SPECIAL RELATIONSHIPS
In the special relationship, we deny our need for God by substituting the need for special people and special things. Our imagined hope for salvation suddenly depends on one individual, so the attention our partner may devote to activities or people outside the relationship feels like a threat to our well-being. An unholy relationship feeds on differences, each partner perceives that his mate possesses qualities or abilities that he has not. Each enters into the union with the idea of completing themselves and robbing the other. They each remain in the relationship until they decide there is nothing left to steal and then they move on.

❡ In these relationships, what reminds a person of past grievances ATTRACTS THEM! Such people are not even attempting to join with the body of their mate. Instead they seek a union with the bodies of those who are not there!

What this means is that you tend to set your mate up as past people who were caretakers, whom you did not complete with.

☞ *A Course in Miracles* discusses what they call a special love relationship; and this, it says is the ego's chief weapon to keep you from God! It starts with the belief that there is something lacking in us that can never be filled. We seek to find the answer outside. We fall in love with someone who we think will fill this need. This is the ego's version of a marriage made in Heaven! As long as you, my special love, continue to act so my needs are met I will love you. The smallest deviation from this arrangement induces terror.

☞ This dependency breeds contempt and we end up attacking those we depend on. If you, the partner, stops meeting my needs, I will hate you.

☞ In the special love relationship our mate is supposed to be our savior, our idol. It won't work.— From our book *Spiritual Intimacy: What You Really Want With A Mate* p. 69. Tomorrow I will go over the special HATE relationship.
Love, Sondra

January 13, 2016

☞ THE SPECIAL HATE RELATIONSHIP
In this case, the responsibility for one's misery is shifted to another. We say, "It is you who has done this terrible thing to me." In a special hate relationship, the hated person's past mistakes are used to justify our attack. All mistakes are used to build a case against them. The ego's plan for salvation here is centered on holding grievances. Anger always involves projection of our separation. Projection, while seeming to deliver us from our guilt, really reinforces it. Our guilt merely becomes strengthened as a result of our unfair attacks on another. The more we attack (get angry), the guiltier we will feel. The guiltier we feel, the more our need to deny and project. Our need to find a scapegoat to hate is overwhelming.

☞ Having projected, we have a fear they will do the same. We unconsciously believe their attack back at us is then justified, so then we build defenses against our fear of retaliation. The problem then is that the defenses attract attack.

₲ In these relationships, people are unconsciously chosen because of their vulnerabilities. Whatever reminds you of your past grievance attracts you.

₲ And what you have not forgiven you attract. Because we believe that we are separated from God, and that is a sin, then we are a sinner. But we do not want to face that, so we project it onto another, like our partner. Now he or she is the sinner. When we threw away our innocence and took up guilt, we made everything a potential threat. We even believe God is going to crucify us and demand our death. Then we also have to defend ourselves against God! But we are going to pretend this is not happening. We now substitute our relationship with each other to replace God.

₲ The ego led you to believe that what you do to others you have escaped. But you have to know the ego is savage and special relationships are brutal. You end up more attracted to pain than to love. TAKE A BREATH—YOUR PLAN WILL NOT WORK.

Love, Sondra

January 14, 2016

₲ WHY DO WE WANT TO BE SPECIAL?
Today I want to review and go over again in another way, what I said the last two days. That is how important it is for us all. It all starts with the fact that we have a "shaky identity" because we think we separated from God. We have thoughts like, "I am not good enough," "I am worthless," "I am bad," "I am guilty," "I am a fake," "I am wrong," "I am nothing,"
"I am a disappointment," etc. These we call personal lies.

₲ Everyone has one suppressed in their subconscious. It is imperative to find out what is yours, exactly. This thought will invalidate your Divinity. (A good breathworker will help you discover it and neutralize it through breathing and affirmations.) So anyway, you become aware that something is bothering you; and you have to get rid of it. The way you get rid of it is by attacking your mate for example. At the same time, you want your mate to make you feel good about yourself, so you won't have to look at yourself. You want your mate to be what you need them to be, so you make them an idol. This is called a special relationship in *A Course in Miracles.*

¶ But in your mind, only certain people can meet your needs, for example a blond or brunette who looks like your mother. Your choices are based upon the past. If your mate does not meet your needs, you think you have a right to get angry. And yet, *A Course in Miracles* says very, very, plainly that ANGER IS NEVER JUSTIFIED, (and Jesus meant NEVER when he said that). So now you have the epitome of conditional love: "If you don't meet my needs, I will hate you. But then I will feel guilty for using and abusing you." So, then you will have fear because guilt demands punishment.

¶ Sooner or later we set up a codependent bargain: "I am going to be dependent on you; and that means I can be helpless. You are going to take care of me, and that means you get to be dominant."

¶ Then the ego's game continues: "By knocking you down, I get elevated. I want to be the king of the mountain in this relationship."

¶ The whole mess started when we attacked our own Self-Identity. We got rid of God on some level because we thought He was not making us special. Then we feel empty and alone. But we do not take responsibility for our own unhappiness. We look for a substitute for God, and that substitute is a special relationship. We find this other special person and take away their specialness. Meanwhile they are supposed to save us. When we make them special, they get to *own our soul!* We set up a psychodrama that re-enacts the past. Of course, this does not happen in the romantic period, in the first few months of our strong attraction.

¶ Try living together for some years and see if you can avoid it. It is all going on at the subconscious level. That is why we need a teacher to point it out and to point the way out. (From p. 72 from our new book *Spiritual Intimacy,* which you can get it on line.)
Love, Sondra

January 15, 2016

❡ OVERCOMING

What is the answer in helping anyone overcome their personal lie? First of all, the personal lie is a deep-seeded negative thought you have about yourself at the subconscious level. Everyone has one.

❡ What is the answer to help anyone who does not love himself or herself? What is the answer to help anyone who is very "needy?" What is the answer to help anyone who thinks he or she is not getting enough love from their partner?

❡ I find the answer in *A Course in Miracles*, Lesson 229 LOVE, WHICH CREATED ME, IS WHAT I AM.
The lesson reads:

> *"I seek my own Identity and find It in these words: 'Love which created me, is what I am.' Now need I seek no more. Love has prevailed. So still It waited for my coming home, that I will turn away no longer from the holy face of Christ. And what I look upon attests the truth of the Identity I sought to lose, but which my Father has kept safe for me. Father, my thanks to You for what I am; for keeping my Identity untouched and sinless in the midst of all the thoughts of sin my foolish mind made up. And thanks to You for saving me from them. Amen."*

❡ If one REALLY got this lesson, how could one be needy? You don't have to desire or search for love desperately. You are it! You don't have to wait for your mate to give it to you or feel badly when it seems he or she is not giving it to you enough. You have it, so give it. Then you will FEEL it! You don't have to ever dislike yourself again. How can you when the truth is that you are love? What is there about you to dislike? All the other negative thoughts about yourself are nonsense.

❡ This especially applies to your personal lie, which is a LIE! You are NOT your worst thought about yourself. You are love and that is all you are. It is so simple really. But can one remember this?   Love, Sondra

January 16, 2016

❡ ON FINDING A MATE

A client we had was really, really eager to have her life mate. She was in her thirties, very pretty and quite enlightened. I found her to be divine and there seemed no reason she was not mated by now. She came to us for a *Liberation Breathing Session* to find out her blocks. She had had some breathwork before, and so she told me her most negative core belief was "I am not good enough". That did not seem deep enough to me. When I took her history, I found out she was born with the cord around her neck. So, I knew I had to go deep. The thought, "I don't want to be here," occurred to me as a cord around the neck is usually a kind of suicide attempt. But even that did not seem exactly to be the block to her having a relationship.

❡ So, Markus and I kept on talking and talking to her about her prenatal trauma. Then she told us she had always had the thought that there was a twin (brother) in the womb with her who had died. THERE WAS THE CLUE! It became obvious that her real preverbal core belief was this: "I am alone." How can you manifest your mate when you are convinced you have to be alone? She had felt totally alone after her twin was absorbed. (Absorbed twins are more common than you might think.)

❡ She went through it in the session also mentioning that she had even told people that maybe she was someone not meant to have a relationship in this life. She was about to be resigned to that. However, that was not what she wanted in this life. She wanted a relationship. I don't know what would have happened had she not come for a session, as she was obviously not at all clear on her preverbal thoughts.

❡ Sometimes it takes a lot of skill on the part of the Breathworker to ask the right questions. When you do, miracles can happen. She left very happy of course. Tomorrow I will share more about finding your perfect mate.

Love, Sondra

January 17, 2016

❡ HOW TO MANIFEST
I promised I would write how I manifested my second husband which some would say was late in life (but not me).

❖ First of all. I was not coming from need. I was very happy all by myself. I had Babaji and that was a lot. (Where need ends true love begins.)

❖ But then I DECIDED I wanted to experience a Holy Relationship in this incarnation. That was the beginning of it all.

❖ I asked myself what FEELING, what term would explain the kind of relationship I would want and I came up with DEEP EASE. I wanted nothing less as I am a public figure and don't have time for the pain. So, I meditated almost a year on becoming that myself first.

❖ Then I asked my guru, Babaji, for an *arranged marriage.* After all, He knows everyone's past, present and future better than I do, and I did not want to make a mistake and choose the wrong man who could not fit my mission.

❖ However, I had been so independent for so long that I had to take certain ACTION to change myself so he could come in

❖ The first thing I did was go out and buy several presents for my future man to make it more real. My roommates thought I was crazy as I wrapped these presents. I got a Brooks Brothers shirt, cologne, wallet, and a ring, the size of which I had to guess of course.

❖ Then I did a mantra, which is written on my blog: *http://liberationbreathing.blogspot.com/2009/08/how-sondra-used-cosmic-dating-service.html#*

❖ Then he still did not come so I decided to write him letters AS IF he was here. This was starting to work! I could feel someone coming.

❖ Finally, I wrote this affirmation: "My perfect twin

flame is here now."
❖ I let go.

❡ Markus showed up in Philadelphia (not where I liked or expected). I had not seen him in twenty years, but we knew each other from the old days. I said, "Oh, are you still in the same relationship?" He said, "No." Two Babaji devotees came in my room and said, "Don't you get it? He is the ONE!"

❡ The rest is the miracle. Incidentally the shirt fit and amazingly enough the ring fit perfectly. I also read him the letters I had written, and we cracked up laughing. The rest was so easy. Our astrologer who did our comparative charts said she had never seen so many sextiles of compatibility. We have the exact same spiritual path. We went right to work on our joint mission!
Love, Sondra

January 18, 2016

❡ SUICIDE
Not so long ago I had a student for a very brief time in Europe. She wrote me later that she was suicidal, all alone and very afraid. As a teacher it was my obligation to tell her that one who commits suicide enters a very deep darkness from which it is most difficult to be released. We reap the consequences of our actions of former births. To try to escape from this by suicide only prolongs the agony indefinitely. It does not solve anything—it prevents us from paying off karmic debts. In other words, I had to tell her that it was NOT AN OPTION as she would just get more and more STUCK in her path.

❡ I also wanted to be a FRIEND to her. Who is called a true friend? He who makes you turn your mind towards the Beloved, he is your best friend. But a person who diverts your thoughts away from the Him and tempts you to progress in the direction of death, he is an enemy. The man who makes no effort to improve himself is in fact committing suicide. I decided to support her by email and help her correct herself. She fortunately listened to me. Every day we made progress. I am happy to say that even she found her true twin flame in the end. One of the big successes I had for the year!

⌘ Part of the training I had by Babaji was VERY TOUGH, you see. The very first Rebirthing client He sent to me sat down and said, "I just want to commit suicide, and don't you talk me out of it." That was her first line—my first client! Imagine. Well, I thought, if she really wanted to commit suicide, she would not bother to come to me.

⌘ So I played the game a bit. I said, "Well let's postpone your suicide one week and you lie down and breathe." So she did. She felt some better, but the second visit it was the same thing. I replied with the same thing. I kept making her promise to postpone her suicide one week. This went on for many sessions.

⌘ By the eighth session, she sat up and said, "Oh, suddenly I feel like living." She had breathed out enough of the unconscious death urge that she changed. I kept track of her. She also got married and became a dancer! So the point is, NEVER GIVE UP; JUST BREATHE! (If you want a *Liberation Breathing* session contact me on my website: bit.ly/LBSession).

Love, Sondra

January 19, 2016

⌘ WHAT I LEARNED ON THE ROAD

We have this student in Spain we have known for quite a few years. Every time we come, we try to get him through his guilt. But every year he gets stuck in it. This time I finally asked him to tell me his fear of giving up his guilt. He replied, "I will die. The Catholic Church will kill me." This brought up something very deep for me. I started coughing. I almost could not finish the training.

⌘ That night in Tenerife I got a deeper cough. We were headed for a holiday in Seville and I wanted to go anyway. I was a wreck on the plane.

⌘ I did not figure out what was going on with me until that night in Seville when we walked by the place where the Inquisition occurred. Then it all came up for me. I was angry at the Catholic Church for its atrocities. The reason this never came up for me before is that I was raised Lutheran in this life. Now I was suddenly processing past lives with the Catholic Church. I thought I probably had karma with that guy also.

ℐ I almost never get sick. I actually had to go to a doctor in Seville. I told my husband that my symptoms were actually the guilt coming out. What I learned is how guilt can make you really ill. Soon we flew to Italy.

ℐ By a miracle we ended up staying at an estate in the country near Assisi, the place of St. Francis. I was excited for Markus to see it and experience it. Years ago I had had a miracle healing in his little church which, is inside a larger Basilica, called the Portiuncula. I was secretly hoping I would have a miracle in there again. And our hostess took us there! They say if you make it to that little church you can have total forgiveness. I went in there and prayed like mad. I asked to be forgiven for my hatred of the Catholic Church. When we left there I heard the words: "My guilt is gone." At that moment I was healed of my cough. What I learned is that forgiveness heals and sometimes you need the support of the Masters—St. Francis was very enlightened, and Masters like him can help us with anything.   Love, Sondra

January 20, 2016

ℐ RELATIONSHIPS AND HEALING
My favorite subjects to teach are relationships and healing. You may not have read what *A Course in Miracles* Text has to say about healing, so I am going to summarize some of it. You need to know this if you want to stay well.

> *"When the ego tempts you to sickness do not ask the Holy Spirit to heal the body, for this would merely be to accept the ego's belief that the body is the proper aim of healing. Ask, rather, that the Holy Spirit teach you the right perception of the body, for perception alone can be distorted. Only perception*

can be sick, because only perception can be wrong." (ACIM, Text; chap. 8; sec. ix*)*

❡ Healing must occur in the place where it is needed, i.e. in the mind that conceived of the insane idea of separation. In other words, the mind rules the body and all symptoms and conditions are due to negative thoughts you made up. All pain is the effort of clinging to a negative thought. Same for all symptoms. And if you keep clinging to the negative thought long enough, you might create a full-blown disease. That is why you must process the thought behind each symptom immediately.

❡ I was shocked when ACIM said, "One thing is not harder to heal than another." As a Registered Nurse, I could not believe that. But then I finally got that if you *ask the Holy Spirit* to heal you, nothing is too hard for the H.S. Here is the explanation: "The Holy Spirit cannot distinguish among degrees of error, for if He taught that one form of sickness is more serious than another, He would be teaching that one error can be more real than another." The miracles that the Holy Spirit inspires can have no order of difficulty because every part of creation is "one order." Healing of the Holy Spirit always works. Unless the healer heals by Him, the results will vary.

❡ Most people are asking for healing of the body and this is a mistake, as the body is just a projection of the mind. Most people are not working with the Holy Spirit either, as they are afraid to do so. What if you ask the Holy Spirit for what you want but you are afraid of it? This is why certain specific forms of healing are not achieved. You wonder why would I be afraid of healing? Because one is afraid of more of God, more of light, more of holiness. We have it all backwards. Sickness is often a problem of guilt. Guilt demands punishment—so we are punishing ourselves by getting sick.

❡ We are afraid of our own innocence. The ego actually will tell you that, if you DARE to think you are innocent, then you are really guilty!

❡ To be healed you have to release fear. How do you release fear? Breathe it out. I often see people get healed of

59

a long disease after only one session of Liberation Breathing!

Love, Sondra

January 21, 2016

❡ MORE ON HEALING

"Health is nothing more than a joint purpose. It reflects the Joint Will. You must overcome the separation to be healed. This is overcome by UNION. To join with Jesus (Holy Spirit) —all things are possible. The ego is the belief in separation. You have to say, 'I renounce the ego in myself.'"

❡ Sickness is based on these two premises of the ego:

> 1) You are the body (you actually are Spirit).
> 2) The body is for attack and defense (anger).

The ego has a profound investment in sickness. A sick body does not make any sense. Sickness isn't what the body is for!

❡ The Holy Spirit teaches you to use the body ONLY to reach your brothers, so He can teach His message through you. The body is only a communication device. Health is the result of relinquishing all attempts to use the body lovelessly. If you are sick, you are withdrawing from the Holy Spirit (Jesus) and yourself. Sickness is Idolatry! When you do not value yourself, you become sick. But His value of you can heal you. Jesus can heal you because He knows you. He knows your value for you. YOU ALWAYS RECEIVE AS MUCH AS YOU CAN ACCEPT! God created you perfect and if you believe you can be sick, you have placed other gods before him (idolatry). If you are God, would He allow Himself to suffer? If you accept yourself as God created you, you will be incapable of suffering. All this above reflects principles in ACIM. Traveling today to Sedona.

Love, Sondra

January 22, 2016

❡ HEALING (continued)

A Course in Miracles talks about the false "god of sickness." Here goes:

> *"The rituals of the god of sickness are strange and very demanding. Joy is never permitted, for depression is the sign of allegiance to him. Depression means that you have forsworn God. Many are afraid of blasphemy, but they do not understand what it means. They do not realize that to deny God is to deny their own Identity, and in this sense the wages of sin is death. The sense is very literal; denial of life perceives its opposite, as all forms of denial replace what is with what is not. No one can really do this, but that you think you can and believe you have is beyond dispute."* (ACIM, Text, chap.10, sec. v)

❡ Depression means that you have forgotten God. It means that you are willing to NOT know yourself in order to be sick. This is actually blasphemy. Say this: "I accept the undoing of denial of God." If you accept yourself as God created you, you will be incapable of suffering. What can the Son of God not accomplish with the Fatherhood of God (Holy Spirit) in him? AND YET THE INVITATION MUST COME FROM YOU. Jesus says this:

> *"Do not set limits on what you believe I can do through you, or you will not accept what I can do for you. Yet it is done already, and unless you give all that you have received you will not know that your Redeemer liveth, and that you have awakened with him. Redemption is recognized only by sharing it."* (ACIM, Text, chap. 11, sec. vi.)

To God all things are possible. Ask yourself this: Do I want the problem, or do I want the answer? As you become willing to accept the help of God by asking for it, you will get

61

it because you want it. Nothing will be beyond your healing power because nothing will be denied your simple request. What problems will not disappear in the presence of God's answer?

❡ Our problem is we have a fear of a miracle healing. That is why we should not ask for a miracle healing overnight. We could not handle it. We must instead ask for the release of the FEAR of the miracle. The correction of fear is our responsibility; but we can ask for help in the CAUSE of the fear. The cause of the fear would always be the belief in separation—so, your prayer for healing must be correct. Tomorrow, I will give you the prayers I have used.

Speaking tonight at Unity Church here in beautiful Sedona, Arizona.

Love, Sondra

January 23, 2016

❡ HEALING AND HOLINESS

I had a lot of conditions in my body I had to heal, and wrote about how I did that in my book *Healing and Holiness*. The hardest one was acute anorexia which I got after my mother died. It took me a long time to figure out the right prayers and affirmations. The job of a true teacher is to save you time. So, I am going to share them with you and save you a lot of time in healing tough conditions. These are worth a million bucks! So here they are:

> **1.** "I know you Holy Spirit can and will resolve this problem now by offering me a miracle. I allow this. I allow healing to happen. I give up my addiction to fear, pain, and death."
>
> **2.** "I no longer deny you your ability to bestow your blessing of healing onto me."
>
> **3.** "I decree, I declare, I determine, I decide, I command, and I order, in the name of the I AM PRESENCE to let go of this condition."
>
> **4.** "I let go of my power trip of not letting anyone heal me so that I could be king."
>
> **5.** "I give up my competition with God."

6. "I am united with Jesus, Babaji and the Divine Mother."

❡ I had to do them in this exact order. Number four was the big breakthrough for me. I was able to get these prayers/affirmations because of studying *A Course in Miracles*. When I got these correct, I created making it to Ammachi for a hug and she finished it all off. But I had to get my mind straight first.

Love, Sondra

January 24, 2016

❡ A MEDIOCRE LIFE

A client came to us who was very unsatisfied with her life. She did not really want to be here in life. She was living a very mediocre life according to her; and not reaching her potential at all. She felt no love in her marriage of 21 years. She was about to turn 50 and she was afraid to leave her marriage because she had tried to separate once before and could not handle it. That was because her house and her routine made her feel somewhat secure. So, she was co-dependent on her husband for kind of a false security. I thought her whole problem was she did not want to be here in life; but she had another thought that she was really stuck on which was, "I am unworthy of life because I am a female." Her father wanted a boy. As a result of this she took the first offer of marriage that came along, thinking she might never get another one. She was not really in love with the man, but she was curious what marriage would be like. To me it was tragic that she was not in love with her husband at all from the beginning. It was a set-up to have such a mediocre life. She had no courage and she was bored to tears and could not stand her life, but she was too stuck to do anything about it. She did not even have the courage to tell her husband what she wanted in the marriage as she felt she was unworthy to speak up. She also had a mediocre career and one of her former teachers had told her that her work was a waste of brains.

❡ It made me wonder how many people are settling for

mediocrity? Here was this woman, about to waste an incarnation! How many people have wasted incarnations? When one is stuck in mediocrity, one's death urge comes up and then one does not want to be here. Then things get worse because if one has the thought "I don't want to be here," one's death urge comes up even more. Then things get worse and worse.

❡ She needed one major adjustment: changing the thought, "I am not worthy" to "I am worthy." I am worthy of speaking up. I am worthy of having a man who demonstrates love to me. I am worthy of moving forward. I am worthy of having a rewarding career. I am worthy of happiness and so on and so on.

❡ She took the LRT training to heart and told us she wanted to go for it with a whole new life. After her private *Liberation Breathing Session* she was shining. She had dropped tons of fear. She felt courage to move on. A mediocre life is one of no satisfaction.
Love, Sondra

January 25, 2016

❡ A TRUE MASTER
In contrast to the mediocre life, let's talk about the opposite. What is it like when you let in a True Master like Babaji into your life?

❡ When your consciousness is awakened by a true master like Babaji, your eyes will discover the beauty of creation. Your ears will hear divine words. You will taste heavenly food. Your hands will learn to create in finer, higher worlds of the Soul. A True Master like Babaji gives you victory over your weaknesses which will give you real power.

❡ Babaji emanates beneficial elements for His group. His sole care is to give you elements of higher nature in harmony with Heaven. You find nothing but blessings near Babaji. He corrects your mistakes. He encourages you, and under His guidance you end up being a virtuoso. With Him you cannot fall back into inertia; you feel continuously stimulated. He draws you along by His words and by His example.

꽃 How can you meditate on heavenly subjects when you have no high ideal which will lift you above your ordinary life? Babaji may have to be severe on His disciples by telling them certain truths for their progress and advancement. (When you are ill, you think it makes perfect sense to swallow disagreeable remedies.) Most people are afraid to tell you the truth. The Master is not. Babaji has to give several injections and a few operations. His motive is never to demolish someone but to help him change to become beautiful and to be saved. What He wants is only the best for you. He wants you to be free to be rich and loved by all.

꽃 Nothing can surpass receiving an initiation and wisdom from Babaji. He will give you love you never found even in your own family. The invisible world sends masters like Him and if you don't accept them, then you might get other teachers in the form of illness, misery or difficulties. Babaji can open doors for you but it is up to you to walk through them. He is an essential tuning fork. You must tune yourself to Him. You end up vibrating quite differently. There is an osmosis that goes on between you and Babaji. You benefit greatly from his light.

꽃 Why do I keep talking about Him? Because all this is the truth; and I want it for you. I don't want you to have a mediocre life. You can best have it by coming to His home in India. (We take a group April every year in March/April.) But do you fear sacrificing your lower nature? Every moment, you can choose a new life!
Love, Sondra

January 26, 2016

꽃 FORMULA FOR HAPPINESS
Babaji's formula for happiness is **Truth, Simplicity, Love, and Service to Mankind.** Then he gave us Liberation Breathing and the mantra (Om Namah Shivaya) for clearing ourselves. He often elaborated on our job as being in SERVICE. He searches for those minds sensitive to His Plan. It is only as we serve that we advance. Service awakens our heart center. Service is not really a quality or a

SONDRA RAY

performance. It is a life demonstration. We must dedicate our whole life to the betterment of human living. True service is a spontaneous out flowing of a loving heart. In order for us to be candidates for initiation, we must have a love for ALL humanity.

ᛃ The work to be done as a whole is the main importance - *never personal status for oneself.* We should be willing to work without recognition. We should pay no attention to personality likes and dislikes, prejudices, attachments, self-pity, defenses, pride, limitations, anger, grievances, selfishness, etc. (Also, worry puts you in the wrong vibration for receiving a Master's guidance.) Circumstances and environment should not be an obstacle. Nor can you have a love for power over others, and you cannot have a fear of speaking about God.

ᛃ The Masters have a plan. This plan is joyful and it will make life easier! Think about how it is a great joy to participate in the Master's plan. Help Babaji, help Ammachi, help Jesus. Jesus says in the text of ACIM, "I am here only to be truly helpful." (**ACIM, Text, chap. 2, sec. V. A.**) If you align with them, Joy will naturally be the quality of your Soul. Being part of the group of World Servers is a magnificent thing. This group has no organization of any kind; no headquarters and the service could be cultural, scientific, political, philosophical, or psychological. Whatever it is you, in your life—a life that is an example to others. You have to recognize the Divine in everyone.

ᛃ What can you personally do to increase your level of service? This is an important question in life. The greatest beings on the planet throughout history have had a love of all humanity, and their actions have made Life better and more peaceful for the human race. What are you doing to serve? Thank you.

Love, Sondra

January 27, 2016

¶ HELLO FROM SANTA FE
Here are some great affirmations:

1. I am alive with the light of God and a blessing wherever I go.
2. I am the living energy of Pure Spirit.
3. I take on the vibration of the Most High right now.
4. When my attention is on the Presence, I bring what I need into this dimension.
5. Every day I am going to be aware of the Presence.
6. My decisions are not made from lack, but from overflow consciousness.
7. I am fasting from that which would bring me down.
8. I am moving from the mundane to the miraculous.
9. What I want benefits others.
10. I wake up in the morning with my mind staying on the Spirit.
11. My consciousness vibrates with the Infinite Invisible supply.
12. I see what is glorious about others.
13. The Eternal fountain of Love showers its blessings on me.
14. I create Heaven wherever I am.
15. I am more interested in the vibration of God than my problems.
16. I am the answer. I stand as a divine exclamation point for what is right!
17. The cosmic good of God expresses as my life.
18. My stand for God has a big significance in the world.
19. I appreciate and celebrate each moment.
20, My conversations are always life affirming.
21. God is revealed through the generosity of my heart and the brilliance of my mind.
22. I gratefully say YES to good, YES to life, and Yes to my greatness.

23. I am getting better and better and better for the rest of my life.
24. I am in the frequency of newness. Behold, I make all things new.
25. I am a strong attractor in the cosmic field.
MORE TOMORROW
Love, Sondra
(Inspired by Rev. Michael Beckwith)

January 28, 2016

𝄞 MORE GREAT AFFIRMATIONS

26. I invite universal wisdom to give me guidance, now.
27. My Joy is the evidence of God.
28, My love is greater than my past. The best is yet to come.
29. I am liberated from conventional thinking.
30. I see the perfect divine blueprint in each person.
31. My body temple is made from genius mind.
32. I incarnated with the brilliance of the universe within me.
33. Lives are changed simply by my walking in a room.
34. I am willing to change according to new information.
35. I unhook from the agreement of mediocrity and make an agreement for excellence.
36. I step into the vibration of a Sage with no age.
37. I am here for something bigger that personal success. I am here for planetary success.
38. My life is a sacred practice of gratitude.
39. I have the sheer happiness of being alive!
40. I release anything that would inhibit the flow of life.
41. I totally let go and let God.
42. I am willing for the shift to occur here.
43. I am an ambassador of the invisible dimensions.
44. God is asking me to do something--He has me

on redial.
45. I have the intention of bliss and ecstasy.
46. I have an intention beyond reason.
47. If I am not happy, I am out of integrity with my soul.
48. I am available to only the highest and the best.
49. I don't want to carry who I was five minutes ago into the future.
50. I am living from inspiration.

This is such a great abundance of good thoughts. You may like to take only a few of them and memorize them and repeat them to yourself for a few days like a mantra. You will be amazed at how good they make you feel.
Love, Sondra

January 29, 2016

¶ THE PERSONALITY TRAITS ASSOCIATED WITH LONGEVITY

1. Conscientious. (That means wishing to do what is right and doing one's work thoroughly; being persistent, responsible, and taking care of one's health.)
2. Easy to laugh.
3. Socially connected.
4. Optimistic and easy going.
5. Happy.
6. Extroverted.

¶ THINKING ABOUT PHYSICAL IMMORTALITY
Dying takes much more effort. Many people chose to die rather than face their inner conflicts and take responsibility for the conflict itself—or for seeking help to get the resolution.
¶ We die because we believe we must. Our computer brain falsely programmed that death is necessary. We have been subjected to mass hypnosis from parents, relatives, the church, the media and so on.

❡ Physical immortality is the first step to Ascension. Our body is an energy system. The difference between a mortal and immortal is what they think about. The body is totally obedient to the thoughts in the mind.

Jesus said: "The power of life and death are in the tongue."

❡ What most people talk about is chronological numbers called age and death. Ascension is a process of completing the merging of the physical body with the higher dimension body or Christ body (light body). Your biology actually ascends. But you cannot think your way to Ascension; it is a heart-centered path.

❡ Where are you at on this subject? Do you really want to keep on dying and reincarnating? Are you working out your death urge?

From our book *Liberation Breathing: The Divine Mother's Gift*
Love, Sondra

January 30, 2016

❡ ARE YOU READY TO BE A LIGHTWORKER?
Are you ready to be among the ministers of God? Maybe you don't realize it, but your work is your ministry. Babaji says, "Work is Worship & Idleness is death." Therefore, your ministry is everyone you meet throughout the day, and everyone in your address book, email list, Facebook, etc.

❡ *ACIM* says, "Forget not that the healing of God's Son is all the world is for." (ACIM Text, chap. 24, sec. VI, 4) This also includes your business, your work. Your business is therefore one of the main avenues for your spiritual healing, since you spend so much of your life there. Your business is also a spiritual healing for others who work with you and those who come to you daily. Those who understand to use business as part of their spiritual path will find that their labors are never in vain.

❡ I already told you that your work should be the highest

service you can think of for mankind. If you are not in a service-type of career, figure out how to make it more service oriented by being a light worker there.

❡ Since the purpose of life is to find God, then this purpose should be an integral part of any career. Otherwise you could end up with what Yogananda calls "a hornets' nest of troubles." Everyone has a role that he or she was designed to perform here. So, it is not as if you go to work and then come home and get enlightened. Every moment is a spiritual opportunity to help raise the consciousness of someone.

❡ Here are some things that raise your light:

- ❖ Generosity
- ❖ Abundance
- ❖ Singing
- ❖ Laughter
- ❖ Being out in nature
- ❖ Serenity
- ❖ Clarity
- ❖ Love
- ❖ Relaxation
- ❖ Hugging from the heart
- ❖ Meditation
- ❖ Joy
- ❖ Thinking good of others
- ❖ Liberation Breathing
- ❖ A Course in Miracles
- ❖ Reading spiritual books
- ❖ Mantras
- ❖ Looking at art
- ❖ Listening to great music

Love, Sondra

January 31, 2016

§ THE MEANING OF GRACE

The dictionary defines grace as "unmerited divine assistance given humans for their regeneration or sanctification." Christianity calls it "divine favor." I think Catholics say you can only get it through the sacraments and so you must go to communion. But I like this definition: *"The empowering presence of God enabling you to be who He created you to be and to do what He called you to do."* (It does not say the word unmerited.) In India they say that grace is "The ultimate key required for spiritual self-realization." I think they say it has to be earned so you can transcend lifetimes of karma.

§ I like Ammachi's definition the best. She says: "Grace is the factor that brings the right result at the right time in the right proportions to your actions. Dedication is the most essential aspect." The more dedicated you are; the more open you remain for grace to enter. The more open you are, the more love you experience. The more love you have, the more grace you experience. Grace is openness. It is the spiritual strength and the intuitive vision that you can experience while performing an action. By being open, your mind is transformed into a better channel through which shakti (divine energy) can flow. The flow of shakti and its expression through our action is grace. The real source of grace is within. Amma says all this; but she also says that grace comes from beyond. I think she means that we won't recognize it is from within until we grasp the beyond.

§ When we read the Divine Mother names during a *Liberation Breathing Session*, we are calling on the grace of the Divine Mother to help our client. I was told this makes a session 9 times more powerful. Why wouldn't it be so? After all, in India they say there is nothing higher than worship of the Divine Mother. I have also read that you can only achieve physical immortality by the grace of the Divine Mother!

Love, Sondra

February 1, 2016

¶ A MESSAGE FOR WOMEN FROM AMMACHI:
BREAK YOUR SHACKLES AND AWAKEN
"Who should awaken woman? What obstructs her
awakening? The truth is that no external power can possibly
obstruct woman on her innate qualities of motherhood -
qualities such as love, empathy, and patience. It is she, she
alone, who has to awaken herself. A woman's mind is the
only real barrier that prevents this from happening. The
rules and superstitious beliefs that degrade women continue
to prevail in most countries. The primitive customs invented
by men to exploit and subjugate women remain alive to this
day.
¶ But the infinite potential inherent in man and woman is the
same. If women really want to, they can easily break the
shackles of the rules and conditioning that society has
imposed on them. A woman's greatest strength lies in her
innate motherhood, in her creative life-giving power. This
power can help women bring about a far more significant
change in society than men can ever accomplish. In today's
world, where everything is being contaminated and made
unnatural, women should take extra care that her qualities
of motherhood (her essential nature as a woman) don't
become contaminated and distorted. Yet, whether woman
or man, one's real humanity comes to light only when the
feminine and masculine qualities within one are balanced.
¶ The forthcoming age should be dedicated to awakening
universal motherhood. Women everywhere have to
actualize the qualities of motherhood within themselves.
This is the only way to realize our dream of peace and
harmony. And it can be done! It is entirely up to us. Let us
remember that real leadership is not to dominate or to
control, but to serve others with love and compassion, and
to inspire women and men alike through the example of our
life. Let us pray that cruel minds which denigrate women be
transformed. May the Paramatma help them to respect the
women of this country and all other countries." —A Part of
Amma's speech when she accepted the Nobel Peace Prize.
Love, Sondra

February 2, 2016

❧ GETTING READY FOR VALENTINE'S DAY
How is your love life? Your love life is connected to your self-worth. So, what does the person you are with say about your love for yourself? There is an old saying, "You are the one you live with." Hopefully you are not staying in a bad relationship. Some reasons people stay in bad relationships are:

1. I don't think I deserve better.
2. I don't deserve to be happy.
3. We have kids and a house together.
4. It is against my religion to leave.
5. My parents would have a fit if I left.
6. I am too scared to be alone, etc.

These are not good reasons to stay in a relationship. You have to ask yourself this: "If I had no fear and no guilt and I did not care what other people said, would I stay or would I leave this relationship?" If the answer comes up "I would leave" then you are out of integrity for staying in that case.
❧ If however, you get that you are an amazing gift to someone, that you are truly worthy and deserving of a great relationship; and that you are truly worthy of someone special, you would not stay in a bad relationship.
❧ And if you are dating or you are alone, what are your thoughts? Do you think there is nobody out there for you? That is so limiting. There are thousands of perfect mates for you just waiting to join, that is IF you get that you are worthy. Say this: "I am now meeting great potential partners." "I am open for a fantastic mate and I allow it." "My perfect mate is here now!" "I am a gift."
❧ If you feel distraught, depressed, and down in the dumps your aura will collapse and you won't have the necessary radiance to meet a mate. You have to have total self-esteem. Your aura has to be radiant.
❧ So, you need to ask yourself if you are with the right partner or if you have the right attitude to find one if you are

looking.

We can help you get very clear on all this. Try a **Liberation Breathing** session.

᠍ I KNOW this is important to you because the most likes I ever got on any post was when I wrote about finding the right partner. Today I am asking you about your self-worth. I want you to create a wonderful Valentine's Day. You have about 11 days to think about it. Why not create a fantastic experience for yourself on Valentine's Day?

Love, Sondra

February 3, 2016

᠍ PEACE = POWER

There is an ACIM lesson that goes like this: "I could see peace instead of this." (**ACIM Workbook, Lesson #34**) Some people think Peace is boring and so they don't want it. They like the juice of arguing and conflict. What they don't understand is that anger makes you weak in every cell of your body. That is what Amma says. She is right. Anger drains your energy. The problem is that the ego is addicted to conflict. So, you really, really have to want peace. You have to make the decision for peace. True power is actually love, safety, and certainty. The result of love is peace.

᠍ A person who is safe is one who is free of anger. A person who has certainty is one who is clear she or he is one with God. What is exciting is to be in your true power. Peace is power. Some people have it backwards: they think anger is power, so they are attached to anger. Anger is NOT power. Peace is power. Do you want to be in anger and push people away, or do you want to be in Peace and draw people to you?

᠍ Once I was studying the lesson "I could see peace instead of this" and I had a huge test. (Usually the lessons test you.) I moved in with a man too soon. I did not notice what I should have noticed because he was wealthy and I was "dazzled." I started to unpack my bags and I was having a good time as usual. He began to pick a fight with me for no reason. I said, "Hey, I am not going there with you, I deserve peace in my personal life." He then stormed out! In

that second, I realized I had made a big mistake. He obviously did not want peace. I had to choose. What would my friends say if I moved out the first day? What would my mother say? Then I decided I did not care what anyone said. I was going to choose peace. So, I started packing my bags. He came back saying this: "Well I thought it over and you are right, you deserve peace. BUT I cannot live like that!" I said, "I can see that so that is why I am packing my bags!" I passed the test even though I could have felt really embarrassed. It is kind of a funny story, but it is absolutely true. Where are you at on this subject? Think about it.
Love, Sondra

February 4, 2016

℘ THE DIVINE MOTHER
The great saint Sri Aurobindo said that "surrender to the Divine Mother is the final stage of perfection." In India they say that there is nothing higher than worship of the Divine Mother. Saints and masters there gained real power and supernatural abilities from Her. However, She is just as available to all. It is said that the Divine Mother releases us from delusion. This is of maximum importance on the spiritual path. To make rapid spiritual progress one must reach for the deep, called MA (the internal) rather than Maya (the external). She will bring us to the nurturing, tender aspects of ourselves, which are so needed to solve problems of the world today.

℘ The Divine Mother will give us the solutions both to our personal problems and to our planetary problems. We need to let Her teach us how. We want to avert catastrophe in our relationships, our bodies, our societies and our countries. How do we deal with our shadows? (Ammachi says you must release your personal shadow, your family shadow, and your religious shadow.)

℘ Logic cannot always find the answer. But the feminine side of ourselves is more capable of harmonizing the light and the shadow. Extraordinary changes take place when the Goddess is accepted for women and men alike. I have interviewed many men whose lives were completely transformed by letting in the Divine Mother.

¶ Everything we possess is a gift of the Divine Mother. Begin by expressing more appreciation to the Source of Life.

> *Praise to you Great Mother.*
> *Make our lives a miracle.*
> *Show us what to do and how to do it.*
> *Let us be innocent and receptive like a child.*
> *Make our hearts Your temple.*
> *I pray that the people will open to You in*
> *Liberation Breathing, as You called it.*

pp. 77, 78 of our book *Liberation Breathing: The Divine Mother's Gift.*
Love, Sondra

February 5, 2016

¶ LIBERATION
What do you want to be liberated from? Is it

- ❖ Pain
- ❖ Negative thoughts
- ❖ Tension or negative mental mass
- ❖ Shallow breathing
- ❖ Symptoms and disease
- ❖ Fear
- ❖ Anger
- ❖ Guilt
- ❖ Sadness
- ❖ The effects of traumatic incidents
- ❖ Blocks to abundance
- ❖ Negative patterns in relationships
- ❖ Birth trauma
- ❖ Parental disapproval
- ❖ Unconscious death urge
- ❖ The past, including past lives

❖ False religious theology and dogma
❖ Depression
❖ The ego

Doing breathwork can cleanse you of all this! Naturally, not in one session. It is a life-long spiritual path. But just imagine how you would feel once you were cleansed of all this!! And it is actually pleasurable to let go of it all. What is not pleasurable is keeping all this in your sub consciousness and body.

℘ Awareness and mastery of the breath are the essential keys for understanding and developing the higher mind. You can use your breath to:

❖ Stabilize yourself
❖ Have more energy
❖ Enhance your immune system
❖ Create beneficial brainwave patterns
❖ Travel into the interior of your being
❖ Acquire transcendent knowledge and information
❖ Seek higher consciousness.

Maybe nobody has told you all this. It is my job to share it. From our book *Liberation Breathing: The Divine Mother's Gift*
Love, Sondra

February 6, 2016

℘ WHY WE NEED VERBAL PROCESSING
One definition of a humble person is that he is willing to recognize his errors, admit them, AND do something about them! It is essential to know when you are stuck, where you are stuck, AND to do something to handle the *stuckness*. When we *process* ourselves, we inquire deeply into the nature of our conditioned and unbalanced ego patterning, with the intention of finding the truth. Processing helps us

- ❖ Find out who we are
- ❖ Become more aware, flexible, and free
- ❖ Function to the best of our ability
- ❖ Cope with the speed of evolution
- ❖ Let go of obsolete teachings from childhood
- ❖ Become free of the past while bringing clarity to future goals
- ❖ Let go of extraneous baggage
- ❖ Cope with life's challenges
- ❖ Have resources for insight and creativity

My friend Leslie Thurston who wrote the above, says, "A cleared consciousness is the most valuable asset to life." Being clear is the best thing you could offer a mate or a child or anyone. It is fun and pleasurable to be around someone who is clear.

¶ Breathing itself is a form of processing. But with verbal processing first, it all goes faster. Most people re-run the same patterns their entire lives without realizing how this weakens them. It slows down your vibrational frequency tremendously.

¶ A simple process to start processing is to say, "The negative thought I had that created this situation was _____." Say that out loud to someone. The answer should never be "I don't know." I don't know comes from not looking. You do know. The answer is within your subconscious mind. But you have to do this process to find it. Another good process is, "I will let go of this condition when _____." (What has to happen before you can let go of the condition?) This question tells you what has to happen for you to let go. You will become better at processing by observing how your Breathworker does it when you have a *Liberation Breathing Session*.
pp. 117-118 in our book *LIBERATION BREATHING: THE DIVINE MOTHER'S GIFT.*

Love, Sondra

79

February 7, 2016

❡ FEEDBACK IN A RELATIONSHIP

Feedback is a delicate and challenging topic. Enlightened beings whose clear goal is total illumination usually welcome constructive feedback because they want to see their shadows as soon as they appear. The art of giving and receiving feedback occurs most successfully between people who have agreed to make it happen between them. In the new paradigm, this is established at the beginning of the relationship. You can open by saying, "You always have my permission to point out things that I do that do not work for you, or that you believe could be detrimental to me or others. Do I have the same permission from you?"

❡ In an intimate relationship with the person you live with, there is the risk of being too critical, too disapproving, and too harsh. This is because we choose mates who are like members of our family we are angry with. We take this latent anger out on our mates. Instead, you have to learn to give feedback that is supportive, tender, and sweet. One agreement you can make is to give feedback on the feedback itself: *"I can hear you when you say it like this, but I cannot hear you when you have that tone. It makes me shut down."*

❡ Remember, criticism can kill a relationship. Try this: Ask the person *why* they are doing something the way they are doing it *before you criticize their action.* Sometimes they have a very good reason, which refutes your judgement. Or, if what they are doing could be improved, the question is gentler, and they often will look at their behavior. More on this tomorrow.

From our book *Spiritual Intimacy*, pp. 111, 112

Love, Sondra

February 8, 2016

❡ FEEDBACK (continued)
Giving feedback:

> ❖ The giver of feedback should first get permission to do so by asking something like: "Do you mind if I share my feeling about_____?"
> ❖ The giver must not speak from anger or "heavy" energy. His heart should be open as if he is speaking to his best friend. The main thing is to be sweet.
> ❖ The giver must also remember that the issue at hand could be his or her projection. The giver should say:
> "What I observe in this relationship is_____."
> "What I feel is_____."
> "What I need is and/or what I recommend is_____."

(This is non-violent communication.)

Receiving feedback:

> ❖ The receiver shall keep his or her heart open and not become defensive.
> ❖ If the feedback is accurate, then he or she should be very grateful for it.
> ❖ If the feedback is a projection, it should not bother, and they can discuss it.
> ❖ The receiver should pay close attention if he or she is getting this same feedback from more than one person. If so, he or she should take action to change it quickly. The receiver shall thank the giver instead of defending or debating.
> ❖ He or she could say, "How do you suggest I change this?" If the receiver gets defensive, chances are the giver is on the right track. The receiver may take action by asking others to help point this out so he can clear the problem more quickly.

If couples can see that gentle feedback is a huge benefit, they will advance more quickly. If, however, the feedback is too critical, hurtful, or upsetting, it can be destructive to the relationship. How would you speak to someone you totally respect? You might say, "Are you aware that—." Remember it helps to know that your partner is your guru, your friend, your teacher and a holy person—someone you are fortunate to live with. If you don't feel fortunate to be living with that person, what are you doing there?

∮ Two people who practice forgiveness on an on-going basis can usually stay together. Can you live by this statement?

"I will not keep any records of wrong doing."
From our book *Spiritual Intimacy*, pp. 113, 114

Love, Sondra

February 9, 2016

∮ AN UPSIDE-DOWN ATTITUDE

Markus and I were doing some interviews by Skype to gather research on views of offering *A Course in Miracles* yearly class—to make things easier for people to understand and apply ACIM. A particular woman had agreed to be interviewed and we were looking forward to it. However, when we asked her questions, she was very resistant. She said she could never commit the time to do the lessons daily for a year. And yet, she did not even have a daily job. She said she had so many social contacts that she did not have the time. I wanted to talk to her about priorities in her life. I wanted to ask her if she could see that getting enlightened should now be put as a top priority.

∮ But we both knew that she would not have the ears to hear. We could not actually figure out why she had even agreed to be interviewed. A part of her must have been curious and yet she stayed in her resistance and defended her position.

∮ The funny part of it all was this: Her camera did not work, and she presented to us *upside down*! Her eyes were below, and her neck was above, and she could not right herself. The whole session was upside down. We had never ever experienced that before! But it was so symbolic of where her mind was at. Markus talks about an innate unwillingness in people. Well, here it was being demonstrated.

❡ Are you one who has your priorities straight? Do you put your spiritual practice first? Once you open the computer it is all over. You almost never will do a spiritual practice AFTER you open your computer. Our suggestion is:

- ❖ Get up a half hour earlier
- ❖ Make the bed
- ❖ Take a shower
- ❖ Get dressed
- ❖ Sit down for a spiritual practice.
- ❖ Then go on to your day

Get yourself right side up!
Love, Sondra

February 10, 2016

❡ ARE YOU APPROACHABLE?
What people see first is your attitude. What they see immediately after that is how you put yourself together, your style. Of course, your attitude affects your style. Your attitude and your personal packaging establish your unspoken credentials. Your authority/approachability quotient determines how other people will respond to you. "Dress for success" is a term often used. Does it really matter? YES.

❡ Image has a real impact. I once took a course called Presentation Salon, or something like that. We had to bring three different outfits: One as if we were applying for a job, one for meeting our boyfriend's parents, and one for evening attire. We had to stand in front of a large group and they would vote and critique us. It was very intense. We women would line up and the teacher would ask the whole class, "Which of these women would you NEVER hire?

Which of these women would you NEVER take home to your parents?" And so forth. Then he had us stand up in categories— Dramatic, Conservative, etc.

ᛉ He did not call me up with any of the categories, so I was scared. Then he said, "Sondra Ray, come up here and stand by yourself." Now I was really scared. Then he said, "You are in a category all by yourself—but DO SOMETHING WITH YOUR HAIR"!

ᛉ He was right. My hair was long and curly with no design. I had let it grow out because I had healed my temporary baldness and I was very attached to it after having had to wear wigs for two years. (The top went bald after a divorce. Breathwork cured even that!)

ᛉ Well, after that I went to India and I wrote that teacher a letter. I said, "Dear Sir, I did something with my hair. I shaved my head!" I guess he cracked up. Well, I did that head-shave to surrender to Babaji. It's called *mundan* in India. I just could not resist sending this letter as I thought it was funny. So, did he. Anyway, as tough as that course was, it worked. I became very conscious of my presentation. Are you?

Love, Sondra

February 11, 2016

ᛉ THE FEAR OF CHANGE

We are not talking about changing the Real Self. It needs no change. What needs to change is the IDEA of who we are—the ego's idea of limitation. If you consider that, why wouldn't we want to change? And what your mate, or anyone else, wants you to change are the illusions—the parts that hurt you or others. Some people don't ever want their intimate relationship to change. They don't want to "rock the boat" so to speak. Couples often think they should stay as they were when they first met. But then they will never experience what they could become together. Furthermore, relationships are about change, about movement and growth.

ᛉ One reason people are afraid of change is because the first change they had to make, their birth, caused pain. To come out from a liquid environment of the womb to the atmosphere was a HUGE change, and, as a newborn, we got hurt. So, people may have the unconscious thought: "change hurts."

❡ Let's say you are in a relationship and you want to be AWAKE, so you are going for spiritual advancement. What you do have to know is this: When you jump to a new level of consciousness, the ego puts up a battle. The ego is fear, so fear has to be faced and overcome. You need effective tools to deal with it or else you will retreat into the past again which is familiar. In *Liberation Breathing*, we inhale love and exhale fear. Breathworkers are trained to help you in this process. Working on enlightenment has two approaches. The old way is to simply let life itself process you. By going through the "school of hard knocks" and by going through incarnation after incarnation, one is finally forced to shift. This approach is very, very, slow. The second approach is easier. One makes a conscious choice to commit to self-correction and spiritual purification on a regular basis. This is easier and more wonderful. Are you doing it the slow way or the faster way?
Love, Sondra

February 12, 2016

❡ WHAT IS YOUR PURPOSE?
I read once that the mother of a prominent actor told him that the purpose of life was intense joy! Imagine having a mother like that! My gurus in India told me that the purpose of life was to recognize the Supreme. Our purpose here is to remove all the fears that block our true nature.

❡ Another purpose of life is to learn. Ram Dass once said, "You are here to take the curriculum." One should use one's issues (one's "case") as a stepping stone. Our world here is a school. The aim of the curriculum according to ACIM is 'removing the blocks to the awareness of love's presence,' which is our natural inheritance."

❡ Yet another purpose of life is to clear our karma. Some great books to read about that are *We Were Born Again to Be Together* by Dick Sutphen and *Other Lives, Other Selves* by Dr. Robert Woolger.

One of the main purposes of life is to serve humanity. This is and will always be considered the first and foremost duty of the mature soul. The is also the purpose of dissolution of the ego. This is a step-by-step process of giving up separation and limitation, and this leads ultimately to experience ourselves as Divine. This leads to Liberation.

The purpose of one's relationships then is to enhance these very goals. Both partners need to discuss why they are here. Many people do not have a good relationship with Life itself. How can they have a good relationship with a mate if they have never thought about the purpose of life? They will continually have their priorities confused. My mother always told me, "Sondra, Life is a Miracle!" I got into the wonder of it all, the joy of it all, and the appreciation of it all.

What are you telling your children?

p. 80 from our book *Spiritual Intimacy*

Love, Sondra

February 13, 2016

CREDO

(From the *Life & Teaching of the Masters of the Far East*)

The Goal is God. You can start your day with God by taking your first thought of God within your own form.

"God, I Am united with universal life and power, and all of this strength is focused in my entire nature, making me so positive with God's perfect energy that I send it out to every form, and I make it so positive that all may be transformed into harmony and perfection. I know that they are all in accord with infinite life and God's freedom and peace.

My mind is fully polarized with Infinite Intelligent Wisdom. Every faculty of my entire body finds free expression through my mind and all humanity does express the same. My heart is filled to overflowing with peace, love, and joy of the conquering Christ. My heart is strong with God's love and I know that it fills the heart of all humanity. God's life fully enriches my entire blood stream and fills my body with the purity of Divine Life.

God is all life. I am inspired with life with every breath and my lungs take in life with every breath and it fills my blood stream with vitalizing life.

❡ I know that all of my organs are infused with God's intelligence. All are conscious of their duties and they work together for the health and harmony of my entire being.
I am Supreme Wisdom, Love, and Power. From the very depth of my heart I shout the glad thanksgiving that I Am this sublime and exhaustless Wisdom, and I demand that I draw it to myself and become completely conscious of this ceaseless Wisdom." (p. 148, vol. 5)

❡ Get your love ready for Valentine's Day tomorrow.
Love, Sondra

February 14, 2016

❡ VALENTINE'S DAY MIRACLE:
BABAJI'S CONSCIOUS DEPARTURE
I said the following to Babaji, "Well, I have said I would follow You, I have said I would surrender to You, I have said I would serve You; and now I am willing to be totally aligned with You." Suddenly He showed me the future and told me that I should hold a chanting evening Monday night after the training on Valentine's Day. I agreed reluctantly though, because I was afraid to sing in public. That was because once in church as a kid I had to sing "Beautiful Savior" as a solo in choir, and my voice cracked, so, I felt I had disappointed Jesus. Well, I thought, the chant is in Sanskrit so people won't know if I make a mistake.

❡ Then I remembered this vision, so I called a close student and said, "Remember the dream your brother had? Well, how about tomorrow night?" His dream was about me conducting a chanting evening. She said, "Fine." I told the LRT group they were invited, and exactly 80 people showed up! Now try to imagine this mansion in Beverly Hills with a living room big enough to hold 80 people easily. There was a thick white carpet throughout, and gold candlesticks so amazing that the bottom of the big candles and the top of the candlestick were about the level of my breasts. I was astonished as the whole place looked like a temple. I could not have imagined a more perfect place to hold my first public chanting.

❡ I explained to everyone the power of the mantra, "Om Namah Shivay," and how it was the highest thought in the universe; how it could purify you, wipe out your negativity, and charge you up at the same time. I played CDs to teach them how to sing; then we began chanting for an hour or more. At 8:00 PM, when it was time to leave, there was a huge phenomenon. The students who had left to go outside began yelling at me to come out immediately. They were all looking up in the sky above the mansion. There was a huge blue cross over the mansion! All of us saw it. There was absolutely no explanation. People who were there still talk about it. I did not have a clue what it was or what it meant until the next day.

❡ I flew to Tucson for some work and then people from all over the world started calling me crying, saying that Babaji had left his body. I was very, very calm, and I was not sad for some reason. I told them all the same thing, "Babaji knows exactly what He is doing; and now we all have to grow up and get to work."

❡ One of my friends was beside herself and could not calm down. I told her I would re-route my flight to Toronto and stop in L.A. and soothe her. When she and her boyfriend picked me up at the airport, we began driving to her place; but I suddenly said, "Stop now and turn in here at this airport hotel and I will call Leonard to find out what is the appropriate public statement." I did not know why I was saying stop, as I could have called Len at home instead. I went in the hotel and turned left. She said, "No Sondra, the phones are over here to the right!"

❡ But going left, suddenly, I was right in front of Michael Jackson and his bodyguard. He had just been injured while making the Pepsi Cola ad; and he looked like a wounded bird. I sent him all the energy I could and then I turned around and went to the phones. Right by the phone I used was a big signpost that read Emergency Departures. My friend's boyfriend said, "He is still out there in the car." "Okay," I said, "Take him my card." Mannie knocked on the window of the limo and Michael actually rolled down the window, with his white glove on, of course. And so, Mannie gave him my card, saying, "Call Sondra, she will help you."

❡ Unfortunately, he never did. He had another chance in Jamaica after that, but he did not go for it there either. Too bad; I could have helped him. I wondered why I would meet Michael Jackson on the day of Babaji's Samadhi. Later I found out from Babaji's high Priest, Shastriji, that Michael and I had been together in Tibet in another life when he was also a devotee of Babaji in another form.

❡ After all this, I calculated the time change, and I figured out that when we saw the blue cross was the exact time Babaji had taken Samadhi (conscious departure). And, I understood that was when He merged his electrons with the universe.

Apparently his last words were, "I am going to explode my heart and give a piece to everyone—and I am leaving everything in the hands of The Divine Mother." It took me years to understand the latter. Anyway, I was instantly clear that He was not really dead anyway. He is always dropping bodies and making new ones. He obviously did not want us dependent on that one any longer.

Love, Sondra

February 15, 2016

❡ CLEAN UP YOUR RELATIONSHIPS DAILY

I recall a couple in one of my workshops who had the following pattern:

❡ Dave would be angry with Janet for something, but he would not tell her. He would pretend to get over it but would be seething inside. Janet had the exact same tendency. She would never tell Dave what made her upset with him. They would both "stuff it." The pressure would build and build until finally they would have a knock down drag out fight and scream out all the complaints they had stored up. This is "dumping" in the highest order. They were always fighting about situations that happened many months ago, sometimes even a year ago. They were never in present time and one or the other would always deny what they said or did back then. Then they would get in a fight about a fight.

❡ After they took the **Loving Relationships Training®**, I encouraged them to start all over and re-conceive their whole marriage. I told them to make the simple agreement to clean up their relationship every night. They both stuck to this agreement and, fortunately, it worked. Besides, they found out that they were not often upset for the reasons they thought. (Often it is an earlier similar event from childhood.)

When you can clean up an upset right on the spot do so. If you cannot, then at least do it before going to sleep. The Bible says to "Never let the sun set on your anger." You can actually say to your mate the following, "Is there anything you need to communicate to me before going to sleep?" Then make your communication a quality communication, a compassionate communication:

> 1. What I observe in our relationship is_____.
> 2. What I feel about that is_____.
> 3. What I need or what I recommend is_____.

Afterwards, acknowledge your partner for something. Then you can drop off to sleep in a happy state or have sex without a lot of psychic garbage in the way.
Love, Sondra

February 16, 2016

❡ FIRST AID FOR YOUR RELATIONSHIP
First of all, remember that "Love brings up anything unlike itself" and that is for the purpose of healing and release. So, when stuff comes up, don't panic. Just process it.

> 1. Call your Breathworker and make an appointment. If you cannot do that, at least try to process yourself.
> 2. Write down all your negative thoughts around the situation and change them to affirmations.
> 3. Become aware of any blame thoughts about the other. Remember that blame is off the track. Disapproval is usually a projection of some kind.

Your partner is your mirror. What does this situation say about YOU? How did you attract this? How did you create this? Say, 'The negative thought I had that attracted this was_____."

4. Don't leave until you understand the pattern at least, or else you might just recreate it somewhere else.

5. Handle your anger in appropriate ways instead of dumping it on another. Write down the thoughts that make you angry and change them. THEN BREATHE.

6. Remember that you are never upset for the reason you think. (**Lesson #5 in ACIM**) Get in touch with the earlier similar situation you are re-living.

7. Lie down and hold each other if possible. When you cannot communicate: STOP, hold each other and breathe gently.

8. When you are calmed down, share all feelings, one at a time. One person talks, the other listens without interrupting for at least eight minutes. We call this "The Eight Minute Process."

9. Use non-violent communication such as:

> *a. What I observe in our relationship is_____.*
> *b. What I feel about this is_____.*
> *c. What I need or what I recommend is_____.*
> *(I deliberately keep repeating this.)*

9. Take **The Loving Relationships Training** if possible, or read out loud our book *Spiritual Intimacy.* If the relationship falls apart, despite all your good efforts, remember this: You never lose someone who is for your highest good. If they leave, they were no longer best for you and God is trying to give you something better. I want to impress you with that: Nothing is taken from you without it being replaced by something better, but you have to LET IT IN. It is called ALLOWING.

You need to really let go, however. You must create a vacuum to receive the new. (All losses are gains not yet recognized.)

Love, Sondra

February 17, 2016

❡ WHAT ABOUT YOUR LIVING SPACE?
Does your living space support your relationship, your self-esteem? What does it say about you?

❖ In the kitchen: Is the stove really dirty and the pots all banged up? Is the food in the refrigerator moldy? Are the cupboards a mess? Is the garbage overflowing?

❖ In the living room: Are the plants dead? Have the cats scratched up the furniture? Are the light bulbs burned out? Is the TV dominating everything?

❖ In the bathroom: Are the towels rancid? Is the shower curtain moldy? Do the shower and bathtub have dirty rings? Are empty shampoo bottles lying around?

❖ In the bedroom: Are there clothes thrown around? Are articles lying around that are not very sensual? Is the bed always unmade? Is it too "techie" and not very romantic?

❡ I am a Virgo, so I like everything very, very neat. But once I lived with a guy neater than I was. He was obsessed. You could not leave one coffee cup in the sink or have one fingerprint on the glass table. He was driving me nuts. I was secretly judging him as being obsessive compulsive. Then I had a brainstorm. Instead of judging him, I decided to interview him. I talked to him like this: "Roger, I am having trouble keeping up with you with this *neatness thing*. Would you please explain your mindset to me?"

He replied, "Sondra, it is very simple: Prepare every room for GOD!"

◊ Wow, I was amazed! That one statement transformed my life: "Prepare every room for God." That was a higher thought than I had. I told him I wanted to go up to his thought and I did. He trained me to be impeccable.

◊ Years later, there was a fire in my building and my apartment was the only one not damaged. Everyone had their stuff ruined and I had not one speck of soot in my entire place! Of course, I also had altars in every room. I had "prepared every room for God," and God protected me. I really appreciated him then for training me. Think about it. Thank you, Roger, wherever you are (I think in Maui). You transformed my life!

Love, Sondra

February 18, 2016

◊ PAST LIVES

On the first page of one of the Dalai Lama's books he says that in the West we keep looking behind all these different doors for the answer to our problems, BUT we don't even have a door called *past lives* to look behind so we are missing out on the answer. Then I found the book *Other Lives Other Selves* by Dr. Roger Woolger. As a psychotherapist he did not even believe in past lives until he had his first Rebirthing session. He saw himself in a trench in a war from another life. This changed him completely. He started regressing people. He wrote a lot about how your past lives influence the type of birth you have in this life. For example, if you had a lot of anesthesia at birth, you were likely to have died in gas chambers before. If you had forceps at birth, you likely died of blows to the head many times. If you had the cord around the neck, you likely died from hanging several times before. I have seen this to be true in my clients.

◊ Another thing I have learned by doing breathwork is that many body conditions are caused by past life traumas. In Iceland we take people to the Blue Lagoon for wet

Liberation Breathing. (It is one of the largest bodies of thermal springs in the world.) One woman who came with us had a history of migraines. They were so severe that she had them sometimes seven days per month! During the sessions I worked with her a lot. Nothing shifted until we got down to a past life where she was gang raped. She never wanted to see this before. (When breathing with a snorkel, in the Blue Lagoon, it is hard to keep something suppressed.) We were able to identify the thoughts she formed in that life and how they were wired together with her birth thoughts. It was complex, but we were able to unravel it.

❡ Because of the clearing I had in India of my own past lives, it is easy for me to help others with this. One year my guru Shastriji tied a vine around my left arm like a tourniquet and shouted a mantra at my third eye for what felt like five whole minutes. So many past lives came out of me the year after that. The next year he did the same around my right arm. More difficult ones came up that year. The following year he did the same on BOTH arms. The really heavy ones came up that year. Good thing I had Liberation Breathing/Rebirthing to release all these! Now I pay a lot of attention to this subject.

❡ If you have a stubborn health condition, maybe you need to consider having a **Liberation Breathing** session to get to the bottom of it.

Love, Sondra

February 19, 2016

❡ DANGERS OF DENIAL

Lately I have noticed that some people come for a session and when we ask them what they want to improve they say, "Everything is okay." This turns out to be ridiculous in the end as later what comes out is that they say their wife is in love with someone else, or they themselves are having an affair to get even, or they are not in love with their mate, or they are out of work or they have kids who are addicted etc.. They have A LOT going on. Or recently we had parents who actually lied, saying they had never had an

94

affair etc. But the next day their teenage daughter came and told us everything about her parents' affairs. Then I realized the parents had lied. Some people come in bragging they have no anger, but we can see they are seething.

❡ My teachers told me if I don't say what I see, it will make ME sick. So, then I have to have the courage to push people out of denial. Sometimes I have to say, "It seems like you are lying to yourself." I have become very alert when people tell me they have nothing going on. Usually it is quite the opposite and after all, why did they bother coming then? Sometimes they really need tough love.

❡ Recently there was a woman in the training who skipped Saturday to play golf and was late on Sunday. I went to her during the breathwork session and she said she had nothing going on. I found out later she came to rip off the training, to teach it herself, and she did not really do it for herself. Well, let me tell you what happened. After the training she apparently had a STROKE. Her denial was huge and look what happened.

❡ The point is: Denial can be dangerous for you. It is a defense mechanism that only makes things worse. Denial is a psychological failure to acknowledge an unacceptable truth. Take a look and see what you might be in denial about.

❡ It is bad for your health as you are stuffing it. Whatever you suppress, you add energy to it. Admitting your weakness is a sign of *strength*.

Love, Sondra

February 20, 2016

❡ JOY

The goal is JOY. It has been said that joy is the highest expression of God that there is. If we wish for joy in our lives, we must remember that we were made in the image of God and we are God like. When you are feeling great and everything is working well, it is easy to feel joy and to love God. But when you don't feel well and things are not going so great and you are not getting what you want, then it seems difficult to feel Joy. Then you have to start by giving up all your negative thoughts about yourself. (Write them down and burn them.) Try to go back to loving God and you will be uplifted, heal yourself and things will start working. Here are some comments from ACIM.

✊ "Joy is the inevitable result of gentleness. Gentleness means that fear is now impossible and what could come to interfere with Joy? The open hands of gentleness are always filled. The gentle have no pain. They cannot suffer. Why would they then not have joy? They are sure they are beloved and are safe. Joy is the song of Thanks." (ACIM, Teacher's Manual, chap. 4, sec. V)

✊ "Living is joy, but death can only weep. You see in death escape from what you made. But this you do not see: that you made death. It is not life in which the problem lies. Life has no opposite, for it is God." (ACIM, Teacher's Manual, chap. 20, sec. V)

✊ "There is one thought in particular that we should be remembering throughout the day. It is a thought of pure joy: a thought of peace, a thought of limitless release. Limitless because all things are freed with it," (ACIM, Teacher's Manual, chap. 6, sec. VI)

✊ "When you have become willing to hide nothing, you will not only be willing to enter into communion but will also understand peace and joy." (ACIM, chap. 1, sec. IV)

✊ "I am teaching you to associate misery with the ego and Joy with the Spirit. You have taught yourself the opposite. You are still free to choose, but can you really want the rewards of the ego in the presence of the rewards of God?" (ACIM, Text. chap. 4, sec. VI)

✊ "Only when you see you are guiltless will you be happy. As long as you believe the Son of God is guilty you will walk along this carpet, believing that it leads to death." (ACIM, Text, chap. 13, sec. I)

Love, Sondra

February 21, 2016

❡ UNDERSTANDING GUILT
If you have the subconscious thought "I am guilty" this thought will make you end up doing things you don't feel good about so you can feel guilty.

❡ You might have different kinds of guilt: Past life guilt, guilt from hurting your mother at birth, religious guilt (thinking you separated from God and having been told you were born a sinner), and or guilt from things you have done in this life. Add it all up and that is a lot of guilt! How can you have any fun in this life if you have not cleared your guilt? You are sabotaging yourself with guilt because guilt demands punishment. Ask yourself, "How am I punishing myself?" Maybe you are not letting in love or getting rid of it. Maybe you are not letting yourself have money or getting rid of it. Maybe you are hurting yourself or punishing yourself with disease. ACIM says, "Guilt is not only not of God, it is an attack on God."

❡ David Hawkins says regret and guilt result from equating the present self that is with the former self that was—but actually is no more. He says it is another form of egotism in which error is inflated instead of being relinquished to a higher power. In this form of egotism, the self becomes blown up, exaggerated, and the hero of the tragedy! Then the ego re-energizes itself through this negativity. Wallowing in guilt feeds the ego and is an indulgence he says. More on how to give up guilt tomorrow.
Love, Sondra

February 22, 2016

❡ LETTING GO OF GUILT
For one thing, guilt is mostly buried in the subconscious, so it is not so easily recognized. You really have to do a truth process and write out what you are guilty about so you can see it. Even if you see it, your ego usually does not want to give it up! In fact, somewhere in *A Course in Miracles* Text it states that the ego will try to tell you that if you DARE to think you are innocent, then you are REALLY guilty! You

have to pass through this big trick of the ego. This is why we need help outside of the ego's system to get rid of it. There has to be a willingness to surrender it. David Hawkins says spiritual alignment is needed. That way the past circumstances underlying the guilt are re-contextualized under the influence of spiritual energy. You either cling to it and get the "juice" of the drama or you give it up. This is the decision you have to make. And this decision has actual consequences on the brain physiology he says.

₰ So then you have to invite in the Divine Mother, Holy Spirit, or the guru; and this invitation transforms by the healing power of grace. You cannot do this with your personality alone. I usually process people this way: Say, "My fear of giving up all my guilt is _____." Once you have expressed your fear, you can let go faster. And remember this Lesson #228 from ACIM, "God has condemned me not. No more do I." God only wants you to give up your guilt and fear. The cause of the guilt is all in the past anyway, and not even here.

₰ Some traditional ways to undo guilt are confession, forgiving yourself, renewal of spiritual principles, good works, selfless service, and humanitarian efforts. In our work, we breathe guilt out of the cells in Liberation Breathing/Rebirthing sessions and do the "Forgiveness Diet" 70x7. You write, "I forgive myself completely" 70 times a day for seven days. You might have to do all of the above if you are really guilty.

Guilt is heavy, and it can make you depressed. Innocence is where the Joy is. (See my book *The Only Diet There Is*.)

₰ Markus and I have another way of getting past guilt in the moment, especially when we have made a mistake. We say immediately, "Even though I made a mistake, I still completely love and accept myself." When you say this, and mean it, there is no room for guilt.

Love, Sondra

February 23, 2016

₰ CHRONIC FATIGUE SYNDROME
A client came to us who had Chronic Fatigue for 25 years!

One reason nobody had been able to help her heal this is because it was totally related to her birth. The obstetrician did not see how he could save the mother and the baby due to a life-threatening situation. At times like this the OB asks the father to choose. But the father was not around so he asked the mother. The mother shouted, "Save the mother," (herself). Then the baby (our client) decided, (and babies do make very sophisticated decisions in the womb) these two preverbal thoughts: "I am nothing," and "I have no value." These two thoughts alone will set up a death urge which will wipe out one's energy. Perhaps you know that Chronic Fatigue is always related to rejection of the life urge.

⚑ We also looked at why she did NOT want to be healed. Her "payoffs" were too great. She also thought people were hostile, as her mother told her that she was cursed the day she was born. Her mother also beat her. She wanted to stay in her room and not come out. So, chronic fatigue was her solution for that one. Later in the session I found out she had been a nun in four lifetimes, so she was also used to being cloistered.

⚑ She also had a fear of joy. If she had joy, she thought she would be punished. I only found this out by processing her deeply. She was run by the worst parts of Catholicism; thinking suffering makes you holy.

⚑ We really made a difference for her, but of course when we left that country, we had to turn her over to other Breathworkers, as she needed a lot of follow up. But the cause of her chronic fatigue was clear to her after just that one session. And she could begin the forgiveness processes to heal it.

Love, Sondra

February 24, 2016

⚑ WHY THE DIVINE MOTHER?

The Divine Mother goes beyond all concepts and dogmas. The experience of the Mother is a presence of calm, power, and blissful unconditional love as the ground of all being, an endless source of deeply rooted peace, the shakti that fuels evolution. Mother is to Father what the shining is to the diamond.

❡ We have done harm to ourselves and the universe, so now we have to open ourselves to the love that heals and saves. She offers us compassion, grace, calmness, and patient encouragement, reverence, and tenderness. In India they say if you want to see Her, you must long for Her with the intensity with which a drowning man longs for oxygen. The best way to Her is direct devotion or "Bhakti Adoration." Adoration itself provides the most profound source of energy of transformation.

❡ The Divine Mother is the universe and all things in it. She not only says, "Adore me," but adore each creature, each being as part of me, each as totally sacred, as brimming with consciousness and light. Ammachi says, "Honor yourself humbly as my child. Bless each aspect of your being. Revere yourself." Give birth to the Divine Child in you. We are here to become the divine human being.

❡ The Mother is JOY. Strip yourself of everything but Her. Seek pure love of Her. If that was all that you wanted, everything would just flow to you, through you, and for you! All protection would be yours. All knowledge. Pray to Her with a longing heart. Persist in your demands to Her. The realized being is like a child at peace in the womb, knowing he or she is fed at every moment by the grace and light of the Mother. You will be in Heaven here. Miracles dance around those who have become like children. Anything can be done by the Mother through us! Humility is the key.

❡ Last night in a dream I was trying to explain this to a student. I was trying to tell her how she could get everything she wanted by understanding this and serving humanity. She could not understand it until she started doing serious *Liberation Breathing/Rebirthing.*

❡ The above I have summarized from the teachings of Ammachi. Try to meet her. When I got a personal mantra from her, I was told I must try to see God in everyone.

Love, Sondra

February 25, 2016

❡ DIVINE MOTHER (continued)
Amma says, "Most of us need a guru to shed light on our inner demons. One has to be purified of lust, delusion, pride, jealousy, anger, intolerance, attachment, hypocrisy, repulsion, crusty wounds, unrealized desires, and impurities. You have to go through a spiritual burning process. This could be a battle of the wills. You may feel crazy, but no doctor or psychotherapist can heal these wounds."

❡ She says that surrender is your final destiny. For all, this means dropping away of every obstruction to peace and contentment. We no longer claim, "I did this," and "I did that." Everything we do is a result of Divine Energy moving through us. Say, "I am a vessel through which Divine Activity takes place."

❡ The guru does not want anything from you. The giving up is for your own inner growth, peace of mind, and bliss. Tomorrow I will say what Amma says about your *shadows*, which is really important. Travelling to San Diego this morning.
Love, Sondra

February 26, 2016

❡ LOVE FROM BAJA, CALIFORNIA
Getting ready for the LRT in San Diego. Today I will complete what I started yesterday. Amma talks about the SHADOW. She says, "What is hidden within must become manifest sooner or later. No matter how much one may try to do otherwise, it is just a question of time. The demons within (inevitable aspects of growth) or the contents of the shadow can become hazardous from neglect. The shadow conceals our divine essence."

❡ Amma says you must go through three shadows:

    1. The religious shadow
    2. The family shadow
    3. The personal shadow

101

But the Mother will not abandon you while you are in the process of clearing your shadows. She says, "After all, the surgeon does not stop until the operation is finished!" I really appreciated that one! And that has been my experience. But you have to ask for help. The Mother comes when we ask.

¶ We must become like little children—then we are more open to the guru's love. And believe me, I was very, very grateful to have gurus when going through my shadows. The best attitude to approach inner work is an attitude of knowing nothing. Otherwise when we think we know a lot we might be closed down.

¶ The religious shadow is all the dogma you were taught in life; lifetimes of patriarchal religious programs. The family shadow is all your programming from your family mind—which is very intense. The personal shadow is your karma and your "case" in this life. This is exactly what Liberation Breathing / Rebirthing is for—to help you eliminate your shadows!

Love, Sondra

February 27, 2016

¶ HI FROM SOUTHERN CALIFORNIA
First of all, we were staying with our organizer Melana Taylor and her husband Joe. They have a gorgeous place on the beach in Baja, California. Perfect for whale watching. To come back to the USA, we had to get in the line. Markus had never crossed the border on land in Tijuana.

¶ What a hold up! Many lines across; people sitting in cars for three hours. I was wondering what they do if they need to go to the bathroom. We were in the fast lane and it still took 1-1/2 hours. The dogs came around first. Then the border guard who checked us was extremely stern. I was nervous that he was going to go through ALL MY LUGGAGE! Not that I had anything illegal in them, but it would have taken ages. So, I was praying to Babaji and we were lucky.

❡ It is great to be doing a training in San Diego. We have people from Las Vegas, Colorado, Oregon, and Texas. I had been praying to Babaji to find someone in Texas, as our astro-cartography is really good for business there. I told Babaji then I want to work in Texas! So, there she is and so I am happy. The LRT ALWAYS works. It is such a pleasure for me to give it.

Love, Sondra

February 28, 2016

❡ THE LRT IS IN FULL SWING
I think the most challenging pattern is the "incest pattern." In most seminars they never discuss it; but I feel it would be out of integrity not to bring it up as it affects everyone's sex life. We are talking mostly about "emotional incest" where there is sexual energy going in families but not acted out. It is psychic. Let's say a mother over-confides in her son or sends unconscious sexual energy toward him and sets him up like a husband. The husband should be getting this, not him. Or a father puts out unconscious sexual energy toward a daughter. Later this could cause problems.
❡ The pattern goes like this: Because you could not have sex with your father if you were a girl, what happens if you grow up as a woman and set up your mate to be your father? You can't have sex with your father so pretty soon you cannot have sex with your own husband because you have turned him into your father. Or, if you have your wife set up as your mother, how can you have sex with your wife if you have turned her into your mother? This is very deep and tricky. It is why some people can have great sex at the beginning of a relationship (because they have the incest pattern suppressed), but when they set up household with their mate or get married, sex goes out the window. That is because this pattern comes up since the relationship is more intimate like the family. Or when a woman has babies—now she is the Madonna. You cannot have sex with the mother so sometimes sex goes out the window after a woman gets pregnant. It takes a long time to explain

and work out this pattern, but the first step is to become aware of it.

♪ I have actually had people faint in this section as they remembered for the first time some inappropriate sexual behavior in the family. Believe me, acted out incest is even a lot more common than you think too.

♪ Please refer to our book *Spiritual Intimacy* to study the whole pattern. Now I have to get back to work.

Love, Sondra

February 29, 2016

♪ THE LITMUS TEST

The New Loving Relationships Training went over really well here. We were invited to work in Las Vegas, so that feels great.

♪ In these trainings, people always ask how long they should stay in a stressful relationship before they throw in the towel. Obviously, I don't want the karma of telling people to leave or not leave. But I can help them decide for themselves. Of course, one should not stay if one secretly wants to leave.

But sometimes people do not know themselves well and they are in denial, so I give them the litmus test. I have them answer this question:

"If you had no fear, and if you had no guilt, and if you did not care what anyone else said, would you stay or leave your relationship?"

If the answer they give me then is "I would leave," then they are out of integrity for staying. If their answer is "I would stay," then we coach them on making the necessary changes to restore their highest good together.

♪ Most people end up staying a lot longer than they should because they are afraid of being alone. However, in the training, we always teach The Cosmic Dating Service, so they get pretty clear that they can create a new partner who is better.

❡ Often though, the relationship can be healed if they really take the training to heart. They have to totally re-conceive it in a new vibration of trust and co-operation; and keep no records of wrongdoing. It depends on whether it is too far gone. It is case by case—there is no *right* answer.

❡ Not all relationships are meant to be long term either. Some are just for clearing karma, and when that is done it is time to move on. So, one should not judge oneself. If it ends, it does not necessarily mean it is a failure. Maybe the karma is complete and that is that. Sometimes separation and divorce are the best answer.

❡ There are so many things to consider. More on this subject tomorrow.

Love, Sondra

March 1, 2016

❡ CHALLENGE

When one partner starts advancing rapidly on the spiritual path and the other person makes no forward movement at all (or worse, resents their partner's growth), the difference in advancement will place these two people at vastly different vibrational levels. This will almost certainly cause great strain on the relationship and can lead to breakdown.

❡ It may be necessary for ties to be severed with affiliations that no longer resonate harmoniously. Would you let go of any of your friends or even your partner if necessary, if you knew that the gap would be filled by higher vibrational people?

❡ There is a metaphysical law that when someone leaves you, they are no longer best for you and God is trying to give you something better! But you have to ALLOW that. If you end in guilt or anger you might block a better one from coming and go backwards. It is a spiritual test how you complete a relationship. Did you become more loving because of it? Or did you become bitter? If you became more bitter, that is a failed spiritual test. If it must end or did end, try to appreciate the person for all the lessons you got.

Love, Sondra

March 2, 2016

❡ IS YOUR LIFE BORING?
It is possible to stay perpetually alive constantly
enthusiastic, and always excited. The method of doing so is
to live all day every day in the company of the Divine. I am
always trying to get people to get close to Babaji and the
Divine Mother. I am not trying to *convert* people. I just want
them to live with the feeling I live with from that. I know how
it feels and I want others to know how it feels. The more
completely their power takes hold of one, the more
wonderful life becomes. It is my observation that this power
definitely enhances the capacity to be excited.

❡ One of my students at the San Diego LRT went to work at
Babaji's ashram in Colorado. She told me she got so
excited and high that it was marvelous. But her husband
could not handle it. Needless-to-say, their marriage is on
the rocks.

❡ I have seen dull and lethargic persons come alive in
Herakhan, when they come to India with us. People for
whom life was only an uninspired routine of one thing after
another, suddenly became vital, even vibrant and excited
about everything. I think it says in the Bible, "If any man be
in Christ, he is a new creature." Every day becomes a new
and thrillingly fresh experience. Awareness gets sharpened
and one gets a keener sensitivity—even light and color
become enhanced. Common things are even endowed with
amazing beauty.

❡ Some people are angry at God though. However, God
never did anything against the person. God is like energy
added to your thoughts. God is the great affirmative that
always says YES to your thoughts. So, you better have
good thoughts.

❡ Devotees of Babaji have so often told me that they never
feel alone after letting Babaji into their life. I try to tell you
what works. I am not interested in what does not work, nor
would I waste my time or yours talking about it. So, do you
want more LIFE? More EXCITEMENT? Take note!
Think about it.

Love, Sondra

March 3, 2016

❡ A SIMPLE SECRET FOR LIVING TO 100 AND BEYOND
While I was waiting for a massage, a mother and daughter
came in. The daughter said, "This is my mom. She just
turned 94." The mother said, energetically, "Are we all
relaxed today ladies?"

❡ The woman next to me said, "You look amazing and full of
life! What is your secret?" Without hesitation the mom
replied, "I have always surrounded myself with nice people.
That's the secret."

❡ I was touched by the power and simplicity of her answer.
There are many studies that support this idea. They show
that increased love and kindness affect our biology in
impactful ways. If there are toxic negative people around us,
this could bring us down and bring disease. You know, I am
sure, the studies of Dr. Emoto, where he showed how
positive and negative energies affect the shape of crystals
formed by water.

❡ We must look closely at what we tolerate. Decrease your
exposure to those people who drain you. Perhaps you CAN
create a shift in them but perhaps you cannot. You can try.
But, "Truth cannot deal with errors that you want." (**ACIM**,
Text, chap. 3, sec. IV-7.) That means if they want to keep
your error of being negative, you cannot change them as
they have free will. Sometimes your compassion and
kindness can shift them, but only if they are willing.
Love, Sondra

March 4, 2016

❡ CHARACTERISTICS OF WORLD SERVERS
We are working with the transmission of divine forces and
this can be extremely powerful. We offer others the chance
to rise up like a phoenix from the ashes of past ignorance
and we invite them to join the mission. In order to do a good
job, we must keep on transcending our own preoccupation
with personal issues to a degree wherein we are able to
align with this higher cause. We must be dedicated to the
greater good of which we have become aware. We have to

keep selflessly seeking the TRUTH and always keep our genuine desire to be of spiritual help to those who come to us. We must have a purity of motive, sincerity, and an unconditionally loving attitude. We have to be aware that we have an important duty to perform.

ℐ We need to keep adjusting our lives so that negative reactions may be avoided. We must keep restoring our own higher frequencies so we won't get triggered by negative influences. It is a LAW that in dedicated and unselfish service, the vibratory rate of consciousness is raised in yourself. The masters look for people like that to give the initiations to. The point is, by serving you are actually raising your frequencies so the masters take note of you.

ℐ Every time you enroll someone into the mission; and bring them to the Truth, you are a blessing to them and the masters. It is an art to find those who are ready to receive it. The results will depend on:

1. *The recipient's degree of openness*
2. *Their willingness to give up old belief systems*
3. *Their thirst to know the higher truths*
4. *Their degree of fearlessness and trust in life*
5. *Their readiness to learn and change*
6. *Their readiness to move forward into greater spiritual awareness*

(From *Serving Humanity* by Alice Baily)

You can easily attract these people if you are that yourself. It is exciting when you can turn them on to the books and seminars and get their commitment. You will reap the rewards and so will they.

Love, Sondra

March 5, 2016

ℐ THE LAW OF KARMA

This is based on the law that for every action there is a reaction. For example, in one life John hurts Mary, and Mary (in a future existence) meets John in a new body with a different name (sometimes a different sex), and she hurts

John back, through a dim awareness (on a subconscious level) that he formerly hurt her. Then comes a new lifetime for both, and now it's John's turn to hurt Mary again—then another life and it is Mary who hurts John again, with each becoming the channel for the other's boomerang karma in a chain of dreary, seemingly endless incarnations. How do they get out of this?

> l. The one most previously hurt was John. He understands karmic law now and refuses to be the channel for Mary's karma. Mary is forgiven by John and the chain of karma breaks. Lucky for her.
> 2. John is not sufficiently enlightened enough to behave as such, but Mary is enlightened to the truth of karmic law and responds to the hurt by saying, "What must I have done to this person to cause him to hurt me so? I have done nothing in this life to cause such hurt, but I must have hurt him in a former life or I would not be in this position".

℟ She decides she must have deserved this. Therefore, she accepts the hurt as her own responsibility and holds no resentment; she has broken the chain. The karmic chain can be broken by either of the two people bound by it. You must be illuminated to receive the gift of karmic memory. (This is summarized from the book *Star Signs* by Linda Goodman.)

℟ Liberation Breathing / Rebirthing is a way you can also remember past lives and take responsibility and learn to forgive.

Love, Sondra

March 6, 2016

℟ A PAST-LIFE BLEED THROUGH

A client came who had fibromyalgia, anorexia, and panic attacks. She was completely stuck in FEAR. She even had paranoia and needless-to-say, catastrophic thinking. In taking her history, there really was not much that happened to her in this life to cause that much fear.

♪ I started getting something about a past life where she was marked for death. Someone was out to kill her and she knew it but she did not know who. So, she was never safe in that life. Her core belief in this life was "I am unsafe." During her session it became clear to me that she was poisoned to death in that life. That explained her fear of eating in this life.

When I processed her on her fibromyalgia, it was also due to fear. When I asked fear of what? She said, "Everything!" She actually thought all of this made total sense and she was very grateful.

♪ Seeing the truth about the cause is always the beginning of the healing. My experience is that when there are phobias one has to always check out past lives. She had it wired that she did not feel safe because of the fear. But the thought "I am unsafe" was causing her fear. Then the fear led to more fear. She needed help in understanding that thoughts precede feelings. We made a lot of progress in one session. But of course, she needed a lot of follow up. When a past life is dominating this life, I call it a "bleed through."

Love, Sondra

March 8, 2016

♪ A GLITCH
We had a big glitch. We are going to Istanbul after Tenerife and then to India. Mark happened to check my visa for India. Since I had a ten-year visa, we had not really been checking it before that day. Turns out it is expired!! So, we have to run around and try to get it here in Canaries. Not easy. Since it takes a couple of weeks to get it, we are under the wire. Please pray for me. Have to go to India! People are joining us there! So maybe now we apply here and pick it up in Istanbul. YIKES. It is a miracle that he checked the visa.

Love, Sondra

March 9, 2016

❡ A MIRACLE
Well, we did have a miracle. Markus figured out how to get the visa on line by paying EXTRA, which we were glad to do. So now we will get a paper e-mailed to us, which we can print out and turn in at the Delhi airport; but it is only for a month. However, we will make it.

❡ One of the ways I try to live is to "not be affected by the external." This is a real challenge on the road in foreign countries. So much can come up that I am always tested. First of all, I brought only summer clothes which I always pack for Spain thinking that it would be even warmer on the island due to being close to Africa. WRONG. To me it is freezing cold here. Secondly the rooms of the house are very cold as no central heating. Thirdly the shower is cold. This is a lot for me. We seemed to solve most of the problems. Bought some cardigans. Got a space heater in the room. The shower is not corrected though. I was having a bit of a hard time with all this, but Markus reminded me that I always tell people in India, "NO COMPLAINING" so I had to get off it!

❡ But we love the people. Our organizer Silke is fantastic. The group last night was fantastic. So as soon as I got back to work I was fine.

❡ I may have to move to the hotel for two days however as I cannot do a good job teaching the LRT without two hot showers per day. Here they are tough; they take cold showers. Life is interesting.
Love, Sondra

March 10, 2016

❡ FEEDBACK BACKFIRING
A student asked for help because her teenage son had actually hit her. I questioned her some about her circumstances and it turned out that her husband had hit her a lot in the marriage in the presence of her son. It turned out also that her father had hit her. I was trying to help her see how she had attracted all this, and I found out after a

process that her core belief was, "I am guilty." I explained to her that guilt demands punishment and that she had drawn this abuse into her life as a punishment for her guilt.

❡ Later I was informed that she was extremely upset by my process and did not want to work with me anymore. I was shocked as I had been extremely gentle with her; patient and loving. To me if I had asked a teacher for help and the teacher gave me the clue, I would be extremely grateful. But suddenly I realized that to her any feedback was interpreted by her as a kind of abuse. She actually must have felt that I "hit" her. It makes it hard for anyone to help her when she is projecting that much. My organizer talked to her about this and apparently, she got off it now. I really don't think I could have been gentler than I was. It just goes to show how much she feels like a victim—when in fact she is attracting this to herself!

❡ One does not get healed if one stays in victim mentality. Apparently, I will get another chance to love her though. We shall see what happens.

Love, Sondra

March 11, 2016

❡ MARKUS'S WRITING HERE IN SPAIN
"In the spaciousness of a Spanish cafe there is a vista overlooking an urban lake. There I have a coffee with my friend Lazaro. He speaks no English, nor I Spanish, so we try to say a few words to each other without much understanding. But there is a language of the heart which transcends words. In this communication, no words are needed. We are here to relax. I pull out my journal and he opens his iPad, as we sip our coffee and enjoy the cool sea air. In Santa Cruz, Tenerife, there is a relaxed atmosphere. It is a city, yet not as bustling as Madrid or Barcelona—on an island off the west coast of Africa. It is a group of islands called the Canaries. We sit near the sea observing the sun peeking through a hole in the clouds. For the most part, the days have been gray, and the clouds roll across the sky in an atmosphere of billowing overcast with little opportunity for the rays of sun to shoot forth. But today there are a few

moments of bright warmth spreading through the gray cotton cover. My friend is busy on his iPad and I am handwriting in my book. It is wonderful to be together with him without the need for words. Hearts join in a camaraderie that does not need speech. We share a silence between us. We share a leisure which does not require any explanation. Human beings naturally commune with one another on a level free of thought. In this space of silence, all of the universe is connected—so together in this quiet is the reality of Boundless Mercy."
—Markus Ray

March 12, 2016

⚐ A SHORT MARRIAGE
A woman came to an evening introductory talk and she was getting a divorce after a year. Her husband wanted it. She complained that he was angry that she would not communicate enough. She said it was because he was angry and that made her shut down. He would get angry and she would shut down. OR, was she shut down and that made him angry? I don't know which came first. I was hoping she would take the training so I could have time to help her; but she did not. Her mother-in-law got sick so she reported to us that she thought if she helped the mother-in-law instead of taking the training, it might save the marriage. I doubt that. This is a typical marriage problem that could be solved with some help.
⚐ There is a way out of this, but it does take two. They would both have to look at their patterns. There is so much one can learn if one studies their anger. But most people just defend it.
⚐ Last night in the training the girl was there who was mad at me for pointing out she was stuck in guilt and the guilt always demands punishment and that was why she was creating her husband and son abusing her. In the Rebirthing she began screaming and thrashing and disturbing everyone. I had to correct her again and I told her we do not do primal scream. Here we pump out anger on the exhale and change the thought that causes the anger. We do not

indulge in it. Drama does not release trauma. If you don't get to the cause, the anger will go on and on.

ᚷ This morning in class we are dealing with the subject of anger. This section is so important that I begin Saturday morning with that right off the bat. It gets heavy in the room because most people would rather defend their anger than let it go. I try to help people see that it is a very low frequency and it keeps you from rising to high states of consciousness. Besides, anger and love cannot co-exist in the same space. So, anger kills love. It destroys relationships and it will destroy one's body eventually. This morning should be interesting in class. Usually Markus helps me field the energy up front because often people get angry that they need to give up their anger! More later. Love, Sondra

March 13, 2016

ᚷ COLD TO THE BONE

The training is going really, really, well. The most unusual moment yesterday was during the emotional incest section. A gal shared that the truth was she was sexually attracted to her brother. He was sitting right next to her and nearly fell off the chair!

ᚷ For me it has not been easy since I am freezing. You would think I would do a better job packing after all these years. However, the big mistake I made was due to the fact that we usually come to Europe in May so I packed as if it was May. We have never come to Europe this early, so I was disorientated when I packed. March in Europe is still freezing cold and here I am with my summer clothes. Even the sweaters I bought are too light as they were for the Spring collection. I am cold to the bone, and I feel stupid about this mistake and disconcerted, and I had a hard time dropping it— because I am uncomfortable. At times like this I have to say to myself, "Even though I made a mistake, I still completely love and accept myself." That usually works to forgive myself. But it did not help me warm up.

ᚷ Even people in the training had on coats during the training, so you get the idea. I don't know why they can't have heating, especially in a hotel! So much for that. I did bring a few shawls which help somewhat. I kept thinking of the people in the concentration camps with no heat and the refugees and wondering how they ever made it.

℘ I am determined to have a great day anyway. Today we cover *A Course in Miracles* teachings and the New Paradigm on relationships, so everyone is excited. I never get tired of the LRT, as it is very, very, interesting. I am proud to say I wrote it but the people are what make it so interesting. The couples are really communicating to each other like never before.   Love, Sondra

March 14, 2016

℘ SUCCESSFUL TRAINING

Successful training thanks to Silke and a marvelous translator named Ana. The translator makes all the difference in the world. Sometimes I have gone through three translators because it is intense energy and their own case comes up. Some have nearly fainted. Once I had to take a student from the audience to translate when three of ours regular translators folded. Ana did the whole thing without a break and she was superb. The highlight for me was when I spoke about Babaji and the whole room LIT UP! There are magic stories to be told.

℘ I am happy everyone went home knowing they could now get what they wanted. People in Spain have so much gratitude. Markus painted a duo of the Divine Mother and of Babaji. I get high when he paints, as he kind of gets into an altered state. And the people love glancing at him painting, as his paintings come alive while I am speaking. He also gave a dynamite speech on *A Course in Miracles*. He often posts them in our **Miracles for You** program. I am going to try to put a photo of his paintings up here.

Love, Sondra

March 16, 2016

℘ ARRIVED IN TURKEY

115

When we arrived at the Turkish airport and I saw everyone in warm coats I knew I was in trouble with my packing error. However at least we have a room with central heating and a hot shower! So, I am very, very, grateful for that. Do you ever appreciate these things we take for granted? Of course, I have no ironing board.

🎵 But anyway, on the plane I read a book that was very advanced. It had been on my shelf for 25 years and I could never read it. Somehow, I grabbed it as we left as I had forgotten to buy books for the trip. This book kept me busy on the plane. It is called EARTH the COSMOS and YOU. Revelations by Archangel Michael. I don't think I would recommend it for everyone. Anyway, I found out things like the fact that I was born under the yellow ray when and where I was born, and I chose that because it is about communication. Before reincarnating, our soul evaluates what needs to be accomplished and sets up certain situations and people to be with in the particular life we are choosing. Certain choices during our life can, of course, free us from karmic debt. If we have unpleasant experiences, it is our soul that has chosen that situation to create a balance regarding something left undone.

🎵 I also found out that there are over 650 million planets that have life on them within our galaxy alone! I had always wanted to know that. So now I have to try to iron my clothes without an ironing board.

Love, Sondra

March 17, 2016

🎵 CASE STUDY

A gal came who said she did not want to be here (in life). There was a miscarriage before her (which was her). She did not want to be with that family. I asked her what her good purpose was in choosing that family and she said it was to bring joy to her mother who was also depressed. She would get in relationships that she did not like and try to bring joy to them (they were downers), but she would never give joy to herself! She was rejecting life so much that she was kind of near suicidal. When I told her that was not an option as she would get more stuck in her process, she did not listen. I had to explain to her that you don't automatically go to a higher place when you drop your body, i.e. "Consciousness seeks its own level." Then I told her she would have to come back, and it would be the same or worse. She listened that time, but she was very, very, stubborn. She said, "What is the use when you are going to die anyway?" I had to show her she was in charge of living and dying—not someone else.

꒹ We talked to her about having a mission, and in fact she was a beautiful singer. We had heard her sing, and it was marvelous. She could not, or rather would not, transfer the joy she had singing to the rest of her life.

꒹ Then she told us she did not want to be in the relationship she was in. So why not move on then? She threw a kind of tantrum wanting to hang on to it anyway—because she did not want to hurt the guy. But we told her she was already hurting him by leading him on. Most of the session she was incredibly stubborn and would not process to higher levels. It was rather disheartening.

꒹ Well, I told her I was going to check on her every week. She liked that support and said that would make a difference. Something about having to be accountable to me started to work. That very day she left that relationship she did not want. I was really surprised as I did not think she had the courage. Now I have to keep my agreement. Maybe when I do check on her every week via my organizer she will start to change. Let's hope so, or otherwise it will be a wasted incarnation.

Love, Sondra

March 18, 2016

꒹ TERRORISM IN ISTANBUL
Istanbul was historically known as Constantinople. It goes back to 660 BC.

꒹ It is a treasure of civilization. The hippodrome was for centuries used for chariot races. In 1453 it was conquered from the Romans and became Islamic. I think it is 99% Islamic—so this is the first time we have worked in an

Islamic country. The Bazaar is the largest and oldest covered market on the planet. It is a true source of wonder. There are 61 streets and 3,000 shops.

❡ Our first evening, our organizer was expecting 100 people, however due to the very recent terrorism the last few days in which a female suicide bomber blew up an area where 34+ people died, there has been terror. People are afraid to go out. I had to really acknowledge the 20 brave ones who came out. They were very alert and had a lot of questions. But due to this, we will likely have a small training. I called some people whose names I had been given from a friend in Athens. They told me they would not come because it is too dangerous. I do not feel this danger. However, we arrived two days after the incident so I might feel differently had I been here during it. We are in a nice area across from a lovely park on the 5th floor. I feel safe here fortunately.

Love, Sondra

March 21, 2016

❡ SHOCKING

We were teaching the anger section of the LRT when our students from Lebanon announced that they heard a bomb go off right in our area. I did not recognize that sound. They are used to it. Then the sirens came and the helicopters. Students ran to their cell phones for news feed. Many killed and more injured—once again. Before it was in the capital and now Istanbul. Markus and I were calm. He kept on painting Babaji and I kept on teaching. I asked students if they could hear me, and the Lebanese said, "Oh, we are used to this." We were all amazed it was in the anger section.

❡ The Turkish students were very upset as this is new to them. The rebirthing was very intense. Some had paralysis—some cried and cried. They were afraid to go home. We stayed in our block and made it to the restaurant which was empty. But the Lebanese were so happy with the training that they have invited us to their country. It just so happens we had a cancellation on the date they can receive us so we are meant to go. This is definitely a new experience. The amazing thing is that the day before all this, I was looking for nylons and people told me to go to that very shopping center (where it happened) to find them. We just could not make it there to that place which was the target for the next day. So, I was not even allowed to see the place.

❡ With so much unrest I was not sure what was the right thing to do. I thought maybe we should leave for India early; however, we suddenly got a lot of requests for private sessions, so obviously we are supposed to stay and help them. The government slowed down Facebook so we could not write for two days. I think that is because they did not want people to organize demonstrations. Now Babaji has us on the front lines of the KRANTI (global revolution). But we are being taken care of by Dina and her team.

Love, Sondra

March 22, 2016

❡ HOW THE SUICIDE BOMBER AFFECTED ME

I was really proud of myself that I had no fear during those days of panic people had. I knew Babaji was protecting me. But then I happened to see a video of the scene with police carrying out people on stretchers and this was filmed in front of Mango clothing store—exactly where we had walked the day before! This kind of got to me. I spaced out and could not find my purse anywhere. I carefully looked through all the rooms of the center where we were staying. Markus looked also. It was nowhere. I was sure I left it at the restaurant on the corner. Markus immediately called to cancel my card and we were relieved no one had tried to use it. I went to the restaurant which is part of a fine hotel. The manager of the restaurant told me it was 90% certain it would be in the safe or 10% in the maids' quarters. Nope. Not either place. I felt badly of course. It put me in a process. Then we searched our living quarters again. Found nothing. Then we went back to the hotel desk again. Found nothing.

❡ Last night we had a Babaji evening at the other center.

We spoke on Babaji and the Divine Mother and meditated on the Aarti (an ancient song sung to Babaji in Sanskrit and Hindi). I said to Babaji, "I want it back." After we finished, I told Markus I wanted to go back to the restaurant and ask the night crew. We had our usual crème brûlée.

¶ Fortunately I had gotten to know the waiters and manager as we had been there each night through the crisis and we would all share. The maître d' asked the manager of the hotel to look at the video camera about the time we had been there the night before and see if anyone went out with my purse. They watched between 6:30 - 8 PM. The hotel manager came in and told me he knew who had taken it.

¶ It was ME! He saw the bag on my arm. This was kind of embarrassing and yet funny. This meant that it HAD TO BE back in our living quarters as we had gone nowhere else during the crisis.

¶ So we searched the apartment again. There was one chair with a kind of skirt around it, and lo and behold I found my purse stuck under there. So then, case closed.

¶ Now we are going back to a normal life. I still don't feel like venturing out too much; but I would love to go to the old market I wrote you about.

Love, Sondra

March 23, 2016

¶ THE PROBLEM IS ANGER

I am trying to do my part helping people we see get over all their anger. So, I give everyone the forgiveness test. Where are they at forgiving the following people zero to ten.
(10 is total complete forgiveness, 0 is none, 5 is half.)

- ❖ Mother
- ❖ Father
- ❖ Sibling you had the most trouble with
- ❖ Ex-spouse or ex-mate
- ❖ Self

It is always astounding to see what low scores people get. Many get below 5 and some even get 0, especially on themselves.

❡ I point out that this means they are still angry. Then I have to go over the consequences of anger. And process them on fears of giving up anger! The problem in relationships is this: what you don't forgive you keep attracting. Also, who you don't forgive, you are stuck with, or in other words, you have psychic attachments with them—and then you become like them! Forgiveness is the key to happiness. Love, Sondra

March 24, 2016

❡ LOW SELF-ESTEEM
We had a client that confused humility with low self-esteem. She thought she was humble if a) she did not have great things and b) if she carried everyone's burden. Needless-to-say, she was tired and her shoulders hurt. Plus, she was not so excited about life because of all that. I had to teach her a new definition of humility.

❡ Yes, the dictionary would say you are humble if you don't think you are too important. But I prefer the higher definition that goes like this:

"A humble person is someone who recognizes his errors, admits them and does something about them."

Too many people don't even recognize their errors. Some do but they won't admit them. Some admit them but then they don't do anything about them. All three parts are important. That resonated with her.

❡ This is the kind of person you want to be, and this is definitely the kind of person you want for a mate. If your mate won't recognize his errors, won't admit them, and won't do anything about them, you are going to have a lot of trouble in the relationship. You may have to discuss this clearly at the beginning of a relationship. Be sure you are setting the example though.

Love, Sondra

March 25, 2016

℔ A CASE OF EXTREME FRIGIDITY
We had a client who had been married a long time and had
a six-year-old child. Her presenting complaint was that she
did not want her husband to touch her. She did not want
any sex at all. At first it is common to think it is a religious
thing (i.e., sex is bad, etc.), but this turned out to be a lot
more complicated. A lot of it had to do with her conception
trauma. At her conception, the father was dating two
women. One he got pregnant, which was her mother. I
immediately knew that he was really in love with the other
one. Later in the interview I found out that the father looked
up the "other one" when she was ten and had a ten-year
affair with the other one until she died. Much later the father
confessed to his daughter (our client), that the other one
was the love of his life!
℔ She was guilty her whole life that she caused him to marry
the wrong woman. (She was not aware that babies pick up
everything telepathically.) She had been a virgin until she
met her husband and said sex had never been good. I kept
pinning her down to see if there was ever a time it was
good. She replied, "Only the time I conceived my child." She
wanted a child more than she wanted sex.
℔ Her case was compounded by the fact that her mother
took it all out on her and beat her. She made the decision
not to FEEL anything. I felt good that we figured it all out;
but obviously, she was going to need a lot of follow-up. The
way I got her to be willing to keep working on herself about
all this was to ask her if she wanted her little girl to end up
the same. That woke her up.
Love, Sondra

March 26, 2016

℔ A THIRTY-YEAR SO-SO MARRIAGE
Take the case of a woman who came to a 5-day intensive.

122

She was very "together," and it seemed too good to be true. (That should have been a sign.) She told her regular Breathworker that she had an absolutely great marriage and felt really safe in it. We thought she was outstanding. But on the last day we were giving her a private session. I got suddenly very suspicious about her marriage even though they were having routine sex. I flat out asked her if she ever had an affair. She said yes and that she had never told her husband.

℥ I began to process her and she finally confessed that her husband was NOT THE ONE for her! She had tried to leave once but she went into a panic as she felt so unsafe. She ran back to where she felt "secure." I asked her then if she was staying with him only for security and she even said, "Yes." I asked her then: "Isn't that USING him?" So, it all unraveled then. She even admitted that her mother once asked her how it was and she had answered, "So-so." She was putting up with 30 years of that. But with the man she had met outside the marriage she had spiritual intimacy and a passion for life, so she knew what that felt like. But of course, that man was not available. She said she did not want to hurt her husband, but I pointed out she was already hurting him by using him. Then she even admitted she was NOT in love with him!

℥ So, I opened a can of worms, as usual. My job is to get to the truth. Decisions made out of fear are not real decisions—I could not play along with her lie. So, we started praying to the Divine Mother and I told her to breathe like mad. Lo and behold, the Mother came to help.

℥ She had a vision of the Divine Mother and the Mother told her she was in total denial and since she knows what real love feels like, she should go for it. This was a miracle as I did not want to tell her to leave her dead marriage. I wanted her to come to that herself and she did. This all came out a couple of hours before her flight to another country. She left very happy and open without any fear. Only 1-1/2 hours earlier she was totally stuck.

℥ Sometimes I wonder why people wait to tell me things until the last minute—things that are the whole key to their situation. They might be driving me to the airport and suddenly reveal the thing they are totally stuck on. I say,

"Why didn't you tell me this a week ago when I came to town? I could have been helping you with this all week!" This happens a lot. They are either in shame or denial or both.

❡ That lady was lucky as I got it out of her just in time. If I don't say what I see, I get sick. So, people have to get used to the truth around me.

Love, Sondra

P.S. Beware when someone tells you their whole life is great and they have no problems.

March 27, 2016

❡ A SEXLESS MARRIAGE

A sexless marriage is the top search marriage complaint. It is 3-1/2 times more common than an unhappy marriage and 8X more common than a loveless marriage. We had a client with a TRICKY SEXUAL ISSUE: The wife claimed they were in a great relationship but upon digging deeper we found she had no interest in sex at all. She had a younger husband who wanted sex. What surprised us was the fact that she was willing to be like that the rest of her life! She even actually created a spiritual teacher telling her that was advanced, and she had let go of all desire in past lives. But the truth was that she was actually frigid and was in complete denial about it. To unravel this case, we had to go all the way back to the grandparents.

❡ Her parents were from a very fundamentalist, almost cult-like church. When they had her, they tried to leave the church and have some joy (which was not allowed in that church); however, both parents' families rejected them for leaving the church. Her basic thoughts were, "If I have joy, I will be rejected." Her man was about to reject her for not giving him what he wanted. He also wanted a family. How these two got together is surprising. So, her pattern was that she would get rejected if she had sex and she would get rejected if she did not.

❡ We finally learned by digging really deeply, that her father was the love child of her grandmother and the priest of this fundamentalist church, for whom her grandmother was the maid! In other words, her father was conceived by this pious priest who was the head of the fundamentalist church! Our client was carrying all the shame of her grandmother in addition to the mindset of the church her parents grew up in. Her core belief was, "I am not acceptable as a woman" since she was supposed to be a boy. Her obsession with being rejected also came from that thought. Her case was all about needing to be rejected.

❡ I did get to interview the husband briefly. His case was, "I can't get what I want" (sex and children). So, their patterns dovetailed perfectly. We gave them a joint consultation which was absolutely necessary. His thought "I can't" dovetailed with her thought "I should not have joy." He seemed very patient with her, fortunately, and in our presence, they did come to some harmony. If they had not, they would have either broken up or been stuck in a miserable marriage. They were both willing to look at themselves and she felt like it was a revelation.

Love, Sondra

March 28, 2016

❡ CLEANING UP
My parents had an agreement to clean up their relationship every night. My mom said to me, "Never let the sun set on your anger, Sondra, it is in the Bible." It is a good policy to have this agreement in your present relationship. Of course, it is good if you can clean it up on the spot; but that is not always appropriate.

❡ But if you want a light, joyful relationship, don't wait another day to communicate something. Each night you can simply say to your partner, "Is there anything you need to communicate to me before we go to sleep?" If you do this, then nothing builds up and each new day starts well. Eventually this process will become integrated into your life as a good habit and you won't even need to ask the questions to remind each other. Of course, you need to use non-violent communication which I mentioned many times:

1. What I have noticed in our relationship is:
2. The way I feel about this is:
3. What I need and or recommend is:

♫ As you keep on doing breathwork, waiting to communicate a few days will become too uncomfortable in your body because you will become more and more sensitive.

♫ After you have done the process, complete by acknowledging each other for something so that you can sleep well.

Love, Sondra

March 29, 2016

♫ HOW DOES YOUR BIRTH EXPERIENCE AFFECT YOUR RELATIONSHIPS?

You probably know I was one of the first Rebirthers in the world and I had the privilege of studying all this. Birth trauma, as we call it in Rebirthing, manifests in various ways:

1. Fear of entrapment in a relationship
2. Womb-like dependency on a mate
3. Fear of pleasure
4. Separation anxiety
5. Fear of letting go around people
6. Fear of receiving love
7. Distrust of people
8. Sexual problems
9. Poor self-image/feeling less than another
10. Feeling like you are dying when a partner leaves
11. Suppressed anger and rage

And more! Liberation Breathing not only heals these fears, but it can heal you in every way. As you breathe out negative mental mass retained from birth, you feel healthier, more alive, more beautiful, and more loveable.

Love, Sondra

March 30, 2016

ℊ PRE-VERBAL THOUGHT
A lot of people do not realize that babies form very sophisticated thoughts already in the womb and at birth. These are often negative and produce negative results. Here are some examples formed at birth:

> ❖ Life hurts
> ❖ Life is too hard
> ❖ Life is terrifying
> ❖ The body causes pain
> ❖ People are out to get me (delivery team)
> ❖ I can't trust men (the obstetrician)
> ❖ I am wrong (wrong sex)
> ❖ I am bad (hurt my mother)
> ❖ I can't or I can't get out
> ❖ I am stuck
> ❖ I am lost
> ❖ I don't know where I am
> ❖ People abandon me (off to the nursery alone)
> ❖ ETC., ETC.

ℊ Then you have to know that, "Whatever you believe to be true, you create." So, you will keep on creating these thoughts manifesting. A good Breathworker will help you uncover your exact thoughts which could be other versions of these.
ℊ A good Breathworker will help you breathe out these thoughts. Most people never uncover their birth thoughts, so you see why they have misery. It is very important work. Liberation Breathing does liberate you from them.

Love, Sondra

March 31, 2016

♪ A CASE OF SEVERE DEPRESSION
We had a client that was not only depressed, but she was depressed her whole life! When examining her life, the only incident we could find that she was super guilty about was when she was seven and had to take care of a younger sibling who got burned. But that did not seem to be enough for depression her whole life. Digging deeper we found that her mother was totally depressed her whole life also. Then we found out that the mother's father was killed when the mother was a baby. He had a horrible death when an elevator crashed and his head was cut off.
♪ During the time we were reading the Divine Mother names Markus had a vision that the grandfather had not crossed over and was deranged as a result; he was possessing the mother of the client and now the daughter. Markus later told me he prayed like mad to Jesus and Babaji to help with this horrible possession. Fortunately, this started working and in the session our client actually saw Babaji; and she also saw the Divine Mother for the first time in her life. That is what she needed as her own mother could not mother her.
♪ I was convinced that the grandfather's soul was finally released, and you can imagine how much better our client felt. Believe it or not, we have seen this more often than you think—where the client was carrying the grief of the parents and grandparents. It is something one has to be tuned into.
Love, Sondra

April 1, 2016

♪ A CRECENT MOON
Last night in Turkey. Our beautiful student Sevgi, who was a Fulbright Scholar to Columbia in Architecture, took us around and about the back streets and side streets in Istanbul. First, we had dinner at a roof top restaurant that overlooked all of the city and the Bosphorus. Then we walked about and ended up at the Baklava Factory.... It was a dream really to be there. These treats were divine. We had the Turkish coffee with mud in the bottom of the little

cups. She turned them upside down and did a reading on the inside of the cups. She was amazed that both Markus and I had the same exact design in our cups—a crescent moon! So, it was a night to remember thanks to her. We would not have felt safe on our own. But with her we were so fine!

Love, Sondra

April 3, 2016

¶ ROUGH DEPARTURE FROM TURKEY
I don't know if is our karma or if it is just the tension in Turkey, but the driver who took us to the airport went on all the back roads and not the freeway, so it took nearly twice the time we had allowed plus he did not know a word of English. (We are used to being seen off by an organizer.) So that was more tension. Then instead of charging us for the extra bag which we are used to paying by bag, they charged by kilo and we had to pay $800 somehow. I don't know if that was a rip-off, but it surely felt like it. Taxis have ripped us off many times in Turkey. Language problem is huge. It crossed my mind about the bomb in the airport in Brussels. We felt a bit skittish, so I grounded myself with Babaji. But we are "never victims" of the world we see, right?
¶ Not sure why we had this intense training in Turkey. However, we met an absolutely great couple— Selin and Mehmet. They treated us like royalty our last few hours before we had to leave. Relationships make up for all the trials. We made some great friends despite it all.
¶ *Now we have arrived in India and it is so sweet and so great.* Went to the spa. Everyone knows me here at the La Lit Hotel, after years of coming to India. I feel so safe here. Thank you for letting me share. I never ever stuff my feelings. Sharing is the key to release stuff. We are now one-step closer to Babaji and His retreat. So happy!

Love, Sondra

♪ PS. Sri Aurobindo said, "For 3,000 years India has been creating republics, kingdoms, empires, philosophies, sciences, creeds, arts, poems, monuments, palaces, temples, communities, societies, religious orders, codes, rituals, systems of Yoga, systems of politics, and on and on." It is so interesting to be here and feel the spirituality behind it all. Even the taxi drivers have altars on their dashboards! One feels that all they really care about is, "How can I love God more?" It is so deep and ancient that it gets under my skin and I cannot stop thinking about it. I always long to come back. It is our second home—well, maybe Babaji's ashram is our original home. The group that is coming with us arrives today.

April 4, 2016

♪ QUOTES FROM GANDHI

❖ "The best way to find yourself is to lose yourself in service to others."
❖ "You must be the change you want to see in the world."
❖ "Strength does not come from physical capacity. It comes from an indomitable will."
❖ "First they ignore you, then they fight you, then you win."
❖ "Happiness is when what you think, what you say, and what you do are already in harmony."
❖ "The weak can never forgive. Forgiveness is the attribute of the strong."
❖ "My life is my message."
❖ "Live as if you were to die tomorrow. Learn as if you were to live forever."
❖ "An eye for an eye will only make the whole world blind."

April 5, 2016

❡ MORE GANDHI QUOTES
Leaving Delhi today toward the ashram. Here are a few more quotes from Gandhi:

- ❖ "Nobody can hurt me without my permission."
- ❖ "Hate the sin; but not the sinner."
- ❖ "I will not let anyone walk through my mind with their dirty feet."
- ❖ "To believe in something and not to live it, is dishonesty."
- ❖ "Whenever you are confronted with an opponent, conquer them with love."
- ❖ "You many never know what results come of your actions, but if you do nothing there will be no results."
- ❖ "There is nothing that wastes the body like worry; and one who has any faith in God should be ashamed to worry about anything whatsoever."
- ❖ "If you want real peace in the world, start with the children."
- ❖ "To lose patience is to lose the battle."
- ❖ "The good man is the friend of all living things."

Love, Sondra

April 6, 2016

❡ OFF THE INTERNET
Leaving for Babaji's ashram early tomorrow. Don't know if we will have any access to internet. Maybe I will be off for 10 days or maybe there will be a miracle.
❡ One gal in our group had the following miracle getting here. Diana was a student of mine when she was 21 in L.A. Now she is 51 and Babaji called her back to me. He put the message in her head, "You are going to India with Sondra." She was shocked.
❡ Later in her room, after she got that message, her white dog's hair stood up on end and then the dog stood up! Then

Babaji came to her in her room and introduced Himself. She saw Him in white robes with a yellow turban. Then she saw an altar appear and fire all around her room. She was given the blessing of a "fire purification." She told us about this very humbly. Needless-to-say, she is definitely supposed to be here.

❡ Tonight, we had a group breathe here in the hotel in Haldwani. Markus and I joined the group on the floor and the assistants led the breathing. I got my instructions from Babaji during the session as to what he wanted added to the book we are writing about Him. It is right now at the publishers and there is still time to add the pages He requested. We hope to channel what He wants written while we are in the cave where He materialized.

Love, Sondra

April 18, 2016

❡ DRIVING IN INDIA

We were at an intersection and it was a huge traffic jam with no traffic lights. On the road there were bicycles, scooters, motorcycles, carts, rickshaws, cars, buses, trucks, tractors, horses, mules, oxen, people, and some monkeys. In the madness Markus made the comments somebody could get killed—the driver turned around and said, "Sir, in India we have 100% trust in God." What a teaching!

❡ Just returning from the ashram where we had a very powerful experience. Jackie from England said to me, "I have waited for this my whole life!" What I love about the nine-day Navaratri is to be able to see how much people change in those nine days. Besides the regular ceremonies we have breathwork every single day, so the group stays healthy and happy. They loved meditating in Babaji's cave, meditating in the Dhuni (Divine Mother fire temple), and meditating in Babaji's receiving room (where he received dignitaries). Jacob, our 13-year-old who was divine, said that when he opened his eyes in there he saw a form of Babaji above each one of us! Every single person in the group made the pilgrimage of climbing up Mt. Kailash. It is a major, major, rebirthing to do so. The elaborate daily fire ceremony is always a highlight. For me, it is a thrill to meet people from all over the world. We got invited to Madrid and Slovenia next year!

Love, Sondra

April 19, 2016

❡ FROM SUTRA #14
This is from Patanjali's ancient Yoga Sutras:

> "O Seeker! Life is a journey. Each living being carries a backpack of karma, both meritorious and non-meritorious, from life after life.
> This life is the result of the past and also to the future. Be careful.
> Change your life through a life of love, prayer and meditation. Transform your life through the practice of God-conscious living. This is the path of blessedness."

April 22, 2016

❡ FROM AGE TO AGE
Sorry, I was in a place here in India with no internet connection the last three days. During that time, I read and re-read the book *From Age to Age*, about a former materialization of Babaji. I want to share some of that.

> "Babaji would undertake difficult and severe penance in secret caves in the Kumaon region, sitting in yogic posture for three to four hundred years. His body was so soft that even by pressing it, one could not feel the presence of bones.
> Whenever He opened his fist, the air all around would be filled with such a fine fragrance that it would bring a joyous mood to all. None ever saw him sleep. Shri Pathak stayed with His Holiness for six months and never saw Him sleep. He wore the

dress suited to the ancient Indian culture (kurta, long shirt, loin cloth and cap.) But when He was seen by Niels Olf Cressander in a hotel in France (while He was still in India), he was dressed in European style and spoke native English." pp.28-29

§ And here is another passage from the book *From Age to Age* about a former materialization of Babaji:

"During the month of Vaishakha (April-May), Haidakhan Baba would pile up wood and cow dung disks and from a great distance, then He would ignite them with His yogic power. He would sit in the midst of the fire, covered only by a thin sheet of cloth, the flames rising from all directions. This penance would go on for days, with the fire continuously charged. The onlookers were suspecting that He would surely be burned. Instead, His body would shine brilliantly, like the rising sun. He got up and shook off His cloth covering and one would see water dripping off His body. Once, His Holiness stayed in the fire for a whole month.
§ Sometimes He would appear as a sixteen-year-old youth with a twining serpent and half-moon on His forehead; at other times He appeared as a century-old yogi." pp. 31, 32

Love, Sondra

April 23, 2016

§ THE DANCE OF THE BEASTS
A well-known family wanted to perform a dance for Babaji. They had a lot of pride doing it. Babaji then told them, "You have seen humans perform and now he would show a dance of the beasts." They did not believe it but soon lion cubs were coming from all directions until there were more than 20 which struck people with fear. The lions danced and then the people fell at Baba's feet regretting they doubted Babaji.

❡ This reminds me of a story which happened to me in Munich: My organizer called me saying he was needing a Rebirthing session as he was very activated. I told him to come over and before I knew it he was having a past life memory of being thrown to the lions. After the breathing, I told him we should go to the Munich Zoo and look at the lions and then go to the stadium. I wanted to get to the zoo before crowds came, so I made sure we were the first ones in at 9 AM when the zoo opened. We were walking toward the lions when a very, very, strange man blocked our path. He was carrying the largest mug of beer I have ever seen. Not normal! He was drinking beer at 9 AM and he was making sounds of the animals in the zoo.

❡ It was very unnerving as the sounds were too accurate for any human to copy those animals. I said, "How did you get here," as it was clear he was not a zookeeper. He said, "I am always here!" Then he pointed to a peacock very high up in the tree, and he told us that peacocks cannot fly that high—which I knew was true. I wanted to run away from him, so I said to my friend, "Let's get to the lion cages." When we did, I realized that strange man had been Babaji. I went back and he was gone. I told my friend that was surely Babaji, and he immediately got a large nose bleed and his whole body was on fire. I told him he was getting a spiritual purification.

❡ Later we went to the stadium which was totally empty. We climbed to the top and looked down imagining what it was like to be thrown to the lions. A man suddenly appeared in front of us from nowhere and asked to take our picture! So, this was one of Babaji's recent materializations in my life. Bhole Baba Ki Jai!
Love, Sondra

April 24, 2016

❡ RAISING THE DEAD
The people of the Kumaon region tell of many incidents of the rising of the dead at the mercy of Sri Babaji.
❡ There was a man named Shri Ramadatt whose brother died suddenly. He went to the lake to bathe before

beginning the funeral rites. He informed Babaji of his brother's death. Babaji followed him home and as Baba stepped in the house, the brother stood up, walked toward Babaji and then prostrated himself at His Holy feet.

❡ Babaji was proceeding with a devotee to the holy ashram at Badrinath. On the way, a devotee had an attack of cholera— with frequent purges of vomiting. His limbs turned cold and he realized he was dying. Babaji told him, "I shall shake off my body instead of you." Suddenly the devotee recovered from his illness and the cholera began its attack on Shri Babaji. On His death, Babaji instructed His devotee that His corpse should be burned, and the ashes floated on the Ganges. His Holiness did die and the devotee, filled with grief, burned the body and followed the instructions.

❡ About a month later, the distressed devotee heard that His Holiness was in Almora, safe and sound staying at another devotee's house. He could not believe it since he himself had performed the funeral rites. He then saw Babaji sitting as usual. He was so shocked he lost his mind and it took him six months to recover.

From the book *From Age to Age,* p. 60 (Summarized in my own words.)

Love, Sondra

April 25, 2016

❡ A TRIBUTE TO MY TEACHER SHASTRIJI
Shastriji was Babaji's high Priest. He was an Ayurvedic doctor; he was an astrologer; he was a palm reader; he was a scholar who wrote many of the great epics in his past lives; he was a poet in all lifetimes and Babaji said he was one of the purest beings on the earth. He always invited me and my staff to his home where he took care of us with so much hospitality that his love was always overflowing to us. Shastriji spent 14 years in the presence of Babaji, serving Him in the highest way. It was Shastriji who recognized the true Babaji and the story goes like this:

> *Shastriji's teacher Mahendra, told him that there was only one being who would know this certain*

mantra and if he heard it, that was then the real Babaji. In 1970 Babaji appeared as a dazzling youth. This youth invited Shastriji into His private room and locked the door. The secret mantra suddenly began to bounce off the walls and hammer in Shastriji's head, leaving no doubt as to the identity of this youthful being. Shastriji made full pranam (prostrating before Him) at Babaji's feet, and then announced to the world that their beloved Mahavatar Haidakhan Baba had indeed returned.

꿍 Babaji would say of Shastriji that he was a true son of Saraswati, Goddess of knowledge, music, the arts, and wisdom, and that in his previous lives he had authored a number of ancient Indian epics and texts. I feel so privileged to have known him so well.
Love, Sondra

April 26, 2016

꿍 FROM THE TEACHINGS OF BABAJI

"In the world today, fire is bursting out on one side while nectar flows on the other. You must decide if you want to choose fire or nectar. While the flames of fire are spreading, it is up to us to save ourselves and others. We must be alert. At this moment, people are jumping into the fire because of their ignorance. We must save these people, and we can do so only if we have great courage. We should give this courage to others as nothing can be done without it. Courage is the most important thing. I have told you many times to wake up. Wake up yourselves and others. Control your mind and have a firm determination. Whoever comes here (to Herakhan) must vow to save himself and the world. Wherever you go, be prepared to save people. Be firm like a rock, deep and serious like the sea. Think of the earth as our Mother. This is one earth. Don't be divided by thinking of yourselves as belonging to

*different countries. We belong to one earth.
Proceed with this in mind. Look to the future with a
vision of good deeds for the whole world, not just
one country. Have great courage and patience
—and be not afraid of water, fire or great storms
—face them bravely."*   p. 63

Love, Sondra

April 27, 2016

♪ NOTE FROM TAJINDER
Hi, Tajinder in the UK sent me this from AMMA. Tomorrow
we are traveling back to the USA. So, I may not get back on
Facebook until May 1. See you then. Sondra.

> *"Our every thought and action has the power to
> bring light or darkness into the lives of many. So,
> we have to be careful that our actions are the kind
> that bring joy and satisfaction to others. We
> shouldn't fall into a state of despair when we see
> the evil in the world. Nor should we allow the
> wrongs done by others to encourage us to do
> similar wrongs. Instead of cursing the darkness, let
> us try to kindle a small lamp. If we can't do this, let
> us at least refrain from causing others any
> discomfort. You may wonder how this can be
> practiced in our day-to-day lives. One way is to
> perform all our actions as an offering to God. We
> should make our every action a form of worship.
> This will give joy to others and will benefit us as
> well." — Amma*

May 1, 2016

♪ BACK IN USA
I wonder if you have ever spent any time in third-world
countries. I wonder if you really, really, appreciate living in a
country where the roads are good. I wonder if you really

appreciate the conveniences you have in the USA or Europe. I wonder if you have gratitude for the hot water, the nice bathrooms, the quality of life. It is so good to hear the customs agents say, "Welcome home."

❡ But one thing we really learned in India is this: They KNOW how to give you hospitality. We have never ever been treated so well as we were with Uday and Retu Chatterjee in Dehradun, India, who are two of our closest friends. We had the most wonderful care in every way imaginable. I grew up with a sick father my whole life, and so I could never have people over to our home as guests. Markus had the same situation. I guess I never learned until now what it is like to truly welcome a guest with the most hospitality imaginable. I feel so moved by how they treated us like royalty.

❡ It made us just want to give back. So today we spent 1 1/2 hours giving back to a friend who is going through a divorce. We were 100% there for her and we will continue to be there for her every single week until she no longer needs our support. Pay it forward they say.

Love, Sondra

May 2, 2016

❡ A PRAYER
I wrote this prayer to the Divine Mother upon returning home from the Divine Mother Festival in India:

> *"Oh, that I may pray properly to you Divine Mother. I wish to express my appreciation to You as the Source of Life. I know that more than in any other relationship, we may rightfully and naturally demand a reply from Spirit in its aspect as You, Divine Mother. For the essence of a Mother is love and forgiveness of her child. I know that a definite conception of God is helpful to receive a clear response and I have made up my mind that You are going to talk to me. In India you were always like a warm shower engulfing us.*

I claim our consciousness be united with You at all times What shall we do (Markus and I) and how shall we do it? Show us the way. You are the key to this day. I know that physical reality is an electronic dream world of You and the physical universe is Your Body. Oh, Divine Mother, it is due to You that we are able to release our sorrows. It is due to You that we will find true happiness. It is due to Your transcendent nature and all-pervading light that You are worthy of being worshiped and adored. Thank you for letting us come to Your Divine Mother Festival (Navaratri) in India this year. We call upon You to keep on igniting us with illumination. You are the personification of intelligence that creates matter. Everything we possess is a gift from You. I address You as though I am still in your actual presence, in as much as You are in every place. In India I felt closer to You somehow. Now I ask that You come to us as much as You did in the fire ceremonies. May everything we do or experience bring me closer to You. Keep on Awakening us."

Thank you.
Love, Sondra

May 3, 2016

❡ ANOTHER PRAYER
To You, Divine Mother, font of all our sustenance:

"Oh, Divine Mother. I am humbled and bowed down as You are revealed to me. You are my ever-lasting light. Yours is the Kingdom and power and glory forever. For in You all things shall be made alive. The last enemy You will destroy in me is death. You have raised me from the dust several times. I know only You can grant the boon of Physical Immortality. I ask for this only so I can serve You more. I sing praises to Your powers because You have revived my heart. Thank you for healing my

group that I brought to You this year. May I speak as an oracle of You. Let me minister with the ability You supply. Let me declare Your glory among the nations that we visit. You have shown me Your greatness. You have removed my burdens; and now I ask You to do that for my wonderful husband today. Don't delay."

Thank you.

May 4, 2016

❡ ON MARRIAGE
Several people asked me on this last trip abroad if people in the USA are still getting married or are they just living together? I understood why people are asking this. Times are changing and marriage does not have a good record and it is scary to think of finances if one is breaking apart. Even one of my friends going through a divorce said her husband quit working so he would have an excuse NOT to pay her!!

❡ I remember when one guru declared that marriage was out of date and that it destroys all possibilities for happiness. He insisted that marriage makes everyone a zoo animal, that it exacerbates the will to die and leads to prostitution! He said it ruined the status of women etc.—and he said this several decades ago.

❡ That wild statement inspired me to explore the whole subject more deeply. Swami Kruyananda wrote in *How to Spiritualize Your Marriage*:

> ❖ *Marriage can help a person achieve inner balance.*
> ❖ *Marriage helps break the confines of selfishness and ego.*
> ❖ *Marriage helps one expand one's identity.*
> ❖ *Marriage provides a "proving ground" for one's inner spiritual development. It tests your spiritual qualities.*

141

❖ *It is a vehicle through which one can achieve union with God in your mate.*

So that is what he said—Yogananda said that the desire for marriage was universal because of the cosmic power of love to draw everything back to oneness.

ʃ Well, all I know is this: I love marriage now. I did not when I was younger and had my first marriage, as I was not clear enough. Matrimony does not solve problems—it accentuates them. What matters is not marriage itself but how you handle it. Of course, you need a holy relationship and that cannot be achieved unless your ego is pretty well blasted.

ʃ Markus and I had very tough teachers who helped us with that. I had Babaji. He had Taraji. I don't think our marriage would be as easy as it is now if we had not been through the fire of a true Master. Furthermore, I asked Babaji to pick my mate and therefore I got someone with the same exact spiritual path which really makes a huge difference.
Love, Sondra

May 5, 2016

ʃ MORE ON MARRIAGE
Studies show that marriage offers many benefits. Married people tend to be healthier, live longer and have more wealth and economic assets, and have more satisfying sexual relationships than single and cohabiting individuals. What I like about it is the intimacy: Closeness with one's spouse emotionally, spiritually, intellectually, sexually and many other ways.

ʃ Especially I like the spiritual intimacy which is why we wrote a book on that subject. It is the feeling of freedom that you can connect at any time and in any way about spiritual matters and issues. There is no walking on egg shells about sharing or raising a question. Revealing your spirituality to your partner and giving them spiritual support is fabulous. It gives one greater warmth, humor, and love. There is less negativity and hostility, and overall greater satisfaction. One is more motivated to be kind and resist the urge to go negative when discussing core issues. I love discussing my spiritual journey with my husband and visa-versa.

❡ Fortunately, we have the exact same spiritual path. We are both devotees of Babaji and the Divine Mother. We are both students and teachers of the Course in Miracles. We are both Rebirthers. We are both students of Hawaiian spirituality. We are both writers and healers. So, it is easy and exciting for discussion. We observe spiritual practices together. We honor the characteristics of intimacy: mutual trust, tenderness, acceptance, open communication, caring, apologies, and forgiveness.

❡ For some people a long-term committed monogamous relationship is one of the scariest things two humans can attempt. Many people would rather do anything to protect themselves from it. And yet, that is what they long for. Besides, the sexes often define intimacy differently. To women, it is talking face to face (after all women spent days holding their infants up in front of them). Men often regard intimacy as working or playing side by side. How often do they share their secret dreams or darkest fears? Men may not look deeply into each other's eyes. Men may even regard debating as intimate. Of course, everyone knows that women generally understand emotions better than men.

❡ But my experience is that men can learn this and then they like it. We don't have to be stuck in these stereotypes. Once a man has been Rebirthed, he is usually quick to be more like his female partner in expression. It is wonderful. He can connect at any time in any way. He feels safe being completely open and honest with his mate. And he knows how to be supportive.

❡ Hope you will read our book: *Spiritual Intimacy: What You Really Want with a Mate.*

Love, Sondra

❡ Travelling to Florida tomorrow.

May 6, 2016

❡ JUST BEFORE MOTHER'S DAY

Thinking about your birth as we approach Mother's Day? What does your Birth Experience have to do with your relationships? You would be surprised how much influence there is:

    1. Fear of entrapment in a relationship
    2. Womb-like dependency on a mate
    3. Fear of pleasure
    4. Separation anxiety
    5. Fear of letting go with people
    6. Fear of receiving love; distrust of people
    7.Sexual problems
    8. Poor self-image
    9. Feeling like you are dying when a partner leaves you
    10. Suppressed anger and rage

❡ There is such a thing as a conception trauma, prenatal trauma, birth trauma, and post-partum trauma. Usually you have something going on in one of these areas or more. You can clear it all up through Liberation Breathing, however. Why not treat yourself to a session?

❡ It was rough getting out of the womb. But did you ever think of what your mom had to go through? If you did, you would appreciate her and your life! But many people are angry about the whole thing and wish they were not even here. If that is you, you are acting as a victim and not taking any responsibility for your own choice to come here. Nothing works when you are acting as a victim. It means you think everyone did it to you and you can't change anything. My own mother kept telling me, "Life is a Miracle, Sondra." And she was right!

❡ IF you want to be safe during the global revolution, I suggest you surrender to the Divine Mother. It is where the real power lies. The original spark of creation is a feminine aspect, they say in India. They also say that surrender to the Divine Mother is the final stage of perfection for a soul. They also say that there is nothing higher than worship of the Divine Mother. But, of course, you have to work out your case with your own mother before you can let the Divine Mother in.

❡ Most people never forgive their mothers completely at 100%. I am here trying to get the people in this training to do that before tomorrow—Mother's Day. They have been sharing all their ISSUES with their mothers with me and they have A LOT going on about their mothers.

❡ One guy brought his own mother with him to the class. He is sharing his issues in front of her. So, it is all pretty intense. When people share that they had horrible mothers who beat them or who were unmedicated bi polar types etc., etc., and all they went through. I have to help them get out of being victims. They want to blame their mothers. But I make them say out loud, "My good purpose for attracting that Mother in this incarnation was_____." It is pretty enlightening to get them to see that.

❡ It is hard work; but if I could only get them to forgive their mothers 100% they might actually have the miracle of letting the Divine Mother in their life. That is my goal.

Love, Sondra

May 7, 2016

❡ A TRIBUTE TO MY MOTHER ON MOTHER'S DAY
My mother's parents came over from Sweden and settled on a farm in Iowa. She used to tell me how they would go to town in a horse and buggy! She never dreamed of being able to go to college at all; but one of her teachers told her she was very, very, smart and she should go no matter what. She got in to Iowa State University and stayed in an attic and became the chauffeur of a Botany instructor.

❡ At a Freshman mixer, my dad saw her sitting with her legs crossed in a sensual way and he asked her to dance. They were engaged for seven whole years.

❡ My mother let me be myself. She let me roam around town by myself even at night. I had no fear. I used to visit the sick and the old people. She had an agreement with my dad never to raise their voices in the presence of my sister and me—and they never did.

❡ They had an agreement to clean up their relationship every night and they did. My dad had rheumatic heart disease and was always in and out of hospitals. It was a real tragedy, but my Mom made ends meet by being a teacher. She never complained. I never heard her complain once. When my dad died, I asked my mom how was it that she held up so well. She said, "Well, I had you girls—some women never can have children." She always had high thoughts.

❡ When I rebelled and got angry at God because my father died, I married a genius, but he was an atheist. Later I found out she silently prayed every day that I would WAKE UP. When I finally did, she came to California and became my student. She took the LRT and everyone found her delightful. At a seminar in Hawaii she rounded up people in the seminar to clean the beach with her at 6 AM. When she was old and on her death bed, Babaji materialized His body to her and blessed her in her hospital room. Later my guru Shastriji told me she was a totally realized soul and never had to re-incarnate.

Love to my mom, Ethel, from Sondra

May 9, 2016

❡ WHAT I DID ON MOTHER'S DAY
Spent Mother's Day at the Kashi Ashram started by Brooklyn-born spiritual teacher, Ma Jaya, who became a mystic and visionary.

❡ When she took a weight-loss class and learned Yogic breath--that brought about her spiritual enlightenment. She had a normal life before that with husband and children. Soon she had an experience of Jesus Christ, Nitiyananda, and then her guru became Neem Karoli Baba. (He was a friend of Babaji and he was also the guru of Ram Dass and Krishna Dass.) Kashi ashram is a beautiful place, which is an interfaith spiritual community dedicated to kindness, compassion, and service.

❡ Every day we had breathing in the yoga studio. We closed the day by Elaine leading us in a beautiful fire ceremony where we offered to the fire (the mouth of the Divine Mother), grains and fruits and incense and flowers while reading the Divine Mother names. It was the perfect way to close our event. After that, the ashram served hundreds of mothers and adult children and young children.

Love, Sondra

May 10, 2016

¶ PRAYER TREATMENT FOR UNEXPECTED INCOME
Everyone can use these prayers to generate more abundance in their lives:

> ❖ I believe God is the source of all supply, and money is God in action and should be used for good.
> ❖ I believe my good is now freely flowing to me so bountifully—I cannot use it all, and I have an abundance to spare and to share today and always.
> ❖ I am expecting "Unexpected Income"!
> ❖ I believe God is now giving this to me and I accept this as Truth, and give thanks.
> ❖ All channels of financial supply are now open to me and I am richly, bountifully, and beautifully prosperous in every good way.
> ❖ I believe true prosperity includes the demonstration of right living conditions, right activity, and right kinds of happiness.
> ❖ This word which I speak in faith, believing, now activates the law of increased universal good for me, and I expect to see rich results now!
> ❖ I visualize the financial good I expect. I see it coming to me now, richly and abundantly.
> ❖ I claim and accept it for myself now.
> ❖ I am grateful in advance! I bless all the good I now have and—I bless the increase.
> ❖ I bless all others in the "Unexpected Income" program, and I know we are all prospering now in every good way, and share the good we receive.
> ❖ I now freely give my tenth to God's good work.

My giving is making me rich!
* God gives me rich, lavish, financial blessings!
* This is so now. I am grateful. Thank you,
Father/Mother/Child as ONE.

(For best results, repeat 2X daily.)
Love, Sondra

May 11, 2016

¶ A RELATIONSHIP SECRET
Lately we have experienced radical hospitality. First in the
home of Uday and Retu Chatterjee in India, and now in the
home of Randi and Tammy Levine in Florida. The dictionary
says this about hospitality: "The host receives the guest with
good will, including reception and entertainment of guests,
visitors or strangers." It also says, "Showing respect for
one's guest, providing needs, and treating them as equals."
Words to describe it are friendliness, welcome, warm
reception, helpfulness, neighborliness, warmth, warm
heartedness, kindness, congeniality, amicability, generosity,
and bountifulness.
¶ St. Benedict said, "Let all guests who arrive be treated like
Christ." Hospitality is an invitation to God to use us in the
lives of others. Have you ever thought about treating your
mate as an honored guest? To me that is one secret of
creating a great relationship.
Love, Sondra

May 12, 2016

¶ A HIGHER PURPOSE
Norman Vincent Peale said, "The more you lose yourself in
something bigger than yourself the more energy you will
have."
¶ This is a very important saying. Choosing to involve
yourself in big things WILL energize you. I know this for
sure. This is why karma yoga is so important (work
dedicated to God). This is how you grow. Picking a project

that is a STRETCH for you will force you to change and move and you will be moving UP the scale of energy. Keeping on doing the mundane can drain your energy.

❡ I once did a training where I asked each participant to pick a project they could commit to that was a stretch for them. Very few could do it. They picked things they already knew how to do, things that they were familiar with because it felt safe. The things they chose were not really bigger than them. I had to push them.

❡ Markus and I just saw a movie about Hemingway yesterday. He kept saying that the only things of real value were the risks you are willing to take. So, if there is something you are guided to do, just start doing it. Help will come. You will be energized. We just wrote a book about Babaji. It seemed like such a daunting task that I put it off for years— how could I do justice to HIM? Well, Markus and I did it together. It will include his paintings and poetry to Babaji. It really, really, has increased our energy. I ended up liking the project so much that I read it twice myself after writing it, something I never used to do. It is called *Babaji: My Miraculous Meetings with a Maha Avatar.* Doing a mission, especially together with your mate, is part of this whole process.

Love, Sondra

May 13, 2016

❡ A STRANGE HOUSE
We had a client who was really depressed. In taking her history, there was nothing that seemed to trigger that depression except that it started when she moved to a certain house. We noted that and commented that there was something about that house that was obviously *off.*

❡ She went on to tell us so many things, but we kept going back to the house. After one hour she suddenly remembered that there was a man who died in that house before they moved in. I told her that was the information I was looking for. Then she admitted that her husband was seeing a ghost. Somehow, she never ever made the connection until she came for this session. There are *earth bound spirits* who, for whatever reason, do not cross over properly and stay bound to their physical place or environment.

℘ Houses definitely take on the energy from the people who lived there before, and this is why you should always get a house cleansed by a spiritual guide before you move in, if the house is not new. She went out saying she was going to look for an apartment on the beach. This made her happy. Love, Sondra

May 14, 2016

℘ IN OUR STILLNESS WE CAN BLESS
Now we are teaching the Loving Relationships Training in South Florida. This passage is something that struck me as very profound:

> *"When you love, you can heal a person just by looking at him or thinking about him, even from a distance. The other person may never even know it. You can walk around the busy streets of New York and impart your stillness. Something takes place because when you are still, you can BLESS. When you bless another, somehow you are blessed too. If you didn't have the blessing in you, how could you bless? By giving, you receive—but not from another person. It is a receiving from Heaven because you feel the need of a brother and you want to give. And you are given what you need to give. It is so swift. Every time you see a need, you are given what you need to impart. You and God become one in that moment. You are surrounded by the compassion of God, lifted and purified, as your giving becomes your laughter and your song."*

℘ This is on p. 75 from *How to Raise a Child of God* by Markus's teacher, Tara Singh. Every parent should read this book.

Love, Sondra

150

May 15, 2016

₰ ASCENSION ATTITUDES
Love, Praise, and Gratitude are the ascension attitudes.
Work at being joyously grateful for every experience of life
as it happens in the present moment. The mastery of
gratitude produces the fastest movement forward.
Frequently radiate energies of gratitude from your heart
toward the Creation. The generation of divine PRAISE
produces real frequencies of energy with specific
wavelengths that help lengthen your life and produce
healing.
₰ One man I know of in Japan totally healed himself of lung
cancer just by bowing to his altar every morning and night
and saying, "Oh God, I appreciate my lungs so much. They
have served me so well." He took no treatment. You can
heal people by expressing appreciation.
Love, Sondra

May 16, 2016

₰ ON MARRIAGE FROM TARA SINGH
We have been in South Florida and I am very impressed by
Tara Singh's book called *How to Raise a Child of God.* Here
is another profound passage about marriage:

> *"In marriage, one is no longer the same. A sense of
> responsibility and caring for another begins to
> awaken; you can no longer be merely physical.
> Another tenderness comes in that you never knew
> existed. It is not sexual; it is a feeling of sacredness
> for another human being by whom you are
> completed.*

> *Both the man and the woman become noble
> through giving and tenderness. Every act speaks as
> love and respect grow. Today, most people only
> know common passion. Seldom do they grow in this
> way, where each person gives the space and*

recognizes the noble goodness in the other. That is marriage."

(p. 66 from *How to Raise a Child of God* by Tara Singh)

Love, Sondra

May 17, 2016

♫ HOW DO YOU SEE YOUR WORK?
There are three kinds of people, it is said:

> 1) Those who see their work as a "job" with its main purpose to provide a living.
> 2) Those who see their work as a "career" with the purpose of advancement upward on a path.
> 3) Those who see their work as a "calling" with the higher purpose of contributing to a larger good.

♫ The third will give you more meaning and bring more enjoyment obviously. Your happiness factor will be much higher. This sense of calling must come from within. Babaji said, "WORK IS WORSHIP; IDLENESS IS DEATH." So, can you see your work as worship? Can you imagine helping people you work with to raise their consciousness, and also people who come to you during your work day? Maybe you can make your current work a calling, or maybe you have to do the affirmation, "I allow the Divine Plan of my Life to now manifest."
♫ You will then be guided to do work that you are naturally good at, work that you enjoy.
Love, Sondra

May 18, 2016

♫ DREAMS COME TRUE

> *"Everybody can make their dreams come true. It takes a dream, faith in it, and hard work. Yet the*

work isn't all that hard because it is so much FUN you hardly think of it as work." (Walt Disney)

Love, Sondra

May 19, 2016

❡ BIG MIRACLES
I am happy to say that people we gave private sessions to in Florida let us know that they had BIG miracles after their sessions. It is amazing how changing one thought can make such a difference. But you have to know what is the thought you need to change to get a new result. It is usually a subconscious negative thought that you are not even aware you have. That is exactly why you need someone who knows how to locate the thought that is sabotaging you. We are experts at helping people find the sabotage. In our work we call this thought the "personal lie." It is you most negative thought about yourself. It is not the truth about you, but part of your mind believes it is so—mostly the subconscious part. It is our work to help you locate this thought to clear it.
❡ Then when you breathe out the thought in a Liberation Breathing Session, you are liberated from it and the miracles can happen. I love doing private sessions for this reason. People deserve miracles. *A Course in Miracles* says you are entitled to miracles, but purification is necessary first. Liberation Breathing is definitely a form of spiritual purification that helps people let go of their personal lie.
Love, Sondra

May 20, 2016

❡ OPTIMISTS
Here are some qualities of *optimists*:

❖ *Optimists are more confident, so they accept challenging goals.*

❖ *Optimists believe setbacks and problems are temporary, so they don't give up.*
❖ *Optimists have confidence that their decisions will turn out right, so they are more decisive.*
❖ *Optimists don't take rejection personally, so they don't waste time on resentment.*
❖ *Optimists know that failure is never final, so they bounce back from adversity.*
❖ *Optimists enjoy life and love their work.*

(p. 21 from *Twenty-one Great Leaders* by Pat Williams.)
Love, Sondra

May 21, 2016

ʃ PHYSICAL IMMORTALITY
Physical Immortality: a thought transformation leading to the achievement of cell regeneration. It is eternal life in the same continually improved transfigured flesh body. If you could live as long as you wanted without being sick and without being in pain and without being old and decrepit, would you want to? Well, most people say NO because it is too painful. And yet, the reason they are in pain is that they never let go of their "death urge." That is what causes the pain and illness. If you strengthen your life urges and weaken your death urges, you will go on living. But WHY? One reason is because you are on a mission of Divine Service and this is the spiritual reason. It is not so you can brag that you are 200 years old.
ʃ People believe death is inevitable because they see everyone dying out there. But those people dying out there never changed that thought. All death is suicide because people kill themselves with their own thoughts and then the body cannot clear itself.
ʃ A yogi taught me this:

> *"SPIRIT is that which cannot be destroyed.*
> *MIND is condensed SPIRIT,*
> *BODY is condensed mind.*
> *Therefore, BODY is utmost SPIRIT."*

154

If you understand that, then P.I. will make sense. But if you think you are separate from Spirit or separate from God, then it won't make any sense at all. If you are interested in this subject, I wrote a whole chapter on it in our book on Breathwork: *Liberation Breathing: The Divine Mother's Gift.* Part Eight is all about it. It also describes how the Divine Mother and your relationship to the Life Force itself is so important to achieving this higher state of ascension. Learn about breathwork and how it can liberate you from your unconscious "death urge."
Love, Sondra

May 22, 2016

❡ BASIC DIFFERENCE
The difference between one person and another (for instance a mortal and an Immortalist) is what they think about.
❡ Whatever thoughts and ideas are in the mind have the power to produce direct results in the body, and in one's life. The body is totally obedient to the mind. So, we say, "All pain is the effort involved in clinging to a negative thought." So then, that is true for all symptoms and would certainly be true for aging and death.
❡ Your body is a self-sustaining electromagnetic battery, forever capable of being re-charged with energy, continually improved. Since your body is an energy system, that is why some souls like Babaji can actually dematerialize and rematerialize. I have seen Him do it.
❡ Did you know that some of the so called "crimes" committed on women during the witch burnings were because some of the women had achieved "agelessness"? Many went up in flames because the neighbors swore under oath as to their birth dates, yet they looked decades younger. Again, the secret knowledge of age reversal was once again buried. (p. 419 from *Star Signs* by Linda Goodman)

Love, Sondra

May 23, 2016

❡ WHO IS CALLED A REAL FRIEND
You might like to think about this. Do you qualify as a real friend?

> *"He who makes you turn your mind towards the Beloved, he is your best friend. But a person who diverts your thoughts away from Him and tempts you to progress in the direction of death, he is an enemy, not a friend. Try to correct yourself. The man who makes no effort to improve himself is in fact committing suicide."*

This is from a book about a great Indian female saint.
(p. 137 from *Matri Vani* - Teachings of Sri Anandamayi Ma)
Love, Sondra

May 24, 2016

❡ MORE ON PHYSICAL IMMORTALITY
I have a friend, an Immortalist who I met in Glastonbury in 1985. He has written great things on Physical Immortality and its achievement. Here is one of his writings:

> *"Physical Immortality is much more about achieving union with God than with avoiding wrinkles. Nor is immortality about being in denial of death or afraid of death. The dissolution of the ego is the beginning of the Immortal pathway. People who have not discovered their highest purpose in life are unlikely to be interested in physical immortality. If you are here to serve the Divine--if your existence is dedicated to the fulfillment of the Divine Plan on earth—then you will want to stick around as long as possible. But a person who is bored, purposeless, and tired of life and living will find the idea of living forever a horrible one indeed! Immortality is about who you are now."*

(From Robert Coon's book *The Path of the Phoenix* – pp. 262,263)

May 25, 2016

♪ ALCHEMICAL MARRIAGE OF TWIN FLAMES
This I read in the book called *Soul Mates and Twin Flames* by Elizabeth Clare Prophet.

> *"Cosmic law requires that we first define our own identity in God before we can completely unlock the joint spiritual potential of our own twin flames. For, until twin flames achieve a certain level of mastery and oneness with their own REAL SELVES, they are often unable to cope with the weight of their negative karma as it is amplified by the presence of their twin flame. The same unique factor that gives twin flames their potential power—their identical blueprint of identity—can likewise cause the amplification of their negative patterns. A Vital Mission awaits such a union in total harmony. If the love is never abated, they could hold the balance for an entire city!"*

I personally have found this to be very true. It took me a long time. But I was patient because of Physical Immortality. If I had worried that it was too late for me, I never would have merged with Markus. So, to all of you out there, I cannot stress enough the importance of learning Physical Immortality. It is never too late, or you are never too old if you gain that knowledge.

Love, Sondra

May 26, 2016

♪ A STORY TOLD BY MASTER KJWAL KHUL
Here is another quote from *Soul Mates and Twin Flames* by Elizabeth Clare Prophet. p.69

"There lived by the sea a gentle soul who was a miller. He and his wife served together to grind the grain for the people of their town. And it came to pass that there were no communities where so much happiness reigned as there. Their countrymen marveled and wondered, for they recognized that something unusual must have happened to make the members of this community so singularly wise and happy. The townspeople themselves where never able to understand this mystery.

♪ Tonight I shall tell you what made these people so happy. It was the service of the miller and his wife and the love which they put into the flour. This flour was baked into their bread. At every meal the regenerative power of love from the miller and his wife was radiated around the table and it entered their physical bodies as they partook of the bread. Thus, like radioactive power, the energy of this vibrant love from the miller and his wife was spread throughout the community.

♪ The neighbors did not know the reason for their happiness and none of the people were able to discover it. For sometimes, although they live side by side, mankind is unable to pry the most simple secrets about one another".

You and your twin flame can also influence countless lives around you through your "radioactive" thoughts, feelings, and actions.
Love, Sondra

May 29, 2016

♪ GOING TO GREECE
Traveling today to Greece—leaving very early. I leave you with these thoughts for today:

> ❖ Give everything in your experience total loving

acceptance.
❖ Keep your sense of humor about everything you
are experiencing.
❖ Love yourself for experiencing everything you are
experiencing.
❖ Totally celebrate everything you are
experiencing.
❖ Be very enthusiastic about everything.
❖ Be grateful for being here to experience
anything.
❖ Open up your heart and let God's energy flow
through you.
❖ Breathe and let love fill your body and soul.

Love, Sondra

May 30, 2016

⚓ ARRIVED IN GREECE
Visiting our friend in Athens and having a ball. Tomorrow we
are taking a holiday by boat to Hydra. We have never ever
been there. We are not even taking our computers. That is
a first!
Love, Sondra

June 2, 2016

⚓ HYDRA
We were captivated by the charm of Hydra. We came on
the "Flying Dolphin" which took somewhat more than an
hour from Athens. What I loved was the fact that there are
no cars allowed; no motor bikes, and not even bicycles on
this island! Only donkeys. (There are some water taxis to
get to more remote parts of the island.) It was so relaxing
that we could hardly believe what we were feeling! The town
is built like an amphitheater around the harbor which is lined
with yachts. You walk on cobblestone streets and alleyways
climbing the hillside. The architecture is
extraordinary—lavish old mansions, galleries, and shops

covered with bougainvillea.

Famous painters, poets, and writers have always come here, and I see why.

꿍 We felt so good we even gave a couple of sessions to our organizer and host/translator. But it was not like work at all. We were so relaxed, and the energy was so high that we have never been able to be so effective in sessions; and it was not like work at all.

꿍 This really taught me something. I can see why the wealthy make more money as they spend time relaxing and then they go to work and get more done at a more profound level which would prosper them more. It is an ideal inspirational destination. I highly recommend it.

꿍 Our last night we dined at the Bratsera Hotel. The name refers to the mothership that brought in the sponges from the sea—it was once a sponge factory. Now it is a gorgeous place to dine and stay. The hotel was preparing for a wedding for a couple from Sweden. I could not help but speak to the interesting woman at the next table who happened to be from Adelaide, Australia where we are going later in the year. She was thrilled that we are coming to her city in November.

Love, Sondra

June 3, 2016

꿍 IN ATHENS

Did you ever do anything really stupid even though you know you are intelligent in the rest of your life? It calls for real self-forgiveness. For example, when I went to the Canary Islands in March I thought it was going to be hot—(being next to Africa and all). I packed light clothes. I was freezing the whole time and had to go out and buy sweaters. I forgave myself for that.

꿍 But lo and behold, when I packed for Europe this time, I had in mind how cold Europe is! So, I brought warm clothes, and now it is really hot. I was obviously out of my body when I was packing because we are going into summer over here of course. I was embarrassed to myself. I confessed it to my husband, and all he said is, "Why did you do that?" I told him it had to be my core belief that I am not perfect. Then he said, "Well, it is what it is," (meaning my "situation"). So then I had to do the affirmation: *"Even though I made a huge mistake, I still completely love and accept myself."* That always helps by the way.

❡Last night we went out on the town to see the night life in Athens. It was so much fun, and I was dressed okay. We decided to go to Delphi in a few days as Markus has never seen it. Greece is in a terrible financial situation, so we have a lot of compassion for the people here, and greatly reduce our prices. Still, few can even afford that. We are giving some sessions for free; but how can we complain? We love Greece.

Love, Sondra

June 4, 2016

❡ DIFFICULTIES ARE NOT NORMAL

I was having a discussion with our friend Yiannis and we were talking about who might want to have a session to clear up their relationships. He noted that most people he knew who were having problems thought that the difficulties in their relationships were just "normal," and not something they needed to seek help over. I got to thinking how true that was. To most people, bickering and even fighting is just normal for a relationship. Even hell in a relationship is probably considered normal. Then we realized how much people just put up with or tolerate; mediocrity, or worse.

❡ Do you tolerate your mate screaming at you or being verbally abusive? Do you tolerate something you secretly cannot stand? Some people even go so far as to tolerate physical abuse.

❡ Hopefully you are not staying in a horrible relationship because you are afraid to be alone! I hear that a lot in this line of work. When I teach people that they do not have to be alone, that they can create a mate easily by the power of their thoughts and by using the "cosmic dating service," they start to see things differently. They often have the courage to let go of a bad relationship when they know they don't have to be alone. However, they might be addicted to

161

misery and suffering, or addicted to a bad pattern and that has to be healed before they can let go also.

❡ Our job as Breathworkers and relationships coaches is to help people get what they REALLY want. Maybe they want to keep the relationship if they can clean it up. Maybe it is too dead and they want to move on. Whatever the problem is, one does not have to just tolerate it. Difficulties are not normal; they are just thoughts that need to be changed. Love, Sondra

June 5, 2016

❡ A PEAK EXPERIENCE IN LIBERATION BREATHING
Had a client yesterday who was so fast, so brilliant, so psychic, so open and so powerful that the problem was most everyone was intimidated by him. We could see why. It required all our knowledge from years of breathwork, all our knowledge of the *Course in Miracles*, a lot of clarity and more, to support him and take him to the next level. You guessed it—he is a film maker and can influence millions of people.

❡ He liked the session so much he wanted another one the next day; but we insisted that he integrate for a few days first. I was so happy that Markus was with me to ground the energy and to take perfect notes and write perfect affirmations so that I could remain l00% focused.

❡ After that we visited the home of an architect here in suburb of Athens, a colleague of Yiannis, and we had dinner directly on the beach.

Today we are back to work in Athens. Going to Delphi tomorrow.
Love, Sondra

June 6, 2016

❡ INTERESTING REACTION
What I find amazing is that whenever I try to teach what Jesus says about giving up anger in ACIM, many people write in protesting—as if they are smarter than Jesus! I

162

believe when He turned over the tables of the money changers, He was not angry, but He did so to shock them. Babaji did stuff like that. Masters do that if necessary. It is different than anger. Shock and Awe! LEAVING FOR DELPHI NOW.   Love, Sondra

June 7, 2016

℘ THE ORACLE AT DELPHI
Did you ever have a day that was absolutely perfect and so magnificent that it would change your life? That, in my opinion is what it is like to go to Delphi, the most important sacred site in Greece. It became the center of the known world, and the place where man was closest to God. Delphi is famous for the Oracle, a female mystic, clairvoyant, and seer, who would answer peoples' questions and give them valuable readings. Delphi is also known for a famous inscription over one of the temple entrances, "Know Thyself," which Socrates often sited. In the Temple of Apollo was the place the Oracle sat, and people came from all over the world—even other countries— to get their questions answered by Her. She did not really give visions of the future, but mostly "right choices" in the now, way back in the 8th century BC. I saw Delphi a long time ago when a spiritual teacher of mine told me I should go, because I had been an Oracle there. The first time I did feel like I was getting "answers," but I thought maybe I was imagining it.
℘ This time I went to embrace the whole place, so I also went into the museum which I had never seen. This blew my mind completely. Markus is putting up some of my favorite photos that he took of the art in the Museum. The very famous *Charioteer of Delphi* is in this museum—just stunning. We felt so connected to beauty and purity that we got very, very, high. When I finally saw a painting of how the ancient Delphi looked back then, it was so exquisite that I could hardly believe my eyes. I felt "at home." Yiannis, Markus, and I did a breathe on the grounds. When we finally pulled ourselves away, we felt so light that we just sailed home in the three hours, feeling ecstatic, really. In the museum I actually saw a woman crying when she stood

before the *Charioteer*, one of the most famous art relics in the whole world. We talked about taking people here one day on a Greek Quest.

Love, Sondra

June 8, 2016

§ REMOVING A CURSE

We had a big miracle our last day in Athens. Maybe it happened because we three (Yiannis, Markus and I) had all been to Delphi the day before. Maybe it happened because Babaji willed it. Maybe it happened because our client was ready, and we got him ready. Who can explain it?

§ Anyway, our client (the film maker); whom I told you was very, very, powerful, came back for his second session. Toward the end of the session he blurted out that he was sure his grandmother had put a curse on the men in his lineage. When we heard the tale, we actually knew that was true. Yiannis was sitting in on this session, as he is also a Rebirther (and a medical doctor), and we wanted him to do follow-up on this client. The three of us were hearing this tale and then suddenly Yiannis was guided to light some very strong frankincense incense (the kind you burn on charcoal). Then we started reading the Divine Mother names for the client, which we always do toward the end of the session. Then we heard a very, very, strange noise. Yiannis jumped up to see what it was. I suddenly saw a fire on the floor! I did know what was going on, but Yiannis informed us that the charcoal had exploded and flew quite far from where it was onto the wooden floor where a kind of fire and sparks started up. The interesting thing is that he had placed the incense in front of the photo that Markus had given him. The photo was of Babaji, Muniraj, and Shastriji. It is the rarest of rarest photos as we have no other photo available of the three of them together.

§ Muniraj is the guru Babaji chose to take over after he took Samadhi. (He was in charge of Herakhan for 32 years.) Shastriji was Babaji's high priest. Babaji said they were two of the purest beings on the earth at the time. So then, we all

felt that they were helping us to take off this curse. We all said in unison, "Your curse is finished." We probably could not have done it without their help. We looked at the burn marks on the floor and the film director said to Yiannis, "Don't remove these marks because you need to look at them often and remember how powerful you are." Needless to say, we felt more than comfortable leaving the film director in the hands of Yiannis for future sessions.
Love, Sondra

June 10, 2016

❡ THREE CIRCLES
There is a Buddhist monk who talks about the three circles:

- ❖ In the center circle is your "comfort zone."
- ❖ In the middle circle outside that is your "challenge."
- ❖ In the outer circle is your "extreme risk."

The challenge circle is where the LEARNING is. How often do you leave your comfort zone? I once gave a training and asked people to pick a service project that was something that would push them to the next level. What would really STRETCH you I asked. Then they stood up to share what they had picked. Most people picked a project that they were already doing in a way and there was hardly any challenge to it at all. Very few really went for a challenge. It takes a really brave person to go for the risk.
Love, Sondra

June 11, 2016

❡ MOST HAVE A "BUT"
A woman came to the training last night who stood up and said she was in a very verbally abusive relationship. I was so glad she was here so we could help her. She got so much out of her first breathing session. But at the end of the evening she shocked me by saying she would not be able

to come Saturday and Sunday – the main parts. I inquired why. She said her husband and daughter do not approve at all of her doing these kinds of things. She is the one in the room who needs this training the most. I strongly encouraged her to come back.

ʃ A man said he was going through a divorce. Then he said he was very, very, upset; if anyone ever criticized him he would get extremely hurt. His breath session was amazing. But then he said he could not return Saturday because he had a very nice invitation somewhere. I encouraged him to come back. I could see he wanted to, but what to do about his "nice" invitation?

ʃ Will these two people change their minds and come back? I could see they really, really, wanted to BUT—most people have a "BUT."

Love, Sondra

June 12, 2016

ʃ OVERCOME THE "BUT"
They both came back to class and everyone cheered. The woman goes in and out which I usually don't let happen; but she is taking in as much as she can, and they are both changing a lot! I said the right things to get them here and I am happy.

ʃ We have a wonderful translator who flew in from Madrid named Anna. She is so outstanding that we are going to take a train to Madrid to hang out with her after this. Last night she told us a great story about what she heard when she was in Babaji's cave. (We met her in Herakhan.) She heard, "All things are okay the way they are, as there is a bigger divine plan which everything fits into." And, "The answer to everything is love." The first line she heard from Babaji and the second one from the Divine Mother. I like that.

Love, Sondra

June 13, 2016

❡ 100% RESPONSIBILITY
All I know to say is when the terrorists bombed the club in
Bali, the priests there all got together and meditated on *how
they created this!* Imagine that. And what they discovered
was that they had missed doing a certain spiritual ceremony
one year back, due to lack of funds. And they saw that
mistake cost them this act of terrorism. They took 100%
responsibility. So, they had to go back and do another
ceremony *that was 1,000 years old* to correct their mistake.
I am sure they will never make that mistake again.
❡ Now you know why we LOVE to go to Bali! It is the
highest place we have ever been—descended from another
dimension! We take a group there every December 3-13,
come hell or high water. People are transformed and we
train people to be Liberation Breathing practitioners at the
same time.
Love, Sondra

June 14, 2016

❡ A REAL MIRACLE
The gal who almost did not come back started applying the
training immediately in her 20-year relationship and it
worked! So, she was smart enough to come for a private
session. I love it when clients have big miracles to report.
She was having a lot of issues because her dad wanted her
to be a boy and she was way too far in her masculine side.
We helped her with this. During our practice of saying the
Divine Mother mantra for her at the end, Ammachi came
and hugged her and helped her get into the feminine side.
Then Babaji came behind her and Jesus was at her feet!
(We call them our Dream Team.) It has never happened
that ALL three of our masters come to a client during the
same session! She said she was totally healed! She was
floating on air after her session. She was very clear her
marriage could be saved. A real VICTORY!
Love, Sondra

June 15, 2016

♪ HAPPY TO BE ALIVE
Shops close here in Spain from 3PM-5PM. After that people go out strolling as I did yesterday. I surprised myself by having the experience of telling God, "I am so happy to be alive." I feel that way most of the time; but I never said it to God like that! I am glad I am not fixated, and I do not drive myself when it comes to making a lot of money. Money flows to us naturally doing the things we love to do without any effort. Therefore, things are simpler for us.
♪ Our last client said she felt SO BLESSED after her session. I think it is so satisfying to see people change. Maybe that is why I said that to God. I felt very good after her session, even though it was not as dramatic as the one before where that gal saw our masters.
♪ I am so glad I can see my work as Worship. Babaji kept saying "WORK IS WORSHIP; IDLENESS IS DEATH." No matter what your work is, make it worship. ACIM says we are among the ministers of God. Who is our ministry? Our address book, our email list, our Facebook friends, and anyone who comes to us during the day.
♪ Try this attitude and you will experience "Vocational Arousal."
Love, Sondra

June 16, 2016

♪ FASCINATION
Last night I was feeling my usual fascination for Markus, my husband. Then I started extending that out and I was able to feel fascination about everything. Fascination makes one feel more alive! (Also, the most fascinating option wins!) It is more intense than "interest."
♪ When I finally got on the other side of most of my karma and my "case," I started seeing life like an amusement park. It is more fun that way. It invokes fascination. Meditate on the word *fascination* and see what you come up with!
Leaving for Madrid—on the train now.
Love, Sondra

June 17, 2016

❡ THE SPLENDOR OF MADRID
I find everything here so elegant. The buildings are majestic. The restaurants are posh. We had a meal in a restaurant with food made by a cook who had travelled all through South America to study cooking. So, we had some venison, Argentine style.
❡ Later we gave a talk in a really beautiful center which was not *new-agey*, like some centers. Markus even loved the art. Today we travel to Toledo, famous for the painter El Greco.

Love, Sondra

June 18, 2016

❡ DINING IN THE SKY
Silke came over from the Canaries and so we went with Ana and Silke to the rooftop restaurant. We are all Breathworkers so we have plenty to talk about. It is so wonderful to be with people who both understand how the mind works (thoughts create results); and who therefore speak with very positive thoughts all the time. We don't indulge in any negative thinking in our conversations. And if one of us needs support in any issue, the others can process us easily. We love to *talk shop* about relationships and check in with each other how we are all doing in that area. Here's to uplifting, inspiring conversations where you always go home feeling good. We can also learn from each other about clients we have had. We also talked about places we love like Iceland and Bali. Today we go back to work—going to give a Liberation Breathing session to Ana's mom. Now that is really something—to get your mom to have a session. Ana is treating her to that; but she was willing and that is the important thing.

Love, **Sondra**

169

June 19, 2016

❡ BACK TO WORK DOING PRIVATE SESSIONS
After all these decades, I am still honored to have been a pioneer for this work. I am even more in awe of Liberation Breathing / Rebirthing, even more excited about it, and even more committed to it. It never ever gets boring to me. I feel that the deeper you go into the Spirit of it, the more interesting it gets. I can only say that I wish everyone could have the experience of it. I want everyone to know how it can heal the mind/body in ways nothing else can; how it brings joy and happiness out; how it increases aliveness and how it has a *youthing* effect on the body. I want everyone to know how it develops intuitive power, and how it releases old hurt, pain, and misery. I want everyone to know how it increases love and prosperity. Who would not want to have such an experience? Who would not want to live longer? (Only someone who was miserable and hated life—and yet Breathwork is here to release the misery and hatred so you will want to live!)
❡ It can lead to an ultimate goal: becoming a true spiritual master. It depends on how far you want to go. Why should one ever stop doing it? It is a life-long spiritual path. Do you want to feel good? Who does not want to feel better? (Only someone addicted to pain and suffering and the payoffs for that; and yet, most of us are here to heal the addiction to pain and suffering.) WHY NOT TRY IT? There are miracles available.
Love, Sondra

June 20, 2016

❡ DO YOU WANT TO SPEND THE REST OF YOUR LIFE ALONE?
This is what I usually ask people who tell me they are not in a relationship and they are not really interested in one; and/or they don't care etc. I often doubt that is true. They may have given up, maybe think they don't deserve one, or

are in denial. When I ask THAT question—"Do you want to spend the rest of your life alone?"—they always say NO. Then they start confessing, forgetting what they had told me at the beginning of the session.

℔ Take the widow we had recently. She said she did not know *if* she wanted a relationship. But later when I asked her THAT QUESTION, she was very clear! She wanted a relationship. "YES." So, then I asked her if she would feel disloyal to her deceased husband if she had one. That was where she was stuck. We carried on with the session and fortunately Silke was translating. The client had travelled over five hours by bus to come and see us and she did not know why, she said. She just had a "feeling" she should find us.

℔ Silke told her that it probably was a case of her deceased husband guiding her to us so she could have a new life. We all agreed and then the client even agreed. She left relieved that she could in fact ask the universe now for a new partner! So then, if you are single, are you telling the truth to yourself?

Love, **Sondra**

June 21, 2016

℔ DEATH IS NO SOLUTION

We so often see clients who do not want to be here. Some have the personal lie, "I don't want to be here," and so their death urge is always up. Here is a quote to note:

> *"When one chooses to die, death does release the weight of gravity and temporarily frees the soul from earth. But it does NOT change the vibration of consciousness from the human level. There is no escape from the vibration of yourself except through practiced change of thoughts. Nor does death cause the released consciousness to go to a celestial level. Consciousness, when departing from the body, automatically seeks its own level." - From* **The Door of Everything** *by Ruby Nelson*

The last greatest evil to be removed from the precious Earth plane is Satan's evil death. Jesus said, "Verily, Verily, I say unto you, if a man keep my word he shall never see death." The soul yearns to be exalted to the vibration of the Ascension Attitudes.

❡ By this, the author of *The Door of Everything* is saying that you do not automatically go to a higher plane by dying...every lifetime you have a new opportunity to be enlightened and to rise above death.

❡ There is a lifetime where re-incarnation will become obsolete and you will choose ascension instead. But you have to want to be here to be able to do it. Otherwise you will have to keep re-incarnating over and over until you get enlightened.

Love, Sondra

June 24, 2016

❡ SELF-LOVE

A lot of people feel they have to "work at" being loving or getting love. This comes from not understanding that we are love. You are love and your partner is love. ACIM says all you have to do is remove the blocks to the awareness of love's presence. It says this in the introduction. This is where one has to do some cleansing. When we become instruments of the loving energy from God, it grows and is a blessing to everyone.

❡ The answer for almost everything is self-love. We were not taught to cherish ourselves. We were not taught to have a deep love affair with ourselves. We were taught this was selfish. But here is a different way to look at this. I found it in a little book called *Dying to Be Me*.

> "Selfishness comes from too little self-love as we compensate for our lack—cherishing the self comes first, and caring for others is the inevitable outcome. To say 'I love you' when you have no matching emotion for yourself is placating. It is not real."

❡ The important thing to remember is to love yourself first. You have to have the necessary radiance to send that love out to others, and you develop this radiance by loving yourself and having intense Pure Joy already.

Love, Sondra

June 25, 2016

❡ IN POLAND
A woman fainted right before the God Training and an ambulance was called. So that is the first time that ever happened. She had travelled about seven hours to come and see me. I thought she fainted because of the trip or that she had sunstroke. It was hot.

❡ She came later, after having her blood pressure checked by the paramedics, and she was okay. She shared that she did not faint due to being tired or hot. She said she fainted at the prospect of actually meeting me! She claimed that she read my books thirty years ago and they changed her life and gave her a wonderful life. So, she was so excited to finally meet me in person that she was overcome with emotions. Well, that is the first time that happened.

❡ The God Training is small because I guess people cannot handle that word, *God*. They have so much going on with that subject that they cannot make it to the training to clear that stuff! So, I probably have to change the name. In a way, it is my most powerful training. But last night I found out that they had not handled the basics: personal lies, forgiveness, thought is creative, and all the stuff about relationships. So now I will go back and teach parts of the LRT anyway, so probably I cannot do this training unless people have the LRT first. They all seem really stuck on relationships too; so I have to shift gears.

❡ Babaji told me to teach the God training so I am doing it; but it seems like I should only have to do it at spiritual retreats when I have a lot of time. At least that is the situation here. The Catholic Church in Poland has a strong hold on them. ACIM is the correction of religion but most have not started it. So, we are back to the basics. Another girl came from five hours away also. She had read my books before also. This is the situation. I have to adjust quickly.

Love, Sondra

June 26, 2016

❡ DO YOU PUT GOD FIRST OR LAST?
Let's say a person lives 70 years. Out of that, they spend:

- ❖ 23 years sleeping.
- ❖ 16 years working.
- ❖ 8 years watching TV.
- ❖ 6 years eating.
- ❖ 6 years travelling.
- ❖ 4 1/2 years in leisure.
- ❖ 2 years getting dressed.
- ❖ 4 years being sick.
- ❖ Only 1/2 year on their spiritual life!

Take note! You might want to make some adjustments!
❡ P.S. I figured out how to do this training perfectly. Then I had a big surprise. An old friend from decades ago showed up unannounced and walked in the door. He took the train over here from Berlin. I was so shocked that I kept spilling coffee and food on my dress. What a highlight!
Love, Sondra

June 27, 2016

❡ MORE FASCINATION
I think it is so interesting that when I talked about "fascination" I had the most hits on my post ever. When I talk about God, I have the fewest. I assume either people:

- ❖ Have trouble with the word God because of religious dogma laid on them.

❖ They are mad at God.

❖ They don't want to face their issues that the concept of God brings up.

❖ They don't like their life.

❖ ?

❡ But God IS LIFE, and a state of being. LIFE ITSELF IS FASCINATING!! Maybe people need to apply the ACIM lesson "I am willing to see this differently." (Lesson #21 in the Workbook.) A spiritually oriented person values all of life's experiences and sees each one as an opportunity to evolve spiritually. Spirituality is one of the highest human needs. It equals ultimate fulfillment. It is the life-line to real essence. To be living in Divine Relationship with God is the absolute TOP. It is the ultimate highest connection you can reach in this lifetime. By the way, another name for God is FRIEND!

❡ Spiritual practices have the goal of recovery from the fractured self. They can be used to heal ourselves and relationships. They can be used to solve our problems. But to be willing to do them, one has to look at one's relationship with God. That is why I bring it up and will keep doing so.

❡ If one wants to actualize one's real potential, they must do the spiritual work of transformation. This group loved the God Training and they really changed—so there you go: The God Training is the ultimate! It is filled with *fascination*. Love, Sondra

June 28, 2016

❡ POLISH MIRACLES
Just have to share some of the miracles we had with the God Training here in Poland.

> 1. One man's relationship was falling apart, and his girlfriend wanted to leave. They totally healed it and are now committed to having a baby together.
> 2. One gal could not sell her extra car. Immediately after the training her car sold.

175

3. One woman was hating her father and could not forgive him at all. During a session her grandmother came to her (the mother of her father), and said, "I gave you total unconditional love when you were young. Why can't you give that to my son?" She called this a total spiritual experience and she totally changed her attitude toward her father.

4. I myself prayed to the Divine Mother like mad during the training for help in marketing books. Monday morning, I received an email from a very advanced young man who offered to market our books for free!

Jai Ma!
Love, Sondra

June 30, 2016

♫ DRESS FOR TRAVEL
Arrived in Estonia! Good thing I love airports as we were in the Oslo airport for a seven-hour layover! I like to watch the people—how they dress, etc. I don't care for men in Bermuda shorts and baseball caps, and I see a lot of that these days. People have become so *casual*. I don't care for women with backpacks—see a lot of that too.

♫ Most people don't dress up in airports. I understand they like the ease of comfortable clothes, of course. We dress up a bit because we are treated better. We treated ourselves to the VIP lounge which made things easy for that long of time. Norwegian air did not charge us any extra for overweight so Markus was impressed.

♫ Pille and Mari-Liis picked us up in two cars which was great because of all of our luggage. It was great to find our room all prepared with a beautiful altar and fresh roses. We are so happy here in Pille's house. Tonight we had quite a group coming for a breathe. Can't wait to go to Old Town tomorrow! Pille and Mari-Liis dress very well, and I'm happy about that.

Love, Sondra

July 1, 2016

❡ WHY MEN LOVE BITCHES

I can't believe I am going to recommend this book. Went to a bookstore in the Oslo airport and there were not very many non-fiction books in English, so I was glad to find any. The title set me back but then the subtitle got me interested. Besides, I read almost any book on relationships. So, I bought the book, and it is called *Why Men Love Bitches.* It is a book for women, but I caught my husband reading it! It is very entertaining and, so far, I am enjoying it and would recommend it for women! She re-defines a bitch as someone who is a mental challenge; definitely the opposite of needy. It so happens that I needed to refer to this book for a few students who were too needy. Here is what it really is: a woman's guide to holding her own in a relationship. I support any book that promotes women staying in their power and self-esteem. Besides, as I said, it is really entertaining! And I caught my husband reading it AGAIN!

Love, Sondra

July 2, 2016

❡ JOY IN ESTONIA

When one is very happy to go to a foreign country it usually means you had good past lives there; and if you really don't like a country you might have had bad past lives there. Markus is incredibly happy in Estonia and feels so at home here. I love seeing him here for this reason. He lights right up. Old Town in Tallinn is an exceptionally well-preserved medieval city on the Baltic Sea. It was founded in 1248 but early settlements go back 3,000 years BC! In Old Town Tallinn, it is like being in a dream—of the best kind.

❡ Last night we went to a Russian restaurant with some of the gals from our training. We had a very lively conversation about all the changes that happened since we gave Angela a session. We had three powerful sessions during the day. Great to be working here. The people are wonderful.

Love, Sondra

July 4, 2016

❡ AKASHIC RECORDS

I read the following about AKASHIC RECORDS. These are the books in the "soul world" that keep a complete record of your soul from all lifetimes. It is up to you how you wish this recorded history of your many lives to read. Your record of service has one side for good deeds (positive karma) and one side for negative deeds (bad karma). The two sides are balanced at the time of death. The result determines where you go.

❡ You came into this life with a spiritual level assigned at birth based on karma and virtues from past lives. We do have the possibility of moving to higher levels by cultivating certain qualities and building virtues through service to others.

Love, Sondra

July 5, 2016

❡ CRITICISM

I am always studying relationships wherever I go. I have often said that criticism kills relationships. John Gottman made studies that predicted divorce. He said criticism can kill your marriage easily.

❡ There is a difference between feedback and criticism. A feedback focuses on a specific behavior, such as, "We don't ever seem to take a vacation." A criticism attacks the character. Such as, "I am fed up with you because you never want to take a vacation." It is a verbal attack inflicting emotional pain. It is destructive, filled with blame. It is not focused on improvement. It is based on only one right way. It is belittling. It will fail at getting a behavior change.

❡ Critical people usually had critical parents. It is part of what we call the Parental Disapproval Syndrome. One should try to turn your criticism into a delightful wish: "It's been so long since we had a vacation. I have planned a trip to the Grand Canyon for us next April." Now there is a real action that will make a difference!

Love, Sondra

July 6, 2016

¶ MY DEAREST MOTHER

I loved the way my mother reared me. When I was a child, she gave me total space. I felt free to grow up without a lot of heavy rules, disapproval, or strict discipline. I did not need discipline; what I needed was a good example and she gave me that. My mother always trusted me completely, and I felt that at all times. She seemed to be saying telepathically, from the beginning, "I trust you. You are good and I know you know what you are doing. I give you space to be yourself." I felt this at a very early age and as a result, I wanted to live up to her highest thoughts about me. I wanted never to disappoint her high opinion of me. I was a good child, eager to be a responsible being like she was.

¶ My mother allowed me to be different—perhaps my greatest blessing of all. She just prayed for me and gave me unconditional love. I do not remember my mother ever complaining. I do not remember my parents ever fighting. In fact, they had an agreement never to raise their voices in my presence and they never did. This I appreciate more than you can imagine. My mother always thought positively and let go of any upset so fast I did not even notice she had an upset. She taught me literally how to go to higher thoughts. She always had faith in me, and that worked. She acted as if I could take care of myself, so she was never guilty of over parenting. This enabled me to be very expressive and creative and to feel happy and free. I must admit I was raised in a very small town and everyone knew where I belonged and parented me if I needed it, wherever I was. I was lucky. My big sadness was that my father was sick and in and out of hospitals my whole childhood. Liberation Breathing® healed me of that also.

¶ wrote a lot more about my mother in our book *Liberation Breathing: The Divine Mother's Gift*. p. 189.

Love, Sondra

July 8, 2016

¶ TIPS FOR FINDING A MATE

A lot of clients are looking for mates. I usually recommend to them the following books:

ASK AND IT IS GIVEN by Esther Hicks
LOVE WILL FIND YOU by Catherine Alice
CALLING IN THE ONE by Katherine W. Thomas
HOW TO CREATE REAL LOVE by Jill Douka
SPIRITUAL INTIMACY by Sondra and Markus Ray!

℘ My friend in Australia, a great Rebirther, suggests that you get a Liberation Breathing session before or during reading these books to work out fear of intimacy.
℘ If you don't find a mate after reading these, you definitely need a private session by us or some great Breathworker to uncover the unconscious blocks.
Love, Sondra

July 9, 2016

℘ LIBERATION BREATHING
People are asking me how we do Rebirthing in a different way. Well, in Liberation Breathing the breathing is the same—however the big difference is this: After the breathing cycle is done, we read the 108 names of the Divine Mother out loud while the client does another cycle. We ask the Mother to help the client clear what came up for them. We always ask the client before if that is okay. (The only person that said no was an atheist.) People love it as they feel safe, protected, and blessed. During this I sometimes receive special messages for them also. Then we have the client turn on their side and change to nasal breathing. While they are on their side, we recite a specific Divine Mother mantra in Sanskrit that is very, very, powerful. Many people have visions during this recitation. Then we all stay in silence for some time. This is the perfect closure.
℘ It is also special to have two Rebirthers (male & female) working with someone at the same time. I do the guidance and Markus is the scribe. He takes notes on all of what they share and writes affirmations for them while they breathe.

This frees me up to give 100% attention for the client, since I don't have to be thinking of what affirmations to write. We work exceptionally well as a team. Together we can unwire someone's patterns easily for them. Then we send the client the transcript of the session and the affirmations that become their homework over the next few weeks.

¶ Incidentally, we ourselves read the Divine Mother names aloud for one whole year to charge ourselves up before we started doing them for clients. People can tell that and appreciate that.

¶ We were guided by our masters to change the name to Liberation Breathing®. The Divine Mother really liberates people. We were even told to do it legally, register the name, and we were given the exact dates according to Vedic astrology to do this by our Master Muniraj. He blessed this work and our action with it. We were told, with the Divine Mother Energy, the sessions are 9 X more powerful and effective than straight Rebirthing. I BELIEVE THAT, AS WE HAVE WITNESSED FANTASTIC SHIFTS IN OUR CLIENTS!

Love, Sondra

¶ P.S. We can also give LB *Sessions* via Skype & Zoom.

July 10, 2016

¶ ARRIVING IN SWEDEN

All my life I wanted to come to Sweden since my mom was Swedish. When I finally made it the first time about 20 years ago, I had a miracle. When I stepped on the soil my organizer said, "There is a clairvoyant who saw you coming and she said your mind is like a crystal and you are ageless." I asked how I could meet her and she said, "She is coming to a party tonight to meet you." I could hardly believe the good news. At the party we had to stand in a circle and interview the person next to us and present them to the group. It was very metaphysical. Then Doris came in and took me to the back room and told me things from Babaji, some of which have not yet happened.

❡ It so happens my sister died when I was here in Sweden and my mother died when I was here in Sweden (which Babaji must have arranged). And so, the Swedish people really took care of me during these tough moments. When my sis died, Doris told me to go to a Botanical Conservatory in Stockholm and sit with the ferns and breathe for one hour. So, I did. This really helped to get all that oxygen. When my mom died, I told the group and they all laid down and breathed with me. That night I was taken to a cabin on a lake where Ammachi spends one day a year (her only day off), and I was allowed to sleep in her bed! That really helped me. Markus and I came here 8 years ago after we were just married and the whole group stood up and sang to us sweet Swedish songs!!

❡ Now we are going to see Doris on our last day here! I am so much looking forward to this meeting.

Love, Sondra

July 11, 2016

❡ PAST LIVES AND RELATIONSHIPS

Originally the founder of Rebirthing, Leonard Orr, identified "5 Biggies"—the five biggest consciousness factors that keep you from being in bliss. Here they are:

1. The Birth Trauma
2. Specific Negative Thought Structures
3. The Parental Disapproval Syndrome
4. The Unconscious Death Urge
5. Other Lifetimes

We did not spend a lot of time on #5, but we are seeing again and again the necessity to do so. Some cases I remember for example:

a. A gal who was non-orgasmic was healed because she recalled a past life where she was burned to death and it was so painful that she decided never to feel again.

b. Another who absolutely could not work out her

relationship with her mother who was verbally abusive to her. In the session she recalled being very mean to that mother who was then a friend and she betrayed her and caused her great sadness.

c. A beautiful gal who could not be married or even committed to a man or get them to commit to her: in another life she was engaged to the love of her life and he went on a mission and died and in that life she decided "I will never commit again."

In all cases, seeing the past life not only explained things but changed things in this life. It is called a "bleed through."

❧ More on this tomorrow.   Love, Sondra

July 12, 2016

❧ MORE ON PAST LIVES
The Dalai Lama wrote that the problem in the West is we look through all these doors for answers; but we don't even have the one door that would give the answer—and that door is past lives.

❧ There are a couple of books I highly recommend:
One is *You Were Born Again to Be Together* by Dick Sutphen. He regressed couples who were stuck in their relationships and found out they could not clear until they went back to the past lives they had together. Fascinating book.

❧ The other book is *Other Lives, Other Selves* by Roger Woolger. He is a psychologist who did not even believe in past lives until he started Rebirthing. In his first session he had a strong obvious past life memory. This changed his life; and he began regressing people and studying about how what happened to them in a past life was related to the type of birth they had in this life. For example, if one had the cord around the neck at birth, probably they were hung several times in past lives. This is a really fascinating book also; and is a must for all Rebirthers to read for sure.
Love, Sondra

July 14, 2016

♪ DEJA VÚ

There is a chapter about deja-vú in Linda Goodman's book *Star Signs*. She gives an example where in one life John hurts Mary. They re-incarnate and in the *next* life Mary hurts John. They re-incarnate *again* and in that life John hurts Mary, again, and so it keeps going for thousands of dreary lifetimes back and forth. Until in one life time, one of them wakes up and decides to forgive the other and stops the pattern.

♪ Had a client awhile back who was still obsessing about the fact that her husband had an affair 30 years ago when she was pregnant—and they divorced when she was six months pregnant. Thirty years ago! She never got over it; and she never stopped seeing those scenes. The problem is she never forgave him, so she was stuck in that. We got her to forgive. FORGIVENESS IS THE MASTER ERASER. It is the only way to stop the obsession and bad memory. And the one who forgives is the one who gets liberated. Love, Sondra

July 15, 2016

♪ ONCE AGAIN THRILLED TO BE A BREATHWORKER

It was so exciting to give a Skype session to a young man about 20 years old. He immediately went back to the memory of himself being in the incubator. He "saw" everything that happened and told us exactly what was going on! He saw how tenuous his life was and he remembered exactly the moment he knew he was going to survive. He was in there nearly two months! He had never had this memory before. It was extremely valuable for him to discover the negative pre-verbal thoughts he had formed in the incubator! It is wonderful to work with someone so fast and so open.

♪ And then we had a client who had a new personal lie. I am always so interested to get a new one. I always think I have heard them all; and now I am up to way over 350! It is so interesting because this gives me new research and the

client gets so liberated. As I have said, finding their deepest negative thought about themselves in their subconscious gives them the key to unlock their life; and I am thrilled for them when we can get it. A great day working here in Umea, Sweden, where it stays light to almost midnight.
Love, Sondra

July 16, 2016

❡ TIRED MIND
There is a condition here in Sweden they call Tired Mind. These people have to quit work and go on welfare. At first, I could not figure out what it was. As I explored it, I realized it is the same as what we term in the USA as Chronic Fatigue Syndrome. You just get exhausted. Sometimes it is too much to even brush your teeth! If you look it up on the internet you will see that the cause is unknown. Some sites say it is due to a virus perhaps. Others do acknowledge that it could be a psychiatric problem. Apparently one million Americans have it!
❡ What we know as Breathworkers is that it is due to the "unconscious death urge." The reason we have results with this condition is that we are pretty clear the "death urge" is the cause, and we work with clients on that. The unconscious death urge includes the following:

- ❖ The thought "death is inevitable
- ❖ All one's programming on death
- ❖ History of deaths in one's lineage
- ❖ Belief systems on death
- ❖ Past life memories of dying
- ❖ Secret wish to die because one hates their life

All this can be breathed out, but obviously not in a few sessions.
❡ The above is also true for depression. At least the Swedes are correct that it is due to the mind! They call it the tired mind. That's an understatement! One has to also study what activated the unconscious death urge in the person.
Love, Sondra

185

July 19, 2016

♪ WET LIBERATION BREATHING
We arrived in Iceland where we are going to do an advanced Wet Liberation Breathing training in the beautiful Blue Lagoon. This is the perfect spot for this. Years ago, my guru Shastriji handed me a paper with the 108 names of the Divine Mother on it. When I landed in Sweden, I sat before my altar in the hotel and recited them for the first time. After that I sat briefly in meditation and received the most incredible knowledge. It was about how to do an advanced wet-rebirthing training. I could have never thought of it myself. I grabbed my snorkel and nose plug and jumped in the bathtub and tried to do it. It was hard at first, and it took me five days to learn it. It has to do with doing prayers, specially designed for each person, and done underwater while you breathe.

♪ Later I tried it on another healer, and he came flying out of the water shouting, "THIS is a stroke of GENIUS." I replied, "It is not from me—it came directly from the Divine Mother." I was then told that I should do it only in mineral springs as that is the real Divine Mother. So, I got the idea to go to the Blue Lagoon in Iceland, because I had heard of a movie director who could never heal his psoriasis until he finally stuck his arm in the Blue Lagoon. So, we came here, and it was so powerful that it took me a long time to integrate it all.

♪ When Markus came into my life, I told him the story and we came back. He was just wild over it all; so here we are again. We have 16 people who came all this way!
Love, Sondra

July 21, 2016

♪ GOING IN THE BLUE LAGOON TODAY
Everyone has a "buddy" who will guide them. First, they will practice the prayer technique and then they will give each other a Wet Liberation Breathing session. That is, they will do the Rebirthing breath through the snorkel, underwater with a nose-plug. The buddy will support them. It is very, very, powerful in mineral water. This is the best in the world

186

really. The tourists leave us alone usually in one section of the Blue Lagoon. They think we are practicing snorkeling.
❡ Before going in this morning I have them walk with their buddy and recite their 10 prayers by memory. This is because they have to say these prayers under water! It is a lot of fun also.
Love, Sondra

July 22, 2016

❡ GOOD TO GIVE SUPPORT
What was delightful was to have the sharing in the afternoon after people had been in the Blue Lagoon for hours. The thing that touched us the most was this: people had been with their buddy supporting them while they breathed. Most had as profound experiences in supporting their buddy as they did in doing the breathing themselves. It was so beautiful. Markus was inspired to give a talk on GIVING, and you can hear it on my Facebook profile. (Similar talks are available in the *Miracles for You: 1-Year Support Network*)
Love, Sondra

July 23, 2016

❡ ICELAND FOOD
Here the food is super delicious. You usually have fish for an appetizer and then more and more fish for a main course; but never have we ever had such amazing tasting fish. Tonight, we are going out to a neighboring little town to have guess what? FISH at a place called the Salt House.
❡ But people love it all and tomorrow we will all have a day off to travel around the island. Yesterday was only the second day in the Lagoon. The guards came over to our side and inquired what we were up to with our snorkels. They got really curious, but then left us alone when Markus explained it. In the afternoon the group shared so deeply of their experiences that at times everyone literally had tears. Now THAT is a real heart opening.   Love, Sondra

July 25, 2016

¶ DROPPING IT

It has been said that a humble man recognizes his errors, admits them, and does something about them. The group that came here is really letting all their stuff get exposed by having sessions every day. Then the question is, "how fast can you drop it?" ACIM says, "Truth cannot deal with errors you want to keep." Meaning yes, all your errors can be exposed but are you wanting to keep them, because you are comfortable with these errors, or are you willing to REALLY give them up? We talked to the group about this today. ACIM also says that the first obstacle to peace is the *desire to get rid of it* (the desire to get rid of the peace in other words). So today, after that talk, I feel everyone went a lot deeper in willingness to drop it all, and practice new affirmative thoughts instead.

¶ I told the group an experience I had back in 1974 when I started this work. Someone did something to me that I felt was totally unfair. A girlfriend of mine tried to steal my boyfriend. I was saying to myself, "How could they do that to me? I would never ever do that to them or anyone." I was stuck on how unfair it was and I was too upset to see how I created it. So at least I called a teacher of mine and told him. I said to him, "You won't believe what so and so did to me and blah, blah, blah." All he said was, "DROP IT SONDRA." I was shocked that he would not allow me to commiserate for even a second.

¶ I said, "Is that ALL you are going to say?" He then added: "DROP IT, SONDRA, AND GET BACK TO WORK!" Then he hung up on me. I shocked! Then I looked at my desire to keep on with the drama. I said to myself, "Well, you called him, didn't you? Are you going to take his advice?" I then realized it was just a decision, and so I DECIDED to drop it. It worked. Afterwards, I calmed down and saw how *I had created it.* I had this gal set up as my sister, and we were always in competition around religion vs. metaphysics. I transferred this competition onto her trying to take my boyfriend away from me!

¶ So today my experience in the Blue Lagoon with the class is that they were going deeper than ever and were more

willing than ever to let it all go. Breathing with the snorkels in this water makes that easier, believe me.
Love, Sondra

July 26, 2016

❡ A REAL DECISION
Markus gave a talk to the group from *A Course in Miracles* on the following topic: "Rules for Decision." It says you should decide each morning that you are going to have a happy day. It says you should say, "If I make no decisions by myself, this is the day that will be given to me." If you find out during the day you are not happy, you have to admit you are wrong." I must be wrong because I am not having a happy day. I want another way to look at this. What can I lose by asking?" You have to decide with the Holy Spirit to have a happy day. The Holy Spirit will grant you a happy day when you stop trying to do it all yourself and decide with the Holy Spirit to have "only that." Then if you are not having a happy day, you have to drop whatever you are doing and ask the Holy Spirit for instant correction. Markus uses a phrase that his teacher, Tara Singh, taught him, that I really like. It is "Love for Correction." (Similar talks are available in the *Miracles for You: 1-Year Support Network*)
Love, Sondra

July 27, 2016

❡ LEAVING ICELAND TODAY
The business card of the Northern Light Inn where we stay says this:

> *"We hope that God will grant you rest while you are under our roof. May this room and Inn be your second home. May those you love be near you in thoughts and dreams. Even though we may not get to know you well, we hope that you will be as comfortable and happy as if you were in your own home. May the business that brought you our way*

*prosper. May every call you make and every
message you receive, add to your joy. May these
days be pleasant for you, profitable for society,
helpful for those you meet, and a joy to those who
know you best. When you leave, may your journey
be safe."*

Since when in the USA does a hotel say things like that to
their guests? It is so thoughtful. Someone who really loves
their customers could only write such a thing.
Love, Sondra

August 1, 2016

❡ MY MAN
I have the sheer happiness of living with a wonderful man
and I want to publicly express my appreciation for him. I
even get to be with him 24/7/365 and that is the real treat. I
see God being realized and expressed through him all the
time. He is in service to the Light and what he does carries
the light. He puts his heart and soul and brilliance into
running the business and takes care of all matters so that
we can have the good life. It works because he is liberated
from conventional thinking. It is never boring to be with him
because he lives from inspiration and does not block his
creativity. As a poet and painter, he is an ambassador to
another dimension. His love for *A Course in Miracles* makes
our life about love, peace, and joy!
❡ He lives in an ocean of devotion to the Divine Mother and
to his teachers Tara Singh, Jesus, and Babaji. Therefore,
he is always willing to change, according to new information
from them. He recognizes his errors, admits them, and does
something about them. He is also very patient about my
errors and forgiving. For every problem, he comes up with a
solution that is a higher frequency. I cherish our friendship
and the way we can place what we think under the
guidance of the Holy Spirit. Because of that we get moment-
by-moment benefits and we also have more fun per hour.
Women are frequently asking me if he has a brother.
In appreciation to Markus Ray.   Love, Sondra

August 2, 2016

❡ UNEXPECTED MEETING
The Divine Mother came to me in a surprising way. A man I did not even know showed up to meet me at a friend's house. He brought me a gift of two white books wrapped in ribbons and flowers. He was lovely to look at, very holy and pleasant to be with. He told us about his son who channels the Divine Mother and had written one of the books. He had obviously given his son TOTAL permission to be who he is (a natural healer since childhood) and spoke with great reverence about his son. His son could not make it to meet me, so he sent the book. The book is called *The Wholeness*. I am going to share some of the passages.

> ❖ *"I AM the Mother of Creation, and I am here to guide you home... In this time, give Me permission to penetrate and love every fiber of your being, every fiber of your sacred physiology. And if there is some discomfort in the physiology then, we view it as an opportunity for it to dance with Me."*
> ❖ *"So, we take this time, this very sacred time. And in this sacred time, we see what our Wholeness does. There is no trying, no effort. Nothing except the gentle intention that our divinity run the show."*
> ❖ *"I promise I am the perfect manager for you. I know the physiology. I know every aspect of this infinite physiology. Don't be afraid of being the Master of the Universe. It is a lot of fun!! And the beautiful thing is you will be given the keys to the car at the perfect time."*

❡ More tomorrow. Written on the new computer Markus bought me yesterday!
Love, Sondra

August 3, 2016

❡ MORE FROM THE BOOK BY THE DIVINE MOTHER

191

❖ *"So when we settle into this silence (and it is a sweet silence), we have given permission for Wholeness, to our Divine Self, to penetrate the physiology. We only give permission to Wholeness to RUN THE SHOW. In one great sweep, Wholeness delivers all of the goods. This means Wholeness brings the healing the body needs. Also contained in Wholeness is insertion for our day, for our life."*

❖ *"The first thing to know about Mother Divine: I embrace all things. I love all things. I resist nothing. I don't even resist resistance. We can start by your embracing a little bit more. We are finished with the old way of doing things."*

❖ *"A good question to ask the self every so often is: 'Am I in Service?' Am I in service to the Divine? Am I in service to the Divine Self? When we are in Service to the Divine it is then that the Divine is in service to us."*

❖ *"On a physical level, on the physical level of the physiology, the ability to perceive deeply is aided by a stronger spine. This means divine awareness is birthed through the spine and comes through the spine on a physical level. It shows the importance of giving some love to the spine every day. The spine is the divine highway on the physical level."*

❧ Some more tomorrow.
Love, Sondra

August 4, 2016

❧ THE WHOLENESS
This is from the book I told you about, given to me by that mysterious man who came to meet me at my friend's house in Santa Fe. This book is called *The Wholeness* by Matthew Reifslager, the man's son.

❧ Here is what the Divine Mother says about breathing—so you will see once again why we are so into Liberation Breathing!

192

❖ *"Whatever is there in the physiology, we breathe it all in. That is what wholeness does. So, breathe ME into the physiology. Breathing your Wholeness deep into the physiology, letting love nurture each corner, each spot of resistance, until there is no resistance left. What you breathe in is My Wholeness. Breathe in your own Divinity."*

❖ *"How can healing occur without a doctor in the room? Very easily. This is how spontaneous healing occurs: permission given, permission received, and direct divine healing is the result. We innocently, gently, give permission to Wholeness to run the show. We give permission to the body to do what it needs to do, to feel what it needs to feel. Let MY LOVE penetrate the physiology. Nothing is needed but permission, and then you let it go."*

❖ *"And when we enter activity, we make sure we are staying rested by breathing deeply. Try breathing a little more deeply than you are used to in all activity. And it makes that activity more restful. Rest is the key ingredient to awakening."*

Love, Sondra

August 5, 2016

❡ FINAL POST ON THE WHOLENESS

This is my final post for now from *The Wholeness* by Matthew Reifslager. I think this one is very important.

❖ *"I invite you to sit with Me [Divine Mother] anytime. I am always happy to provide some guidance and I will never steer you wrong. If you have a question about anything, ask Me. You cannot do anything, think anything, feel anything without Me. Breathe deep My silence. Allow it to transform and open your heart. My love is here for you always. Breathe me in!"*

❖ *"If you let go of controls, I promise to take them over. This is the deal and it is always on the table. All suffering is born of resistance. When an experience is rough, this is the time to call on Me. The Earth is shifting so dramatically that alignment with Wholeness must be established for maximum smoothness. I am on call all of the time!"*

❖ *You do nothing. I do everything. That is our agreement. Recognize that life lived in the ego is profoundly powerless. For that means you have chosen to identify with a life that is guaranteed to end, a body that is guaranteed to break down, and fortune that is guaranteed to be spent. To walk around surrendered in your heart at all times to God, knowing that I will take care of you and your every need—this is the most powerful place a human being can be."*

ॐ Jai Ma!

Love, Sondra

August 6, 2016

ॐ BABAJI SAID "FAITH IS EVERYTHING"
How can you have faith if you are filled with more fear and doubt than love and trust? Fear cripples you; it makes you paralyzed. When I feel fear, I feel suddenly weak and I know I need to breathe it out immediately. You can see that lack of faith is the cause of many troubles. Without faith, you have no feelings, no heart, and no love. People tend to place faith in someone's qualifications, in certificates, in a piece of paper hanging on their wall. People have faith in a doctor's or scientist's words even though the doctor or scientist is likely to be stuck in the intellect and therefore limited.

ॐ A person who has no faith will be unduly sensitive and fragile whereas a person with faith can keep in good spirits and strength all the time. No matter what the circumstances you find yourself in, your faith protects you.

❡ There are people with no faith who lead normal lives, but you cannot know what is going on inside them. It is likely there will be a dryness within them, that they will lack a zest for life, and will rarely be relaxed. They can be rather mechanical. Such people can come off as narrow-minded and loveless.

❡ You can only fill the gap of the unknown when the heart is filled with faith in a Supreme Power. Without love and faith, such people lack vitality, they are like living corpses. Nobody will be attracted to them.

❡ Some doubt a Mahatma (great soul) because he has no credentials; and yet he has delved deep into the deeper mysteries of the Universe. This is why I have total faith in Babaji. Once, when I had some doubt, He asked me this: "Have I ever let you down?" The answer was no; He had not. I was embarrassed about my doubt.

❡ Some of the things I have done in my life (like joining the Peace Corps, going to India by myself, taking rebirthing to Russia while the iron curtain was still up, etc.) took a lot of courage, but I had a strong faith which got me though it all. Love, Sondra

August 7, 2016

❡ COMMUNICATION
We see a lot of couples who have communication problems. It seems that people just don't listen to each other. Oprah said that after 25 years of doing her show, the main thing she learned is that people just want to be heard! The other problem is criticism. Criticism kills relationships and shuts down communication.

❡ Everyone should know Compassionate Communication, as taught by Marshall Rosenberg. It goes like this:

> l. "What I observe going on is this:___." (Say it without any judgement or evaluation.)
> 2. "What I feel about this is___."
> 3. "What I need is___." or "What I request is___."

It is so simple, and it works! We are accustomed to thinking about what is wrong with others when our needs are not met. Then what we want comes across as a demand. Then others either submit to it, resent it, or rebel. It is good to get others to trust that we are *requesting,* not demanding. You cannot have the slightest indication that they will be blamed or punished or made guilty when they don't comply. We must let them know that we only want them to comply if they can do so willingly. They will be a lot more willing if you don't demand.

¶ Markus and I came up with The 8-minute Communication Process. One speaks for 8 minutes straight, using non-violent communication as above. The listener must observe these rules: No interrupting at all. No bad faces. No rolling of the eyes. No rehearsing what you are going to say back in a rebuttal, just 100% conscious listening. After the first in the couple speaks for 8 minutes, then switch. The other person speaks for 8 minutes. You would be amazed how this process defuses an argument, or a disagreement. And, this process makes sure each of you are heard totally in peace.

Love, Sondra

August 8, 2016

¶ FIVE LOVE LANGUAGES

Have you ever read *The Five Love Languages* by Gary Chapman? I reviewed it yesterday and I can give you the gist of it. The point is you should know the way your mate feels the most love. Is it through mostly one of these ways:

1. *Words of affirmation*
2. *Quality time*
3. *Receiving gifts*
4. *Acts of service*
5. *Physical touch*

For example, if your mate feels loved by receiving gifts and you think your acts of service prove your love, it will be a disconnect.

196

₰ For me, I like quality time. I am not interested in receiving gifts really. I prefer to pick out the things I like myself. I even buy my own birthday gifts and show Markus what he bought me. I know that sounds crazy, but I don't want him to have to figure out what I like, and he does not like shopping anyway. He gives me quality time since we are always together. I am fortunate.

₰ For him, he likes physical touch. He loves to put his head in my lap and have his head and hair stroked. It makes him SO happy. So, I always am generous with that.

₰ Words of affirmation are nice of course but neither of us really need a lot of acknowledgement because we have total self-esteem.

₰ So think about it. This is probably not as important for a relationship as having your case cracked; but it is sweet to know the love language your mate desires.

Love, Sondra

August 9, 2016

₰ A MEDITATION

Recently in a meditation I "saw" myself coming toward Babaji for several lifetimes. It was a very winding, curvy, difficult road and at the end of the experience I saw myself on a straight road going directly to Him. How long this has taken, only He knows. But it was exhilarating. A false master is just a tranquilizer. You come to him and he consoles you. But the REAL MASTER, like Babaji, will help you grow rapidly. Growth can be difficult—you have to pass through many tests. A true Master will HAUNT YOU! There is no transformation without fire. Friction is the right word for the inner war. You have to become uprooted so your family no longer has power over your mind. All that has been before must be disrupted. A real Master helps you do this.

₰ Unless you are ready to encounter yourself, you cannot become a disciple because a Master can do nothing if you are not ready to face yourself. All that you have denied and repressed will come up and that gives one fear. That is why people avoid going to Babaji. They are not willing to go through fear. (We have breathwork to release this fear and we do Liberation Breathing every single day in Herakhan.) You only become a disciple when you are ready to expose your whole being to yourself. I always felt totally exposed around Babaji; but He was the most exciting thing on earth!

ɠ Are you ready? Are you courageous enough? I am daring you to be great!

Love, Sondra

August 10, 2016

ɠ SPIRITUAL MIDWIFE

The Master is like a midwife. He helps you pass through a new birth and be reborn. But you have to trust—you cannot doubt. You have to drop your armor completely. The openness has to be total, otherwise nothing can happen. You have to pass through great training. To me, it is the greatest training on earth.

ɠ The Master is the one who awakens you. He wants to birth you into His or Her dimension. But when there is a Master like Babaji or Ammachi or Jesus, people try to escape from Him or Her in every way possible. I see this all the time. People say they want to go to Babaji with me and then they back out!

ɠ People think it is dangerous to encounter Him because He can see right through you and the false life you made up. You become transparent and cannot hide yourself. I used to become a trembling leaf before Babaji. I had to be very courageous around Him. But I took the jump into the abyss and I gained everything. I want that for you.

ɠ Babaji is saying to you: "The door is open right now. My love is available. You can take it or not." I say WHY NOT? If you postpone the entry, your mind will remain the same. People have tried every which way to change themselves —but is there really much change?

ɠ The Master offers total freedom. The Master is fire and you have to become like liquid so all that is wrong is burned. At times I felt like my bones were on fire for days and weeks on end. But I knew that this fire purification was what I needed. I came out different from what I was. A transformation is discontinuity with the past. It is not patchwork. How do you think I ended up with such a great relationship?

❡ If you are courageous enough to pass through the fire of Babaji, a new world will open up for you. The other choice is to remain in the nightmare. But one has to decide. The mind is afraid of the unknown. But the unknown is ecstasy. Would I kid you? Babaji invites you once again. Are you going to reject the invitation?

Love, Sondra

August 11, 2016

❡ SOME IMPORTANT NOTES

Here are some of my own paraphrased notes from *A Course in Miracles:*

❖ No evidence will convince you of the truth of what you do not want.

❖ The ego loves us to be unhappy.

❖ What seems like bad news is really a call for celebration—it means that the ego's foundations have been shaken. This is good!

❖ The ego's capacity to use anything and everything to delay your awakening cannot be underestimated.

❖ You have to learn to gently laugh at the ego.

❖ What matters is what is driving our behavior: Is it love or fear?

❖ We are inclined to think some people are more special, valuable, or lovable than others = tricky territory.

❖ The ego is attached to outcomes. The Holy Spirit fully accepts all situations knowing that each one is the perfect classroom for learning.

❖ There is nothing that happens to us that cannot be seen as holding a gift or a miracle within it. Once we change our mind, there are no problems—only opportunities.

❡ My goal is to be at peace regardless of externals. This is not a course of love and light, but one that holds up a mirror to your unflattering side. The work of the Course is *undoing* of blocks, not a dismissal of them. The Course actively warns us against denial, which would only keep the blocks in place and give them more power.
Love, Sondra

August 12, 2016

❡ SOME THINGS I HAVE LEARNED LATELY
I know these may seem obvious, but lately I've been thinking:

1. My ideas are not as high as Babaji's.
2. Sometimes I have the tendency to think that other people think like I do. They don't; and I have to handle that.
3. Some people would rather stay in the struggle and their personal hell than face Babaji and get liberated even if I think that is dumb.
4. Not all lawyers are the same. Some are actually very spiritual and extremely high. I have met two like that.
5. Some decorators can decorate a very plush mansion and have the best of everything but ruin it with a very angry painting and not get it.
6. Many people say things and do not keep their word and I still get shocked at that.
7. Some people are even threatened by a Buddha statue.
8. The India Quest never fails to produce miracles.
9. I have to be a lot clearer up front about what the financial deal is.
10. When Mark and I can stay in hotels, I feel much better and can do a better job.
11. The "personal lie" is even more insidious than I even thought and it continually causes people to do things they regret.
12. Some people are very competitive but won't admit it.
13. There is nothing like wet rebirthing in thermal waters.
14. Sincere sweetness is such a refreshing quality and

wonderful to work with.

15. Some people do not like to communicate as much as I do.
16. Some people who seem simple can be higher spiritually than those who think they are very spiritually advanced.
17. People are somehow afraid to be "empty." They think it is somehow bad. They do not get they can fill that space with love, which is infinite.

Love, Sondra

August 13, 2016

❡ MORE THINGS I HAVE LEARNED LATELY

18. I need to have even more gratitude despite the fact I think I am grateful.
19. Even if it looks like things are falling apart, it might be good, as the ego needs to fall apart.
20. I feel better every single time Markus writes a poem and especially when he reads it to me.
22. I have to keep giving up expectations and attachments.
23. Even if it looks like someone is quitting and that could make me nervous, they are almost instantly replaced by someone better who Babaji sends us.
24. When someone withdraws and shuts down, it is often covert hostility.
25. Too many people are totally stuck in their marriage and even are sleeping in separate bedrooms and still pretending they have a good marriage.
26. People are attached to their anger and get mad at me when I try to help them give up anger. I have to keep on trying anyway.
27. I need to learn a lot more about discrimination and how much energy a person can tolerate.
28. Sometimes people run away from me for 15 long years and then they come back, regretting they did that. Others never come back. I notice some of them die.
29. Ammachi said: "The Ashram is a battleground. Some people make it and others don't." I *now* get what she

means.

30. When people avoid communication, the vacuum might be filled with negative assumptions.
31. I should assume the BEST.
32. I am getting better at helping people create a mate!
33. Bali remains the highest place I have been in the world.
34. ALL THINGS are lessons God would have me learn.

Love, Sondra

August 14, 2016

♪ WHAT I HAVE LEARNED LATELY (continued)

35. When there is a problem, I should ask the person involved how they see it.
36. Diplomacy is the ability to tell someone something that is difficult to hear and have them thank you for it.
37. I have to decide if I have more faith in a problem or the miracle to solve it.
38. 33% of girls in America are molested. Molestation is rampant all over the world and I am still shocked.
39. A house can be "clean" but overly cluttered. I have trouble thinking clearly in those houses.
40. It is so wonderful to be with people who can handle feedback and who enjoy looking at themselves.
41. Mark's paintings have been creating miracles for those who bought them. I love that!
42. The Dalai Lama says that the highest happiness is when one reaches a state of liberation where there is no more suffering. Well that is exactly what Liberation Breathing is for!
43. Oprah said that the main thing she learned in 25 years is that *people just want to be heard*.
44. It is more of an honor to be on Babaji's team than I have been saying.
45. Sometimes I just don't know how to get people over their fear of Him. I need to learn that.
46. People who organize and bring others to the work are

JEWELS.
47. Sometimes people just need a break from me.
48. Sometimes I am too tough and sometimes I am not tough enough.
49. The most crucial interaction with a person is the first four seconds!
50. Until you chose Heaven you are in Hell.

Love, Sondra

August 15, 2016

❧ KARMA AND ANOTHER REASON WE NEED A TRUE MASTER
I read this in Meher Baba's Discourses:

> "Fate is really man's own creation pursuing him from past lives. Karmic determination is the condition of true responsibility. It means that the individual will reap what he sows. According to karmic law he can neither avoid the debts or dues. It is through his own binding karma that he invites upon himself pleasure or pain. He keeps reincarnating to pay off his debts and recover his dues. But even then he may be unable to clear his account for two reasons:
>
> 1. All the persons with whom he or she has karmic links may not be incarnate when he has taken a body.
> 2) Due to particular limitations of his capacities or circumstances, he or she may not be able to meet all the complex circumstances. He may even go on adding to his karma!
>
> The result could be that there is difficulty getting out of his karmic entanglements. These entanglements would be endless if there were no provision for release. The help of a Perfect Master is enormous for this. The Perfect Master can bring emancipation.

Another way out is spiritual purification and service to humanity."

℣ So, now you see why I am always harping about Liberation Breathing as a form of spiritual purification and trying to get people to Babaji.
Love, Sondra

August 16, 2016

℣ PAST LIVES AGAIN
I mentioned before that the Dalai Lama said that in the West we open a lot of doors to find answers, but there is one door we don't even have, and that door is to past lives. I do often see a need for this with clients. We had a client who kept telling us she was an "illusion." I thought that was a really strange personal lie. In this life she was a doctor. She had a lot of fears and one of them, after a deep process, came out to be fear of being burned. That was the first clue I was dealing with a past life. She also thought she was dirty and confessed she had had a very thick hymen which had to be opened by doctors. Her first sexual experience was more or less rape. Turns out she was engaged in orgies in past lives.
℣ She had some special healing power in past lives, but she always ended up being wrong with sex or being persecuted for her healing powers. So, she had it wired up that her sex was bad. That is, she was in her female power, and she was bad and wrong. So, she hid her healing powers behind being a doctor. Her ego solution was to remain small and helpless. So much so that she became "not here," really, and an "Illusion" to feel safe. She was convinced that her REAL Self was dangerous and bad. Of course, we know that one's Real Self is good and holy, so she had it wired backwards.
℣ Markus was surprised how much I had to "grind up" her mind; but it was necessary. We even had to get out the vomiting pan. But she loved the session!

Love, Sondra

August 17, 2016

❡ THE NEW LOVING RELATIONSHIPS BOOK
I am so happy that I could finish a new book yesterday. The book *Loving Relationships* was very, very, successful in the 70s. I totally rewrote the whole book from scratch—*The New Loving Relationships Book.* I read it yesterday and loved reading it myself. I liked it.
Love, Sondra

August 18, 2016

❡ SOME MORE OF MY NOTES FROM ACIM
I have paraphrased some important points I learned from over 40 years of reading *A Course in Miracles*:

❖ The real purpose of relationships is to let them be used by the Holy Spirit for the healing of our minds. Is your relationship for making your ego comfortable or for transcending it?

❖ Anger is profoundly disempowering and dishonoring of ourselves. Neither suppression nor expression of it is of any value.

❖ The past can have no hold over us unless we bring it with us. ACIM offers us a way of letting our past go, through forgiveness.

❖ Every moment of our lives is the perfect opportunity for us to make a new start. Each new moment can symbolize a rebirth.

❖ Everything that happens to us can be used either by the ego for our crucifixion or by the Holy Spirit for our salvation.

❖ Fundamentally using someone to meet our needs is stealing from them. Many subtle bargains are then struck in the name of love; often we are giving to get. This is not love at all but manipulation and theft.

❖ No human can fully satisfy us when we are actually seeking what only God can provide. Yet we keep looking. This is an addiction.

205

❖ The ego's motto is "seek but make sure you do not find."

Love, Sondra

August 19, 2016

❡ ANOTHER CASE OF SEVERE CHRONIC FATIGUE
A client came to us with a case of this and she had this condition for 25 years! Nobody had been able to help her at all because it was definitely related to her birth. That is where we came in.

❡ At the time of her birth there was a life-threatening situation and the OB doctor decided he could not save both the baby and the mother. Usually in such a case the doctor would ask the father to decide, which is horrible enough; but the father was not around. So then, he asked the mother herself. The mother shouts, "Save the mother!" meaning herself. The baby, our client, heard this and babies can make very sophisticated decisions in the womb. The client in that moment decided, "I am nothing; I have no value." Those two thoughts alone would set up the death urge which will wipe out one's energy. Of course, Chronic Fatigue Syndrome, in our experience, is related to rejection of life. But any good Breathworker would also have to look at why she did not want to be healed.

❡ There were so many reasons. She also had the thought people were hostile, as her mother beat her. She just wanted to stay in her room and not come out. Chronic Fatigue Syndrome would fit that pattern, as usually they cannot move about. She had also been a nun in four lifetimes; so she was used to being cloistered. Further, she had fear of joy. If she had joy she thought she would be punished. This I found out by processing her deeply. She was also run by Catholicism —thinking suffering makes you holy!

❡ I really think we made a big difference. Of course, I turned her over to Rebirthers in the area where she lives, because she needs tons of follow-up. One always has to start by getting the exact right causative factors whenever there is

an illness. The reason doctors can do nothing for this condition is because they don't understand how the death urge operates and they don't look at the birth trauma.
Love, Sondra

August 20, 2016

❡ GUILT
People have all kinds of guilt: past life guilt; guilt for hurting mother at birth; religious guilt; guilt about things done wrong in this life; etc. ACIM says guilt is not only not of God, it is an attack on God! But it also says in order to get rid of it, you have to pass through the trickiest part of the ego—where the ego says: "If you dare think you are innocent, then you are REALLY guilty."
❡ David Hawkins also said that excessive guilt is a disguised form of egotism in which the self becomes blown up, exaggerated and the hero of the tragedy! The ego regenerates itself through the negativity. Wallowing in guilt, he says, is feeding the ego and another form in which error is inflated instead of being relinquished to a higher power.

> "By spiritual alignment the past circumstances underlying the guilt are re-contextualized under the influence of spiritual energy. The question one has to face is either one wishes to cling to it and thereby get the juice from it or give it up. The alleviation and recovery from guilt is confession, forgiveness, penance, and the renewal and re-dedication to spiritual principles as well as good works, selfless service, and humanitarian efforts." —David Hawkins

❡ How can you have any FUN in a relationship if you are guilty? The thing to know is that guilt always demands punishment!
❡ Driving today to Omega Institute in NY to speak at a Congress for Breathwork.

Love, Sondra

August 21, 2016

❡ DRIVE TO OMEGA
We arrived at Omega Institute which is out in the boondocks in upstate New York. We don't mind the drive if we can listen to Esther Hicks tapes all the way, which we do. Otherwise I would want to fly. But she keeps us in a very high frequency. Today she talked again about these 5 steps:

      1. You ask
      2. It is given
      3. You allow it
      4. You master this, (and the contrast)
      5. You maintain it no matter what is going on

❡ The other thing to really get is that most people want something so they can be happy getting it. But you have to be happy first, in order to get it. It is basic metaphysics; but so good to have her remind us. If you are going to order her tapes make sure they are of the actual seminars and not someone reading her books. It is easy to make that mistake so watch out.
❡ Planning to see Leonard Orr tonight. Tomorrow we begin. Love, Sondra

August 22, 2016

❡ BREATHWORK CONGRESS
Today we start the Breathwork Congress. Leonard will speak.
❡ Of course, I acknowledge him for my wonderful career and for teaching me Physical Immortality. I acknowledge Jim Morningstar who is also speaking this week for giving me one of the best Rebirthing sessions I have ever had. He got me down to my conception. I acknowledge Jessica Dibb for taking care of me when I went through the dark night of the soul and for producing this Congress. We shall see what comes up!

♫ I am really looking forward to meeting the people who come. We met one last night who came all the way from South Island near Christchurch, New Zealand!
Love, Sondra

August 23, 2016

♫ OFF TO A GOOD START
Today we shared about Liberation Breathing and the miracles of the Divine Mother. Then we processed everyone on personal lies and how to overcome the addiction to them. Then we presented the channeling that Markus did from the Divine Mother on Christmas Day in Bali. That was really deep and a very intimate experience of our time together alone after a 10-day intensive. I like it because it has the music in the background that we love to listen to alone. Buddha Bar and Indian Classical music.
Love, Sondra

August 24, 2016

♫ MY BIRTHDAY
For my birthday, Markus gave me a beautiful white crystal watch from Swarovski. Then we went out to dinner in Rhinebeck with Ana from Spain and Lauren from Washington D.C., both of whom will organize for us in the future. It is so exciting to think about opening in a new area. I love it! We had dinner in a restaurant that was an old church converted into a very nice dining place.
♫ My birth took place in the little town of Grafton, Iowa, population: 300. I was born on the kitchen table at home. The whole town came to see me afterwards, and my mom said even people from neighboring towns came to see. Later I asked her, "Why?" She said, "Well they had never seen a Swedish baby before." I guess I was a public figure right away!
Love, Sondra

August 28, 2016

❡ RECOMMENDATION

After we listened to all the Esther Hicks tapes, we still had a really long drive. So then, we listened to some beautiful Babaji music, which I highly recommend you get. The music is played by Goma and the chants and bhajans are simply exquisite. You can order these:

1. *Ocean of Devotion*
2. *Sacred Source*
3. *River of Grace*

Even the titles are magnificent as you see. We turned this music up really loud and I also chanted with the songs. We got very high doing this and I suggest you try it!

❡ After that we listened to Indian classical music. The musician who plays the reed flute is called Hariprasad Chaurasia. The whole purpose is for your spiritual awakening and evolution. They are so precise that if they miss one note they could have a heart attack! That is how perfect it is.

Love, Sondra

August 29, 2016

❡ SPIRITUAL HEALING

The post that I had the absolute most response to was the one I did in Iceland on Spiritual Healing. I am going to write more on this. When I had anorexia after my mother died, it was the hardest thing I ever had to heal. Here are some of my old notes: (It now occurs to me that you can borrow this for any problem, not only physical.)

❖ "The solution is available this moment because there is no separation. I release all fear that keeps me from being able to access the solution. I am perfect Love so therefore fear cannot reside in me. I recognize and invite my connection to You, God, into my consciousness. I am the temple of God and the Spirit of God dwells in me. I bring truth to this situation."

❖ "This condition has no power. Instead of asking you to heal me God, I commune with this eternal presence that You are in me. I am therefore unconditional, non-judgmental love. I am harmony. I am in your hands God."

❖ "I use prayer to open the gates of my Soul to your Divine Presence. I use prayer to reside in that one power of your God Consciousness."

❖ "I ask you Jesus/Babaji/Divine Mother how to pray about this. My life is Yours to use as you see fit. Water me like a flower. I want to know You intimately God. I want to engage with You Heavenly Father/Mother/Child like never before. With You, God, all things are possible. That is the promise You made. I give no power to this perceived problem. The light dissolves all my darkness. I do not give energy to this problem."

❖ "There is but One Power. Now I will bring the One Power of good to these thoughts of anguish. I bring Spirit to them. In silence and stillness Your energy God, becomes mine. I free my mind of endless chatter. I allow the faster vibration of Spirit to enter." More tomorrow.
Love, Sondra

August 30, 2016

℘ MORE ON SPIRITUAL HEALING

❖ "I want to be born again for you God. I no longer feel guilty or angry about my condition. I know my body is my curriculum, God. I unite in Wholeness with the healing capacity of You, God. I use my spiritual essence to maintain a sense of perfect health. I let go of the negative thought causing this condition which is _____."

❖ "I bring Spirit to this error. I bring the highest healing energy of pardon to this. I accept the miracle of my perfect _____. My Spirit is perfect. My body is a manifestation of God's knowledge. My body is firmly rooted in Spirit. All my frequencies are in harmony with perfect health. All negative frequencies are dislodged and removed now."

❖ "I have returned to my normal state of Grace. This condition is unreal, i.e. it does not exist as a part of God. I know you are not withholding health from me God. I activate my Chi to remove all imbalances. I am a channel through which all healing moves. I am connected to Source. My thoughts are on You, God, not on my condition. I no longer enjoy talking about my malady. I renounce this egotism. I am problem free."

❖ "The relief for my despair is already here. Please redeem my mind and body. I give up control. I give up my own agenda. I do not know what to do in this instance, but I am willing to let go and turn this entire thing over in the knowledge that its solution rests in the hands of the all-knowing power of infinite intelligence. CHARGE ME UP! Angels are in front of me, behind me, and all around me now. Here is my life submitted to your perfect plan, God." Love, Sondra

August 31, 2016

✯ A SIMPLE SECRET FOR LIVING AN EXTRA-LONG LIFE The other day I was sitting in a parlor waiting for my massage. Another woman sat down to my left just as two ladies entered arm in arm, one helping the other into a chair. I could see right away that they were mother and daughter. The daughter looked to be in her seventies!

✯ The woman next to me asked them if they were mother and daughter and the younger woman answered, "Yes this is my mom. She just turned 94." She looked in really good shape. The 94-year-old mother said energetically to us, "Are we all relaxed today, ladies?" She was full of light and joy. The woman next to me said to her, "You look amazing and full of life! What is your secret?"

✯ Without even one hesitation, the mom replied, "I have always surrounded myself with nice people. That is the secret."

✯ I was touched by both the power and the simplicity of her answer. I have often written about how allowing negative people into our lives can affect our emotional and physical well-being. I am a big believer in being very mindful about what we tolerate. But I had not thought about putting nice people together with longevity!

❡ It makes total sense. Kindness is an expression of Love and love is the most powerful force known to us. There actually are many studies that support this, including a recent one at the University of N. Carolina at Chapel Hill. Half the participants were assigned to take part in a loving-kindness meditation each week for six weeks. The other half was assigned to a control group. There was increase in the vagal tone in the first group (the activity of the vagus nerve, our longest cranial nerve). The greater the vagal tone, the greater the physical health. The more kindness, the more positive emotions, and the more of an upward spiral dynamic. And you probably know that Dr. Masuru Emoto showed that kindness affects water crystals and thus our cellular structure. So get the lesson, and hang out with kind people. Don't tolerate toxic relationships.
Love, Sondra

September 1, 2016

❡ A VERY INTERESTING DAY
Our Uber driver informed us that our city (Nashville, TN) was voted the "most friendly" in all of the USA.! We agree. So that is great to know. Plus, he said 78 people a day are moving here! It is fun!

❡ Where were we going? We were headed to the County Court House to see the judge so Markus could change his name from Mark Sullivan to Markus Ray! We had to sit in the courtroom for hours watching the judge handle many cases before us. At least he was not boring. He was actually funny. Our name was not called so I figured we would have to wait until the end because we were not lawyers like the others.

❡ But finally, we were the last ones in the room. He said we were not on the roster! Turns out we had the wrong day! It was embarrassing but we immediately did the affirmation: "Even though we made a mistake we still love and accept ourselves." We thought maybe he would make us come back another day; but he decided to take us on.

₲ Markus also did not have his birth certificate so we were facing the possibility of him not taking on the case because of that. But the judge was really nice and he said there were enough documents.

₲ Then, when he realized Markus was taking my name, he actually acknowledged him for being on the cutting edge! (He is.) Then Markus acknowledged him for entertaining us with his humor. He said, "I take my job very, very, seriously, but I don't take myself seriously." Then he pronounced him as Markus Ray.

₲ After that we went to the driver's license place to update Markus's new name on that, and after that we went out for lunch at our favorite Hermitage Hotel to celebrate. It is great when you let go of your past this way. I did it when I became an author and it gave me a whole new life. The numerology of his name went from a 6 to a 1. So now I am looking forward to seeing Markus's changes!
Love, Sondra

September 2, 2016

₲ NEGATIVE BEHAVIORS THAT CAN CONSTRICT YOUR ENERGY FLOW

- ❖ *Withholding or lying*
- ❖ *Blaming each other or anyone else*
- ❖ *Thinking loss is real*
- ❖ *Holding onto guilt*
- ❖ *Manipulations through guilt*
- ❖ *Holding on to the past and/or using it as a reference point*
- ❖ *Acting out of obligation (generally leads to resentment)*
- ❖ *Saying Yes when you mean No, or visa-versa*
- ❖ *Doing things you really do not want to do in order to get approval*
- ❖ *Struggling*
- ❖ *Defending and justifying*
- ❖ *Judging*

❖ *Making yourself wrong*
❖ *Sacrificing*
❖ *Being motivated by fear, guilt, or anger*
❖ *Needing to be needed*
❖ *Perceiving others as lacking*
❖ *Saving or rescuing people*
❖ *Needing to be right or making right more important than being happy*
❖ *Indulging in anger*

Love, Sondra

September 3, 2016

❡ A CASE OF DISCONNECTION
A woman came who is a coach and she helped others get their goals and get in their power; but she told us she did not feel her own power at all. She was not easy to process and did not communicate well—so we really had to ask a lot of questions. It seemed like she did not really believe in God and she did not feel anything at all. She claimed she was in a great marriage, but she was very flat in her tone.

❡ There was not much in her history except she did not feel connected to her mother. The one thing suspicious was that she casually mentioned that an older man had been sexually inappropriate with her, but she claimed it was not a big deal. In the session I asked her about her sex life, and she said she got mad at her husband during sex after her daughter was born. Markus brought up again the issue of the older man being inappropriate with her. It was obvious to us she had not processed that and did not like talking about it.

❡ I finally asked her how it stopped. She said, "He died." We were able to see that her personal lie was "I am disconnected."

❡ She could not feel connected to her mother because of that thought, nor to God because of that thought. She also could not feel connected to her power because of that thought. BUT she did feel connected to the old man who

215

died. It ended up she was more connected to death than to life! When she was in the womb, her mother had an actual allergy to her and broke out and scratched herself during the whole pregnancy. The mother did not have that with previous pregnancies. It seemed to be some big past life karma with her mother and she never really got connected as a result.

Ʂ So she unconsciously found the neighbor to connect with and it was in fact a HUGE deal, even though she played it down. Her anger at her mother came up when she had her own daughter and she took it out on her husband during sex. It was difficult to unravel all this because she tried to disconnect from us and from her feelings.

Ʂ We were able to help her a lot in the end because we asked the right questions. It was very tricky though. One affirmation Markus gave her was, "I am connected to LIFE through my feminine power." I was so glad we were skilled enough to help her. She had no idea that she was stuck on that thought! I learned a great deal from this case.
Love, Sondra

September 4, 2016

Ʂ EMOTIONAL INCEST
We have seen quite a few clients recently stuck in this pattern. The term describes a relationship between parents and children that is sexualized, without actual sexual contact. It is a *covert incest* on the emotional/mental level. It involves dynamics much like a relationship between sexual partners.

Ʂ For example, a mom is communicating too intimately with her son, and kind of setting him up as a husband replacement. Jr. becomes seduced emotionally into a power position without realizing it. In other words, it is a parent responding to a child's love with adult sexual/intimate energy. Problems between the parents often facilitate emotional incest. As the parents' distance themselves from each other physically, sexually, and emotionally, one parent then begins focusing more and more on the child. The child becomes the surrogate partner and source of emotional support for the parent. Forcing the emotional role of a spouse on a child means the child's own needs get ignored and the relationship is for meeting the needs of the parent.

ꝺ The parent is not often even aware of the damage being done and begins over-bonding with the child as an equal or buddy. A mother might tell her daughter they are like sisters and they see this as wonderful. It occurs when a parent sucks dry a child to fill their own inner emptiness.

ꝺ Also, Dad's hugs with his daughter can become weird over time. All this will later produce stress in sexual relationships when the child grows up. A girl chooses a guy like her dad for sure, and then it gets tricky because everyone knows you cannot have sex with your dad, so the sex goes out the window because she cannot stop setting up her mate to be her Dad. Sounds wild, but it happens.

Love, Sondra

September 5, 2016

ꝺ AN EMOTIONAL AFFAIR

Related to the emotional incest pattern is the possibility of an emotional affair (or also a direct affair). That is because one can get stuck in triangles if one has not cleared emotional incest. Here are the signs of an emotional affair:

❖ *You find yourself thinking about that person a lot.*

❖ *You find yourself fantasizing about what it would be like to be with that person.*

❖ *You find yourself having sexual fantasies about them and substituting the fantasy for your real partner.*

❖ *You feel gripped by intense longing, wanting, and yearning.*

❖ *You feel a sense of grief and loss when you think you might never be with them.*

❖ *You secretly worry they might be your actual soul mate, but in the wrong time and wrong place.*

❖ *Secretly you believe you or your life would be happier if you were to have a romantic sexual*

relationship with them.
❖ *Secretly you believe that being with you would make them happier.*

And perhaps the biggest sign is that when you mentally compare the fantasy with your current partner, you feel like your current partner falls short.

ℱ The person may say to himself, "I am not really cheating because we are not having sex." But when you start telling things to this person that you would not even say to your mate, then how hurtful is that? How hurtful is all of the above?

ℱ It all happens in the mind. An emotional affair is very dangerous. The allure of it is very subtle. It is like a spider's web. They usually wane because they are not rooted in reality. I know of a case where the gal was having an emotional affair with someone she had not even met, i.e. a celebrity. It happens.

ℱ To get out of it, one must have self-awareness and realize that nobody outside can cause you to have all these feelings. We usually help the client see how this is related to emotional incest and the need to be in a triangle. Because a girl, for example, was in love with her father and he was taken by the mother and right there is the original triangle. Of course, this also applies to an actual affair acted out. Both kinds of affairs are dangerous. We see a lot of female clients who are attracted to married men. It is very alluring also.

ℱ This whole thing is such a can of worms that I broke out in a sweat just writing it. My whole point is to get you clear on what can happen when you don't handle the emotional incest pattern I wrote about a few days ago.

ℱ Get a **Liberation Breathing Session** to clear your incest pattern.

Love, Sondra

September 6, 2016

ℱ STUCK IN GRANDPARENTS' MIND

Sometimes it is tricky to unravel a case, and you have to look at the grandparents. We had a client who was a real woman; beautiful inside and out. She was married with two kids for six years and very happily. The sixth year her husband had an affair and then all was ruined. This was the same pattern that happened in her parents' relationship, so that part was easy to look at. However, all her relationships afterwards went sour fast, even though the men loved her madly. This was harder to figure out. Her personal lie was, "I am not worthy," so that was part of it. However, this personal lie was more stuck than usual. It turned out the family gave all the love to the brother (the "boy"). Nobody acknowledged her although she was outstanding, and we could see this. There had to be something else, so we studied the grandparents.

❡ The paternal grandmother did not approve of her son marrying her mother, and therefore rejected her also as the first born. BUT the maternal grandmother really loved her and gave her many endearments and much good attention.

❡ The problem was that this grandmother was a drunk (because her husband had died), and the family deemed that grandmother unworthy of being in the family. So, our client had it wired that she had to be like her to be loved. "I have to be unworthy like she is to keep her love." She had love and unworthiness wired together. (We so often think if we are somehow like a family member, they will love us more.) In her case, she was loved mostly by her grandmother who was drunk and unworthy. This made her personal lie stuck X2! Fortunately, our client was smart enough get this when we pointed it out.

❡ She had to do the forgiveness diet on her maternal grandmother to whom she had bonded, and also forgive the paternal grandmother who rejected her and her mom. She had forgiven all others, but not the grandparents. What you don't forgive, you attract, or emulate.

Love, Sondra

September 7, 2016

§ CASE CRACKING
A woman came who is in her late 40s and had never been married but she wanted to be. To crack her case, we had to once again study the grandparents. Her grandmother told her mother (mother-in-law telling daughter-in-law) to have an abortion. She did not want our client to even be born. I thought this was VERY controlling since the client's mother and father were married, and it was not a case of being illegitimate. The idea that children are a huge burden went all the way back to the great grandmother!

§ Here we had to study preverbal thoughts. What thought did our client form as a result of being an attempted abortion? She decided, "I have to hide." "I have to be alone to survive." "I must be alone." Therefore, she would push away men because of those thoughts that she was unaware of.

§ She had another issue we needed to discover. Her parents
were not very happy together; BUT when they were happy, they would always exclude the children, (because children are a burden).

§ So our client had another thought, "I am excluded from happiness." She did not really want to be alone; but according to her wiring she had to be alone. It was a definite no-win situation. Many people who are alone don't realize that their subconscious thoughts are forcing them to be alone. This is why one has to be aware of the thoughts blocking a relationship or one could end up alone for years, and not understand why.

Love, Sondra
September 9, 2016

§ FUN IN FLORIDA
Had an amazing dining experience in Tampa. Cassandra and Rhett told us about their wedding on the beach. We were floored to hear the great idea they had. They asked the guests to read the 108 names of the Divine Mother out loud to them, as a blessing, and they gave all the guests

each a mala. The guests got so high doing this and I really loved the idea.

♫ At dinner Cassandra and Rhett were in a very exalted state, and we all got really high together—it is so great when four people, who all love each other equally, never speak with any negative thoughts.

♫ The food was also exquisite. Fun to be back in Florida since I went to the University of Florida College of Nursing. I recall the first day I came in from the Midwest and saw the palm trees and college students wearing thongs and Bermuda shorts. I had been in the Midwest, freezing while walking to the library, so I thought I had arrived in Heaven. Love, Sondra

September 10, 2016

♫ ACKNOWLEDGING MEN
I want to acknowledge all men who are willing to come to seminars and do self-introspection, and all those who are presently willing to get breathwork and really look at themselves. In this training we only have two men, Cassandra's husband and my husband. So, then it is a training full of willing women. I guess men think it is courageous to remain stoic and not show any feelings or vulnerability. But what is truly courageous in a man is when he is willing to do self-inquiry and look at his part in relationship issues.

♫ I once asked a clairvoyant if there was something in me that prevented more men from coming to trainings like this. She said, "No, men more or less have to be encouraged by other men to get to a seminar." This is a very common problem to see so many more women in a training than men. I hope to somehow solve this riddle and get more balance in the trainings. Once we get a man to cross the line and have his first Breathwork session, he really will go for it. It is just tricky to get them to the first one.

♫ So to all of you men who have crossed the line, I would like to honor you today and say to you that what women want is a man who will come and who will look at himself. A woman wants Spiritual Intimacy, and this includes self-introspection. Being humble and changing your thoughts is essential.

ℐ A humble man is someone who recognizes his errors, admits them, and does something about them. Being willing to come and being willing to get a Breathwork session is doing something about them.

Love, Sondra

September 11, 2016

ℐ FEAR OF GIVING UP ANGER

When I ask people in the training to tell me what their fear is of giving up their anger, they often say, "I am afraid of being vulnerable, and I would not be protected." I have to point out that the truth is just the opposite. Anger never protects you.

ℐ ACIM says that anger is a defense, and defenses attract attack. That means when you hold on to your anger, you actually get attacked more. So, people usually have this wired backwards.

ℐ Another thing they often say is this: "If I gave up my anger I would not be heard." Then I ask them if they like to listen to people with anger, and, of course, they say no. They obviously came from a home where there was a lot of yelling, and to be heard they also had to yell.

ℐ Anger has only negative consequences. Some say they cannot control their anger. That is false also. So, then I ask, "Who is in control of it then?" Then I ask them, "If you were in a heated argument with your wife and someone knocked on your door, would you continue to shout?" That usually stops their minds. Back to work.

Love, Sondra

September 12, 2016

ℐ TAMPA LRT THE DAY AFTER 9/11

Friday night we had a woman in the training who was in a real war with her ex-husband for years. She was coming from being a total victim of the situation. She was the highlight for me because by Sunday morning she had totally, totally shifted, and she shared with the whole group a letter she wrote to her ex. When she read it, several people cried. This was just one of the miracles we had. Her X had actually been in the Twin Towers during 9/11. She gave me permission to put this up:

> "Dear B,
> I am hoping you're well with 9/11 here. I can't imagine what it was like to be inside that horrific scene. I want you to know that I prayed so hard & when that building came down, I fell to my knees begging God to bring you home to us. I am happy you came home that day! I'll not ever forget you running into my arms, telling me things that no eyes should ever see! I am still praying for you & thankful that you made it home. I believe that you did once love me passionately as I love you, but the same passion you had went into hate for me in the end. I've come to realize that we seek in our partnership to recreate the context in which we were wounded so that we can finish the business of our childhood. Our old wounds are re-opened by our partners. Thank you for being my greatest teacher for I am an amazing woman, stronger & more beautiful thanks to you! I am sorry how things turned out, it was so hard asking you for a divorce while I was still in love with you. I want you to know that I will always love you & pray for the best for you, after all, you made my dreams come true & gave me the greatest gifts, our kids, W. & S. I only remember our good times, I cherish them always for we created master pieces together in W. & S. I am sorry, please forgive me, I love you & thank you." Love, V.

This letter is what I would call a perfect Ho'oponopono. She took full responsibility for her feelings, and there was no blame in the letter. She expressed her regret, but also her deep gratitude, still intact. THANK YOU, V. for making the Tampa LRT a huge success.

Love, Sondra
September 15, 2016

¶ ON THE WAY TO SANTA FE
We landed in Albuquerque and rented a car to drive to Santa Fe where we have some amazing friends, Darlene and Tommy. They have a gorgeous new home with breathtaking vistas all around. The energy is perfect, and the sunsets are amazing. They have adopted us in a way and treat us to meals at the club every night, where we have amazing discussions. We have become their "Karma Yoga." They take care of us when we need rest. They are also Babaji devotees, so this is their wonderful service. We are all a family. It is the perfect place for us to rest and write. Markus is relaxing by painting watercolors of beautiful wings.

¶ On the plane I saw an extremely interesting movie called *All the Way with LBJ.* I learned so much about the time after Kennedy was shot. I was devastated then as I had just joined the Peace Corps to serve Kennedy and the USA. My ex-husband and I had passed all the difficult tests and we were landing in Peru to begin our service. Just before we landed in Lima, the pilot told us the news. We were in shock but had to go immediately to the barrio as there was a plague epidemic. We had no time to grieve. The Peace Corps was my "boot camp" to world service.

¶ I am reading the book called *On the Road* by Gloria Steinem. It is so interesting. We kind of have a life like hers. Markus is reading *White Eagle on the Divine Mother.* I am so happy he is surrendered to the Divine Mother. Both of these books are about the place of the feminine. The ancients adored and worshiped the Mother. She is the antidote for suffering. We could not live without her bounty. When we return to the worship of Her, there will be more happiness. More tomorrow.

Love, Sondra

September 16, 2016

❡ WHITE EAGLE ON THE DIVINE MOTHER

"Until man and woman live in perfect partnership, each playing their part in the evolution of the race, there cannot be real progress. With the coming of the FEMININE ASPECT and the balancing of life there will be great progress on your earth. In every woman soul living, there is the expression of wisdom, and in the male soul the expression of power or will. The ultimate perfection in human life occurs when the Love is so perfected in each soul that there will be no separation.

❡ The Father or Will must be balanced by the Mother, or the Intuition. The place of the woman in the world will have to be recognized completely. In ancient Egypt, man and woman ruled together. They worshipped the Mother God because the Mother was the giver and preserver of life and provided the continuation of Life. A Mother has the antidote for the child's suffering.

❡ Turn your thoughts to the Mother God (Divine Mother), the expression of all that is compassionate, warm, kindly, loving and understanding and remember that the wise Mother knows what is good for the child (you) and does not fail in Her duty. Why have people for so long been presented with God as a masculine God? It is not strictly correct to do so.

❡ The Mother gently administers correction if need be. She sees clearly the child's need for experience. So then, get this in your mind: Karma gives you the opportunity to experience God more. Whatever you are faced with in life will take the form of an experience planned to bring to you in the end the joy of God."

Love, Sondra

September 17, 2016

225

ℐ A YOGI VISITING MY PLACE

A yogi of Babaji's visited my place and I asked him if he wanted to write something for my book on the Divine Mother. After he wrote it he tore it up in tiny pieces thinking it was not good enough. During the night while he slept, I went through my wastebasket and put all the pieces together like a puzzle and taped it together and wrote it down. I thought it was so fantastic that I published it. Here is an excerpt:

> *"A very dear friend of mine was crossing Germany by foot during the second world war. One day she found herself in the situation where a Russian soldier entered the room in which she had taken shelter. He was ready to rape her. Instead of going into fear and terror, she stood calmly sending her prayers to Mother Maria. The soldier stood immobilized for a while; then he suddenly sank onto his knees and burst into tears and begged for forgiveness. What happened? Remembering the Mother changed his entire behavior. Perhaps he also remembered his own mother.*
> *ℐ To have the blessing of Her sight, the saints and scientists of all ages have undergone great penance. In order to have the blindness of our inner eye to be lifted, we have to pray to Her with the full power of our heart."*

ℐ He wrote a lot more, which was very beautiful, but he closed it with this prayer:

> *"O Mother of Bliss, Thou fillest me with supreme joy. Thy mercy is boundless. O Mother, forever I bow to thee. Teach me. Teach me how to be more loving. Teach me how to be a caretaker of this planet."*

Love, Sondra

September 18, 2016

❡ TOO MANY DRUGS AT BIRTH

Awhile back we had a client whose presenting complaint was she was exhausted and burned out and that she thought it was due to being a workaholic. It turned out to be a lot more complicated than that. Seven years before her, her mom had given birth to her brother and claimed it was such a horrible birth she would never do that again. The father wanted another child, so it took the mom seven years to get up the nerve. A doctor convinced her it did not have to be the same and left a prescription of a lot of drugs to be given to the mom at birth, so she would not feel anything. She had Scopolamine, Demerol, and another drug. This "cocktail" certainly knocked out the mother, but the baby (our client) was over-drugged at birth, and also had the cord around her neck on top of that! I thought her adrenals got shot right at the beginning—right at her very birth.

❡ She complained that "everything goes crazy the last minute in her life." I recognized this as a side effect of Scopolamine. She actually had a subconscious thought we pulled out that went like this: "I have to burn myself out to stay alive." Now that clearly does not make sense, but it is typical of a cord around the neck. They nearly die but they live, so they have the thought: "I have to die in order to live." And coupled with the drugs at birth, quite a *birth trauma*.

❡ It is extremely tricky to rebirth a cord around the neck. You have to know what you are doing as a Breathworker. It took us a long time to get her personal lie. It turned out to be, "I am powerless." That is how she felt at birth with all those drugs. She also felt powerless to stop burning herself out, and powerless to say no to work assignments. She felt life is too much and too huge.

❡ Not surprisingly, she had problems with alcohol in her first marriage. (Addictions often start later on when there have been too many drugs at birth.) Her whole issue with burnout and exhaustion was related to her birth. Markus had to be very, very, precise in the exact right affirmations for her to work on. She has now written us how much this session helped her.

Love, Sondra

September 19, 2016

♩ A CASE OF SEVERE DEATH URGE

A new client came for the first time, and when she sat down, I had the thought: "I want to kill her." This has never happened in my career since 1974! I thought perhaps her mother wanted to abort her and I was tuned into that. Then she handed me a paper with all her ailments on it. She had Rheumatic fever for 6 years as a child and in the last 12 years she had mitochondrial myopathy. She had intolerance to activity, muscle pain, muscle fatigue dysphagia, intestinal parasites, slow digestion, severe weakness, problems with attention and memory, insomnia, sacral meningocele, scoliosis, and asthma. Imagine that!

♩ She told us that in a regression she had a womb memory and thought she was dying in the womb. After quite a while she finally verbalized the truth for her, "I want to die." Of course, I knew part of her wanted to live or she would not have bothered coming to us.

♩ Usually people say they want to die because they are suffering from so many ailments as she was. But in her case, the thought, "I want to die," was like a personal lie, and her ailments came from having that thought first. I tried to get her clear on this.

♩ It turned out her grandmother died when she was in the womb, which caused great suffering for her mother. But worse than that, her grandfather had been shot and killed, then her mother's brother was shot and killed by the same man. Fifteen years later, her grandmother was shot and killed when our client was in the womb. She was carrying all this weight of the family karma obviously. Furthermore, her father had a gun and kept threatening to kill the mother. Then I realized why I had had the thought, "I want to kill." So much killing in her family!

♩ In a case like this which is absolutely overwhelming, the best thing one can do is to get one thing accomplished. The main thing we did was get her to see that her thought, "I want to die," was making her really sick. (This case was so tragic it made me sick.) She cried a lot during the session, and we were so glad to read the Divine Mother names and do the mantra. She actually liked the session and wants to continue. Markus told her she was carrying the murders in

her consciousness. When people are shot, they often do not cross over right away, and they were probably hanging around attached to her mother and her. Can you get the power of the mind to come up with complicated diseases?
Love, Sondra

September 20, 2016

❡ YOUR RELATIONSHIP AS A TEACHER
In a book called *Partnering*, Hal and Sidra Stone talk about the fact that any relationship can be a teacher once you know how to take advantage of the teachings. I agree so much with this approach and have always said your mate is your guru—your real teacher in Life.

❡ You are not really surrendering to your mate as a person but to the process of the relationship itself. This relationship is a *joint venture.* It emphasizes cooperation and equality, mutual respect and mutual empowerment. This relationship includes (besides love, romance, and chemistry) personal growth and spiritual evolution. You are together for the evolution of your souls. You have love and commitment, but you also have mutual exploration of consciousness. The fundamental equality of both partners is key.

❡ Most relationships exist in a hierarchical form where there is one who adopts a role of wielding power over someone weaker. Look into your parents' relationship and see who was dominating whom? Maybe your father dominated your mother or maybe your mother dominated your father. You have to be willing to look at your family patterns and clear them.

❡ In my first marriage, I was married to a man with a genius I Q. (He was unfortunately stuck in his head.) We used to have long debates to see who could get in the last word. It was a competition. After I was divorced, I decided I would never again waste time competing like that with a man. But then I got in a business relationship with a very smart man. We seemed to be equals. But then, if he wanted things his way, he would RAISE HIS ENERGY. I would back down because I did not want to debate or argue. In many ways, he slowly took over my business. Not good.

❧ Now finally I am truly with my equal and there is no competition and no hierarchy. It is such an amazing relief. I feel like I was able to create this because I knew for sure what I did NOT want. I did not want what I had before. I did not want arguing and debating. I DID want what we call *a* conflict-free relationship. I had decided that I wanted "deep ease" above all else. I prayed for that. I asked my guru for that.

❧ The miracle was this: Markus had spent years working on himself and his consciousness before we got together. I had done the same. He had a tough teacher named Tara Singh. I had one named Babaji. We became used to having teachers and we continue to surrender to them. And to this day and we teach each other as teachers. Markus is my teacher and I am his teacher. And we both have the love of correction. We understand that until we are like Jesus, "walking on water and raising the dead," we have something to clear. We go to India every year to surrender to the process of self-realization.

Love, Sondra

September 21, 2016

❧ LOOK TOWARD THE SOLUTION

I had a client who repeatedly attracted men who abused her or left her. I decided to send her some quotes from the book, *Vortex* by Esther Hicks. I think these words are very valuable:

> *"Nothing good ever comes from focusing in opposition to what you desire. It is possible to walk away from an unwanted situation without repeating it again, but that would require not talking about it, not thinking about it, and not pushing against it. It would require a complete deactivation of the Vibration of the troubling experience. And the only way to deactivate a thought or Vibration, is to activate another. The way to avoid repeating unwanted situations is to talk about WANTED situations. Talk about what you do want; and*

discontinue dialogue about any unwanted experiences, situations, or results.

⨍ Monitoring thoughts can be tedious and tiring, so the best approach to deliberately change the direction of your thought is to reinforce your desire to feel good. Once you are determined to improve the way you feel, you will catch yourself in the early stages of negative attraction. It is easier to release a negative thought in the beginning stages of it than after it has gained momentum.

⨍ The only way to solve a problem is to look toward the solution. And when you are looking in the direction of the solution, you always feel an improvement in your emotions. Looking back at the problem always feels worse. Spend no time complaining about where you are. Nothing is more important than your feeling good. Your desire for a mate keeps them coming, but your belief in bad relationships pushes them away." (Esther Hicks)

Good, Yes?
Love, Sondra

September 22, 2016

⨍ PERSONALITY TRAITS FOR LONGEVITY
I was reading some research on the personality traits associated with longevity. They are kind of obvious, but I still want to share them.

> 1. Conscientious (That means wishing to do what is right and doing one's work thoroughly, being persistent, responsible, and taking care of one's health.)
> 2. Easy to laugh
> 3. Socially connected
>
> 4. Optimistic and easy going
> 5. Happy (This counted very strongly.)
> 6. Extroverted

Check yourself on these.

❡ Of course we are going for more than longevity. We are considering Physical Immortality which is the ability to live as long as you choose, WHILE improving your body, and while living a happy and purposeful life. Where are you at on that subject?

❡ Do you like it? Do you want it? Are you thinking about your love for life daily? Do you want to stay here and serve as long as you can? Are you reading the books on it? Are you having breathwork on it?

❡ I just looked up Physical Immortality on Google. I was astonished there was so much about me on there and I did not even know it!

I have met so many people—even some very high—and they did not care if they lived or died.

❡ Read *What Is Death?* in the teacher's manual of *A Course in Miracles.* (Jesus talking). There is a whole list of books I recommend on the subject in our book *Liberation Breathing*. If you read nothing but those books for a whole year, you would feel so much better as it would strengthen your life urge. Become a sage with no age!

Love, Sondra

September 24, 2016

❡ AT BABAJI'S ASHRAM IN COLORADO

So, now we are in the "Shambala of the Rockies." People make their pilgrimages to this sacred land. The Baca Grande in Colorado is a 200,000-acre tract of land where there are spiritual centers, shrines, ashrams, monasteries, retreat centers, and environmental organizations. The land was acquired by the UN Undersecretary Maurice Strong, and his wife, Hanne, set up the Manitou Foundation. Our Babaji ashram—the Haidakhandi Universal Ashram—is here.

❡ The land sits at a convergence of ley lines (Earth's electromagnetic energy system). Energies for healing and higher consciousness are here, so there is a strong vibratory frequency. This was originally the home of the Ute and Comanche Indians; but nearly all indigenous early tribes came here for healing and meditation. They all had to drop their war-like behavior here and get along. So they never fought on this land and that is why it is called "The Bloodless Valley."

❡ We are more or less half-way between Santa Fe and Denver, but very off the beaten path. It is a deliberate act to come here; you don't end up here just driving. The valley landscape is flanked by the San Juan Mountains to the West, and the Sangre de Cristo Range to the East. There are crystals below the water table, and the gold in the mountains will never be discovered, I was told by my Indian Teacher, Shastriji. So, they say you can evolve rapidly here. There is absolute quiet.

❡ We came obviously to go to Babaji's Divine Mother Temple, hoping to be more connected to the Great Ones and to the energy of this place.

Love, Sondra

September 25, 2016

❡ PRAISES TO BABAJI AND THE DIVINE MOTHER

Today we are singing the praises to Babaji and the Divine Mother. Some paragraphs translated are here:

> To Babaji—
> "Thou art a never-failing spring of bliss, the infinite essence of Truth. Thou art the form and base of everything pervading the world. Thou art worthy of being served by Lakshmi and Vishnu, yet you are their selfless servant as well. Divine love is given to those who always repeat Thy name. Remove poverty, pain, and doubts, Have compassion."
> ❡ To Divine Mother:
> "You are the energy of Shiva, all auspicious, fulfilling all desires. You are the refuge, with three eyes. Salutations to You, Narayani. You are creation, preservation and destruction, the eternal, living energy. You are the support of the three

233

*qualities of Nature and they are Your form.
Salutations to you, Narayanti. You always protect
everyone. You remove every pain. You remove all
obstacles. Salutations to You."*

Love, Sondra

September 27, 2016

❧ ARE YOU STUCK IN THE OLD PARADIGM?
Fifty-four percent of first marriages end in divorce. Sixty-seven percent of second marriages end in divorce, and Seventy-four percent of third marriages end in divorce. Of the remaining marriages, only fifteen percent are truly romantically married. Fifteen percent have just become roommates and just cope, and fifteen percent are miserable but stay together. This is a clear argument that the old paradigm is not working. The old paradigm is all about the following:

- ❖ Roles
- ❖ Domination and control
- ❖ Manipulation
- ❖ External power
- ❖ False security
- ❖ Codependency
- ❖ Projection of the past onto mate
- ❖ Blame
- ❖ Anger and conflict
- ❖ Victim consciousness
- ❖ Conditional love
- ❖ Getting weaker

❧ The old paradigm is full on upsets. The subconscious contains wounds from the past we are upset about that are projected onto the relationship in the present. It is NO FUN! More tomorrow.
Love, Sondra

September 28, 2016

❧ MORE ON THE OLD PARADIGM
Some of the subconscious issues that come up in a relationship are to do with the following:

- ❖ Birth traumas collide
- ❖ Family patterns dovetail
- ❖ Preverbal negative thoughts clash
- ❖ Past lives are re-lived
- ❖ Death urges kill off the relationship
- ❖ Church dogma interferes

And of course, as you know anger causes hell. Today I will be speaking on Facebook broadcast on the subject of the unconscious death urge.
Love, Sondra

September 29, 2016

❧ IS YOUR RELATIONSHIP UPLIFTING?
Is your relationship lifting you up into more happiness in your life, and with a sense of well-being—or is it taking you down?
❧ You have to be the one to initiate the change if your relationship is not working. You have to be the one to take responsibility first for your part in any malfunction. You have to be willing to leave behind the old paradigm for relationships inherited from your parents and ancestors for a totally new model. If you just go ahead and handle your part, then you are not creating karma, you are clearing it and that is what you want. Hopefully your mate will follow suit. There may be a transition period from the old to the new.
❧ You may need to reconceive the relationship with mutual effort in a new purpose and frequency. You may need to clearly evaluate if you want to stay in a relationship,

especially if you have even thought about leaving. The way you find out your REAL intention is to do this truth process:

If I had no fear, no guilt, and I didn't care what anyone thought, and if I knew I could find another relationship, would I stay or leave this relationship?

ℐ If the answer is I WOULD LEAVE, then you are out of integrity for staying. You are most likely just using your partner for some "payoff" you have, or you are not facing your fear, or both—and that is not really fair to you or your partner. Tell the truth to yourself.
Love, Sondra

September 30, 2016

ℐ WHAT IS A PERSONAL LIE?
Do you really know what a personal lie is? Do you know what yours is?
ℐ I have been mentioning the personal lie in my case studies; but now it occurred to me I have not really explained it well here. Your "personal lie" is the cornerstone of your ego. It is the one thought that invalidates your Divinity right off the bat. It is your most negative thought about yourself—but not one on the surface. It is usually a preverbal thought that can be formed in the womb, or at birth, or even it may be dragged in from a past life. This negative thought is a huge addiction. It holds you back, ruins your self-esteem, kills off your energy, destroys relationships, and leads to failure. All of that is part of the ego. (The ego is a false self that you made up to replace God. It starts with the idea that you think you are separate from God.) You can release the personal lie, but it is usually so suppressed in the unconscious mind it is hard to locate and even admit, let alone give it up.
ℐ Anytime you release ego you are ascending, and you are going toward more holiness. By cracking the case of your personal lie, you get more intimate with your mate and more intimate with God. By changing this thought, you stop invalidating your Divinity and you start to WAKE UP and

understand who you really are. It is really hard to be close to your mate or to God when you are stuck in your personal lie. (I have heard over 350 different ones.)

❡ Everyone has a personal lie (unless you are a spiritual immortal master who has been totally liberated). Personal lies begin with "I am_____." Instead of saying, "I am one with God," which we should be saying, people instead are saying for example these personal lies:

- ❖ I am not good enough
- ❖ I am wrong.
- ❖ I am bad
- ❖ I am a disappointment.
- ❖ I am a failure
- ❖ I am unwanted
- ❖ I am a burden
- ❖ I am guilty
- ❖ I am a fake
- ❖ I am illegitimate
- ❖ I am stupid.
- ❖ I am slow.
- ❖ I am an intrusion
- ❖ and on and on

❡ You have to get the exact right one in order to be liberated, and that is what Liberation Breathing is for, for one thing. This thought has to be identified, changed, AND breathed out of the cells. Yes, we hold negative thoughts in our cellular memory. That is why breathwork is so important for clearing ourselves of the past. More later.

Love, Sondra

October 1, 2016

❡ CLEARING YOUR BIRTH TRAUMA
You may wonder why on earth you have to look at your birth script to improve your relationships. Most of us had some

trauma in our conception, pregnancy, birth, or post-partum. All this is your birth script. I can tell you that your birth trauma is one of the biggest saboteurs you have going. But most people have no idea about that.

❡ That is why you have to look at it and study it. That is why we called breathwork "Rebirthing" in the beginning. We were clear that conscious connected breathing could get people in touch with their birth scripts, and we were aware that people needed to go back to clear these things with the breathing. The breathing actually helps people release the unconscious birth trauma.

❡ Even in a "normal" birth there is a lot of trauma. You could have been terrified coming down the birth canal and then there were the bright lights, and they handled you roughly, and they did all kinds of tests on you. The worst thing was the umbilical cord was cut too fast, and then you were choking on your amniotic fluid. Your first breath was then horrible, and most people breathe shallowly today as a result. They may have hung you upside down and slapped you to get the fluid out. All this is intolerable for a baby. Then separation from your mother was the worst thing that could have happened.

❡ All babies form pre-verbal negative thoughts through all this. These thoughts later ruin your life and definitely affect your relationships. The great thing is this: we are trained to pull out these damaging thoughts from your subconscious and help you breathe them out in a Liberation Breathing Session.

❡ We can liberate you from them, hence we call it Liberation Breathing now; and we do prayers to the Divine Mother that help in this. In the womb we were in bliss and really connected to the Source. All this changed when we came out, as it felt like all hell broke loose. Can you imagine the difference when you let go of all this trauma? Think about it. We can help with this!

Love, Sondra
October 2, 2016

❡ CONCEPTION TRAUMA

What if during your conception you were unwanted, unplanned, or a mistake? What if it was forced in a rape-like manner? What if your mother went off birth control without telling your father? Any of this would of course be a conception trauma.

❡ You or your mate could have this situation. If you were unwanted at conception, you may choose mates who do not want you. Or if someone wants you, then you don't want them! If conception was unplanned or a mistake, then the conception of your relationships could be off. The conception of your business projects could be off. The whole conception of anything could be "unconscious."

❡ If your parents did not consciously choose your conception, maybe you have never really chosen to be here! You could have a preverbal thought "I am not wanted" or "I shouldn't be here." That would be your *personal lie* related to your *conception trauma*. Remember that consciousness exists before conception. Anything that happens at your conception is recorded in your memory and is still repeating its negative effects until it is neutralized through forgiveness.

Love, Sondra

October 3, 2016

❡ PRENATAL TRAUMA

It could start when your mom took her pregnancy test. Was she glad? Upset? How did your father react? All this is recorded in your consciousness, as consciousness exists before conception. Did she have terrible morning sickness? How were your parents getting along when you entered your body?

❡ If anything unusual happened while you were in the womb, you may have wanted to get out of there quickly. You could have been premature as a result. If something very traumatic happened while you were in the womb, like an accident or a death in the family or whatever, you could have had a lot of shock and formed negative decisions such as "I am not safe" or "the universe is dangerous."

❡ Prenatal and Preverbal thought is formed early in your

239

incarnation and it affects you a lot later. What if your mother smoked or drank during your prenatal period? This could have led to a toxic womb. If she was very negative herself, you could have experienced an emotionally toxic womb. You may attract toxic environments or toxic relationships if your womb was toxic. If you did not like it in the womb and had wished you were not there, you could fear entrapment in a relationship or resist it. You may need to demand space in a relationship. If your parents were fighting while you were in the womb, that would surely affect you.

❡ If you would *really* like to explore this whole subject more, read the book *The Secret Life of the Unborn Child*, by Dr. Thomas Verney. If you know anyone who is thinking of getting pregnant, or just found out they are pregnant, please refer that book to them or buy it as a gift for them.
Love, Sondra

October 4, 2016

❡ ANGEL FIRE, NEW MEXICO
Angel Fire, NM, is named for the fiery afternoon light on the peaks. The Ute Indians used to gather to renew their ancestral ties with the Great Spirit here. During one of those celebrations during the 1780s, three young braves returned to camp from a hunting trip and told of a strange glow at the tip of a peak. The Utes were unsettled as they gazed at this mysterious splash of orange and red flickering in the Northern Sky. Then the awed silence was broken as one of the elders exclaimed it was an omen and blessing—the "fire of the gods." Thereafter, whenever that rosy glow was seen, it was called the fire of the gods. Kit Carson said he too had seen the *angel of fire* at dawn and dusk.

❡ It is a very beautiful ski resort now. Markus wanted to bring me here to show it to me, as he once had taken a forty-day retreat here with his teacher, Tara Singh, who taught him *A Course in Miracles*. Now we are on our way back to Santa Fe after having our Skype client from Istanbul.
Love, Sondra

October 6, 2016

❡ BIRTH TRAUMA
If your mother had tremendous pain upon delivery, you could end up thinking you hurt women or hurt people (primal guilt). This is unconscious of course, but you could end up with the preverbal thought, "I hurt the one I really love." These kinds of preverbal, subconscious thoughts produce heavy results for you. This could cause you to shut down your aliveness.

❡ You could also decide you are *bad* because you caused your mother so much pain. The thought "I am bad" creates bad experiences then.

❡ If your mother had drugs, you might have been heavily drugged as an infant, and this can cause addictions for you later on. Once I rebirthed a psychiatrist in Paris, and so many drugs came out of his body that I had to run and open the hotel window for air. He swore he had no drugs in his life and no surgeries. The smell was all due to the drugs at birth which came out of his body when he breathed. He kind of shouted, "I have had no idea what it feels like to be really alive until now!" He was thrilled with the session,

❡ So much goes on in the first five minutes of life that it is important to look at how all this affects you. We can get people down to that memory and clear it in Liberation Breathing. What if you got stuck in the birth canal? You could have a preverbal thought "I am stuck." Then you are not moving forward in your life, or you are feeling stuck all the time. Think about it.
Love, Sondra

October 7, 2016

❡ OBSTETRICIAN SYNDROME
The obstetrician is the first person who physically supports, guides, coaches, and controls us; they may also manipulate us or hurt us at the same time. A baby roughly handled at birth may become mistrusting later on of any form of authority figure or may even dislike positive support from a

partner (if the partner is "set up" as the obstetrician). You may resent relationships that are at all like *authority figures*. Your mate might try to support you, but you interpret it as hurtful. This can cause confusion. I had a client who disliked physical affection/touching because of the way her obstetrician originally handled her.

¶ Then there is the big problem of being taken away from your mother and being put in the nursery. This causes tremendous "separation anxiety" later on. A baby should be next to the mother at all times during the first weeks of life, and especially the first minutes of life, unless there is an extreme medical reason that prevents that.

¶ In Bali babies are held next to the parents' bodies for months, and when the baby is finally put down, they have a religious ceremony. They grow up with tremendous self-esteem and safety. Think about it.

Love, Sondra

October 8, 2016

¶ NIGHT SCHOOL
IT IS VERY EXCITING to be in the Las Vegas LRT. There are 30+ people in the room, thanks to our organizer Mike, and his wife Ali. They are very good organizers to put it mildly. We had around five or six people who were having their very first Liberation Breathing session last night. They had amazing experiences. One had a memory of her birth and her postpartum period, and that totally explained her life pattern. She was astonished. And she was able to let it all go!

¶ During the night I dreamed the following: I had each person come to me and tell me their biggest problem. Then I took it from them, transmuting it, and they were released of it. Working all night in my sleep—I call it my "night school."

Love, Sondra

October 9, 2016

¶ TWINS AT THE LAS VEGAS LRT

Saturday the LRT went exceptionally well. We were amazed to find we had so many twins in the training. This gave a special effect.

❡ In one case one was left behind and the other adopted. In another case one was left behind for months very sick, while the other one got to go home. In another case the mother delivered one plus the placenta, and then went back to her room. Only later after she was "done" with the birth did she discover there was another one in there coming out! You can imagine how all these cases were complex and affecting the remaining twin. Other people had twins in their family who were not there, so they were very affected by these stories also.

❡ Afterwards, we went out to the luxurious Bellagio Hotel, which is incredibly beautiful with its showcase of beautiful floral art which is so breathtaking. There are also 2,000 hand blown glass flowers from the artist Dale Chihuly hanging from the ceiling, which cover 2,000 square feet in the lobby! I have never seen such a large casino in my life. Las Vegas was hopping on Saturday night!

Love, Sondra

October 10, 2016

❡ HUGE SHIFTS

People made huge shifts in the Las Vegas LRT. I found that there were many people who had chronic pain in their body—especially in their backs. I taught them how to process that with the Ultimate Truth Process:

> Step One: The exact negative thought that caused this pain was_____.
> Step Two: My *payoff* for hanging on to this pain is_____. (A payoff is a *neurotic benefit*.)
> Step Three: My fear of giving it up forever is_____.
> Step Four: If this pain could talk, what it would say is_____.
> Step Five: I will let go of this pain when_____.

Step Six: The affirmation I need to think to heal this condition is_____.

¶ All this information is extremely helpful in clearing the pain. It is also important to look at when you first became aware of the condition, and what was going on in your life at that exact time. In other words, what was the triggering factor? The mind is often stuck back at that incident, and the memory must be forgiven and breathed out.
¶ People were so happy to get out of pain, and everyone had great breathing sessions.
Love, Sondra

October 11, 2016

¶ FORMULA FOR HAPPINESS
Wouldn't it be nice to have an actual *formula* for happiness? I can give you one. But each person in a relationship is responsible for his or her happiness. In ACIM, Jesus says, "God's will for you is perfect happiness." That's from Lesson #101 in the Workbook. (Some people learned in church that there is holiness derived from suffering and they site Jesus's suffering as an example.) It has been said that Joy is the highest expression of God that there is. If we wish for Joy in our lives, we must remember that we were made in the image of God, and we are God-like. Loving God is Pure Joy!
¶ Babaji Himself gave us the actual *formula for happiness*, and here it is: TRUTH, SIMPLICITY, LOVE & SERVICE TO HUMANITY. Then he gave the mantra Om Namah Shivay, and the breathwork process of Liberation Breathing / Rebirthing as the tools to keep ourselves clear.
¶ But He constantly repeated that our highest duty was service to mankind. He used to proclaim that, "Work is worship, and idleness is death." Work dedicated to God is called Karma Yoga. Your line of service could be cultural, political, scientific, religious, philosophical, psychological, financial, or whatever. Your current work could be your service if you have the right attitude. If you are unclear what

it should be, start offering up your willingness for the Divine Plan of your life to manifest.

ℐ Are you willing to be one of the new group of world servers? For me the Peace Corps was my boot camp for world service. Read the book *Serving Humanity* by Alice Bailey.

Love, Sondra

October 12, 2016

ℐ SOME DYNAMITE AFFIRMATIONS

I am always on the lookout for positive thoughts which can transform our consciousness and our life. Here are some that I have written down and have been using for myself lately:

1. I am alive with the light of God and a blessing wherever I go.
2. I am the living energy of Pure Spirit.
3. I take on the vibration of the most-high now.
4. When my attention is on the Presence, I bring what I need into this dimension.
5. Every day I am going to be aware of the Presence.
6. My decisions are not made from lack; but from overflow consciousness.
7. I am fasting from that which would bring me down.
8. I am moving from the mundane to the miraculous.
9. What I want benefits others.
10. I wake up in the morning with my mind staying on the Spirit.
11. My consciousness vibrates with the infinite, invisible supply.
12. I see what is glorious about others.
13. The Eternal fountain of Love showers its blessings on me.
14. I create Heaven wherever I am.
15. I am more interested in the vibration of God

than my problem.

These were inspired by my minister at Agape, Rev. Michael Beckwith.
Love, Sondra

October 13, 2016

♪ DYNAMITE AFFIRMATIONS (continued)
Here are more affirmations I have been using lately:

1. The cosmic good of God expresses as my life.
2. I appreciate and celebrate each moment.
3. My conversations are always life affirming.
4. God is revealed through the generosity of my heart and the brilliance of my mind.
5. I gratefully say YES to good, YES to life, and YES to my greatness.
6. I am getting better and better and better for the rest of my life.
7. I am in the frequency of newness. I make all things new.
8. I am a strong attractor field.
9. I invite universal wisdom to give me guidance now.
10. My Joy is the evidence of God.
11. My love is greater than my past. The best is yet to come.
12. I am liberated from conventional thinking.
13. I see the perfect divine blueprint in each person.
14. My body temple is made from genius mind.
15. I incarnated with the brilliance of the universe within me.
16. Lives are changed when I walk in the room.

♪ I particularly like these two combined: "My Joy is the evidence of God, which changes lives when I walk in the room." More tomorrow.   Love, Sondra

October 14, 2016

❡ MORE FROM REV. MICHAEL BERNARD BECKWITH

1. I am willing to change according to new information.
2. I unhook from the agreement of mediocrity and make an agreement for excellence.
3. I step into the vibration of a Sage with no age.
4. I am here for something bigger than personal success. I am here for planetary success.
5. My life is a sacred practice of gratitude.
6. I have the sheer happiness of being alive.
7. I release anything that would inhibit the flow of life.
8. I totally let go and let God.
9. I am willing to let the shift to occur here.
10. I am an ambassador of the invisible dimensions.
11. God is asking me to do something. He has me on redial.
12. I have the intention of bliss and ecstasy.
13. If I am not happy, I am out of integrity with my soul.
14. I am available to only the highest and the best.
15. I don't want to carry who I was five minutes ago into the future.
16. I am living from inspiration now.

❡ Thank you Rev. Michael, for these affirmations. And thank you for my all-time favorite words of wisdom from you in these: "Be *not against* anything, but *be for* something."
Love, Sondra

October 15, 2016

❡ NOTES ON HEALING FROM ACIM - PART 1
I take a lot of notes out of ACIM for my healing classes. I also study this material for myself! ACIM is the most important book written in 2000 years. These passages are paraphrased from my 40+ years of studying it. Are you studying it? If yes, I bow to you. If not, why not?

❖ *"When the ego tempts you to sickness, do not ask the Holy Spirit to heal the body, for this would merely be to accept the ego's belief that the body is the proper aim of healing. (The mind is what needs healing.) Ask rather then that the Holy Spirit teach you the right perception of the body—Wholeness heals because it is of the mind."*

❖ *"All forms of sickness (even unto death) are physical expressions of fear of awakening. Waking is joining. Healing is the release from fear of waking, and the substitution of the decision to wake. The decision to wake is the reflection of the will to love, since all healing involves replacing fear with love."*

⸚ As a nurse, it was hard for me to understand what ACIM says—that one thing is not harder to heal than another. I could not imagine healing cancer was as easy as healing a common cold. Here is ACIM's explanation:

❖ *"The Holy Spirit cannot distinguish among degrees of error, for if He taught that one form of sickness is more serious than another, He would be teaching that one error can be more real than another."*

❖ *"The miracles the Holy Spirit inspires can have no order of difficulty because every part of creation is of one order. Healing must occur in the place where it is needed, i.e., in the mind that conceived of the insane idea of separation."*

Love, Sondra

October 16, 2016

⸚ NOTES ON HEALING FROM ACIM - PART 2

❖ *"Healing is the one ability everyone can develop and must develop if he is to be healed. Healing is the Holy Spirit's form of communication in this world, and the only one He accepts. Healing only strengthens. Healing that is of the Holy Spirit ALWAYS works. Unless the healer always heals by HIM, the results will vary."*

❖ *"The unification of purpose (Christ Mind in the world = forgiveness) is the Holy Spirit's only way of healing. It is the only level at which healing means anything. The Bible says you can accomplish all things in His Name; but it is not His name alone. The name of God's Son is One. Since sickness is a problem of guilt in the mind, healing must be of the mind as well."*

❖ *"When a brother perceives himself as sick, he perceives himself as not whole and therefore in need. If you, too, see him this way, you are seeing him as if he were absent from the Kingdom or separated from it; thus, making the Kingdom itself obscure to both of you. Sickness and separation are not of God, but the Kingdom is! In the Kingdom there is only Certainty. To be in the Kingdom is merely to focus your full attention on it."*

❖ *"Health is the beginning of the proper perspective on life under the guidance of the Teacher who knows what life is, being the Voice for life itself."*

❡ These passages are so beautiful. I hope you enjoy reading them as much as I do!
Love, Sondra

October 17, 2016

❡ NOTES ON HEALING FROM ACIM - PART 3
❖ *"What if you ask the Holy Spirit for what you want, but you are afraid of it? THIS IS WHY CERTAIN SPECIFIC FORMS OF HEALING ARE*

NOT ACHIEVED EVEN WHEN THE STATE OF HEALING IS."

¶ Why would people have a fear of healing and often not realize it? The answer could be because they are not used to the Joy the healing would give. People are not aware that they are afraid of Joy. They don't think they deserve it, or they are too guilty to let it in, that is my opinion.

¶ When Markus and I first got together it was hard for him to just relax and have fun. In his family there was a thought, "It's no fun to have fun." There was a lot of fear of having a good time! Can you imagine? So, he had to work with the affirmation, "It's fun to have fun!" Really! ACIM says its purpose is to escape from fear.

> ❖ *"Healing gladdens and always produces harmony. Healing can be counted on if it is inspired by HIS VOICE. Healing reflects our joint will. Healing is the way separation is overcome. Separation is overcome by union. ALL THINGS ARE POSSIBLE BY OUR JOINT DECISION. To join with me (Jesus) is to restore His power to you because we are sharing it. Health is nothing more than a united purpose."*
>
> ❖ *"Say this: 'I renounce the ego in myself'. Healing is the result of using the body solely for communication. Sickness is based on these two premises of the ego:*
> *1) the body is for attack 2) you are the body. However, DO NOT let the body reflect your decision to attack (by getting angry)."*
>
> ❖ *"Sickness is a way of demonstrating that you can get hurt. The ego has a profound investment in sickness. A sick body does not make any sense. Sickness is not what the body is for. Affirm "I choose not to accept anything but the truth."*

¶ Health is a natural state of everything when interpretation is left to the Holy Spirit.   Love, Sondra

October 18, 2016

❡ NOTES ON HEALING FROM ACIM - PART 4
I'm on a roll here when it comes to what *ACIM* says about
healing and health:

> ❖ *"Health is the result of relinquishing all attempts
> to use the body lovelessly."*
> ❖ *"If you are sick, you are withdrawing from Jesus
> and yourself. When you limit yourself, you are not of
> one mind, and that is sickness. Yet sickness is NOT
> of the body, but of the mind—a sign that the mind is
> split and does not accept a unified purpose."*
> ❖ *"To believe that a Son of God is sick is to
> worship the same idol he does. Sickness is
> IDOLATRY. Sickness is idolatry because it is the
> belief that power can be taken from you. When you
> do not value yourself you become sick, but His
> value of you can heal you."*
> ❖ *"When a brother is sick, it is because he is not
> asking for peace, and therefore does not know he
> has it. The acceptance of peace is the denial of
> illusion— and sickness is an illusion."*
> ❖ *"Jesus can heal you because He knows you. He
> knows your value and it is this value that makes you
> whole. YOU ALWAYS RECEIVE AS MUCH AS
> YOU CAN ACCEPT."*
> ❖ *"Sickness and perfection are irreconcilable. God
> created you perfect and if you believe you can be
> sick, you have placed other gods before him;
> (idolatry). The god of sickness is the symbol of
> deciding against God. If you refuse to worship this
> symbol, sickness will disappear into nothingness."*

❡ Wouldn't that be awesome! Enough on healing for now.
Hope you learned something.
Love, Sondra
October 19, 2016

❡ AN APPEARANCE OF THE DIVINE MOTHER

I am so happy today because Ammachi (the Divine Mother Herself) came to me during the night! This kind of darshan is rare; you cannot make it up. If you see Her, she really came to you!

♪ I had to make a difficult decision yesterday and She came to show me I had done the right thing! I was honored to be able to bow before Her. Except in the vision I was embarrassed as I had only my pajamas on. That was because someone had taken all my clothes! I could not find them anywhere. I wanted to ask Her what that was about. A yogi stopped me as I was getting in line. He had seen that I had already had the opportunity to bow to Her, so he wanted to know what was my rush. I told him what had happened, and that I needed to find out who took my clothes. He said, "Oh, it is because you have become so pure." Then I quipped, "But I have already been a sadhu in too many lifetimes," (not wanting to do that again). We both laughed. Then I woke up.

♪ Today I feel good that I did the right thing and that I saw Her. I have not really had the opportunity to go to Her locations on Her tour this year, as I was always booked when She was anywhere near. So, She came to me, knowing I had a troubling situation. What a blessing.

♪ In India we sing this awesome passage to the Divine Mother:

> *"Destroyer of pangs, illusions and fears of the world,*
> *Remover of obstacles on the way to spiritual perfection,*
> *Your heart easily melts with mercy, Goddess of all.*
> *Hail to Thee, O Universal Mother, Consort of Shiva."*

Love, Sondra

October 20, 2016

♪ LIFTING OURSELVES TO THE FREQUENCIES

OF LIGHT AND HARMONY

By embracing gratitude, we can easily do this. A grateful heart is a radiating force field of light that adds light to the world. As light workers, we should be saying and feeling this: "My whole life is a sacred practice of gratitude. Every breath is a divine privilege."

❡ When we feel gratitude, our energy is so harmonious that it permeates our bodies and blesses people around us. It is proven that love and gratitude transform the molecular structure of water. Our body is made up of water. We know this. But do we remember that EXPRESSING gratitude is very therapeutic? It raises our consciousness, creates a happy mind, a healthy body, and sustains the gift of life. Someone said: "All things are in a state of silent rejoicing that their consciousness is an expression of Divinity." If we realize this, we will see why everything deserves reverence.

❡ Ammachi told a story about an old man who was planting mango trees. When his neighbor saw what he was doing, he came to him and said, "Do you actually think you will live long enough to taste the mangoes from those trees?" "No, I doubt it," said the old man.

❡ "Then why are you wasting your time?" asked the neighbor. The old man smiled and said: "All my life I have enjoyed eating mangoes from trees that have been planted by others before me. This is my way of expressing my thankfulness to the people who planted them."

❡ Have you read the book *The Magic* by Rhonda Byrne? Have you read the book *The Path of Wealth* by May McCarthy? If not, order them today! They are all about living and expressing gratitude.

Love, Sondra

October 21, 2016

❡ LAST NIGHT MARKUS GAVE ME A SURPRISE TREAT Markus's spiritual Teacher, Tara Singh, and his teacher, Krishnamurti, lived in Ojai, CA. Since we will be doing a training in Ojai, he came up with an old movie filmed there. It was filmed in 1935. It was in black and white and some parts of the film did not even work, only the sound. The title was *Lost Horizons*.

❡ It was about these people whose plane went down over Tibet. They were rescued by Tibetan people who took them to a secret valley which was called Shangri-La. Everything was pure beauty and had been materialized to perfection. The energy and beauty were so perfect that nobody aged. This was fascinating. All needs were met, and there was not one thing one could complain about.

❡ They got so happy that most of them could not stand it. They ended up trying to escape and go back to their country. But the leader of the party really got what the place was, and he was chosen to take over by the head Llama. However, his team eventually tried to talk him out of staying there.

❡ He had fallen in love with the goddess there, and her name was actually Sondra—spelled with an "O." During one weak moment, his brother convinced him to leave, and he got the porters arranged.

❡ The trek out was very, very difficult, and the team perished except for him. He spent years trying to get back there—and finally made it in the end.

❡ His younger brother stole a woman of Shangri La away with him, and as soon as she left the valley, she started aging suddenly. She turned into an old hag with her face shriveling, to reflect her real age. This freaked his brother out, and he got himself caught in an avalanche. All but the older brother died. Fascinating.

❡ How often we try to get rid of bliss. What a plot! We sabotage it; this is what *A Course in Miracles* talks about. We turn heaven into hell all the time, and then we try like mad to get back to heaven. But because we chose to leave heaven consciousness, it is more difficult to get back to heaven than just learning to stay there.

Love, Sondra

October 22, 2016

¶ DANGER OF DENIAL

I have noticed that people come for sessions and yet, when we ask them what they want to improve, they may say, "Oh everything is fine." This turns out to be really ridiculous because after probing, I find out that they have so much going on that it is overwhelming—even to me. They don't want to admit it; and yet they finally tell us their wife is having an affair with someone else, or they themselves are having an affair to get even. They may be out of work. They are not getting any sex. Their kids are addicted to stupid on-line games or drugs. They cannot communicate with their mates. They are stuck in their *personal lies*, etc., etc., etc. They have A LOT going on!

¶ I might tell them to write down their fears, but they say they have no fears; and yet I can clearly see they are frozen. They say they have no anger, but they are seething and withholding on their mate as a get-even tactic. As a Breathworker, I feel it is important to point out that they are fooling themselves. I cannot hold back what I see. If I don't speak up, it makes ME sick. It sometimes takes courage to push people out of denial; but If I don't do it, who will? Lately I have gone as far as to say: "It sounds to me like you are lying to yourself."

¶ I have become very ALERT when people tell me they have nothing going on—usually this means it is quite the opposite. So, I am studying denial as a defense system. Obviously, they want help, or they would not bother coming to the seminar or for a session. I flat out don't buy it at all. Perhaps they think it is easier to stay in denial than face deep stuff. But, of course, it is harder to keep the deep stuff because sooner or later it will catch up with them and they will be sick or whatever.

¶ Sometimes I say, "Your mind is set up to not have things work." People often need a shock to get out of denial. There was a woman who came to the LRT who skipped Saturday to play golf, and she was also late on Sunday. Friday night, when I had gone to her during the breathe, she said she had nothing going on.

¶ Sunday, after the training, I heard she had a stroke.

¶ A humble person RECOGNIZES HIS ERRORS, ADMITS THEM, AND DOES SOMETHING ABOUT THEM. So, what are you in denial about?
Love, Sondra

October 23, 2016

¶ MORE ON AGORAPHOBIA
Agoraphobia is extreme or irrational fear of crowded places, with the need to stay inside and not go out. For our client, to even get to us for the Liberation Breathing Session took extreme courage. I felt she must be ready to be healed in order to get herself to us. Nobody had been able to help her with this condition; but now she felt like she absolutely had to leave her marriage, as she just did not feel accepted and she could not stand that any longer. She wanted to move out from him and move in with a friend, but she had to handle her condition first.

¶ Her interview took a long time. She had an extreme case of self-hatred, and said she felt like garbage. It took a long time to unravel her mind; I would have to say that she really did need someone who was a Breathworker who understood birth scripts.

¶ It turned out that right before her birth, her father's father died. So, when she came out, there was only death. That was one factor.

¶ She was afraid to go out also because she would be rejected, she thought. She had been bullied when she was young, and she did not feel good about anything in her life. The odd part is that at home she was already being rejected by her husband, and yet she was afraid to go out as she might be rejected. She had it set up to get rejected no matter what.

¶ She kept telling us she was garbage, but in the end her *personal lie* was "I am unacceptable." She kept creating rejection to prove she was unacceptable garbage. This horrible fear of rejection and fear of death being all around added up to being the cause of her condition. The amazing part is that she totally got it after one session. She was fortunately so ripe for change that she was completely open

to us. She was ecstatic to have the understanding and she saw how she was even creating being unaccepted at home. She chose to move out and start over, however. Once again, Liberation Breathing worked miracles.
Love, Sondra

October 24, 2016

❧ A SUICIDAL CLIENT
A suicidal woman came to us in a foreign country. She arrived in worse shape than any client had ever arrived. She could not even tolerate breathing. She just wanted to drown herself and she cried the whole time. There was only one approach we could use, and it was this: We took turns holding her in our arms and loved her with all our might. Then we told her to lie down, and we read the Divine Mother prayers and recited the mantra. Eventually her negative thoughts came out: "I am too weak," and, "I should not even be here." We must have gotten through to her as she said suddenly: "I think my boyfriend would like you to come to his Indian restaurant."

❧ We accepted this invitation as we wanted to get clearer on her situation and see what else we could do. She could not work so we of course did not charge her. I knew she did not really want to die, or she never would have bothered to find us. She was not able to drive so she had taken a bus to the place where we were, a whole hour out of city center.

❧ The next night we went to the restaurant. She was much better. Her boyfriend was a wonderful, a brilliant man who had gone to Yale. During the dinner we suggested she come back for another session. She even drove her car by herself that day, something she had not done for ages. We had her do gentle nasal breathing. We told her how great it was she had manifested such a nice boyfriend and we worked further in helping her release those negative thoughts.

❧ The miracle was that she breathed the whole session and when we did the Divine Mother prayers, joy came out of her for the first time in years, she said. She told us she wanted to get strong enough to marry this man and have his child!

257

Right then he called us and asked for a session himself. Of course, she needed follow up by other Breathworkers, which we arranged. This is someone who had been in a mental hospital twice, but no therapy had helped her because nobody had ever processed her thoughts. I love the victories of Liberation Breathing.
Love, Sondra

October 26, 2016

❡ I WONDER WHY
Hmm, I wonder why I got 184 hits when writing about suicide? Is it because people like the macabre or is it because people are depressed? Now I want to balance that by writing about Joy. But will as many read it? Maybe Joy seems too far out of reach? To me it is definitely not boring. Since JOY is the highest expression of God that there is, wouldn't people want that? ACIM says this:

> ❖ *"LIVING IS JOY, but death can only weep. You see in death escape from what you made. But this you do not see: that you made death. It is not life in which the problem lies. Life has no opposite, for it is God."*
> ❖ *"There is one thought in particular that should be remembered throughout the day. It is a thought of pure joy; a thought of peace, a thought of limitless release. Limitless because all things are freed within it."*

❡ Maybe here is the answer to my question:

> ❖ *"The ego is afraid of Spirit's Joy, because once you have experienced it, you will withdraw all protection from the ego, and become totally without investment in fear."*
> ❖ *"When your mood tells you that you have chosen wrongly (and this is so whenever you are not joyous), then know this need not be."*

❖ *"I am teaching you to associate misery with the ego and Joy with the Spirit. You have taught yourself the opposite. You are still free to choose, but can you really want the rewards of the ego in the presence of the rewards of God?"*

❖ *"Only when you see you are guiltless will you be happy. As long as you believe the Son of God is guilty (that would be you), you will walk along the carpet leading to death! And the journey will seem long and cruel and senseless, for so it is."*

Love, Sondra

October 27, 2016

♫ FOR FUN
Just for fun, we watched a documentary on the life of Elvis Presley. It is very interesting to look at his "case" as we say in Breathwork.

♫ He was born a twin, but his other twin was born dead. This birth trauma ran his whole life, as he never ever got over survivor's guilt. And as a result, his mother over protected him and made him totally dependent on her, (We call this the *emotional incest* pattern.) When his mother died at 42, he never really recovered from that. His personal lie was obviously, "I am guilty for being alive."

♫ When he married Priscilla, he totally set her up as his mom. When she got pregnant, he no longer could have sex with her because it was too incestuous. (That I read in an article by Priscilla herself!) So then he had a lot of affairs which added to his guilt. He suppressed all his guilt by taking drugs which eventually killed him. The amazing thing is he died exactly the same age as his mom: 42! (That is being a conformist.) So, this great talent was destroyed by his case. We could have helped him with this in Liberation Breathing. Too bad!

♫ Same with Michael Jackson. In fact, he actually had two chances to have a session with me. He did not do it. His personal lie was obviously, "I am bad." That was his hit record that made him millions, you know, and that thought

he acted out plenty. I asked my guru Shastriji why he was planted in front of me twice. He said that Babaji had given him a chance to get healed because he and I had been with Babaji in another materialization in another life. Too bad I did not get to help him in this life.
Love, Sondra

October 28, 2016

❡ GUILT KILLS PEOPLE
Since guilt kills people (like Elvis), let's talk about it. There is past life guilt, primal guilt for hurting one's mother at birth, religious guilt (for thinking you are separate from God when you took a body), and whatever else one is guilty about. That adds up to a lot of guilt.

❡ The one thing we have to realize about guilt is that all guilt demands punishment. The main way people punish themselves is to get sick and ultimately die. Other forms of punishment may be getting rid of love, getting rid of money, failing in general, or hurting yourself emotionally or physically.

❡ ACIM says guilt is not of God, it is an attack on God.

❡ David Hawkins wrote that regret and guilt result from equating the present self that IS with the former self that WAS, but actually is no more. He says it is another form of egotism in which error is inflated instead of being relinquished to a higher power. In this form of egotism, the self becomes blown up, exaggerated, and the ego re-energizes itself through the negativity. Wallowing in guilt feeds the ego and is an indulgence!

❡ There has to be a willingness to surrender it. By spiritual alignment, the past circumstances underlying the guilt are re-contextualized under the influence of spiritual energy. Giving it up is a decision. One either clings to it and thereby gets the juice of the drama of guilt or gives it up. This is the point of the decision without which healing cannot occur. This decision has actual consequences in the brain's physiology. One has to invite in the Divine Mother/Holy Spirit/ guru.

❡ The invitation starts the transformation through the

presence of the healing power of grace. But you have to know that the ego loves suffering a wrong and perpetuates the suffering. The ego will tell you that if you DARE to think you are innocent, then you are really guilty! You have to pass through that trick of the ego. The ego cannot lift you out of this mess with all its might. Only the grace of the Holy Spirit can. Guilt becomes like the lightness of feathers if you surrender to the grace of God.

Love, Sondra

October 29, 2016

❡ THE REAL DANGER OF THINKING YOU ARE UNWORTHY & GUILTY

Here is what *ACIM* says:

> *"Remember, if you have judged yourself unworthy you have condemned yourself to death. The death penalty is the ego's ultimate goal, for it fully believes you are a criminal, as deserving of death as God knows you are deserving of life. The death penalty never leaves the ego's mind, for that is what it always reserves for you in the end. Wanting to kill you as the final expression of its feeling for you, it lets you live but to await death. It will torment you while you live, but its hatred is not satisfied until you die. For your destruction is the one end toward which it works, and the only end with which it will be satisfied. It is a traitor to you who believes you have been treacherous to our Father. That is why the undoing of guilt is an essential part of the Holy Spirit's teaching.*
>
> *❡ For as long as you feel guilty, you are listening to the voice of the ego, which tells you: "You deserve death." You will think that death comes from God and not from the ego because, by confusing yourself with the ego, you believe you want death.*
>
> *❡ When you are tempted to yield to the desire for death, REMEMBER THAT I DID NOT DIE [Jesus speaking]. You will realize that this is true when you*

look within and see me. Would I have overcome death for myself alone? And would eternal life have been given me of the Father unless He had also given it to you? When you learn to make me manifest, you will never see death!"

ᔎ These very powerful words are from the Text in a Section called "Looking Within." (ACIM, Text, chap. 12, sec. VII) Love, Sondra

October 31, 2016

ᔎ LOOKING GOOD ALL THE TIME
Can you see that I am trying to lighten up? Here is what I feel like talking about today: Looking good all the time. When you feel wonderful you are likely to look wonderful. This makes you feel even more wonderful. Looking fabulous raises your self-esteem and energy and makes you feel more alive. In this way you also attract more prosperity and fun to yourself. Besides, when you look good, feel good, and smell good, people are often healed in your presence and you are an inspiration. Today I was in a store and a black man started asking loudly, "What is that wonderful smell? From where is it coming?" He seemed to be dancing into it. "Well perhaps it is my perfume," I said. I told him it was Rose Oil from India. He told me I made his day.
ᔎ It is often said a person "wears his mind." Some people do not even care to iron their clothes or think about design. The way you dress is your art, and it says a lot about you. People form an opinion of you in 5 seconds, you know. Do you care about other people's experience of you? Are you willing to give them a pleasant experience? I live with an artist and that is very uplifting. He inspires me to dress up even at home, whether I go out or not. He does not require this, but I am inspired myself to dress up, regardless of who might see me. Dressing up makes me feel good! I even wear costume jewelry.
ᔎ Markus really appreciates my taste. He deserves to see me always looking good at home in my opinion. In my neighborhood, people see me walking around and always

make a lot of good comments. When I go to the grocery store the checker announces, "Author on the floor." It is really fun. I get a lot of compliments because most people don't dress up to go grocery shopping. Now, I am not dressed to the nines. It is always appropriate. But people like Pizzazz.

♪ Why not put yourself out there? If you get a compliment, hand them your business card. That is what I do. Once I went into a bar waiting for a movie to start across the street. A man at the bar came up and actually told me this, "When I saw you, I decided not to kill myself."

♪ I said, "Oh, were you at my book signing last night?" He said, "No, I am talking about right now!" That is the immortality factor he tuned into, and I was dressed just right.

♪ See, how you dress could save someone's life!
Love, Sondra

November 1, 2016

♪ A SPEECH BY BABAJI

> *Love and serve all humanity.*
> *Assist everyone.*
> *Be cheerful. Be courteous.*
> *Be a dynamo of irrepressible happiness.*
> *See God and good in every face.*
> *There is no Saint without a past.*
> *There is no sinner without a future.*
> *Praise every soul.*
> *If you cannot praise someone—*
> *Let them pass out of your life.*
> *Be original. Be inventive.*
> *Dare, dare, and then dare more.*
> *Do not imitate. Stand on your own ground.*
> *Do not lean on the borrowed staff of others.*
> *Think your own thoughts.*
> *Be yourself.*
> *All perfection and all virtues of the*
> *Deity are hidden inside you.*

Reveal them.
The Savior, also, is already within you.
Reveal Him.
Let His grace emancipate you.
Let your life be that of a rose.
Though silent it speaks in the language
of fragrance.
   —Sri Sri 1008 Haidakhan Wale Babaji

Love, Sondra

November 2, 2016

❡ SITTING IN MY LIVING ROOM
I am so happy sitting in my living room doing my spiritual practice every morning; because everything I look at is beautiful. I have collected this sacred art over the years and Markus loved all of it.
❡ On the left wall are three Balinese goddesses who are praying. (In Bali, they actually place them in the rice fields to pray over the rice.) To the right is the Divine Mother Altar. The painting of the Divine Mother above the altar is simply gorgeous. The first time I saw it years ago it emitted the smell of roses for 15 whole minutes. People are mesmerized by it. On the top level of the altar is a small lovely statue of Quan Yin, modeled after the famous Quan Yin at the Nelson-Atkins Museum in Kansas City. On the left of Her is a photo of the Virgin Mary. On the right of Her is a photo of Ammachi. The altar cloth itself is a sheer nude beauty with sparkles on it done in Mexico, but of exquisite design. On the lower shelf are very wonderful photos of Babaji, Muniraj, and Shastriji, who are my main male teachers. There is another Balinese statue praying over them. In the corner is a tall wooden carving of Quan Yin placed on a special stand. (Once, when we lived in Los Angeles, there was an earthquake. I shouted out, "What do I do?" Markus said, "Grab the Quan Yin," and so I did. (Otherwise, she would have toppled off her stand.)
❡ Next to the lovely sofa is a small table which is hand-crafted. On it stands a statue of the Snake Goddess from

the island of Crete.

❡ On the floor is a gorgeous rug from Kashmir, India. The design is gorgeous, and the colors are soft blue and very soft rose. In front of me is a beautiful Chinese blanket chest carved with scenes of immortals. It is placed like it is a coffee table. Above the door facing the swimming pool is a painting Markus did of Babaji, Jesus, and Ammachi. We call them the Dream Team; I love looking at that.

❡ To the left is a smaller altar to Babaji. Above that altar is a painting of Madame Pele, the Goddess of Volcanos. Her hair is formed by streams of molten lava flows and fire is going up her chakras.

❡ I suggest you consider making everything you look at in your living space something beautiful. It makes such a difference in your mood.

Love, Sondra

November 3, 2016

❡ DO YOU HAVE A MONEY REJECTION COMPLEX? Money is an effect. When you concentrate on the effect, you are forgetting the cause, and when you forget the cause, the effect begins to diminish. When you focus your attention on getting money, you are actually shutting off your supply. You must begin this very moment to cease believing that money is your substance, your supply, your support, your security, your safety. Money is not. God is. When you understand and realize this truth, the supply flows uninterrupted into perfect and abundant manifestation. You must look to God alone as THE Source and take your mind completely off the outer effect. If you look to your job, your employer, your spouse, or your investments as the source of your supply, you are cutting off the real Source. Don't shut down the flow.

❡ You must think of money simply as an outer symbol of an inner supply. Money is a symbol of an Idea in Divine Mind—the idea of an all-sufficiency of supply to meet every need. If your mind is on the Source, the Cause, the supply flows freely. People who have evolved consciousness attract all good things to them in overflowing measure and

continually experience the joy of abundant living. How rich can you be? As rich as you think you can be. Don't be content in just getting by. Critical thoughts and fear will hold back your good. Summarized from *The Abundance Book* by John R. Price.
Love, Sondra

November 4, 2016

♪ ON THE SUBJECT OF FEAR
I awoke in some fear that the training in California was not going to happen. I do not like the feeling of fear (nobody does), and so I knew I better start reading *ACIM* fast to get myself out of it. Here are some of the things I just read:

> ❖ *"The correction of fear is your responsibility. When you ask for release from fear, you are implying that it is not."*
> ❖ *"These conditions always entail a willingness to be separate. At that level you can help it. You are much too tolerant of mind wandering."*
> ❖ *"Before you do anything ask if your choice is in accord with mine [Jesus's]. If you are sure that it is, there will be no fear."*
> ❖ *"Fear is always a sign of strain, arising whenever what you want conflicts with what you do. Fear cannot be controlled by me [Jesus], but it can be self-controlled. Fear prevents me from giving you my control."*
> ❖ *"The presence of fear shows that you have raised body thoughts to the level of mind. This removes them from my [Jesus's] control. The fearful mind must miscreate. Any attempt to resolve the error through attempting the mastery of fear is useless. In fact, it asserts the power of fear by the very assumption that it need be mastered."*
> ❖ *"The true resolution rests entirely on mastery through love. Fear is really nothing and love is everything."*
> ❖ *"No one who lives in fear is really alive."*

❡ These are all powerful statements, yes? We all need to listen to the Masters to overcome fear in this world.
Love, Sondra

November 5, 2016

❡ MORE ON FEAR FROM ACIM

> ❖ *"A separated mind must be confused. It is uncertain about what it is. It has to be in conflict because it is out of accord with itself. This is the essence of a fear-prone condition. The ego's purpose is fear because only the fearful can be egotistic. Anything that engenders fear is divisive Fear does not gladden."*
>
> ❖ *"Healing is release from fear of waking. The decision to wake is the reflection of the will to love, since all healing involves replacing fear with love. The purpose of the course is the escape from fear. Do not be afraid then to look upon fear, for it cannot be seen. Clarity undoes confusion. To look upon darkness through light must dispel it."*
>
> ❖ *"The ego is fearful to you because you believe the ego has power. Yet in truth all power is of God, not the ego."*
>
> ❖ *"For only the insane would choose fear in place of love. Blessed are you who are willing to ask the truth of God without fear, for only thus can you learn that His answer is the release from fear. Fear and love are the only emotions of which you are capable. One is false for it was made out of denial. Deny its power to reveal love."*

Love, Sondra

November 7, 2016

❡ TRUE POWER

❡ We have had a lot of clients lately who are afraid to be in their power.

❡ They have past life memories for being killed or tortured when they were in their power, so they are holding themselves back in this life and shutting down. For them we have to start by redefining power.

❡ And then we have to show them that they were in the wrong kind of power in their past lives. What they called power before was really control and manipulation probably with anger thrown in.

❡ True power (spiritually) is LOVE/SAFETY/CERTAINTY A person who is safe has no anger whatsoever. A person who is certain, is certain that they are one with God. When you are in this kind of power, it is not dangerous at all. People get healed in your presence and you can lead.

❡ True power also lies in releasing resistance. Most people do not understand that there is power in relaxation; in letting go into love joy and bliss. If you hang around a Spiritual Master long enough you will experience the supreme relaxation they have, and you will see how much power they have to heal people. A truly relaxed person can let in the stream of well-being!

❡ The other reason people got killed or died who were misusing power is because they were guilty about that misuse and they had a death urge. Power and fame do not kill you. The death urge and the wrong thoughts kill you.

❡ Work toward consistent release of resistance, release of the death urge, and don't hold yourself back!
Love, Sondra

November 8, 2016

❡ MY THOUGHTS ON ELECTION DAY
Take time to remember the children, women, and men everywhere who live with injustice, poverty, and violence as constant companions.

❡ Take time to remember all the people in our country who have spent their lives helping make our world a community of justice, peace, and joy. What do we owe those who came here before us? We owe a lot of gratitude and determination to keep our nation safe.

𝔍 We have freedom, joy of friends, and opportunity. We are blessed to be part of this nation. We should keep progressing and try to be the best we can in our professions. We should approach any problem or duty with concentrated energy and execute it to perfection. The greater our will, the more inexhaustible the energy. As long as you work to serve the people and to please God, all cosmic forces will harmoniously assist you. Do everything with the greatest pleasure and spirit of service. Love your country. Every day do some good to help others. Keep your mind on the resolve to never lose your peace.
Love, Sondra

November 9, 2016

𝔍 THE KRANTI IS COMING
BABAJI said, "The KRANTI is coming!" We would say: "What is the KRANTI?" He would say it is a world-wide revolution.

𝔍 He said, "At all times, peace was established only after revolution. The earth has been crying out for it. This desire of the earth will be fulfilled. The revolution will come quickly. Great courage is necessary. No power in the world can stop this revolution. It will not be confined to any particular country, but the whole world will be engulfed."

𝔍 He talked about the fact that the leaders were busy safeguarding their positions, ignoring their people's needs, and were misguiding the public. New leaders, He said, would take over from the corrupt ones and will restore proper order. Prayer will be your safeguard, He said, plus the mantra "Om Namah Shivay." He said, "If you chant that, you can even defy death. Only he can survive who has spiritual courage. Without that, one is dead, though he is living."

𝔍 He kept on telling us how brave we must be. He told us to work hard to elevate humanity. He even said a time would come when there will be big cities where there was sea and there will be sea where there were cities. Babaji said he is in charge of the Kranti. Wouldn't it be great if you could be connected to Him then? Now you know why I encourage everyone to come to His home in Haidakhan, India, with us, at the end of March. See my website and come! India Quest.

❡ Other psychics say we are at a beginning time of a new civilization. Everything that is out of harmony will be dismantled. The earth will be restructured. This election is really a seismic evolutionary event. And we should embrace it no matter which way it turns out.

Love, Sondra

November 10, 2016

❡ WHO HAS THE LOVE OF CORRECTING THEMSELVES?

Markus told me that is always what his teacher Tara Singh used to ask. I wonder if people really can take in that question? Most people are just afraid of feedback and take it as criticism. But there is a difference between harsh criticism that hurts and instead someone pointing out something that needs to be corrected so the person can lift themselves higher.

❡ A long, long, time ago I saw the movie *Reds*. I was stunned that Warren Beatty could pull that off at such a young age. I had to let go of my judgement of him, then being the big Casanova of Hollywood. Later I read an article which was an interview of him. He was asked about making *Reds*, "How did you do that?" His answer was amazing. He said that he deliberately invited the toughest movie directors all over the world to come over and criticize him. Wow, I thought, that is really someone willing to have the love of correction. Ever since I read that, I ask my teachers in India to please correct me.

❡ Markus and I are used to it more than some, perhaps as we each had very tough teachers: Babaji and Tara Singh. One of the immediate benefits of living like this is you save time. Our teachers saved us decades of time by blasting us. Once Taraji's teacher, Jiddu Krishnamurti, was studying yoga. The yoga teacher asked him to demonstrate what he had already learned, which he did. Then the yogi told him everything he had learned was incorrect. As if on que, Krishnamurti said, "Dropped sir. Let's begin." That is *a love of correction!* A humble person recognizes his errors, admits them, and does something about them.

❡ Maybe your mate has been pointing our something you do not want to hear or handle. But they could be right about the matter you know.

Love, Sondra

November 11, 2016

❡ THE FIRST THING TO DO IS TO INTROSPECT

I am in an introspective mood. We must look and see what is standing in our way. Are there habits that need to be weeded out? Introspection is a mirror in which to see recesses of your mind that otherwise would remain hidden from you. If you cannot see what the block is, you can be sure you can get the help of a Breathworker who is very good at what we call "processing." Self-analysis is one secret to progress.

❡ Here is what Yogananda says on the subject:

> *"Millions of people never analyze themselves. Mentally they are mechanical products of the factory of their environment, preoccupied with breakfast, lunch and dinner, working and sleeping, and going here and there to be entertained. They don't know what or why they are seeking, or why they never realize complete happiness and lasting satisfaction. By evading self-analysis, people go on being robots, conditioned by their environment. True self-analysis is the greatest art of progress. Everyone should learn to analyze himself. At least write down your thoughts and aspirations daily. Most people don't change because they don't see their own faults. Don't hide from yourself. You must know yourself."*
> *Paramahansa Yogananda, (*From the book *Where There is Light)*

❡ When you have a result you don't like, ask yourself, "What was the negative thought that created that result?" (Try not to say, "I don't know." That comes from not looking.) The answer is within to why you created a situation or result you don't like. The answer will always be some negative thought you need to change.

❡ P.S. Today is my husband's birthday. I really, really acknowledge him for having the "love of correction" and willingness to always do self-analysis. I am surprising him by taking him to some very special live music here in Nashville with fine dining.

Love, Sondra

November 12, 2016

❡ I JUST RECEIVED THE ANSWER

❖ I just received the answer to solving "neediness" in a person.

❖ I just received the answer to solving a person not liking herself or himself.

❖ I just received the answer to helping a person who thinks he or she is not getting enough love from their partner.

❖ I just received the answer for people who think their personal lie is real.

❖ I was just reviewing this lesson in ACIM. Lesson 229 says:

"Love, which created me, is what I am." It further reads this way:
"I seek my own Identity and find IT in these words. Now need I seek no more. Love has prevailed. So still It waited for my coming home, that I will turn away no longer from the holy face of Christ. And what I look upon attests the truth of my Identity I sought to lose, but which my Father has kept safe for me."

❡ Well, if one really got this lesson, how could one be needy? You don't have to search for love desperately. *You are it.* You don't have to wait for your mate to give it to you. *You have it.* So, give it! Then you will feel it. You don't ever have to dislike yourself again. All other negative thoughts about yourself are just a bunch of nonsense.

> *"Father my thanks to You for what I am; for keeping my Identity untouched and sinless in the midst of all the thoughts my foolish mind made up. And thanks to You for saving me from them."*

Love, Sondra

November 13, 2016

❡ THE LAW OF ATTRACTION
Remember that the law of attraction cannot bring you a well-balanced, happy person as a mate if you are not that already yourself! The thoughts you think about yourself determine the relationship you attract. AND not only does the power of your thought determine which people make their way into your life, BUT it also determines how they behave! We are leaving for Australia today. We do have time for our usual broadcast at 11 before we leave.
Love, Sondra

November 14, 2016

❡ FLIGHT TO MELBOURNE
Arrived in Melbourne after 15 hours of flying. Even though we had lousy seats for such a long trip, I was fine watching documentaries and reading the book *When God Steps In, Miracles Happen* by Neale Donald Walsh. But these lousy seats did enable me to sit next to an interesting Australian woman who may join us for the LRT here. Of course, no one comes to you by accident. There is no such thing as a coincidence. Nothing occurs at random. No one sits next to you by chance.

❡ Then I got off the plane and it was cold. I said to myself, "Oh no, I brought all the wrong clothes AGAIN." This is the second time in two years I have done this. Remember Canaries? I was almost upset, but then we got to Zeroum's (cozy house). He turned on the central heating. You cannot always count on that here. So now I am really, really, happy to be here.

❡ More later.

Love, Sondra

November 15, 2016

❡ LATELY I HAVE SEEN PEOPLE "SETTLING FOR LESS" It seems people think they have to "put up with their lot," as if life just happens to them; and, as if they are afraid to stand up for what they really deserve. We have all done this at times, I suppose. But let me tell you— it is not necessary, and it is NO FUN.

❡ Once I did a training called "The Ruthless Relationships Training." I had people write down what they actually wanted in a relationship on one side, and what they actually had on the other side. The sides did not match at all! Almost no one in the class had created what they REALLY wanted in their relationships. They were just tolerating what they had, rather than going for what they really wanted. I don't remember the exact reasons people were settling for less; but I presume these are some of the reasons:

1. Low self-esteem, i.e., "I don't deserve THAT."
2. Not even asking for what they really want from the universe—just taking what comes along.
3. Addiction to one's personal lie.
4. Punishment, i.e., "I am guilty, so I have to have a crummy life."
5. Fear of asking your partner to shape up.
6. Copying parents' relationship.
7. Thinking it is not okay to leave.
8. Fear that if they left to try to get something better, they would end up alone instead.
9. Being addicted to suffering.

10. Letting the ego rule instead of the Holy Spirit.

11. Fear of being really alive and really in one's power.

12. Staying in the "comfort zone" of what is familiar (even though it is bad!), instead of going through temporary discomfort of change.

13. Getting some kind of "neurotic pay off."

14. Thinking it is not possible to have a great relationship.

15. Struggle patterns.

16. Past life karma.

17. Fear of joy, total aliveness, and bliss.

18. Wanting to stay angry for not getting what one wants.

19. Fear of jealousy of others.

20. Not having any idea of how to create enlightenment in a relationship, nor conflict resolution.

21. Just plain ignorance of creative thought.

22. Being too preoccupied with one's career.

23. Loving to complain.

24. Not forgiving parents or past relationships.

25. Spiritual laziness.

❡ Wow, I did not expect to write a *whole chapter*. More on this tomorrow.
Love, Sondra

November 16, 2016

❡ CHECK YOURSELF—WHAT IF YOU TOTALLY WENT FOR WHAT YOU REALLY WANT?
What if you really went for it, and asked for what you really want in a relationship and did not let anything stop you? One of the reasons you are here is to create exactly what you want! Start demanding that of yourself. Why hold yourself back in any way? Why let a mate hold you back? Why let anyone hold you back?

❡ Of course, it is easier if you and your mate want similar things. But it is possible to be in a good relationship where both of you get what you want even if that is different. You have to be smart about it though. You have to be at the point where you can say to your mate, "Let's both get what we want. I don't want to interfere with your love for yourself." All kinds of things can be worked out if you are in a holy relationship and both of you want to be enlightened as a priority.

❡ You help each other get what you each want; and you help each other get enlightened. (To understand all that, read our book *Spiritual Intimacy*.) The main thing is that neither of you should be selling out. Neither of you should be under the ceiling of the other. Where are YOU with all this?

❡ Be a cheerleader for each other in the process of evolution. Your relationship is a spiritual workshop! Pray every day for God's help in making your relationship work. The purpose should be to share love, accelerate your spiritual growth, and have more joy on your spiritual path.

❡ The thing people complain about most in a relationship is lack of communication. Let's talk about that tomorrow.

Love, Sondra

November 17, 2016

❡ TRUE COMMUNICATION

True communication is a bonding of spirits. We become in touch with the essence of the other. But true communication takes courage. You care enough to be affected more, enlarged more, and transformed by what you have heard. You exchange feelings that can open both people to more awareness. There is

     a. The Message
     b. The Listening
     c. The Response
     d. The Acknowledgement

❡ You need to say exactly what is in your heart. What is it that you are NOT saying? You have to be emotionally brave to say that. It is precisely the things you are afraid to say that will show you who you really are. There should be no withholds.

❡ You want to have the kind of relationship where you can say ANYTHING without fear. Be tactful, as you would with an honored guest. That is the secret.

❡ Words can heal or wound. Criticism kills relationships. Criticizing in public is degrading to another person's essence. Never make fun or rudely fight in the presence of others.

❡ Reprimands always have a painful reference to childhood. Verbal acknowledgement works. You need to verbally express why you deeply love your mate. Simple things, like saying *PLEASE,* are a way of respecting the person you love. It is a way of holding your beloved in high regard. If you cannot find 20 minutes a day for intimate communication, your relationship could go down-hill fast. Not resolving something takes an incredible amount of energy. Defensiveness keeps the problem going. And the silent treatment—well, need I say anything about that? Love, Sondra

November 18, 2016

❡ COMMUNICATION IS TO A RELATIONSHIP
WHAT BREATHING IS TO LIVING
Communication is the key to keeping a relationship committed. When communication lines are not open, a relationship is doomed to failure. But you have to be a *love finder,* not a *fault finder.* It is never appropriate to judge or criticize. It is fine however to have an observation. You can say, "Honey I have an observation I would like to share with you if you are open to hearing it." Spiritual honesty is communicating what is appropriate and loving in a respectful manner.

❡ A child may blurt out everything with no self-control. But as an adult, this is "oral diarrhea." Never punish each other. It is childish behavior. Never let attack come from "you" sentences! (Like, "You did this, and you did that.") Never communicate when you are caught up by negative emotion or anger. There is no such thing as righteous anger. ACIM says anger is never justified. Arguing is a manifestation of negative ego.

ᵹ Know the difference between asking and demanding. I have shared this before, but I will share it again—*non-violent communication* (or also called "compassionate communication") goes like this:

I. "I observe this happening in our relationship_____."
2. "The way I feel about this is_____."
3."What I need or recommend for this is:_____."

ᵹ If you both are willing to just practice these simple things above, your communication will be great and on track.
Love, Sondra

November 19, 2016

ᵹ ROMANTIC RELATIONSHIPS ARE THE FAST TRACK TO GOD
Anyone can maintain Christ Consciousness living in a cave. But can you do it with a mate? That is the challenge. For example, each time you want to react with negative emotions to your partner's behavior, can you bless him or her instead, allowing you the opportunity to pass another spiritual test? Do you want God or your ego? Do you want harmony and spiritual evolution, or do you want self-centeredness and narcissism?

ᵹ Are you defensive? People who are ego sensitive will most likely get defensive and insulted by just about anything you say to them, no matter how lovingly it is presented. Do you use anger as a manipulative tool to control your partner?
If one of you gets angry, STOP the conversation and tell your partner you are unwilling to communicate unless it is loving and respectful.

ᵹ Can you let go of the blame game? Try the Eight Minute Process we came up with (explained in an earlier post) in which you both get to voice your feelings for eight minutes without any interruption from your partner. Don't let anger and resentment rule your relationship. Practice real communication instead, in which both of you are owning how you feel, not blaming, and implementing the life together that you really want.

℘ Try this prayer: "Help us to see that everything is either love or a call for love." (ACIM says, "Every loving thought is true. Anything else is a call for help.") The Fast Track To God is a Loving Relationship. All your stuff will come up, but for the purpose of healing and release, can you hang in there and get through it? I hope so. The rewards are tremendous.

Love, Sondra

November 20, 2016

℘ MIRACULOUS TRAINING IN MELBOURNE
This LRT in Melbourne was successfully organized by Zeroum and Tina, with the help of Aimee and her yoga studio. We had about 20 in the room, which was just right for lying down to breathe. I was really happy because almost everyone had Breathwork before, so I was able to move fast and go deep. Several are in Zeroum's Rebirthing class, fortunately. Our friend Adrianna came over from Canberra to assist. We even had a young gal of 18 years old. Imagine waking up so early to all this information!

℘ In love we get what we deserve. These people deserve a lot. Now they are ready to be light workers. I told them to create heaven wherever they go. Several told me it was the best experience of their life!

℘ Markus did a beautiful painting of Babaji I liked a lot. Also, Markus gave an amazing talk on ACIM. It was one of his best. It was a real Divine Offering. We all felt like we were breathing in the Divine. I also made my deepest offering of Love. We all offered our best. I think everyone got that they needed—to give what they are waiting to receive! At one point I played Astarius's *Spirit Rap*, cuts #3 and #4.

℘ This was marvelous, and some people had spontaneous rebirthings with Kundalini Rising! I felt like Markus and I gave our deepest gifts. We came home and found an invitation to come to Slovenia!

Love, Sondra

November 21, 2016

❦ KNOW WHAT YOU WANT
It is okay to *know what you want,* and have it fulfilled.
Wanting comes first; getting comes second. But we are
often taught it is not okay *to want.* We shouldn't want what
we want.

❦ Or maybe one is taught "You will never get what you
want." Maybe one is taught that "You should not even ask
for what you want because asking is demanding." Maybe
one is taught "Nice girls and boys don't ask; they should
wait until it is offered." Or maybe it is implied that "Other
people's wants are more important than yours." Or you
might conclude: "If I get what I want others will be deprived."
"Wanting is selfish" "Wanting is greedy."

❦ A popular song says, "You can't always get what you
want." Buddhists say, "Desire to be desire-less." In other
words, don't have any wants.

❦ Basically, we are taught that satisfying ourselves is wrong.
You are supposed to be strong and not need anything.
However, if you listen to Esther Hicks, or read her books,
she always talks about having "Rockets of Desire," and that
is a good thing because it makes you evolve, grow, and
expand!

❦ I like that. Read her book A*sk and it is Given.* The
affirmation we use is this: "I am willing to know what I want;
I am willing to ask for it; and I am willing to receive exactly
what I ask for." Imagine you can have everything you want
that you can write down in 10 minutes! That would be
something!
Love, Sondra

November 22, 2016

❦ DO YOU KNOW THE DIFFERENCE?
Do you know the difference between a special love
relationship and a special hate relationship? The *special
love relationship* starts when we believe there is something
lacking in us that can never be filled—we feel incomplete.
So, we embark on an endless search to find satisfaction

external to ourselves. We say, "There are special needs I have that cannot be met with myself or by God, and I cannot find happiness without them. But YOU, a special person with special characteristics, can meet my needs." Those who we perceive fill these needs, we love. "As long as you, my special love, continue to act so my needs are met, I will love you. But don't ever stop meeting my needs or I won't love you." Here we have placed our hopes for salvation on this one special person. If they put their attention elsewhere it is a big loss. This is co-dependency to the max. Dependency breeds contempt. We feel guilty for using others to meet the needs of our "shaky identity."

♪ In the special hate relationship, the responsibility for one's misery is shifted onto another. "It is YOU who has done this terrible thing to me". There is an *IF ONLY* orientation. If only my parents had been different. If only something outside of me were changed. The ego's plan for salvation here is centered on holding grievances. "Look at the terrible things you have done to me." (This is a projection; while seeming to deliver us from guilt, it only reinforces it. Our guilt merely becomes strengthened as a result of our unfair attacks on another.)

♪ The more we attack the guiltier we feel. The guiltier we feel, the more our need to deny. Our need to find scapegoats to hate is overwhelming. Then we built defenses against our fear of retaliation. Defenses attract attack. In the special hate relationship, the hated person's past mistakes are used against him to justify our attack. All mistakes are used to build a case against him. (Whatever reminds you of your past grievances attracts you.)

♪ From *ACIM*. Summary: In the special love relationship, you make your mate your savior, your idol. In the special hate relationship, you make your mate your enemy. None of this is any fun. It is brutal.   Love, Sondra

November 23, 2016

♪ HAPPY THANKSGIVING.
I AM SO HAPPY AND GRATEFUL FOR ALL OF YOU READING THIS POST. I AM SO HAPPY AND GRATEFUL

FOR ALL OF OUR FRIENDS AROUND THE WORLD. I AM
SO HAPPY AND GRATEFUL FOR THE ORGANIZERS
WHO HAVE INVITED US AROUND THE WORLD. I AM SO
HAPPY AND GRATEFUL FOR MY HUSBAND MARKUS
AND MY MARRIAGE. I AM SO HAPPY AND GRATEFUL
TO HAVE BABAJI, AMMACHI, AND JESUS OF ACIM IN
MY LIFE. I AM SO HAPPY AND GRATEFUL TO HAVE
THE BALI QUEST, THE INDIA QUEST, AND THE
ICELAND QUEST FOR SPIRITUAL RETREATS. I AM SO
HAPPY AND GRATEFUL TO HAVE THE MARVELOUS
STUDENTS WE HAVE WHO ARE STICKING WITH IT. I
AM SO HAPPY AND GRATEFUL TO HAVE READERS
FOR OUR NEW BOOKS. I AM SO HAPPY AND
GRATEFUL THAT THE BOOK ABOUT BABAJI HAS JUST
COME OUT. I AM SO HAPPY AND GRATEFUL TO HAVE
ENROLLMENTS IN ALL OUR EVENTS. I AM SO HAPPY
AND GRATEFUL I CAN LISTEN TO THE AARTI RIGHT
NOW. I AM SO HAPPY AND GRATEFUL TO ZEROUM
AND TINA WHO ARE HAVING US IN THEIR HOME. I AM
SO HAPPY AND GRATEFUL TO EVERYONE WHO TOOK
THIS LRT AND THOSE WHO ARE COMING TO PRIVATE
SESSIONS. I AM SO HAPPY AND GRATEFUL WE ARE
ALWAYS SAFE WITH BABAJI. I AM SO HAPPY AND
GRATEFUL WE ARE HAVING A LOT OF FUN ALWAYS. I
AM SO HAPPY AND GRATEFUL FOR OUR HEALTH. I AM
SO HAPPY AND GRATEFUL TO BE AN AMERICAN. I AM
SO HAPPY AND GRATEFUL THAT WE HAVE A SIMPLE
LIFE IN NASHVILLE. I AM SO HAPPY AND GRATEFUL
THAT WE CAN SERVE HUMANITY IN THE WAY WE DO.
THANK YOU.
LOVE, SONDRA

November 24, 2016

ॐ WHAT ABOUT MANA?
Do you know about MANA? Mana is the life force or
spiritual power that the Hawaiians believe to inhabit all
things and creatures. It comes streaming in from another
universe and is also absorbed from the environment by
eating and breathing. The Kahunas (Hawaiian spiritual

masters) said that the most effective way to gather mana is to do deep breathing. Look how fortunate we are to be into Liberation Breathing! Chanting also generates tremendous mana, which is why Babaji keeps insisting we chant the mantra Om Namah Shivaya.

❡ Mana can be directed to flow outward for the purpose of healing. It can also be directed to our own goals and projects. Mana is stored by the body and manifests as VIGOR. The goal the Kahunas had was to acquire and guard one's personal mana. It was believed that the amount of one's mana determined one's success and luck (or lack thereof). Mana is considered to be an inherent quality of command and leadership. Once a yogi told me I had the fortitude of the Founding Fathers, so I was happy I was on track as a leader with my mana!

❡ The blocks to having mana are anger, resentment, guilt, fear, anxiety, and negativity. Mana will give you a reservoir of strength. It will give you a personal magnetism. It will make you a high-impact personality. It will give you charisma. For sure it is the genius and inspiration of a king. No leader wants his mana diluted. Hanging out with the wrong people can dilute your mana. So be careful. Think about it. Love, Sondra

November 25, 2016

❡ TAKING ON YOUR PARTNER'S CASE
There is an issue in relationships in which you take on your partner's karma, or his/her "case" (negative stuff). This could occur without you realizing it. It could ruin *your* health. Some of the reasons this occurs are:

❖ You think you can heal your mate or visa-versa.
❖ You are unconsciously trying to heal your mate or visa-versa.
❖ You feel sorry for them or visa-versa.
❖ Your frequency is low and you are very susceptible to "stuff."
❖ It is all transferred during sex.
❖ They don't want to work on themselves, so you

are the martyr doing it for them or visa-versa.

❖ You feel angry at them or visa-versa, and this makes your "aka cords" (psychic attachments) stronger and you get more hooked in.

❖ You are unconscious of the above and did not even know of this possibility.

❖ Your partner dumps his stuff on you and you are the scapegoat, or visa-versa.

¶ The first step to avoiding all this is to become aware you are doing it, and then *stop it!* This case comes to mind:

> *I had a client (woman/wife) who was really going for it in Breathwork. She loved it and kept going for it. Her husband, however, refused to even try it once. The trouble with this is that his case came up telepathically in her presence as she changed. He was the one with a difficult birth (cesarean) and his cesarean memories were coming up, but he was not clearing them. She felt this, and it was not getting processed. One day she went wild and grabbed a knife and started slicing up the stuffed furniture! Now, she was not an angry person at all, and she was not crazy at all. She was shocked she did this, so they called me. It was easy for me to see that she was unconsciously acting out his obstetrician who performed the cesarean.*

¶ So that is another problem. When one is getting Breathwork and the mate is not keeping up—the difference in growth is too strong and they are no longer on the same page. Pretty soon they are not even on the same elevator. It becomes the "different elevator syndrome" and the relationship can break down!
Love, Sondra

November 28, 2016

¶ WHO SHOULD AWAKEN WOMEN? WHAT OBSTRUCTS HER AWAKENING?

A woman's mind is the only real barrier that prevents this from happening. Amma tells this story:

> "An elephant can uproot huge trees with its trunk. When an elephant living in captivity is still a calf, it is tethered to a tree with a strong rope. The calf elephant tries with all its might to break the rope. When its efforts prove futile, it finally gives up. Later when the same elephant is fully grown, it can be tethered to any small tree with a thin rope. It could easily free itself by uprooting the tree or breaking the rope. But because its mind has been conditioned by its prior experiences, it does not make the slightest attempt to break free." — Mata Amritanandamayi*

§ This is what is happening to women, she says. The infinite potential inherent in man and woman is the same. If women really want to, they can easily break the shackles of the roles and conditioning that society has imposed on them. A woman's greatest strength lies in her creative lifegiving power. This power can help women bring about a far more significant change in society than men can ever accomplish. Women everywhere have to actualize the qualities of motherhood within themselves. This is the only way to realize our dream of peace and harmony. And it can be done! Let us all pray that cruel minds which denigrate women be transformed.

§ Yet, whether woman or man, one's real humanity comes to light only when the feminine and masculine qualities within one are balanced. That is why Babaji asked Markus and me to add the Divine Mother prayers to Liberation Breathing. He wants the patriarchy to be balanced out. Real leadership is not to dominate or control, but to serve others with compassion.

(From Amma's speech when she received the Nobel Peace Prize).

Love, Sondra

November 29, 2016

❡ CHANGING A SITUATION
If you are upset about a situation, you are looking at it wrongly. You can correct it by:

1. Undoing: Admit you actively decided wrongly, and you can actively decide newly.
2. Return your thinking to the point where the error was made.
3. Turn it over to the Holy Spirit. Say this: "I must have decided wrongly because I am not at peace. The only way I can be at peace is by changing my mind about what happened. Help me change my mind about why I am angry.
4. See that the problem is not "out there." It is in your own mind. Say, "I am willing to see this differently." When things go wrong, don't feel guilty, change how you look at it.
5. The ultimate goal is to have your unforgiven mind healed. Forgiveness erases the ego.

❡ If you don't forgive this situation, another one will come along. There is nothing outside of you that can hurt you except by your own thoughts. If we don't feel peace it is because we have chosen not to identify with it. There is a way to check if you have learned the lesson: A) You are without fear. B) You are at peace.
Love, Sondra

November 30, 2016

❡ TRAPPED BUT UNWILLING
We saw a lot of clients this year who felt trapped in horrible relationships but were hesitant to get out of them. Some of the reasons they were selling out were:

1. Low self-esteem: "I don't deserve better."
2. Not even asking for what they really want from

the Universe—just taking what came along.

3. Being addicted to their *personal lie*, such as "I CAN'T get what I want anyway. And, "I CAN'T leave."
4. Needing punishment: "I am guilty, so I have to punish myself with this crummy situation." (That is usually unconscious.)
5. Fear of asking the partner for a change.
6. Copying parents' relationship of bad habits.
7. Thinking it is not okay to leave, for whatever reason.
8. Fear that if they did leave to try to get something better, they would end up alone instead.
9. Being addicted to suffering.
10. Letting the ego rule instead of the Holy Spirit.
11. Worried about what other people would say.
12. Staying in a "comfort zone" of what is familiar (even though it is hell), instead of going through temporary discomfort of change.
13. Getting some kind of neurotic "pay off".
14. Sheer laziness.
15. Staying together for the kids even though the kids are suffering terribly in the situation.
16. Staying together for the money.
17. And on and on, as I have mentioned many time before.

❡ Sure, it takes courage to leave a situation; but most of these people are headed for some illness as they are so stressed out. Then they get more stuck. All these reasons can be handled by practicing a change of thought. There is always a spiritual solution.

❡ Nobody has to put up with a horrible situation that is living hell. But you have to have the courage to face yourself and make some kind of adjustment or change.

❡ I don't tell people what to do when they come to me complaining they are stuck in a bad relationship, but I ask them this: "If you had no fear and you had no guilt and you did not care what anyone else said, and if you knew you could get someone better, would you stay or leave?"

❡ They usually say, "I would leave. So then I say, "Aren't you then out of integrity for staying?" This helps them get clear. Breathwork supports them through the change. If any of the above is you, we can be of great help! There is a Loving Relationships Training coming up somewhere in the world. You can make it! Or you can schedule a **Liberation Breathing Session** over Skype or Zoom and really get clear! We can help you. Bit.ly/LBSession is the link.
Love, Sondra

December 1, 2016

❡ BALI IS BLISS
Arrived in Bali! Our plane was 8 hours late so fortunately we were able to check our bags and go back to Zeroum's house in Melbourne. I used the time to re-write my book on *Physical Immortality.*
❡ Arrived at our villas at 2:20 AM. Here we are in the lovely Nefatari Villas. Each villa is huge and has a gorgeous outdoor bathroom enclosed with exotic plants. Everyone is so very sweet and holy. It is so amazing to have these sweet Balinese people bowing to you like angels. Each villa has its own swimming pool, and all is enclosed. You can swim in the nude if you want to, all completely private. There are flowering trees hanging here, and over the veranda where we are dining for breakfast. Everything is open air, so we have the birds singing and the smell of exotic flowers and fruits.
❡ Every morning all over Bali the family sits down together and makes offerings to the Divine Mother. They weave little baskets and put fruit and flowers in them. The whole family participates. Then they take these offerings to the work place where they place them carefully on an altar after doing a ceremony. Each family relates to 7 different temples! There are 10,000 temples in Bali and they are all used. Can you imagine what it would be like if every family in America did this spiritual ritual?
❡ In the morning they totally clean and bless our villa. A young woman in beautiful Balinese dress comes in with offerings and does a puja to the Divine Mother. She is like a

dancing Goddess, making hand gestures with lit incense sticks that are absolutely exquisite. We are blown away by the beauty of it all.

❡ Bali is Bliss. Being here is like being constantly on another dimension! People are starting to arrive with all their dramas getting here. More later.

Love, Sondra

December 3, 2016

❡ STARTING THE BALI QUEST

Today we started the Bali Quest. After morning class, in which we recite the names of the Divine Mother, we are taking the group to the lovely bead shop where they can choose precious stones and have malas made. The women do them correctly with a knot between each stone so it's easier to do repetition of the mantra.

❡ Then we plan to visit the Elephant Cave, a holy shrine dating back to the 8th or 9th century. It is an archeological site of significant value not even excavated until 1954! There are five big statues of angels holding vases next to the bathing pools. Inside the cave there are indentations in the walls where the priests used to meditate. There is also a statue of Ganesh, the Elephant God considered the lord of removing obstacles.

❡ The entrance shows a giant face with wide open mouth at the door, considered to be the elephant's mouth. We are all going to choose an obstacle we want to let go of. After that we come back to the villas to do paired Liberation Breathing sessions. People get practice learning to give someone else a session. More later.   Love, Sondra

December 4, 2016

❡ THIS IS A TRUE STORY

In Herakhan (Babaji's ashram in India), we met a man from Bali and he invited us to come here. When we came, we met this amazing woman, Swasty, who told us the following: One day Babaji materialized to her in person, and walked her out to her yard and pointed to a place where He asked her to build a fire pit. He told her exactly how to build it. She said she did not have money for the supplies, and He told her not to worry about that. The very next day a crew arrived with the supplies and built it. So now we can go there, and it is like a Babaji ashram here in Bali.

ᘔ So we are taking the group there for an ancient fire ceremony. It is very, very beautiful and they do it exactly like in India. They decorate the fire pit with gorgeous Balinese flowers, and then they have the ingredients for us to offer into the fire—that is grains, fruits, flowers, incense, etc. It is kind of a Thanksgiving where we give back to the Divine Mother an offering in all our gratitude for what She gives us. While we make the offerings, very ancient mantras are read out loud. They are so powerful that they can even change the weather.

ᘔ We are taking the group there this morning. So, watch for the photos.
Love, Sondra

December 5, 2016

ᘔ A REAL DARSHAN
Darshan is receiving the blessing of a Holy Master. We were greeted with so much love at the home of Swasty and her husband. The fire ceremony was done perfectly by her husband with her help. It was as if Babaji Himself were doing it. At one point when they blew the conch shells together, it was magnificent. I hope this comes out on the video. We were so blessed as everyone in the group got to make the offerings together. This went on for over an hour.

ᘔ We had a big surprise that turned out to be a miracle. Swasty, who has six children, told us there was a new addition to the family. We saw a little boy being carried around. Turns out Babaji had told Swasty to go to the hospital and get this new born and adopt him. Babaji told her that the boy had been a high priest in a past life. When we got close to him, we were amazed. We felt like bowing; but then we were so stunned we forgot to do it. He was beautiful beyond words and his ears were that of an angel.

In other words, they were not human ears. They were shaped differently and gave the appearance that he could fly like an angel. Last night we could not sleep because we knew this being was going to change our lives and we would not be the same. Only a Master can have that effect on you. Quite frankly, I have never seen anything like that of him. It was like being with Babaji.

❡ We kept saying to each other last night the following: "THE MASTER IS BEAUTIFUL." Markus will write a book with that title. We were so startled that we failed to get a photo of him. But he will be forever in our minds.
Love, Sondra

December 6, 2016

❡ TAKING 100% RESPONSIBILITY
Remember when that nightclub in Bali was bombed and many Australians died? I cried. I found out later that the Balinese people did not feel like victims. They immediately asked, "How did we attract this?" The Priests met to figure it out. After deliberation they realized that they had omitted one ceremony a few years before that due to lack of funds. This mistake was the culprit. Then to correct it, they took an extreme action. They went back to an original ceremony from 1,000 years ago and started anew. This ceremony apparently takes 14 continuous days and is very expensive. So, they had to raise the money from the people. They did the 1,000-year-old ceremony perfectly, and now they feel like the correction is made.

❡ People in this retreat are astonished at the traffic of motor cycles and nobody is getting hurt. We have told them that last year we were able to witness the ceremony for cars and motorbikes which is done every year. They drape the car hoods and the bikes with altar cloths and put on those cloths flowers and fruits, making an altar. Then they do a puja to the machine. They are certain this protects the machines and people on them.

❡ Today we go to the Immortal Springs. More on that tomorrow.
Love, Sondra

December 7, 2016

❡ TIRTA EMPUL
Yesterday we went to Tirta Empul, the Holy Immortal Springs. It was built in 960 AD. On top of the hill overlooking this is the presidential palace of the Indonesian president. This holy water spring is something to behold! There are lush gardens and tropical plants everywhere. The bathing pools are so wonderful you cannot believe it. There are 13 elaborate sculptured spouts running with cold mountain crystal clear spring water. This is curative water. Before you go in you must make offerings. So, our fabulous driver, Agung, had already made these beautiful offerings. Then he did a ceremony for us before we went in, asking that we be blessed, and that our prayers would be answered and that we would be in total harmony.

❡ There is a dress code as it is an outdoor temple. So, you must wear a Balinese sarong in the water. We got in line and we bowed three times under each spout. This is a very amazing experience. Everyone felt that they would have a "new life" after this. Some went into spontaneous rebirthings after, and later their Liberation Breathing sessions were extra deep. Watching the Balinese people bow and bathe made us feel we had a long way to go with devotion before we get to the level they are at.

Love, Sondra

December 8, 2016

❡ MARKUS WRITES ABOUT BALI
Here is something beautiful Markus wrote that I want to share with you. It is from a book he is writing called *Boundless Mercy.* It is so lovely. Sondra

> *"I am in Bali for the sixth time, each visit deeper than the last. At Nefatari Villas we have a family of Balinese who take care of us in all aspects of our stay. Their care is beyond mere hotel service, verging on a divine dedication that is common in the Balinese culture. Before cleaning our room in the*

*morning, sacred offerings are made to cleanse the
atmosphere as well. A young woman came this
morning to make them, and she looked like a
Goddess—so pure and serene. Could you imagine
this happening in the West? All over Bali people
place God at the top of their daily purpose, so their
"first thought" is worship. It is their "work" of the day
to honor the Divine. The young woman came into
our villa with a woven tray of offerings—each in a
small woven grass basket of its own, with flower
petals and sticks of burning incense. She placed
one small basket of buds and petals by the pool. I
watched the smoke of the incense waft upwards
above the turquoise water of our pool, as the lady
moved like a dancer toward the covered veranda.
There did she pause before a small altar built out
from the wall. Offering flowers with various hand
gestures, time stopped in my observance of this
profound beauty of her sacred movements. A
blanket of peace came over me; a light of pure
gratitude emanated from my heart into the space
surrounding our villa. This girl of the Goddess
expressed only the truth of Boundless Mercy."*

Love, Markus Ray

December 9, 2016

❡ THE BALINESE DANCE
The essence of Balinese culture is contained in the dance
and drama, so we went to that last night. This cannot be
separated from their religion. Even dances done for tourists
are preceded by the dancers praying at their shrines. The
dances are performed for local people at festivals. They
may be a welcome for visiting gods, they may be a channel
for visiting gods or entertainment for visiting gods. They are
breathtakingly beautiful and unique. The dancers are
trained when they are young, and the training is rigorous
and disciplined. All parts of the body are used: faces, eyes,
hands. You are put in a trance watching this, and some

dances stir up your dark side! The costumes are out of this world. Flowers are scattered over the audience and sometimes it is all too much to take in. The musicians play bronze and bamboo xylophones, gongs, cymbals, bells, flutes, and drums. This music sounds like none other on the planet. See the video Markus made on my Facebook.
Love, Sondra

December 10, 2016

♪ THE BESAKIH TEMPLE
Today we go to the Divine Mother Temple, Besakih Temple. For 1,000 years it has been sitting there on a 1,000-meters high slope of Mount Agung. It is a complex that comprises 86 temples, including the Great Temple of the State. It is the biggest and the holiest of the island's temples surrounded by breathtaking rice paddies, mountains, hills, and streams. To the Balinese, visiting the place is a special pilgrimage. It is also with us. It has a mystical quality and is open to all castes. There are 70 ceremonies held there each year.
♪ In 1963 there was a huge eruption of the volcano of Mount Agung on the island, and the lava missed the temple by only a few meters. Apparently when it came to the temple it divided in half and went around the temple! It is believed to be a miraculous signal from the deities demonstrating their power. The name, Besakih, actually means *Congratulations*. The largest temple has areas representing seven layers of the universe, each with their own shrine.
♪ The tourists are not allowed to go to the two top layers. But the first time I came with Markus and a group, a very holy priest approached me out of the blue and told me that he "got" who I was! He led us to the very top where there is a surprise. Every year since, he somehow finds me. We shall see if it will be the same this year.

Love, Sondra

December 11, 2016

♪ ARRIVING AT BESAKIH

After a long drive we arrived at the Divine Mother Temple on the slopes of Mount Agung. The priest I love was there to greet me and the group once again. He took my hand and led me and the group up the many stairs and levels. When we got to the third level we stopped and read the 108 names of the Divine Mother. Our driver placed a beautiful offering for our group once again. This time he even made a small offering for each one of us. That never happened before. We all recited the 108 names together there. We were also blessed this time by a female priest who gave us holy water to drink three times, and three times to put over our heads.

♪ Then it began to rain a lot. The rain was so heavy that I feared he would not take us to the top level. Since we were sitting underneath a small temple, I asked him if we were going to wait until it stopped. He said it was not going to stop so we were going. We all purchased umbrellas from villages along the way. I knew there was only open space at the seventh level (and therefore no coverings or roofs), so I imagined standing in the rain and doing the vows. It seemed impossible as the rain was so heavy. But off we went. The top level is not available for tourists, so it is such an honor that we get special dispensation.

♪ When we got to the top, Markus and I stood in the rain and recited out loud a Divine Mother Mantra to prepare for our ceremony. Eight students had prepared themselves to take the VOW for Physical Immortality.

♪ Each stood between us in front of the top altar and said the vow, and then stated ten reasons they wanted to live. It was very, very moving, especially in the drenching rain. Then they all bowed three times. I know it is something they will never ever forget. Taking the Physical Immortality Vow was such a strong experience, something more than just an empty religious ritual.

Love, Sondra

December 12, 2016

❡ AT THE OBEROI HOTEL
We are going to celebrate the completion of the Bali Quest tonight at the Oberoi Hotel in Seminyak, where two of our students from Lebanon are staying. The Oberoi is on a 15-acre spread along the beach, and it is very unique among luxury hotels. That is because the grounds are dotted with ancient Balinese temples, and daily offerings are made to them. There is a natural stone amphitheater and a venue for Balinese dancers. It is a very magical atmosphere.

❡ The very first time I came to Bali alone decades ago, I stayed at the Oberoi the first night. The following morning at breakfast on the beach, the waiters were bowing to me. I said to myself, "Dear God, what has happened to the Western world?" It was my introduction to this place. Later when I brought Markus to Bali, we stayed there a couple of nights. It was raining, so the dancers came directly into the dining room where we were sitting and danced very, very close to us. It was so mesmerizing, as they had the best dance group of young girls in puberty doing the Legong dance. They were so sensuous that Markus started writing poetry that night. He became a poet before my very eyes. Then he ended up writing a whole volume of poems to the Divine Mother after that! This began his three year sojourn of writing *Odes to the Divine Mother.* Our lives changed that night. Going back to the Oberoi tonight, for the first time since then! (You can order it at bit.ly/OdesDM)
Love, Sondra

December 13, 2016

❡ THE GOD TRAINING IN BALI
The first time I came to Bali I had a huge miracle. I came because Babaji had asked me to create a "God Training." He said, "It is not *can you do it*, or *will you do it*, but this MUST be done." I agreed, but I never could figure out what that was for a whole year. So, I told my staff, "I am going to Bali, the Island of the Gods, so I can get it."

❡ The day it came through me was amazing. I channeled it

296

in about twenty minutes. Then I looked out the window of my bungalow right after I channeled it, and I saw one hundred gorgeous women, all dressed in colorful batik clothing, walking in procession and each carrying on their heads a high stack of fruits. They walked in perfect unison and the fruit did not fall off. It was such an amazing sight, I decided to follow them. They walked down to a beach and then they kneeled down and carefully took off the fruit from their heads—and still nothing fell to the ground. They laid down a long batik cloth on the beach for an altar. Then they carefully placed the fruit on the cloth for an offering.

₰ I was desperate to figure out what was going on. Finally, I found a woman from the embassy who spoke English. She said, "You are so lucky to see this. This is the day the whole island prays for families." I could hardly believe my ears. I learned that they do this every six months. Can you imagine if every single person in America did this twice a year? They not only pray for their own families, but they pray for all families on the island, and in the universe. Think about it. Love, Sondra

December 14, 2016

₰ YOUNG MASTER
Yesterday we went back to Swasty's place for a second time to see that little boy I told you about, that "little master." We did not expect to have another fire ceremony, but there was one which was a wonderful completion. Wijaya, her husband, was doing a special elaborate prayer ceremony himself in Balinese. It was hours long and she told us he does it every single day. He told us it was for the whole universe! Can you imagine?

₰ We all took turns holding the precious little boy, Satya Wijaya. His name means: TRUE LOVE THAT BRINGS VICTORY AND GOOD FORTUNE. That is the name Babaji told her to give him. He was so calm and beautiful, and we felt that we were receiving a darshan (holy meeting) from him. In fact, his mother talks to him telepathically like to an adult. When she sent her older son to the US for a new job recently, she told us she said the following to the little boy (6 months old): "What are we going to do now, as we have no money left since we sent your brother to the U.S.?" She said he answered her telepathically by saying to her: "Don't worry Mom, someone is bringing you money tomorrow." So, then that happened! She then commented to us, "Babaji provides everything to us." So, we went away with this in our mind. We felt our prosperity consciousness was enhanced there yesterday. We decided then and there to tithe to the family to help raise him.

¶ And so, last night we were treated to a wonderful dining experience by an Italian Babaji devotee, named Prema Chand. I had met him in India long ago. He has an Italian restaurant named Spaccanapoli, here in Ubud, as he is married to a Balinese lady. We took along Jodi, Magdalena, and Silke, and he treated us all! Delicious! I recommend it!

¶ Now we have days-off in Bali as the training is over. Let's see what happens!

Love, Sondra

December 15, 2016

¶ THE MALA SHOP

We went to the mala shop today to pick up the malas we had made for presents. They are of semi-precious stones, and we like to have them made with knots between each bead. This makes it really nice to do japa (reciting the mantra). There are 108 beads on each mala. It is very powerful to say Om Namah Shivaya 108 times every morning, plus other mantras our gurus have given us.

¶ The meaning of Om Namah Shivaya is Infinite Spirit, Infinite Being, and Infinite Manifestation. Also: "I bow to Shiva, destroyer of my ignorance (ego)." So, what happens when you say the mantra on your mala beads? You release negativity at the same time you charge yourself up! If you do 10 rounds it is really dynamite. Babaji says this is the highest thought in the universe. With it you can even conquer death! He said it is more powerful than the atomic bomb. Which means, you should always carry your mala beads with you. For example, when an airplane gets bumpy, we always pull out our malas and start reciting the mantra.

ʃ You can get mala beads at any metaphysical bookstore, or order them on line. You want the kind with 108 beads, and with tiny knots between each bead.

Love, Sondra

December 16, 2016

ʃ RELAXING WITH A GOOD BOOK
Now our group has left Bali and I can relax with a good book. I love to read. I am reading *Living with the Himalayan Masters* by Swami Rama. Here is a little story in that book:

> "When I received my second step of initiation at the age of fifteen, I had nothing with me. I thought: 'All these rich people come with baskets of fruit, flowers and money to offer to their teachers, but I have nothing to give.' I asked my Master, 'Sir, what is the best thing for me to offer?' He said to me, 'Bring me a bundle of dry sticks.'
>
> ʃ "I thought, 'Surely, if someone brings such sticks to his teacher, his teacher will kick him.' But I did as he instructed. He said: 'Offer it to me with all your heart, mind, and soul.'
>
> ʃ "Then he said, 'This is the greatest gift that you can ever give me. People want to give me gold, silver, land, and a house. These valuables mean nothing to me.' My master explained that when you offer a bundle of dry sticks to a guru he understands that you are prepared to tread the path of enlightenment. It means, 'Please relieve me from my past, and burn away all my negative thinking in the fire of knowledge.'
>
> ʃ "He said, 'I will burn these dry sticks so that your past karmas do not affect your future. Now I am giving you a new life. Do not live in the past. Live here and now, treading the path of light.' What a total blessing I had that day."

❧ Most people brood on the past and do not know how to live here and now. That is one cause of their suffering. But by the grace of the guru, your past karmas get destroyed. Who would not want that?
❧ Come to India with us and see for yourself!

Love, Sondra

December 17, 2016

❧ FALLING IN LOVE
I am enjoying relaxing and reading. Today I read the following about relationships:

> ❖ *"A man cannot fall in love with a woman who is not already in love with herself! (If a woman was well loved by her father, it helps her fall in love with herself.)"*
> ❖ *"The reason men fall in love with the ideal part of a woman is because they have a natural craving to raise their own spiritual standard. When a man falls in love, he is wishing and striving to be a better man."*
> ❖ *"It is a woman's responsibility to raise a man's level of consciousness from the concrete level of money and sex, where he is comfortable, to the spiritual level of love and relationships where she is comfortable."*
> ❖❖❖❖ *"Whether they admit it or not, men want women to set the spiritual standard in the relationship." (I put 4 points by that line on purpose. I think women need to hear this instead of making their men wrong for not being as spiritual as they are.)* From *Getting to I Do* by Dr. Patricia Allen

❧ I am always reading books on relationships as that is my field. Sometimes authors word something I already know really much better.   Love, Sondra

December 18, 2016

❡ GANUNG KAWI
There is a place in Bali I saw 31 years ago that I could not stop thinking about. I wanted to take Markus there this time; but I could not remember the name of it or where it was. Finally, a few days ago, I figured it out! It is called the Valley of the Kings. The Balinese name is Gunung Kawi. This is the only place where the shrines are carved into mountain rocks in Bali, and each is 23 ft high. These temples are named after the Goddess of Death, Chandika, a consort of Shiva. They are not tombs, they are monuments to a king and his consorts. When I saw it the first time, I was unaware of its significance. I was like a tourist then. There are 400 steps down to the river and all I remember is the beautiful scenery. Today it will be different for us. I know the significance. So last night we prepared ourselves to face *Death* and we talked a long time about the book we are writing on physical immortality.
❡ We also prepared ourselves fully in another way; as I received the message that we should shave our heads there today to be initiated into our new mission. Markus had no resistance at all. We once did it together for a whole year when we first got married and started working together. Now it is time to go to the next level. So, Markus texted our wonderful driver Agung about this. We shall see if he brings a barber or if he will do it himself. Stay tuned!
❡ Meanwhile, looked up on the internet Gunung Kawi and the Valley of Kings in Bali, and you will be amazed when you see these temples.
Love, Sondra

December 19, 2016

❡ HAVING OUR HEAD SHAVED
On the way to our mundan (head shave), our driver, Agung, stopped to get a new pair of scissors. Then when we got to the site, Ganung Kawi, we had to go down, down, down 400 steps into the bowels of Bali. There we got to the ancient

stupas cut into caves in the walls. He told us to kneel right there. (The tourists stayed away, really.) He began cutting our hair. Even though this is my fifth time in this life, it was still very, very powerful. He cut it as close as he could for both of us. Silke, our organizer from Tenerife, was there to assist. Then we went down by the clear swift river placing the hair in the stream. We went in the water and did a total immersion. Silke held the big beach towel for me so I could change my clothes. It felt so good, and I knew we had done the right thing. Since we did not have the proper razors, we had to stop at a local Balinese barber and go the next step and finish it off. After that we could get the shave really close with our Gillette razors.

ℊ Having a mundan purifies you. It rids you of past life negativity. It bestows long life and rejuvenates you. It protects you. It cleanses the body and soul. It improves your intuition. It sharpens your mind. It is always an initiation into the next level, which is precisely why we did it, since Babaji now told us we must move to Washington, D.C. Obviously He is giving us a new powerful assignment. I don't like the snow and the weather, but I always told Him I would go wherever He wanted me to go; so, when this move came to us, (and we both got the message at the same moment), we surrendered. Two nights later we got the instruction to shave our heads. It feels so good and liberating. The staff at our villa were really shocked as we had not told them ahead of time. I do feel younger and more alert, and my meditation is much better.

ℊ Now, by doing this, we have said to Babaji, "We accept our new assignment and we are willing to do whatever it takes to let You know that. We also did it because we are working on a book on Physical Immortality. So, we wanted to face Death at that particular temple. Bole Baba Ki Jai! (Victory to the Sweet Father, Babaji!)

Love, Sondra

December 23, 2016

ℊ A PRAYER FOR OUR NEXT STEP
Divine Mother, I address you as though I am in Your actual

Presence (which I am):

> *"Divine Mother, what shall we do? How shall we do it? Show us the way. We give up what we thought we were supposed to be. We surrender to Your love. In the bliss of Your lap, we know You will take care of us. Give us the strength, the perfect energy, peace and healing power for our next step. Give us what we need to serve You. We let go and let YOU run things. You are the road under our feet. Let us hear Your voice. May everything we do bring us closer to You. Purify our aura and vibration please. Let Your Divine Light shine in us as we start this new mission. We ask You, Jesus and Babaji, to heal our minds completely. May all our actions be that of worship. Teach us the feminine way. You are one with Supreme Truth. Teach us the language of your Heart. We are so grateful that You trust us. Show us what to write. Tell us what to say. Send us all the highest people possible to help with this Mission."*

❡ Everything we do is a result of Your Divine Energy moving through us.
Love, Sondra

December 24, 2016

❡ MORE ABOUT MUNDAN
Mundan (head shave) is a radical method of altering one's false identification with a body. It gives us a chance to see that *something* in us that appears constant, regardless of any change in the physical. It stimulates all the psychic centers on the head and creates a singular unit of cosmic reception that has a clearer relationship with the universal vibratory state.
❡ The first time I did it was to surrender to Babaji's lineage and take Him as my absolute Master, by which He agrees to be responsible for your liberation. It was an initiation. I did it for nine months. The second time I did it was after my

sister died. The third time I did it was after my mother died. (It is very, very helpful to clear the death urge that gets activated in one when a family member dies.) The fourth time I did it was when I got married to Markus. We kept our heads shaved a whole year then, as we entered our mission of working together. It was very intimate to shave each other's heads.

ℐ Now, the fifth time we did it again together as we are approaching a new mission. We wanted Babaji to know we are accepting that and taking it seriously.

ℐ Some of the other benefits are these: You get a better future. You get a longer life. You are protected more. It cleans your body and soul. It improves the strength of your nervous system. It helps you let go of the past and past lives. And it actually boosts your confidence. Why? Because you have to rise above what everyone thinks—and when you do that, you get a lot stronger and more confident. Mundan also forces you to change; and you know it is often hard to change. This works.

ℐ The best place to do it is in a holy place. It is most auspicious to do it in Herakhan by the Ganges River. Come with us on the India Quest and find out for yourself.
Love, Sondra

December 25, 2016

ℐ CHRISTMAS INVOCATION
Today why not invite God to come and celebrate with you? The meaning of Christmas is not only to celebrate the birth of Christ. It is also to give of one's very self—to truly think of others and of how to bring happiness to others. Why not also look at what you are giving to yourself:

> ❖ *Are you giving yourself the gift of becoming enlightened?*
> ❖ *Are you giving yourself the gift of a Holy Relationship?*
> ❖ *Are you giving yourself the gift of perfect health?*
> ❖ *Are you giving yourself the career you absolutely love?*

❖ *Are you giving yourself the finances you deserve?*

If not, why not? When you give to yourself so your own cup is filled, you can give more to others. Try saying to the people you are with today the following: "I am so grateful you exist."

ℐ Merry Christmas.

Love, Sondra

December 26, 2016

ℐ AN IMPORTANT REWRITE

We are just finishing up our rewrite of the book on Physical Immortality. Our new title is *Physical Immortality: How to Overcome Death.* The belief that death is inevitable and beyond our control is still the biggest killer of all. Many people have no desire to conquer death because they imagine themselves living in an ill and aged body. Of course, who would want that? But what if you could improve your body and keep improving it? Then would it interest you? Or is your life in general not so happy? Then you would not want it either. BUT if you were improving your body AND being really happy, you might want it. What if you understood that your body is a self-sustaining electromagnetic battery, capable of being recharged with energy? What if you could have cell regeneration? Well, it all begins in your mind.

ℐ I have found that the more I meditate on this possibility, the better I feel and the more I want to be here. Of course, it is important that you have a great mission and that is the very reason why you will want to stay here. Tell the Masters you accept a spiritual mission, and so you are here to help others and serve humanity. Otherwise this topic probably won't interest you, or you would be into it for the wrong reasons.

ℐ Naturally you cannot get the *boon* (blessing) of Physical Immortality unless you have forgiven everyone. You cannot make it to long life if you still have anger. This is the first prerequisite. NOT going for it leads to gloom, as then you

305

will end up sick and suffering in the end and dragging out your death. Isn't it a relief to know that you don't have to end up suffering in later years? Of course, this is yet another reason to have a Master like Babaji in your life. He helps with all this. He pushed out of me so much death urge—I might have gotten totally stuck in it if He had not helped me. Another reason to come to India with us in March and take the Vow of Immortality at the Immortal Tree. Love, Sondra

December 27, 2016

❡ ANSWER TO A PROBLEM
What would you do if you knew there was someone you could go to who knew all the answers to all problems? Someone who had mastered life completely—someone who could put you in instant joy—someone who would heal you—someone who could even teach you how to conquer death? Would you go find him? What would you do if you knew Jesus was still around and you could find Him? Would you check Him out, even if you were not raised a Christian? I would think you might.

❡ What would you do if you knew there was a book written by Him in the last few decades? A book for modern times—a book that cleared up all the confusion about religion—a book that explained everything, answered all questions, and taught you how to heal yourself completely—a book that taught you how to have perfect relationships? What if the book itself was a miracle? Would you read it?

❡ That book is here. Jesus is here through it. The answers are in it. That book is *A Course in Miracles* and it is available. You can be healed now. Imagine having *Liberation Breathing*, *A Course in Miracles* (Jesus), Babaji and Ammachi all in your life. That is what I have. We call them the "Dream Team." That is what you can have. You can receive *salvation*, or the ultimate solutions, now. Your life can work now.

❡ The reason I am writing this today is this: If you have not started *A Course in Miracles* you have time to get it right

now before the New Year and you can start Lesson 1 on New Year's Day. If you have it, you probably need to do it again, so start over on New Year's Day. It is also available online, but I like to have the actual books. Start with the Workbook Lessons first. Don't read the Text first as it is too deep. Read a few pages, or one chapter of the Text for every 10 Lessons. Never jump ahead on the Lessons. Do them one at a time in order. Each one builds on to the next lesson. Trust me!
Love, Sondra

December 28, 2016

❡ RECOGNIZING IF YOU ARE STUCK

> ❖ *Do you feel unhappy and isolated?*
> ❖ *Do you feel anxious or moody, rarely experiencing joy?*
> ❖ *Do you feel helpless, can't move forward, or accomplish things?*
> ❖ *Do you feel sick, in pain, or is your vital energy blocked?*
> ❖ *Do you feel a nagging urge to attack someone verbally and stay angry?*
> ❖ *Do you feel you cannot get your personal relationship clear?*
> ❖ *Do you feel you cannot find a relationship?*
> ❖ *Do you feel your financial situation is shaky?*

If so, you need to give yourself some special attention. The situation calls for spiritual purification, Liberation Breathing, reading ACIM, and/or prayer. If you cannot do any of these immediately, then just write down all your negative thoughts on a piece of paper and change them all to the opposite affirmations. That will help right away.
❡ Or perhaps you need to write a letter to God or Jesus, or Babaji, or Ammachi, or Mother Mary and bare your soul and put it on your altar under your altar cloth. Confessing your case is always good. Whatever you do, don't stay the same

and get more and more stuck.

ᛦ Chanting Om Namah Shivaya, or reciting it on mala beads is another immediate thing you can do. Always have your *mala* handy. If you don't have one, get one asap. Let's not carry our crap into the new year!

Love, Sondra

December 29, 2016

ᛦ RECEIVING CORRECTION

Are you willing to receive correction of all your problems? Think how great your release will be when you allow all your problems to be solved! If God is just, then there can be no problems that justice cannot solve. Each time you keep a problem for yourself to solve, or judge that its one that has no resolution, you have made it *great* and passed the hope of healing it. Your problem will recur, and then recur again, and yet again, until you hand it up to a higher Power. The Holy Spirit offers you release from every problem you think you have. It has no greater difficulty in resolving some than others. Every problem is just an error to the Holy Spirit. And all errors can be corrected. This is the promise made by Jesus in *A Course in Miracles.* However, you have free will to hang on to problems rather than let them go to the Holy Spirit for correction. THIS IS THE REAL PROBLEM: TRUTH CANNOT DEAL WITH ERRORS YOU WANT TO KEEP.

ᛦ So instead of complaining that one of your problems won't go away, look at WHY you are keeping it. Say this: "The reason I am not allowing this problem to be solved is_____." You will get an answer, and you have to change that thought. When you change it to an affirmation, the light will come into your mind, the angels will come in to help you. The holy angels hover over you to keep away all darkness and hold you in the light where they have entered. Why not give your "problems" to them to solve now.

Love, Sondra

December 30, 2016

❡ APPLICATIONS OF CHAPTER 2 IN ACIM TEXT
I am processing myself on giving up my *personal lie* ("I am not perfect.") Here are some of my notes from reading Chapter 2 in the Text of *A Course in Miracles* that are helping me do that:

❖ *I remember that I was created perfect and still am. Any of the things that seem to me imperfect are really lies, and I confess i made them up to usurp the power of God. I had the notion that if I made myself less than perfect, it proved I was more powerful. This is insanity.*

❖ *I was wrong when I thought putting walls around me would make me strong. I was wrong when I thought I needed protection. I was wrong when I added fear, guilt, and pain as defenses against God. These things only made me weaker and in need of more protection, which made me still weaker.*

❖ *Defenses attract attack, so I now choose to remain totally open and vulnerable to be safer. Since I am one with God, I have all the safety I need. In my perfection I am safe. In my defenselessness I am perfect.*

❖ *I can heal myself totally by remembering I am one with God, and by allowing all my wrong thinking to be undone and accepting the miracle. In order to heal myself I can aid the situation by locating the ego thought causing the condition "I am not perfect," and by letting it go.*

❖ *I do not expect anyone else to take away my fears. I take responsibility for making them up. In general, I made them up because I thought I was separate from God. This was a mistake. I forgive myself for thinking I was separate. I forgive myself for thinking I was not perfect. I am forgiven for this.*

❖ *I am perfect; I am God-like.*

❡ This is not blasphemy. It is not blasphemy to think that I am perfect in God's eyes. I forgive whoever taught me that it was blasphemy against the church to think I was perfect. It is time to start living my perfection, as GOD would have me BE!
Love, Sondra

PS. Insert your personal lie in the parentheses.

December 31, 2016

❡ COMPLETING THIS YEAR
Here are some fun questions to ask your mate over dinner tonight before the New Year comes in:

❖ *What was your biggest triumph this year?*
❖ *What one word best sums up and describes your experience this year?*
❖ *What was the greatest lesson you learned this year?*
❖ *What was the most loving service you performed this year?*
❖ *What is your biggest piece of unfinished business this year?*
❖ *What are you most happy about completing this year?*
❖ *Who were the three people that had the greatest impact on you this year?*
❖ *What was the biggest risk you took this year?*
❖ *What was the biggest surprise this year?*
❖ *What important relationship improved the most this year?*
❖ *What compliment would you liked to have received this year?*
❖ *What else do you need to do or say to be complete with this passing year?*

❡ Tomorrow I will go over creating a new year.
Happy, Happy, New Year's Eve!
Have a lot of fun tonight!!
Love, Sondra

January 1, 2017

❡ CREATING A NEW YEAR

What would you like your next year to look like? Here are some questions you and your mate could ask each other on this New Year's Day.

> ❖ *What would you like to be your biggest triumph in this new year?*
> ❖ *What advice would you like to give yourself in this new year?*
> ❖ *What is the major effort you are planning to improve your financial results in this new year?*
> ❖ *What would you be the most happy about completing in this new year?*
> ❖ *What major indulgence are you willing to experience in this new year?*
> ❖ *What would you most like to change about yourself in this new year?*
> ❖ *What are you looking forward to learning in this new year?*
> ❖ *What do you think your biggest risk will be in this new year?*
> ❖ *What about your work? Are you most committed to changing and improving in this new year?*
> ❖ *What is one of your undeveloped talents you are willing to explore in this new year?*
> ❖ *What brings you the most joy and how are you going to do or have more of it in this new year?*
> ❖ *Who or what, other than yourself, are you most committed to loving and serving in this new year?*
> ❖ *What one word would you like to have as your theme in this new year?*

❡ Markus and I wish you the best year ever. May it far exceed your expectations and dreams. Remember, "God's will for you is perfect happiness."
Love, Sondra

❡ P.S. Think about treating yourself to a major life-changing experience by coming on the **India Quest** with us in the Spring!

> *"India was the motherland of our race, and Sanskrit the mother of Europe's languages; she was the mother of philosophy; mother through the Arabs of much of our mathematics; mother, through Buddha of the ideals embodied in Christianity; mother, through the village community of self-government and democracy. Mother India is in many ways mother of us all." (Will Durant)*

January 2, 2017

❡ APPLICATIONS FROM CHAPTER 3 IN ACIM

> ❖ *Since God's will for me is only perfect happiness, I am no longer afraid of God's will. (When bad things happened, that was not God's will for me, it was the creation of my own poor subconscious mind.)*
> *God's will brings me everything I want. God's will and my will are one now. Now I can care for my subconscious mind in better ways.*
> ❖ *From now on, in every brother I see God. I recognize myself in him. I recognize God in him. I do not wish to ever attack myself or God, therefore I do not attack my brother in any way. Since I know my brother, and my brother knows me, we are in a loving relationship. There is no need to play the game of "strangers."*
> ❖ *I pray for forgiveness regarding the distortions I have made that kept Spirit out. I choose not to maintain these distortions that cause separation. I*

do not want this error any longer. I am one with Spirit, one with joy, one with life, and one with abundance and all that God is.

❖ *I can totally give up the fear that God punishes people. Therefore, I can totally relax. I forgive the church for teaching me that insanity.*

❖ *Whenever I am tempted by my ego, I do what Jesus did saying, "Get behind me negative thoughts. I will not indulge in you or believe in you. I relinquish you. My mind is God's mind."*

❖ *I know Who I am and I accept my own inheritance.*

I꒜ f you have not started *ACIM,* do it today and start on Lesson 2 and keep going.
Love, Sondra

January 3, 2017

꒜ HAPPINESS OR MISERY

Leonard Orr was my first Rebirthing teacher. He wrote a book called *Breaking the Death Habit.* He says that "people can live in either happiness or misery." Here are some other thoughts he expresses in that book:

> ꒜ *Ignorance leads to misery. Wisdom can produce happiness. We choose life or death every day. Every month we are happier and more alive, or more miserable, and more dead. People rarely die in one day; they spend a lifetime dying by poor-quality living.*
>
> ꒜ *All the body systems are created with the principle of renewal and regeneration built in. However, the mind can frustrate this principle and cause the body to malfunction and even die. Believing that death is inevitable and beyond our control is the beginning of the ignorance that causes death. Believing that the body is the perfect and eternal work of God is far more intelligent.*

♪ Since we are naturally divine, we forever have the power to destroy the body, but we don't have to use this power. We can just as easily use our natural divine power to heal and rejuvenate the body. This is its natural tendency. When we injure the body, it heals itself automatically. This is our normal experience.

♪ The mind is a powerful goal-achieving mechanism. We must always consciously select a goal for our mind to work on. Reaching one worthwhile goal after another is success consciousness.

♪ People can get away with negative thinking for a while, but sooner or later it manifests in some way and the punishment continues until our thoughts are changed.

♪ You don't have to die to feel God. Your body is the Temple of God. To feel God in your body is the best place to feel Him or Her. Conscious energy breathing is often called a biological experience of God. It is easy to practice when you learn connected breathing and learn to breathe from the breath itself.

(From Leonard Orr's Book, *Breaking the Death Habit*; Leonard Orr is the Founder of Rebirthing.)

January 4, 2017

♪ AT THE HERMITAGE
We went to Andrew Jackson's home because we are trying to prepare for our move to Washington, D.C. (Babaji has asked us to move there as an assignment.)

♪ I did not know my history very well, so I did not get how important the Battle of New Orleans was to save our country from the British during the War of 1812. Andrew Jackson was the commanding general who won that battle. When you think about the war with the British, you have to really appreciate all those who gave their lives so we could be the America we are today. How many people are grateful?

❡ And think of what Andrew Jackson had to deal with. He was poor, fatherless, and his mother died of cholera when he was young, so he was an orphan. Then his wife died right after he became president! Imagine that. He had to deal with a lot of death and abandonment.

❡ His estate was incredibly beautiful. He earned his money on land dealings. Don't worry, I know about this Trail of Tears with the Indians. That was not good. But I needed to see this place. Some think Donald Trump is an incarnation of Andrew Jackson. For better or worse. You decide.
Love, Sondra

January 5, 2017

❡ PRACTICING GRACE
"Grace means that we have an abundant Life-Force-God who takes care of us whether we deserve it or not. To practice grace means to be always thankful for Life and its lessons, even when they are unpleasant. The kicks in life are for the purpose of teaching us something. When we learn the lesson, then we deserve grace and we can enjoy God's love for us.

❡ Grace means practicing the Presence of God. It means to realize that God is always present in the space between our thoughts, as well as in our thoughts. We are always the Eternal Spirit, thinking and living.

❡ Practicing grace should make us a gracious person. Devotion to God earns grace. Each time we discover that God loves us, it is a pleasant surprise.

> ❖ *Grace is when our love for God meets God's love for us.*
> ❖ *Grace means falling in love with God.*
> ❖ *Grace is the power of forgiveness that sometimes prevents our mistakes, sometimes prevents our mistakes from harming us, and*

sometimes heals the damage done by our mistakes.

❡ The paradox is that the more grace we have, the more we trust grace, and the more perfect we are. Grace is the power and energy of Infinite Being.

❡ Earth, air, water, and fire practices are the eternal vehicles of grace. They work for us whether we believe in them or not. Taking a shower or bath removes spiritual dirt automatically. Exposing our aura to an open flame removes pain and tension automatically and nourishes us with fresh life energy. Energy breathing is pure grace. Fasting heals whether we believe in it or not. These simple practices restore our life energy, our Joy of Life, and introduce creativity."

—Leonard Orr, founder of Rebirthing

January 6, 2017

❡ TWO TOGETHER ASCENDING

If you and your partner are both rather advanced on the path of Ascension, the work that can be done is tremendous and of extreme value to humanity. If you both make God the center of your work and life together, you will have a relationship of the highest order.

❡ Merging with the Master, you invoke His or Her Divine Presence to permeate your being, thus making those extremely high energies available to you as well as to all of humanity and the earth herself. When two of you join in Divine intent, a third entity is created comprised of yourselves, your I AM Presence, and the Master who is working with you.

❡ Hilda Charlton said that the ecstasy of God union far surpasses any type of sexual union. The Masters wait to be invited. You must invoke that yourselves.

Love, Sondra

January 7, 2017

§ PAST LIVES AND HEALING
One of the best books I have ever read on the subject of past lives is the book, *Other Lives, Other Selves* by Dr. Roger Woolger. Here are some of my notes from that book:

> *"Even though the physical ailment may have very specific origins in a person's current life, I have found more and more there are certain layers to every major syndrome of physical illness, accident or weakness. The existence of a past life level of physical problems has been confirmed over and over again in the cases I have seen.*
> *§ A woman in her early forties relived an unfulfilled life as a woman in the pioneer days which ended tragically when a horse and trap overturned; she broke her back and died when she was twenty-seven in that life. In this life, at the age of twenty-seven, she was in the hospital with a very serious kidney infection which they could not properly diagnose, and she nearly died. The pain was absolutely terrible and was in the same place where she had broken her back in the other life."*

§ I have found, as he did, that it is especially true for phobias. When someone has a very deep fear which cannot be explained, I have found as he did, that behind that fear is a past life trauma. In sessions people can remember deaths from poisonous insects, snakes, sharks and more. Many who have a fear of heights can remember being thrown off cliffs in past lives. Sometimes to get the cure, we have to guide the client through the whole memory of that particular death in their Liberation Breathing session. Going through it in their session and breathing out the charge, helps them to be free in the present of the related conditions.

Love, Sondra

January 8, 2017

❡ APPLICATIONS OF CHAPTER 4 IN ACIM TEXT
These are some of the strongest empowering passages:

❖ *It is safe to change completely. I can change without separation or pain. (In other words, our first change of taking a body made us feel separate from God. Our second change at birth was painful.) The more I change (by letting go of the ego), the safer I am. The more I change, the more I am united, and therefore the safer I am.*

❖ *I do not let my ego keep me from the joy I deserve. When I feel fear around joy, it is not because joy is fearful. It is just my ego trying to keep me away from that joy. I will not run from joy (because it is unfamiliar). I will go toward joy, not letting my ego prevail. I trust that joy is safe.*

❖ *I will not let the ego convince me that death and temporary existence are the right goals and results. I know that Spirit is eternal and that God loves me, therefore I deserve eternality. I no longer hate myself in any way, therefore I accept what the Spirit offers: permanence.*

❖ *I choose to let go of fear. I can do this by changing the thoughts I have that produce the fear; I can also breathe out the fear on the exhale.*

❖ *When I am not feeling joyous, I remember I have chosen wrongly. I can clear this by asking myself: "What have I thought that God would not have me think?" And then let those thoughts go.*

❖ *When I feel upset I can command, "This need not be." I can remind myself that I am not "stuck with it." I am never stuck with any situation. I can correct it.*

❖ *Whenever I am tempted to fight or be witness to an argument, I remind myself that it is my ego wanting to disrupt communication and keep me separate. I can change this situation with a higher thought.*

Love, Sondra

January 9, 2017

❡ SAINTS AND TEACHERS
These are some great passages from my Rebirthing
teacher, Leonard Orr:

> ❖ *"Sometimes we discover a very wise or good
> person. It is wise to spend time with these people
> and honor them and learn as much as we can from
> them. We can consciously choose high quality
> friends*
>
> ❖ *We also need to realize that some people in
> teaching positions are not wise and don't really
> understand life. Some people in a position of
> authority don't really deserve to be there.*
>
> ❖ *I have met Babaji Who is the Eternal Father in
> human form. He is called the Angel of the Lord in
> the Bible. He appears to thousands of people all
> over the world every day. He can appear to you.
> And I have met several immortal yogis and some of
> them thousands of years in the same body. They
> are very, very wise and deserve to be called Saints.*
>
> ❖ *It is good to constantly look for saintly and wise
> people and learn from them. Making my own
> daughter my guru, my therapist and healer was one
> of the best decisions I ever made.*
>
> ❖ *Having enough pure people in our life makes life
> easy and more pleasurable. It is an intelligent thing
> to give ourselves enough support. Having at least
> one enlightened spiritual teacher in our life makes
> the 'school of hard knocks' less bumpy.*
>
> ❖ *God the Conscious Self, our personal connection
> to Infinite Intelligence, is the ultimate guru for all of
> us."*

Thank you, Leonard.

Love, Sondra

319

January 10, 2017

❧ PERSONAL SHARE
I thought this head shave would be easy since I had done it
four times before—WRONG! Since we deliberately did it at
the temple to the Angel of Death (down 400 steps in Bali),
we were really asking for it. We wanted to confront anything
left in us about the unconscious death urge. WOW. Markus
went through bronchitis in Bali. It hit me later.
❧ I came back and went through an internal Kranti
(revolution). I had insomnia a couple of weeks, which was
disconcerting, as I would fall asleep in every movie—and
that was not fun for Markus. Then I could not swallow as I
had some kind of abscess on my tonsil. This went on for 9
days and nights and it was extremely painful. I had to use
every trick in the book I had learned to heal myself. It was a
real battle. I used:

- ❖ Wet rebirthing
- ❖ Dry rebirthing
- ❖ Hypnosis X2
- ❖ Chanting
- ❖ Mantras
- ❖ Prayer (LOTS)
- ❖ Healing Codes
- ❖ Ho'o Ponopono X3
- ❖ Consults with other healers
- ❖ Lords of Karma Process
- ❖ Letters to Babaji
- ❖ Getting processed by my husband
- ❖ Begging for help from God, and you name it

❧ I went through the crisis last night. The fear came out.
Markus said I was saying in my sleep that I was going
through a "psychic seizure." This was terrifying. I felt like I
was having convulsions and falling apart, and I could hear
strange noises in my brain. (The ego has to fall apart if you
want to be healed.) I woke up and my pajamas were all wet;
but I could finally swallow.

❡ What was this fear anyway? Turned out to be fear of the next level where Babaji would speak through me. Hence the throat stuckness. I was afraid that people would be totally shocked. Markus assured me that I would be shocking people out of their misery, and they would need it. He told me Babaji shocked people. WHY? Because they were going the wrong way and were not in touch with their higher Self. It helped to hear that.

❡ You have to be brave to shave your head. I don't want you to think that your mundan would be like this. It is always worth it. Mine was deliberately provoked to be this—and it was worth it. Otherwise, I would be stuck at the same mundane level for years and how could I do our new mission?   Love, Sondra

January 11, 2017

❡ THE 5 "BIGGIES"
Some of the clearest teachings Leonard Orr taught us at the beginning of Rebirthing were what he called the "five biggies."

❡ These are the major consciousness factors that prevent you from achieving and maintaining bliss. Liberation Breathing / Rebirthing helps people clear out these consciousness factors. They are 1) birth trauma 2) specific negatives 3) parental disapproval 4) unconscious death urge, and 5) other lifetimes. Today I want to talk about the parental disapproval syndrome. There are several vehicles by which this syndrome is transmitted. Three of the most popular are bedtime, mealtime, and toilet training.

The Parental Disapproval Syndrome:
> ❖ *There is a lot of unpleasantness connected with beds and it is no wonder some people have difficulty having fun in bed and in the bedroom. Not only have you recreated the womb like experience by going to bed (which could bring up the tension of the birth trauma), but there is also this fact: Children get punished by being sent to their room. They go*

there and feel unloved. That is why some people can have good sex only outside the bedroom.

❖ *Mealtime is the time when most kids get the bad news. That is when you also learn that if you don't clean up your plate you are not loved.*

❖ *Then there is toilet training: Problems of constipation, diarrhea, etc. are probably connected to toilet training. I have had clients who became anally fixated and could only get turned on by anal sex. One client took enemas constantly.*

❖ *Being aware of parental disapproval is very important as you are likely to set your mate up to be your disapproving parent(s), and you will "pull" disapproval out of them and then resent them. You could have disapproval wired up with love, and then you don't want to give up the disapproval as you might lose the love. It gets very distorted.*

pp. 60-61 from *Rebirthing in the New Age*
By Leonard Orr and Sondra Ray
Love, Sondra

January 12, 2017

⁋ BAD THOUGHTS AT BIRTH

At the moment of birth, you formed impressions about the world which you have carried all of your life. You even may have formed some very strong thoughts about life itself. These impressions control you from a subconscious level. Many of them are negative:

- ❖ *Life is a struggle*
- ❖ *The universe is a hostile place*
- ❖ *The universe is against me*
- ❖ *I can't get what I need*
- ❖ *People hurt me*
- ❖ *There must be something wrong with me*
- ❖ *Life is painful*
- ❖ *Love is dangerous*

❖ *I am not wanted*
❖ *I can't get enough love*

❡ Your parents and others who cared for you didn't know what you needed when you were born; they gave you a lot of things you did not need. Lights that were too bright for sensitive eyes, sounds that were too harsh for your ears, touches of hands and fabric that were too rough for your delicate skin. Some of you (despite the fact that your spine had been curled up for nine months), were jerked upside down by your heels and beaten, which produced excruciating pain. Breathing became associated with pain and your breath has been too shallow ever since. The cord was cut too fast and you were in shock. This is why we need Liberation Breathing / Rebirthing to be liberated from our birth trauma.
Love, Sondra

January 13, 2017

❡ THE HIGHEST REALITY
The highest reality is that you are one with God and your mate is one with God. God is life and love and bliss. Everything else is not real.
❡ The ego is the thought that you are separate from that. It makes you experience fear, guilt, pain, misery, struggle, conflict, worry, depression, disease and death. You can dispel it by withdrawing belief in it.
❡ When your mate is experiencing his limited mind (ego states), you must be careful not to agree with his/her illusions about himself/herself. See your mate as healed. See your mate as perfect, alive, loving, joyful, peaceful and immortal. This is precisely how Jesus healed people. He would not go in agreement with their limited mind. He only saw the Holy Spirit in them; and His reality was so clear and strong that, in His presence, people could not maintain their old reality.
❡ However, when your mate is having a crisis, he believes it is real. He experiences fear and the fear seems real. Give

him or her space to feel it and express it without cutting him off; but then suggest he has a breathing session. Gently remind your partner who he is and what he can do. This is the encouragement he or she needs.

♪ Sometimes reading ACIM out loud to your mate will remind him of his highest reality.

P.S. We went out on the town here in Nashville to hear live music with our house guest Patty. Ended up at a late-night burlesque show! Fun! Fun! Fun! I think having fun is God —like no matter how.

Love, Sondra

January 14, 2017

♪ BLESSING INSTEAD OF JUDGING
Although that is an ancient practice, it might be new for you to develop the habit of blessing those whom you want to judge.

♪ The kahunas of Hawaii teach that even MENTALLY criticizing others affects your body. They teach that criticism of the self, or of others, causes stress and inhibits awareness, memory, and energy flow, making you weaker and more susceptible to illness.

♪ The Bible teaches us that someone who is thankful for all things will be made glorious and thus attitudes of love, praise, and gratitude fill one with an incomprehensible power of the Spirit. These are called "ascension attitudes."

♪ We may know these ideas but applying them all the time is another story. When someone displays a behavior that is intolerable, we usually don't feel like praising them for it, of course, or blessing them. But to break the habit of judging that person, just try blessing the situation instead.

♪ Support the person in moving through the offensive pattern, bless them, see them as healed of it and honor and respect their God Self. This is easier to do if the relationship is already placed in the context of conscious blessing. Blessing what you want daily and focusing on praise as a habit will create a safe space in your relationship. A sense

324

of peace and relaxation should be the context of any
relationship; and this should be re-established
daily—telepathically and verbally. Try praise saturation!

Love, Sondra

January 15, 2017

¶ ATTRACT A MATE, OR NOT
If you are single and not in an intimate relationship, you are
either enjoying your freedom or perhaps longing for a mate.
Hopefully you are not suffering while not being open for a
change. Since you are single, it is good to accept that you
have chosen solitude and realize that it was not forced upon
you by bad luck, fate, lack of potential mates, or something
being wrong with you. You are never a victim of your
circumstances. For some reason your higher self has
chosen to be alone for this period, OR you are too afraid of
an intimate relationship. Which is it? Whatever your
reasons, you CAN create a mate any time you wish,
whenever you are ready. You can process your fear of
intimacy any time. If you cannot do it yourself, we are glad
to help.
¶ Here are the books that make it very clear how to attract a
mate:

1. *Spiritual Intimacy* (by Markus and myself).
2. *Love Will Find You* (by Kathryn Alice)
3. *Calling in the One* (by Katherine Woodward)
4. *Ask and It is Given* (by Esther Hicks)

¶ All these books give different formulas. In our book I tell
exactly how I created Markus in my life. I had to take steps,
as I was too independent for too many years. If you read
these books and it still does not happen then you are
blocked, and you really need a Liberation Breathing
session. I have become very good at helping women find
their man. And it is never too late.

Love, Sondra

January 16, 2017

❡ WHAT IS YOUR MISSION TOGETHER?
Imagine what would happen if a couple sat down and decided right from the beginning, what kind of mission they were going to accomplish together, for the world—and they actually did it! This spiritual mission could be a joint career of service. If they were already in different careers, they could still decide what kind of service they could offer the world together apart from their careers.

❡ When people are deeply in love, they feel a natural concern for the state of the world, and they want to do something about it. If love has waned and the relationship is stale, it might just be because the couple never acted on a sense of purpose.

It is never too late to infuse your marriage or relationship with this gift. It is not only a gift to the world; it is a gift to the relationship. What is your mission together?

❡ It gives the relationship true meaning. I have studied successful relationships of partners who were equally powerful people. With all that combined power it can be a real challenge together unless they commit to some mission. The ones that have stayed together have done this.

❡ Missions are satisfying. In my case, finding mine felt like the beginning of my true life. However, I always had a natural desire to serve. I started out as a waitress in college, then I became a nurse, then I joined the original Peace Corps. Then I became an Air Force nurse. Then I became a Breathworker. Then I became a healer. Then I became a writer and international speaker, always studying relationships and helping people with that. Then when Markus and I joined, things really took off! It was wonderful.

❡ Once I held a class where I asked each student to select a mission that would be a stretch for them. Almost everyone totally underestimated their abilities. Big stretches make you expand, and at the same time they heal you. And what is your contribution?

Love, Sondra

January 17, 2017

❦ APPLICATIONS OF CHAPTER 6 IN THE TEXT OF ACIM
Here are some of the highlights I picked out from Chapter 6
in the Text of *A Course in Miracles*:

> ❖ *No one can hurt me or attack me but myself. I
> forgive myself for making attack real when it is not.*
> ❖ *instead of expressing or repressing anger, I will
> locate and change the thoughts causing anger. I will
> not lower my vibration to that of anger because it is
> destructive to my energy body.*
> ❖ *I wish to follow the example of Jesus because He
> leads me out of pain.*
> ❖ *I forgive everyone who misinterpreted the Bible
> through the ego and those who confused me. I
> forgive myself for "buying into" this confusion.*
> ❖ *I forgive myself for projecting my thoughts onto
> others. I am forgiven by them. I now choose to
> extend love rather than project; I also remember
> that all blame is off the track.*
> ❖ *I am no longer concerned about getting. I am
> committed to giving all that I can. This is the way to
> be saved.*
> ❖ *I choose peace over conflict. I am careful not to
> create conflict, add to it, or support it in my space.*
> ❖ *I am willing to change. I am now an inspiration to
> others to change.*
> ❖ *I always reach for the highest, most spiritual
> thoughts. I identify with that which is good for me.
> Heaven consciousness is a decision I am willing to
> make now.*
> ❖ *I am willing to promote peace, spread and teach
> peace. I give up all conflict in myself, so that I am
> becoming the peace of mind fully. Peace is who I
> really am.*

Love, Sondra

January 20, 2017

❡ ON A BOAT IN L.A.
Last night we had a mini-seminar on Greta's boat where
she lives full time. We had around 15 people who just fit in.
It was so much fun. I taught a healing seminar and people
were very interested. I had everyone pick one condition they
wanted healed in their body. Then I taught them the
Ultimate Truth Process, which I myself developed—which
they loved. It is a writing process:

1. The exact negative thought that caused this condition
   was_____.
2. My payoff for keeping this condition is_____.
   (A "payoff" is a neurotic benefit you are getting out of it.)
3. My fear of giving up this condition forever is_____.
4. If this condition could talk, what it would say is_____.
5. I will let go of this condition when_____.
6. The affirmation I need to think to heal this condition
   is_____.

❡ This is the information you need to know. There are 3
steps to spiritual healing

1. Find the cause (see above).
2. Confess those thoughts to God, your guru, or another.
3. Do spiritual purification practices to release the above.

❡ Then I go over the spiritual purification practices to use for
self-healing.
❡ We got up at 6 AM this morning to watch the inauguration.
Since we are moving to Washington, D.C. as per Babaji's
request, we have to be informed.
Love, Sondra

January 21, 2017

❡ IN SOUTHERN CAL

What I like about Southern California is that everyone is having SO MUCH FUN!

❡ We were celebrating life ourselves. So, last night we went to the Italian restaurant of a client of ours. Sal's restaurant is called Scopas. It is so famous that they don't even have any sign on the building. The place was packed. This was the best Italian food I have ever had, seriously. And we have been to Florence, Rome, and Milan! I had stuffed squash flowers and squash ravioli. Could not believe it!

❡ Despite what you think of Trump, you have to admit that yesterday was a great American day. I was really feeling like serving our country again. I did it for the Peace Corps. And I did it when I was an Air Force Nurse during the Viet Nam War. So now by going to Washington, I will be doing it again and that feels good. However, we have no idea yet what Babaji wants us to do in Washington, D.C. Nevertheless, I felt happy we had a peaceful exchange of power yesterday and we had a beautiful ceremony to watch. Celebrating last night felt good.

Love, Sondra

January 23, 2017

❡ IN A RAIN STORM

It was a rain storm when David Stark and Sue drove us all the way to Pasadena. They were angels. We were thrilled to see Maile, and she had our meal all prepared. Then we gave another seminar on healing. People loved it. I am now convinced I must keep doing this evening seminar around the world as everyone tells me how much they got out of it. Almost every single person came up and thanked me profusely. There is nothing like RESULTS.

❡ A few years back we made two trips to India in one year. The first trip we took a group as usual. The second trip we went alone to have a private darshan with our guru Muniraj. We asked him if there was anything he wanted us to do. He said that it was very important that we help people with relationships and healing. He said that people were really, really, going to need that in coming times. I was so happy as we were already doing that! People are getting healed in

Liberation Breathing; but I never had a healing seminar per
se. Now I do. Once again, California made me break
through!
Love, Sondra

January 24, 2017

❡ DIVINE MOTHER OF LIFE IMMORTAL
My husband is a poet. Words come out of him naturally to
honor the Divine. Here is one poem from his book, *Odes to
the Divine Mother:*

> *Divine Mother of Life Immortal, make me a vessel
> of Your Love in a body that sees no death. You
> infuse me with Your strength that created a whole
> cosmos, a strength flowing in my veins and
> permeating my thoughts with absolute freedom. Let
> not the thoughts of death touch my soul in a world
> of men obsessed with death's apparent inevitability.
> Turn my mind around in this belief that all things in
> nature have an end, and we will surely die as part
> of cycles already set, already decided for us in a life
> with certain end. Make me certain of immortal life
> instead—the will You have for me that brings
> perfect happiness. Give me absolute dominion over
> my cells, over my thoughts that are their royal
> monarchs. Keep me aligned in my rule so my
> kingdom of physicality is ever an expression of Your
> Immortal Life of peace and Joy. Make all my actions
> consistent in this one purpose to extend the truth
> that there is no death, and Love is the law of the
> land that abolishes all need for conflict and strife.
> Put me into a frequency of deep ease, of relaxation
> destined to be my leisure divine. Keep my mind
> ever calm, with no reactions to the illusions of
> appearance, as others choose to die and fight for
> life around me. There is no fight for life needed. You
> give Life and only Life. What could there be in me
> that still would need release? Take from me all the
> last remnants of tattered conflict and doubt, of fear*

and limitation. Make me fully aware I am Your Holy Son of God Himself.

Written by my husband Markus Ray. Pretty cool, huh?

Love, Sondra

January 26, 2017

ꆯ ON THE PLANE BACK HOME
I read this on the plane:

> *A lady once wrote her autobiography in four very short chapters:*
> ❖ *Chapter One: "I walked down a new street. There was a deep hole in the sidewalk. I fell into it. It wasn't my fault. It took me a long time, but I finally got out."*
> ❖ *Chapter Two: "I walked down the same street. There was a deep hole in the sidewalk. I fell into it. It was my fault. It took me a long time, but I finally got out."*
> ❖ *Chapter Three: "I walked down the same street. There was a deep hole in the sidewalk. I walked around it."*
> ❖ *Chapter Four: "I walked down a different street."*
> (From the book *Fresh Start* by Joel Osteen)

Love, Sondra

January 28, 2017

ꆯ ARE YOU PART OF A SPIRITUAL COMMUNITY?
For the first training in Portland we have a small group but that does not matter as I can start a community with just a few people. There is nothing as important as being part of a spiritual community. I love starting those. People have a refuge where to go to get help and support. You don't have

to rely on your mate to give you everything. You have a like-minded group where you can share what is going on with you, and where you can get "processed" to go to a higher level. It is important to hang out with people who are getting clear, who are positive, who are up-beat.

§ In your spiritual life this is called "the principle of right association." In other words, it is important to put yourself with the highest people you can find who force you to adapt upward. This is precisely why we go to India every year. We are forced to adapt upward. Don't associate with people who bring you down. If you want to ascend, you should not even hang out with angry people. Their vibration will bring you down. People who are working on themselves and who are positive will help you stay positive.

§ Be careful who you spend time with, who you live with, and especially who you have sex with. If you belong to a spiritual community, you easily meet the right people. Your city might have an Ammachi group and a Babaji group. Find a breathwork community. Go to the right meet-up groups.
Love, Sondra

January 29, 2017

§ BEAUTIFUL VENUE
We are literally in the most beautiful venue I have ever had in my whole career. It is right on the river and the architecture is gorgeous. The room faces the river and the whole inside is gorgeous. I notice what a positive effect this has on me.
Beauty can really change how I feel. It makes me feel fantastic.

§ People act differently around beauty also. Beauty should be the start of things really as we yearn to commune with the beautiful. It changes your emotion in a positive way. It makes you feel happier, less stressed, and less frustrated. In my apartment at home, I make sure that everything one looks at is beautiful. Try this: the Chinese say if you have only two pennies left in the world, buy a loaf of bread and a lily.
Love, Sondra

January 30, 2017

♫ EIGHT MINUTE PROCESS

I have shared this before. Sometimes I repeat things because they are SO IMPORTANT and I want you to get them. I teach the eight-minute process in the LRT, and people really love it. You can use it easily in your relationships—any relationship, but especially the one you have with your life partner. It is a communication process one can count on. Markus and I use it a lot, especially when we are stuck on something.

l. Set aside a private time for just the two of you alone at a beautiful place like a restaurant with soft music and a carpet on the floor so it is not noisy.

2. Make an agreement to take eight minutes each to share. The one listening must be totally present and practice non-judgmental listening. The one listening must be willing to follow these rules:
a. Absolutely no interruptions.
b. Absolutely no making bad faces or rolling eyes.
c. Absolutely no rehearsing in the mind a rebuttal.
d. Absolutely saying only THANK YOU at the end.

3. Then switch and apply same principles.

4. Use non-violent communication at all times:
a. I observe this in our relationship: _____.
b. The way I feel about it is: _____.
c. What I recommend and need is: _____.

5. After both have spoken each for 8 minutes, then you are ready to have a peaceful discussion. Some couples in extreme stress have had to do this process every day for some days.

♫ P.S. Yes this can be done in the nude in a hot bath.
Love, Sondra

January 31, 2017

❡ ARE YOU ASCENDING?
A couple should cultivate their capacity to enjoy life. There needs to be an intention for feeling good. Keep asking:

Are we ascending the ladder of holiness or are we descending?

❡ Is what we are doing life-enhancing or life-depreciating? If what you are doing is descending the ladder of holiness or is life depreciating, you are going to feel badly. If what you are doing is ascending the ladder of holiness and is life enhancing, you are going to feel good.
❡ I hope I have made the point that relationships viewed from the soul level (holy relationships) are very different from those viewed at the personality level (unholy relationships). A relationship that is soul mated has a lot of passion naturally. One that is not soul related may be lacking in passion so that a couple might create a lot of drama to get a rush. How will you ever get out of your karma that way? Your karma can bury you. From our book *Spiritual Intimacy.*
Love, Sondra

February 1, 2017

❡ THE IDEAL SCENARIO
The ideal scenario for a relationship, in my opinion, is where both are actual trained Breathworkers. I cannot stress enough how wonderful this is. Let's say one partner is activated or going through something. He or she can then ask his or her partner for a session.
❡ This is wonderful as it avoids dumping one's stuff on the partner. This is wonderful because one does not have to suppress stuff, nor does one have to wait until he or she can get some kind of help from someone somewhere. We are training Breathworkers at events around the world: The Glastonbury Quest in England, The India Quest, The Bali

Quest, The Iceland Quest. These are my favorite places on the planet. Although a Breathworker is in training for life, we can get you started on one of these *Quests*. You will be able to practice giving another a session. Every day of the Quest people are under our supervision; it is really fantastic. Think about it.

Love, Sondra

February 2, 2017

❡ CONSIDERING MARRIAGE
There was a guru who said that marriage is out of date and destroys all possibilities for happiness. He insisted that marriage makes everyone into a zoo animal and exacerbates the will to die.
❡ However, Swami Kruyananda said the following:

> ❖ *Marriage can help a person achieve inner balance (especially between reason and feeling).*
> ❖ *Marriage helps break the confines of selfishness and ego, helping one to learn to live in a larger reality than one's own.*
> ❖ *Marriage helps one expand one's identity.*
> *It provides a proving ground for one's inner spiritual development. It tests a married mate's spiritual qualities.*
> ❖ *Marriage is a vehicle through which one can achieve union with God (after achieving union with the God in your mate).*

❡ Of course, marriage is a sacred bond only if it is made sacred. I like being married because I have a holy relationship first. What do you think?

Love, Sondra

February 3, 2017

♂ YOUR ENEMY IS YOUR SAVIOR

This is from Lesson #78 in the Workbook of *A Course in Miracles.* The lesson is, "Let miracles replace all grievances." It is one of the most confronting lessons, because it asks us to take someone with whom we have a lot of grievances, and make him/her our "savior" for the day:

> *Begin by holding someone who is difficult in your mind as you now consider him. Review his faults, the difficulties you have had with him, the pain he has caused you, his or her neglect, all the little and larger hurts he or she has caused. Regard his or her body with its flaws and better points. Think of his or her mistakes and sins.*
> *♂ Let us ask of the Holy Spirit who knows this Son of God in his reality and truth that we may look on him in a different way, and see our Savior shining in the light of true forgiveness given unto us. Visualize this. Then say, "Let me behold my Savior in this one You have appointed as the one for me to ask to lead me to the holy light in which he stands that I may join with him. You stand with me in the light (say the person's name). The light in you is all that I would see (say the person's name)."*

♂ This person is your teacher—to show you something in yourself you would not have seen.
Love, Sondra.

February 4, 2017

♂ FORGIVE EVERYONE

Love is impossible where there is no forgiveness. ACIM says that the unforgiving mind is full of fear with no room for love. It is sad with no release of pain. It suffers and abides in misery. It is torn in doubt, confused. It is afraid to go ahead, afraid of sound, afraid of stillness. It is terrified of the dark but especially terrified of the light. It is angry and sees only sins. It wants to live but wishes it was dead. It sees no hope of escape. When you have an unforgiving thought, you make a judgement, and the mind is closed and cannot be released.

꩜ Furthermore, by failing to forgive, we are condemned to a seemingly endless cycle in which the past repeatedly recurs in the present. It could be called repetition compulsion, and what you don't forgive you attract.

꩜ Say this: "I forgive EVERYONE for whatever they did to me, and I know that whatever they did, I alone invited and now accept full responsibility for it. I requested the lessons, and they helped me to learn that which led to my further unfolding of light and love."

From our book *Spiritual Intimacy*
Love, Sondra

February 6, 2017

꩜ APPLYING CHAPTER 12 IN THE TEXT OF ACIM
Here are some of my notes from reading Chapter 12 in *A Course in Miracles*:

> ❖ *I no longer weaken myself by creating illnesses to replace God.*
>
> ❖ *I awaken to the fact that I am already at home in God right now, and that I am perfect in God. I place no other gods before Him (such as the god of sickness).*
>
> ❖ *Sickness and death were bad habits that I have had. As I remember my own identity, I realize that these things are unnecessary.*
>
> ❖ *I am now completely forgiven for the blasphemous times I denied who I was. I forgive the church for teaching me the wrong definition of blasphemy.*
>
> ❖ *I acknowledge that, since God has given me freedom to choose (free will), I am the one totally responsible. Now I accept myself as God created me. I acknowledge Him as my Creator.*

❖ *I can help heal others by seeing them as healed. I do not go into agreement with their belief systems, and I do not add fear.*

❖ *I see in sick people the love of God and peace. I strengthen that in them. My presence alone, grounded in Spirit, will make them strong.*

Love, Sondra

February 7, 2017

❡ THE TRUE HERO
The True Hero is distinguished first by his (or her) warm and radiant personality; second by his good manners. He also has charm, high good humor, and infinite capacity for compassion and attention to human detail. A well-trained Hero has these 10 powers:

1. He (or she) lives as long as he pleases.
2. He enters deep meditation at will.
3. He can shower immensely valuable necessities on all living beings.
4. He improves destiny everywhere.
5. He lives in and is of the world and purifies it by his existence.
6. He straightens the bent, frees the bound, and releases energy wherever he goes.
7. He goes the way of peace.
8. He can perform miracles if necessary.
9. He understands the purpose of love, its intrinsic meaning and implications.
10 He stills doubt, opens eyes, dissolves pain and guilt. He bestows understanding which leads to insight and higher wisdom.

❡ He shows the way to fulfillment of every loving wish.
From *The Masters of Destiny* by James Allen

Love, Sondra

February 9, 2017

❡ WHAT I LEARNED BY GOING THROUGH THIS MOVE
Basically, I really got that staying with what is familiar is the
easy choice. Doing something big and different is such a big
stretch that you are forced to change. This is the harder
thing. One wants to avoid it. You have to go through a lot.
Your ego puts up a fight. It is a test to see if you are really
courageous.

❡ For example, we had every single convenience in walking
distance from our apartment in Nashville. It was easy. It was
so nice. It was simple. Just to arrange everything for the
movers made us nervous.

❡ In D.C. we are going to have to pay double rent. We are
not able to count on things being that close. We have to get
our friend Amy to see that the packers do everything right
as we are on tour. We have to count on Prema to meet the
movers in D.C. which she also is kind enough to do. She
found our apartment and we have to trust by looking on the
internet that it is going to be okay. It is *complicated*. It made
us nervous. I am not used to being nervous ever. I am
usually totally relaxed.

❡ I was saying to Markus: "Now I see why people stay in
bad relationships and don't move on. The familiar is easier."
But life is about change and progress. We have accepted
the new assignment and there was no way we are not going
to do it. However, we even created people telling us we are
crazy to do this. I got some symptoms. We have to lie down
frequently and rebirth ourselves. This move won't take place
for a few weeks so now we don't even have a home. It is
weird. But we have a lot of work to do on the road.

❡ In my dream last night, I was going to a clairvoyant to ask
her where I should live to be of greatest service to mankind.
She said the following: "You need to be on the road just like
Ammachi!" So here we are finally surrendering to the
unfamiliar.

Love, Sondra

February 10, 2017

❡ COURAGE AND LONG CONTRACTS

If you want to play in the *big leagues*, you may have to deal with leases or contracts that are 45 pages long! (We only had a one-page contract in Nashville.) It is tempting to think it is scary. But we keep on meditating on courage. That is a vibratory emotion of a very positive nature and all are attracted by it. We don't want to transmit a bad feeling to those whom we contact. We cannot afford to remain afraid. Markus keeps saying to me that we must be fearless. Babaji told me "FAITH IS EVERYTHING." Babaji Himself was fearless, believe you me.

❡ If we remain courageous, we cannot indulge in self-pity or complacency. How can we lead others out of darkness and confusion unless we maintain courage? When courage is lost, all is lost. We would become weaklings without it. Self-pity leads to being a coward.

❡ Right now meditating on courage is feeling like a constructive power for me. Whenever I let myself go into any fear in life, I feel weak and that feels terrible. Courage gives me strength and power. I have to really acknowledge my husband for dealing with all this paperwork!

❡ Every time Babaji has pushed me to jump levels and I did, I looked back and wondered why I was so hesitant, as the next level always felt better. But when you jump levels, at first you are at the bottom of the next level. It is like learning to walk. After we get through this move and get beyond the bottom of the next level, I know we are going to feel better than we did before.

❡ And what happens when you move on from a relationship that is not working? You get a better one if you courageously change your thoughts. If you remain afraid or bitter, you could descend and get something worse. So, it is a spiritual test.

Love, Sondra

February 11, 2017

❡ MORE ON VERBAL PROCESSING
One of the big contributions I originally made to Rebirthing in the old days was the art of verbal processing, a form of self-inquiry. It is essential to know where you are stuck and to be able to clear the *stuckness*. One definition of a humble person is that he is willing to recognize his or her errors, admit them, and do something about them.

❡ Through processing, one can learn to recognize errors that may be hidden. When we process, we inquire deeply into the nature of our conditioned and unbalanced ego patterning with the intention of finding the truth. The results are that you:

- ❖ *Become more aware, flexible, and free.*
- ❖ *Function to the best of your ability.*
- ❖ *Cope with the speed of evolution.*
- ❖ *Let go of obsolete teaching from childhood.*
- ❖ *Become free of the past while bringing clarity.*
- ❖ *Let go of extraneous baggage.*
- ❖ *Cope with life's challenges.*
- ❖ *Have resources for insight and creativity.*

❡ Leslie Temple Thurston, a friend of mine says this: "A cleared consciousness is the most valuable asset to life." We can teach you how to do it. Check out our book *Liberation Breathing* for starters, or come take a seminar with us.
Love, Sondra

February 12, 2017

❡ PREVERBAL DECISIONS AT BIRTH
Here are some preverbal decisions made by babies at birth:

- ❖ *Life is a struggle.*
- ❖ *The universe is a hostile place.*
- ❖ *Love is dangerous.*

341

> ❖ *I can't get enough love.*
> ❖ *Men hurt me.*
> ❖ *I can't trust people.*
> ❖ *I have to struggle to survive.*
> ❖ *I can't get out (of the womb or the relationship which becomes womb).*
> ❖ *I have to get out of here.*
> ❖ *I am not wanted.*
> ❖ *There must be something wrong with me.*

What you have to remember is this: WHATEVER YOU BELIEVE TO BE TRUE, YOU CREATE—especially what you believe in your subconscious mind. So now you see how a person could go on creating these preverbal thoughts and make them real. Your birth script has more power over you than you realize.
Love, Sondra

February 14, 2017

❡ WHAT IS THE UNCONSCIOUS DEATH URGE?
The *unconscious death urge* is a conglomerate in the unconscious mind that includes the following thoughts:

> ❖ *I am separate from God.*
> ❖ *Death is inevitable.*
> ❖ *Belief in one's personal lie.*
> ❖ *All anti-life thoughts.*
> ❖ *Family traditions on death (what ancestors died of).*
> ❖ *False religious theology.*
> ❖ *All guilt.*
> ❖ *The belief in sin.*
> ❖ *Past life memories of dying.*
> ❖ *The secret wish to die if you hate your life.*

THE RESULTS OF THE DEATH URGE ARE:
> ❖ Fear
> ❖ *Sapped vitality and fatigue*

- ❖ *Lack of clarity*
- ❖ *Inhibited creativity*
- ❖ *Illness*
- ❖ *Aging*
- ❖ *Blocked wisdom*
- ❖ *Anger*
- ❖ *Depression*
- ❖ *Helplessness*
- ❖ *Failure/ loss of money*
- ❖ *Anything not working in your space*
- ❖ *Warfare (social statement of group death urge)*

(p. 193, *Liberation Breathing* by Sondra Ray)

February 14, 2017

♫ HAPPY VALENTINE'S DAY

The Catholic Church recognizes three different saints named Valentine. One legend is that Valentine was a priest who served the 3rd century Rome. When Emperor Claudius the Second decided that single men made better soldiers than those with wives and families, he outlawed marriage for young men. Valentine realized the injustice of that decree and defied Claudius and continued to perform marriage for young lovers in secret. He was put to death for this! Pope Gregory declared Febrary14 Valentine's Day because it was the beginning of the birds' mating season. Written Valentine's Day did not appear until after 1400. Hope you have a lot of fun today. Also see below which I wrote today.   Love, Sondra

February 14, 2017

♫ CAUSES OF AGING AND DEATH

Here are some other causes of aging and death, which make up the *unconscious death urge*:

❖ *Invalidation of personal divinity*
❖ *False religious theology (such as sin is real/belief you are separate from God/ death is inevitable.*
❖ *Lack of Immortalist philosophy*
❖ *False belief systems (medical belief)*
❖ *Family traditions*
❖ *Addictions and over-eating*
❖ *Anger and non-forgiveness*
❖ *Unresolved tensions and birth trauma*
❖ *Anger at God*
❖ *Denial of the unconscious death urge*

❡ No *youthing* shot or magic health elixir will process your *unconscious death urge*. This is a mental and spiritual matter. Spiritual purification clears the death urge. Remember this: The power of God is stronger than any disease.

Love, Sondra

February 16, 2017

❡ TRAVEL GLITCH
Our driver (who was kind enough to drive us here to the other side of Florida), taught us something on the way. We were a bit disturbed because we found out our travel agent had gotten us tickets to St. Thomas instead of St. Croix. This is going to cost us $250 each to change tickets which adds up to $1,000 both ways. He took no responsibility for this mistake as he claimed he had sent us the itinerary to check. We saw how we attracted this because we were already "disturbed" that our rent was going to be double in Washington, D.C. of what it was in Nashville, TN. It is obvious that when one does "mental grumbling" like that, one just creates more messes.
Jeanine told us that she heard from some teacher this: "If you make money your issue, it will always be your issue!" We had to thank her for stopping our minds on that one. Well, we are forgiving ourselves because our chiropractor

Lynn, pointed out that moving is #3 on the stress list after divorce and death. So, we needed some correction and we got it from friends. So last night before going to sleep we both stated everything that we are grateful for and that helped.

❡ I decided I must review the book *The Magic* during this time. Gratitude will always get you out of a funk.

❡ Getting ready to do the New LRT here in Ft. Worth, Florida, at Jai Star Studios. Starting tomorrow night.
Love, Sondra

February 17, 2017

❡ ALL ABOUT WORRY

It is a psychological fact that thoughts must be either positive or negative. Negative thinking results in real disease or disturbed mentality, either of which is destructive of health and happiness. Worry, being negative, is an enemy and should be eliminated. If we allow worry to dominate our consciousness, intelligence must, of necessity, be submerged. It is only when we use our God-given reason that we are able to remove this useless and antagonistic force from our consciousness. Not only is worry a disease condition of consciousness but interfering as it does with the normal functions of the bodily organs, it is the cause of many physical diseases, and also of many mental disorders of a trying kind and degree.

❡ If a period of concentrated thinking offers no solution to a difficulty, the natural cause of action pursued by the AVERAGE person is to begin worrying, as though such a reaction would produce an answer to the problem. The individual begins to fret; then enters the fear of consequences followed by mental depression, despondence, and brooding, and soon the whole organism is disturbed. Like the emotion of fear, worry directly affects the physiological processes.

❡ Strange symptoms are the result of worry, and immediately the individual begins to attach these symptoms to serious causes. Worry is a destroyer of health, wealth, love, and expression and then creates bigger difficulties to worry about—all the outcome of negative thinking. Nature did not intend that we should worry. Worry, like fear, will disorganize the whole being—body, mind, and soul. Most people who are ill are the victims of worry. Either their illness is a direct outcome of worry or this destructive force is associated with the condition in some degree.

ℑ Worry is responsible for more disease than all the germs that exist upon the face of the earth. Worry is not only created by physical conditions but itself creates bodily sickness. It hastens the breakdown of the organic functions. In order eliminate worry from his experience, the individual must face life with courage. Life presents the opportunity for joy and happiness in equal measure with discontent and worry. We can avoid this suffering.

(From an old book I have called *Rays of Dawn*)

February 18, 2017

ℑ NEVER GO BACK!
Markus and I were having a discussion last night about the problem of going back to people and things that are familiar. This reminded me of the most dramatic teaching I had on this subject. A long time ago, two years after my divorce, my ex-husband called me and wanted me to come back. My thought was, "Yes, I should try it again and make it work." (There are seven stages of divorce and one is where you think you should go back.) I was in Arizona, and so I actually sent a lot of stuff ahead to Florida where he was. I was actually planning on going back the next day. I was sitting on the floor of my apartment talking to a friend about how I felt going back the next day. Suddenly I was filled with light and I heard a voice talking in the air (not in my head). I would have thought I was going crazy; but my friend heard the voice also. The light got stronger and I could not move. The voice said: "NEVER GO BACK!" I was stunned. Then the voice in the air got louder and said, "NEVER GO BACK. GO TO CALIFORNIA NOW."

ℑ My friend looked at me and said, "Sondra! I think you better go to California." I replied, "If I don't follow this voice, I will regret it my whole life." I did not know who was talking to me—God? (Later, after I met Babaji, I realized it had to be Him.) He *saved my ass*, so to speak. The next day I headed for California! I did not know anyone, and the California Nurses' Association had written telling me not to bother to come to California looking for a job as the waiting list was two years.

♪ I went anyway. The rest is history. I found everything there, mainly my enlightenment and Rebirthing. It was the best thing I ever did. If I had gone back, I would have gotten sick and it never would have worked out. I know that for sure now. I had nothing but miracles happen to me the moment I crossed the California line.

♪ I have had so many clients confess that they "went back" and it did not work. Be careful.

Love, Sondra

February 20, 2017

♪ PEACE INSTEAD

I once lived with a man for less than one day! He was one of the few men I ever dated who was extremely rich, so I was a bit dazzled and dazed, and did not see what I should have seen before I moved in.

♪ I started unpacking and I was having a good time as usual. He began picking a fight with me for no reason. I said to him, "Hey, I am not going there with you. I deserve peace in my personal life." He got mad at that statement even more, and stormed outside. I thought, "This relationship did not last very long." I started re-packing. He came back in and said, "I thought it over and you do deserve peace in your personal life—but I can't live like that!" I said, "I can see that. That is why I am re-packing my bags!"

♪ It was funny, but also a test. My lesson from *A Course in Miracles* that day was, "I could see peace instead of this." (Lesson #34) I was determined to learn that lesson, and since he even admitted he did not want peace, I was out of there! Of course, I had to face what my friends would think. What would my mother think etc., but I was proud of myself for passing the test and forgiving myself for making the mistake of moving in.

ʃ I am glad I did not stay because of what others would think. It would have been one fight after another. The ego is addicted to conflict. Some people like to fight. Others don't know how to stop fighting. I am not willing to do it. Why tolerate something like that?

Love, Sondra

February 21, 2017

ʃ YONI EGGS
The dinner discussion last night with our friend, Sula De Paula, turned to the topic of *yoni eggs*. I had to come home and look that up. At least I did know that *yoni* is the Sanskrit name for female genitalia. But I did not know that yoni stone eggs have been used for 5,000 years by empresses and concubines in the royal palaces of China.

ʃ Apparently, they increase libido, awaken sensuality, increase lubrication, balance estrogen levels, help you get to know your yoni, promote nerve growth, help overcome infertility, ease childbirth, reduce PMS, and work well in Tantric practices. They also increase your feminine intuition and make you more psychic.

ʃ She is going to bring me one tonight. They are made of jade, rose quartz, and black obsidian. Guess I will try one out!

Love, Sondra

February 24, 2017

ʃ A PROPHET FOR OUR TIMES
I was reading a book called *Prophet for Our Times* by Peter Deunov, and here are some lines that stood out to me:

> ❖ *Every human thought, every human feeling and every human action has to express gratitude to*

God, to all sublime beings that have bestowed the good things.

❖ *If we are grateful for the small good thing, the greater one will come.*

❖ *Do not express your opinion about people, because you are doing so about the work of God. You do not know what God is going to do with those people. God has not finished His work on them. There is no worse thing than to look for the faults of other people. It is another thing though, if you are ready to pray for them.*

❖ *Do not criticize one another. Look for each person's good characteristics. (I always teach that criticism kills relationships.)*

❖ *Every person is an object-lesson. Whether you like him or not, you should not judge him, you have to learn something from him.*

❖ *It is better for you alone to judge yourself and correct your mistakes.*

❖ *The tongue of a person should become so soft that every word which passes through it sounds harmonious to the human ear.*

❖ *If you say something to a person, and you feel joy in your mind, then what you have said is true.*

❡ How beautiful these saying are! From the **book** *Prophet for our Times* by Peter Deunov

Love, Sondra

February 25, 2017

❡ WHAT I AM LEARNING IN ST. CROIX
At first nothing was turning out the way we expected or wanted. We expected the island to be gorgeous since it is a US territory. We thought it would be romantic. But instead it appeared to be very run down and with a lot of ruins. It seemed very, very poor, and we had no idea of that. It made us feel depressed when we tuned into that poverty. I

349

thought "Poverty = no joy." Then we found out the turn-out was going to be very low because of that. So, we were not very satisfied with that. Of course, we did not blame our organizer and he tried very hard. But we still felt down and out.

¶ There is no air conditioning in the house where we are, none in the car, and none in the place we are working. The roads are absolutely pot-hole ridden. If we were beach people that would make a difference, but I have not really been a beach person ever. We were wondering why we were creating all this. There seemed to be a lot to complain about; but we were trying to change our attitude.

¶ What worked was getting to work. As soon as we started working my attitude changed completely. I love the people and I am now enjoying myself. No wonder Babaji says, "Work is Worship." The main thing I learned is that work gets you out of any funk, and serving people is always the answer. The other thing I learned is that people who live in the mainland USA often don't have any idea how lucky they are, and we all need a lot more gratitude for being American.

¶ Like everywhere, the people need so much help with relationships and health. We are here to give that. After I got back to work, I changed my attitude, I saw the charm of the place after all.

Love, Sondra

February 27, 2017

¶ A FUNNY THING
A funny thing happened in the St. Croix LRT. We were in an open-air yoga studio upstairs. Sunday afternoon, after the meal break, a parade started going by. I think it was the Dominican Republic parade or something like that. The music was so loud that I could not be heard. I mean REALLY LOUD! (Souped-up cars with loudspeakers.) Finally, I told everyone to just lie down and breathe to the music. I had no choice.

❡ I could not even go around and help people as they could not hear me at all, so I decided to lie down and breathe with everyone. It was not the time for the rebirthing, as I usually do it at the end of the day. But I had no choice. This went on for over one hour and 15 minutes. It got wilder and wilder. Well, the music pushed something out of me, and a very loud sound came out of my body. It was a hoot. It was lucky we did that. What would we have done during all that time? It was either that or watch the parade. Apparently, they have a lot of parades on this island.
Love, Sondra

February 28, 2017

❡ LEAVING NASHVILLE FOR GOOD
Tomorrow, on March 1st, our 8-year tenure in Nashville will come to an end. The movers are coming and Amy Lynn is meeting them, and by March 4th our things will be delivered to our new home in Washington D.C. met by Patricia Henderson. We have not even seen our new place yet—can you believe that? Patti arranged the whole thing! Meanwhile, we will be in Las Vegas when our stuff arrives in D.C. teaching the Loving Relationships Training. I hear we have over 30 people in the training, and it could be more, thanks to Mike Orci and Ali Ames Orci, Juanita Curiel, Jodi Friedman, Magdalena Brandon, Rikki Queso, Janelle Collard, and many other friends. We are so grateful to all of you. SEE YOU ALL SOON. HUGS.
Markus Ray & Sondra Ray

March 4, 2017

❡ THE DREAM STAGE
Do you know why the dream stage (romantic period) of relationships lasts only about two months on the average? That is because love brings up anything unlike itself. When your new partner is in love with you and you with them, that is a lot of energy entering your consciousness. Love is

351

energy for one thing. That energy is so powerful that it pushes up all kinds of junk from your subconscious: (past lives/ birth trauma/ parental disapproval syndromes/ death urges/ anger/ guilt, etc.). You are pushing up all that in them and they are pushing up all that in you. When all that stuff is coming up, people usually don't know what to do—so they fight. Then the dream stage ends rapidly.

ℊ It is kind of like if you have a glass of water with mud in the bottom. When you add more water, the mud gets all stirred up. This is when you need a spiritual purification technique to handle all this stuff. You keep pouring in more water (spiritual purification) and eventually the water gets clear and the mud gets washed away.

ℊ Our main spiritual purification method is Liberation Breathing—breathing it all out is a safe, effective way to handle all the stuff coming up. If you don't do the breathing, you get stuck. It is no fun. Liberation Breathing is also fun. If you never have had a session, we can give you one by Skype or Zoom. It takes about an hour and a half.
Love, Sondra (Teaching Las Vegas LRT). People had big miracles last night during the **Liberation Breathing session**!

March 5, 2017

ℊ AN INTERESTING DREAM
I had such an interesting dream I did not want it to end! I encountered this very, very interesting group of people who were fascinating to no end. They were very happy and healthy. They were from all walks of life. They were very entertaining. Brad Pitt was one of them, but they were not all actors at all. I wanted so much to be part of this group. But they said it was up to the leader. I could never find the leader. I kept lobbying for myself to get in this group. I told them they needed to expand and let me in. I told them not to let the leader control them. They were leaving for Bali together; but they became really interested in me and could not stay away from me.

ℊ I told them I could rebirth them all and they would love it. But they seemed unable to have me join without the leader's permission. I could not figure out where the leader was. Brad Pitt did a funny performance for me and the group got closer and closer to me. I finally told them that if they could not let me join, they should at least have me as a visiting professor!! Then I woke up. Markus said maybe I was supposed to be the leader.

❡ Today our things are being unpacked in our new apartment. It is going to be a new life.

Love, Sondra

March 6, 2017

❡ BABAJI IN YOUR LIFE

What is it like to have Babaji in your day-to-day life? Since Babaji materialized His body directly from the Source, He is not a "go-between" for you and God. You are able to go to the top and have a human face put on God. This is very helpful, as you can have Him as a friend and you never feel alone. You can talk to Him all day long and get answers. He makes an ordinary life into an extraordinary life.

❡ With Babaji you can feel bliss walking around in your own space at home, especially when you might otherwise feel alone. Of course, you have to be willing to go there where He comes from. There are some people who just don't let Him in. He says, "My love is available, you can take it or not." I say, "Why not? We need all the help we can get."

❡ Babaji can know you inside out. He knows what your karma is and He can take some of the load off, but He knows what you still have to do for yourself. He arranges leelas to help you clear it faster. (A *leela* is an arrangement by the Master to help you clear your issues.) This way he saves you lifetimes of struggle. You see what is unfolding in front of you and it is so clever you could never have dreamed it up yourself. Instead of a big crisis, you get a lesson that you end up appreciating. It is a consciousness training exercise.

❡ Babaji shows you when you are going down the wrong road before you end up hurting yourself.

From our book *Babaji: My Miraculous Meetings with a Maha Avatar*. If you order this book, you will never be the same. Love, Sondra

March 7, 2017

ʃ SOMETHING VERY MOVING
Patty Henderson has been unpacking our things in our new apartment. BLESS HER. She sent us the following text yesterday:

> *"The movers were very intrigued about your story. They were fascinated by Markus's paintings. This move touched their lives."*

You never know who you are going to reach and how. I am really happy that the movers were moved!

Love, Sondra

March 8, 2017

ʃ TRAVELLING TO OUR NEW HOME
We are travelling to our new home in Washington D.C. today. What can I say? A New adventure.

Love, Sondra

March 9, 2017

ʃ ARRIVED AT OUR NEW HOME
Patty had everything unpacked so you can imagine how nice that was. The way she arranged the kitchen was perfect. The only thing we had to really straighten out were the books and hanging the art. We felt totally overwhelmed when we awoke. The thing I did first was prepare the altars. I learned that in Bali. As soon as the altars were in place, I

felt inspired to go to work.

❧ I love these high ceilings. They are about fourteen feet, as we live in an old foundry loft.

❧ Markus is in shock. We need some time to integrate this. Our neighborhood is fantastic, however. We have all that we need right across the street. I feel good about this. We did it all very fast with the help of Amy and Patty. Can't say enough about these kinds of girlfriends!

Love, Sondra

March 10, 2017

❧ WHY MOVING IS SO GOOD

After recovering from the stress (moving is right up there with divorce and death regarding stress levels), one can really get the benefits. Staying in the same city all one's life can be boring. You get in a rut.

❧ Moving detached us from the past. Now we are in a state of discovery and inspiration. We see the beauty of new beginnings. This has forced us to make the decision to move forward in life which is always good for health and career. A new city means a new you. We are looking forward to discovering the new us. This has forced us to change. Change is good for you. Not only can we open up to new opportunities, but we can make new friends.

❧ We can have new food experiences, especially here. We can get a fresh start financially. I think one of the benefits for sure is I get to throw out stuff. I am amazed how much I am throwing out. We were starting to get into a rut, and we could have gotten STUCK. Never stay stuck. You can always make a change and lighten up!

Love, Sondra

March 11, 2017

❡ BRINGING BABAJI & THE DIVINE MOTHER TO WASHINGTON

Now we see that as our mission. It is so obvious. We have been preparing our loft for this. We have a lovely hallway where the Balinese Goddesses are hung. They are beautiful with praying hands. They are facing paintings of The Virgin of Guadalupe, Madam Pele, and Durga, the Divine Mother of India. The Goddesses are praying to the Mother and when you walk in it is VERY dramatic. I don't think people will ever forget visiting us. Then we have a large hanging of Babaji, life size photo, plus an etching of him standing on a mountain top with his garment blowing in the wind. These are very large and very beautiful, and it is the next thing one encounters. There is a nook where we have a large wood carving of Quan Yin on a stand. It is the one I "saved" during an earthquake in L.A. When I felt the tremor, I said to Markus, "What do I do?" He answered, "Grab the Quan Yin," which I did, or else it would have toppled over and crashed. When you turn the corner, there are paintings of the Balinese dancers.

❡ Since we have such extremely high ceilings in the main room, it is very spacious and there we have a large painting of Jesus, painted by Markus. The living and dining area are all together in one very spacious room. We have yet to hang the painting of the Divine Mother over the main altar as it is very heavy, and we need special things which Patty will bring tomorrow. It is looking like a temple.

❡ Also, tomorrow we are going to meet the main Rebirther in town. She is having a welcoming party for us and we are certainly looking forward to that. We hope to have a strong community going with her.

Love, Sondra

March 15, 2017

❡ IN ENGLAND
We just arrived in England. On the plane over I read this:
"Nearly all rich and powerful people are not notably
talented, educated, charming, or good looking. They are
rich and powerful by wanting to be rich and powerful. Your
vision of where or who you want to be is the greatest asset
you have. Without having a goal, it is difficult to score."
Think about that. If you don't set a goal, how can you
score?
Love, Sondra

March 16, 2017

❡ CHAOS LEADS TO MORE CHAOS
What I learned about myself today was that chaos in my life
just creates more chaos—and that does not work for me.
Although our apartment was beautiful enough to do a video
before we left, there was one room only half finished as we
had no time to do it before leaving. There are books stacked
on the floor and loads of papers that need to be filed and
straightened out. I did not like leaving it that way but had to.
When we travel it helps ground me to think of our place as
impeccable and totally organized. The sight in my mind
makes me relax thinking about the beauty we have. But we
could not get it all done before we left as we had to
purchase extra bookends. Maybe most people would not
care about this, but I do.
❡ I close my eyes and see that chaos. The worst thing was I
could not find my check list. So, I got here and realized I
had no pajamas! That felt like a disaster for the whole trip.
But by a miracle I had packed two pair for Markus so now I
am wearing his.
❡ Dulles airport was also something we are not used to. I
could not sleep on the night flight over, so we arrived here
tired, and my room felt in chaos this morning. But after we
got situated, we had fun going out with our organizer Lucy
Pattinson and her partner Michael. They drove us to see the
private school where they met, which was one of the very

best in the whole world. Then of course we all went out to the pub in the little town, by the babbling brook.

Love, Sondra

March 17, 2017

❡ SAINT PATTY'S DAY IN SURREY
There is a line in my LRT script that says:

> *"You are the writer of the script of your life; and everyone else in the universe is playing the part you have assigned to them!"*

Lately I have to emphasize to people the last part of that quote—what does it mean? It means that you are even creating every reaction people have toward you. If someone hit you, you assigned them to hit you. If someone had an affair on you, you assigned them to do that. If someone ripped you off, you assigned them to rip you off. This teaching is often very difficult for people to accept. They tend to want to be victims and blame the other. And yet, if you get this teaching (and I mean totally), then you will become very enlightened as you will learn what your subconscious is ordering out there.
❡ I constantly hear something like this, "My husband does not give me what I want." For example, he may not be generous to her but why did she attract that? ACIM says, "Beware of the temptation to perceive yourself unfairly treated."
❡ Another related teaching is, "You are the one you live with." Decades ago I went to a therapist and all he wanted to know is what was the man like, whom I was dating. He did not want to know anything about me. I said to him, "This is ridiculous. I might as well bring every boyfriend in here to see you." But I was not getting it at first. He knew everything about me by what I was attracting in my boyfriend. Think about it deeply.
Love, Sondra

March 18, 2017

❧ SHARING BABAJI

My favorite part of giving the **Loving Relationships Training** is when I can tell people about Babaji. If you surrender, Babaji will push you to be all that you can be. I had no idea who I could really be until I met Babaji. I was a nurse and I might have never realized all the talents I have now had I not let Babaji into my life. I let Him mold me like clay. This actually feels good because you always feel like you are progressing and not stuck in a rut. He gets you clear on your mission and keeps you on track with it. He gave us the miracle of Liberation Breathing / Rebirthing, and He gave us all the spiritual practices we need to stay clear. (The main practices are the Breathwork and the mantra Om Namah Shivaya.)

❧ My experience is Babaji also keeps you out of danger. You feel safe with Him. You feel protected no matter what happens. This is worth its weight in gold, to put it mildly. Many times, he has prevented me from doing things that would not have been good for me. That is quite a long list. So, I can be really relaxed, and this is wonderful.

Love, Sondra

March 19, 2017

❧ A NEW PATTERN

I have learned a lot of new things by doing The Loving Relationships Training myself, over the years! One is a new pattern of family and relationship dynamics. I am calling it the Over Tolerance Pattern. I see people putting up with things in a relationship I would never put up with. Tolerance is a good thing, such as in India where the driving is impossible, but people do not get road rage because they tolerate the traffic. They are also very tolerant to let in-laws live with them, etc. But one has to ask oneself what one is tolerating in a relationship that maybe they should not be tolerating. I would question:

> ❖ *Is it right to tolerate verbal abuse? I don't think so.*

❖ *Is it right to tolerate the silent treatment? I don't think so.*

❖ *Is it right to tolerate smoking? I question that.*

❖ *Is it right to tolerate lack of cooperation? I don't think so.*

❖ *Is it right to tolerate alcoholism? I don't think so.*

❖ *Is it right to tolerate an affair or emotional affair? I don't think so.*

❡ When is one over-tolerating just to keep the relationship? When is one really unhappy about certain things? Interesting to look at this.
Love, Sondra

March 20, 2017

❡ IS GOD OUR GOAL?
Markus gave a talk in the England LRT today on Lesson #256 from *A Course in Miracles*: "God is the only goal I have today." This lesson states:

> *The way to God is through forgiveness here. There is no other way. If sin had not been cherished by the mind, what need would there have been to find the way to where you are? Who would still be uncertain? Who could be unsure of who he is? And who would yet remain asleep, in heavy clouds of doubt about the holiness of Him whom God created sinless? Here we can but dream. But we can dream we have forgiven Him in whom all sin remains impossible, and it is this we choose to dream today. GOD IS OUR GOAL. Forgiveness is the means by which our minds return to Him at last.*
>
> *We have no goal except to hear Your Voice and find the way Your sacred Word has pointed out to us.*

❡ This is pretty profound. Can we make God our only goal today?   Love, Sondra

March 22, 2017

❡ TREATED LIKE A QUEEN
I have to admit it is great being treated like a
Queen—almost a Goddess in fact, here in India. That is the
service we get in the Lalit Hotel in New Delhi where I have
been coming for over 25 years. They all know us, and the
staff is just amazing. We have the group here for a few days
so they can rest in luxury and feel safe. India is rather
shocking the first time you come.
❡ The **India Quest** group enjoys feeling good at this hotel,
after going out on the streets to shop and look around. I like
to have the group take India in stages.
❡ There is an incredible spa here where you can take steam
baths and get massages, manicures, and pedicures etc.
The group is beginning to trickle in today. We have 21 of us
all together.
❡ VERY SAD watching the London Attack on TV. We just
came from England. Sending them Love.
Love, Sondra

March 24, 2017

❡ A NERVOUS BREAKDOWN
Something very shocking happened. A student who was
coming on the India Quest broke up with his girlfriend just
before coming, and on the plane he had a breakdown. The
plane was taxiing to the runway, and the pilot actually
turned the plane around and brought him back to the gate.
So, you know that it was serious. In this case we can only
try to help him telepathically through thought transmission.
❡ We can have communion with another this way. To
establish rapport; we must call on the subject mentally. We
can do this by focusing our attention on him and mentally
call his name. We then can imagine that he has answered,
and mentally hear his voice. What we sincerely believe as
true of another we can awaken in him. We therefore
imagine he is being healed. We must mentally see him in

the calm state we hope for him. We imagine that he is telling us back that he is now okay and feeling better.

₲ We must speak in confidence to awaken a corresponding state in him. We do not really give to him, but only *resurrect* the sanity which was temporarily asleep in him. We cannot regard space as an obstacle. A friend (a thousand miles away) is rooted in our consciousness, through our fixed ideas of him. The state we transmit to him has to be believed by us. So, this is what we are trying to transmit to him; *that he is going to be okay and sane and happy.*

₲ We are imagining that he is telling us now that he is that way. We send our blessings to him.

Love, Sondra

March 25, 2017

₲ GOD REALIZATION

India has discovered the ways by which God can be known. The greatest of all achievements is to find God. God Realization is a primary concern in India.

₲ Doing the "work" on oneself to clear the ego is the lifeline to real existence, *without which one remains undeveloped.* You have to do the work of transformation to actualize yourself. That is why these students came here to India. It is the fast track to God. But one has to give oneself to the work completely and un-hesitantly. The ego does not want us to give up anything. It wants to GET. So, our unconscious raises hell when we commit to the work. It tries to maintain defenses. So that is why I admire those who actually made it here. The work threatens the false life one made up. You have to be courageous to come here.

₲ One has to have a proper relationship with the spiritual msters, with Babaji, the Divine Mother, and with Jesus of *A Course in Miracles* to get liberated. One has to have *respect, consideration, love, appreciation, gratitude, service, and humility.* If one has rebellion and doubt, one cannot benefit. The channel is then closed.

₲ The ashram life is designed to force you to change. If one does not go along with the program, one goes back to one's old ruts. So, is a person going to be loyal to old conditioning or to one's freedom? In India one learns God is the Source of all happiness. Complete surrender to God is the only goal in life. Only God satisfies. If one wants to be saintly, one has to mix with holy people! This is what we do here on the India Quest.

Love, Sondra

March 26, 2017

❧ ADORING THE DIVINE MOTHER
Today we are on our way to Herakhan to participate in 9 days of adoration of the Divine Mother here in India. I saw this article on Adoring Shakti, which is the Living Energy of the Divine Mother. The ancient traditions here are to honor the Mother. Men and women alike worship the Divine Feminine aspect of creation that is the Source of all manifested form. Here we go to Herakhan, on the India Quest, to "adore Shakti."

Love, Sondra

March 27, 2017

❧ SURRENDER TO THE GURU
Surrendering to the guru is *the secret way to wisdom*. The relationship between friends is the greatest of human loves. Yet, the relationship between the guru and the disciple is the greatest expression of Divine love and friendship. The disciple bares his soul to the master and the master bares his heart to the disciple. Doing this inner work is the most important thing in your life, but it threatens the false life you made up.
❧ We are leaving our hotel here in Haldwani today for Herakhan. There will not be any more posts until we get back in ten days.
❧ Bhole Baba Ki Jai!

Love, Sondra

363

April 6, 2017

ℐ THE MUNDAN CLUB
We left the ashram yesterday, after ten days of worshipping the Divine Mother in the sublime Presence of Babaji and the Holy Masters. We had 14 people out of 21 in our group shave their heads. That is called getting a *mundan*, which is a complete head shave; an offering to the Divine of our vanity. *It is also a sign of surrendering and new beginnings.* Babaji said that it was easier for Him to enter our head with a mundan. The recommended time to keep one's mundan is nine months. You get maximum value if you do that, and you release all prenatal trauma. Jokingly, we call all the people who received mundan in Herakhan our "Mundan Club." But it is really no joke. These people are very seriously committed to their spiritual evolution and awakening.
ℐ Mundan is important for clearing one's karma. It is also an agreement between you and Babaji. You are surrendering to His lineage and you are allowing Him to take responsibility for your total liberation. Who wouldn't want that? I did my first mundan for nine months and I got so much out of it. I became so much more creative and I could write books so fast after that.
Travelling to Dehradun today. More later.
Love, Sondra

April 7, 2017

ℐ IN A PROCESS
Please pray for me, as I was in a huge process during this Navaratri (Divine Mother Festival). At one point I actually got laryngitis! This was rough as I was the teacher. Fortunately, Markus covered for me and the group was very supportive. I wrote letters to them and Markus read them to the group. In looking at the cause, it became clear that I was afraid of speaking out on outrageous subjects (like physical immortality) to the masses and authority figures. I had no fear of speaking to new age people—but to the masses? I did not feel any fear per se, but it got acted out in

my body, and my larynx became paralyzed. I confessed it all to the students and they just loved me. That really helped and then I got my voice back! Amazing what confession can do.

¶ After I got my voice back, I got a bad cough because I felt guilty about my lack of faith. This cough has persisted and it is hard for Markus to sleep at night. So, I am still in a process even though the Navaratri is finished. I tell students it may take them a year to integrate Navaratri. Usually I am fine and can go back to work immediately; but not so this year. I have gone very deep and I just hope I am okay for the work we have to do in Lebanon. Please pray for me. We have to fly to Beirut in four days, so I need a miracle.
Love, Sondra

April 8, 2017

¶ FIRE CEREMONIES
There are nine fire ceremonies offered, one each day to a different manifestation of the Divine Mother, during the Navaratri. They are dedicated especially to the Divine Mother and Babaji.

¶ This is the most powerful ceremony of all. It should never be missed when you attend the Navaratri. Offerings and mantras are given at the fire, which transform one for sure. Each person can offer a coconut to the fire, and psychically put into the coconut that which we want to let go of. The fire burns it up. The power of this ceremony reaches far and wide, as it helps balance the relationship between the 5 elements. We all say "Swaha!" each time an offering is put in the fire. This is a time one can give thanks and say the affirmation you want to manifest at the same time. Putting your affirmation into the fire is very, very, effective. It gives that thought *more power.* If your mind is focused you can create a miracle for yourself during this fire ceremony. The Priest reads the mantras very fast, calling on the aspects of the Divine Mother to accept the offerings. One can clearly feel the auspiciousness of this ritual.

Love, Sondra

April 9, 2017

❡ STARTING OUR DAY IN HERAKHAN
The daily program for the Divine Mother Festival starts with a morning bath in the river between 3 and 4:30 AM. This time is called Brahma Muhurta (Divine Moment) and is considered the most auspicious moment of the day to connect with the Divine. This bath is not only to become clean, but also to rinse ourselves of the accumulated mental activity during the night, and start with a fresh day. The water is highly energized running down from the Himalayas over the rocks of a sacred river—one feels vibrant and refreshed. The process of going bathing there, with the stars as your witness, puts you in touch with the beautiful energy that Herakhan and Mother Nature are offering.
❡ After that, Chandan is offered in the temple. Chandan means sandalwood in Hindi and is the main ingredient in the yellow paste applied to the forehead. This is considered prasad (Divine Nourishment offered), as it has already been offered to Babaji's padukas (silver shoes) in the early morning puja. The yellow paste has a cooling, calming effect on the mind that can easily be sensed when you meditate afterward. The three lines of Chandan symbolize Shiva. The red dot placed on the third eye, Cum Cum, is the sign for the Divine Mother, and is applied to open up your spiritual vision. Rice is also put on this spot, and has the quality of attracting Lord Ganesh, the remover of obstacles. Chandan is applied to each person, with everyone waiting in line in silence, while bhajans and mantras are being played in the background. After this we all chant the Aarti.
❡ I am writing these posts after the fact of Navaratri, because we had no internet in Herakhan. Thought you might like to know what goes on there.
More later.
Love, Sondra

April 13, 2017

❡ ARRIVED IN BEIRUT

We arrived in Beirut last night—crashed and couldn't wait to get sleep. Now we are back to work. There is so much to learn about this country and all the religious conflicts which are very complicated to me. Most of our clients went through the civil war and the overtaking by Syria and Israel. I am realizing how ignorant I am as an American about what is going on in the Middle East.

❡ Tonight going out to a real Lebanese restaurant and joining our gang: Thanks to Jad and Oumayma we are here to learn and serve.

Love, Sondra

April 14, 2017

❡ EARLY PHOENICIANS

Beirut is one of the oldest cities in the world, inhabited over 5000 years ago. Back then the Phoenicians were here, and they were great masters of trade in the Mediterranean region. The name comes from a Greek word that refers to the "purple cloth" the Phoenicians were so well known for making. Scholars now concur that modern-day Lebanon is where the Phoenicians lived and developed.

❡ It is pretty intense to be in the Middle East. Our clients have suffered through a lot in recent years. There was the Lebanese Civil War in 1975, and also Beirut was under siege from Syria in 1978 and under siege from the Israelis in 1982. They tell us what it was like. No fun. Some have family members killed or tortured.

❡ There are 18 religious groups here—4 Muslim sects, 12 Christian sects, and a couple of Jewish sects. What is most shocking to me is the fact that divorce is still handled by religious authorities. Our clients are wanting a divorce but telling us how nearly impossible it is. Some have paid off the priests to the tune of $30,000.

❡ We find it all a bit edgy, but people here are very passionate about their country. We really had a great time with our wonderful organizers. I have met some really powerful women here already. Going to work to do the LRT tonight. More later.

Love, Sondra

April 15, 2017

❡ HAPPY EASTER
I read this in *A Course in Miracles* today about Easter:

> "This day we celebrate Life, not death, and we honor the perfect purity of the Son of God [you and your brother] and not his sins. Offer your brother the gift of lilies, not the crown of thorns; the gift of love and not the 'gift' of fear. You stand beside your brother, thorns in one hand and lilies in the other, uncertain which to give. Join now with me and throw away the thorns, offering the lilies to replace them. This Easter I would have the gift of your forgiveness offered by you to me and returned by me to you. We cannot be united in crucifixion and in death.
> ❡ Nor can the resurrection be complete till your forgiveness rests on Christ along with mine. Easter is not the celebration of the cost of sin but of its END.
> ❡ The time of Easter is the time of JOY. For Easter is the time of your salvation. This Easter look with different eyes upon your brother. The way to the Peace of Easter is to join in glad awareness that the Son of God is risen from the past and has awakened to the present. Now are the lilies of innocence untouched by guilt and perfectly protected from the cold chill of fear. You shall be led past fear to love when you release your brother from crucifixion. Walk with your brother now rejoicing. (ACIM; Text; chap. 20; sec. I; ❡2.)

Love, Sondra

April 17, 2017

❡ LEBANON LRT
This Lebanon LRT turned out to be a lot better than I expected. On Sunday we always start by clearing religious

dogma. Then Markus talks about ACIM then I talk about Physical Immortality, and then I talk about Babaji—in that order.

❡ A lady in the training said my aura increased dramatically when I was talking about Babaji. The highlight for us was the couple from Saudi Arabia. We have never met anyone from there before. They were delightful. The wife was very, very, beautiful and sexy but of course she has to COVER UP in her country. She cannot even drive a car there! This is still shocking to me. If we accept an invitation to come there, I will have to cover up also. Really—can you believe that?

Love, Sondra

April 18, 2017

❡ RISE ABOVE IT ALL

One thing I have had to get over as a public figure is worrying about what others think of me. If I were to worry about what others think of me, I would be owned by them. I require no approval from the outside. I have an affirmation I use for this:

"I rise above the need for approval or disapproval."

❡ I think this is why people have a fear of public speaking. They unconsciously set up the audience to be their disapproving parent. They assume the audience is disapproving of them, and this makes them nervous. I had to handle that or else I would not have any fun at all being a public speaker.

Love, Sondra

April 22, 2017

❡ GIVE WHAT YOU HAVE

Yesterday we gave a free session to a new friend. She needs all her money to take care of her sick parents. It is always good to give some things away. The act of your giving something, anything, causes you to experience that you actually *have it* to give away. You cannot give to another something you do not have.

> ❖ *If you choose to be happy, cause another to be happy.*
> ❖ *If you choose to be prosperous, cause another to prosper.*
> ❖ *If you choose more love in your life, cause another to have more love in theirs.*

❡ But you have to be sincere—not just for seeking personal gain. We really wanted this person to have that inner peace and clarity one gets from a breathing session with the Divine Mother and us, and she got it and loved it. People so often say they get more out of one *Liberation Breathing* session than they did in 10 years of therapy! Go figure.
Love, Sondra

April 23, 2017

❡ LOVING WASHINGTON, D.C. NOW
Only two more boxes to unpack. Our apartment is so beautiful and everything I look at in it is beautiful. That gets me high. We feel more powerful here. Yesterday we went to a mixer in our club room. We met a black minister who was kind enough to give us two tickets to the White House Garden Tour for today. So off we go.
More later.
Love, Sondra

❡ THE WHITE HOUSE GARDEN TOUR WAS SO COOL
What a treat that we were in town for the White House Garden tour, which only happens for two days in the Spring and two days in the Fall. It was so amazing. I had no idea we could walk right by the Oval Office. We could not go inside, as apparently you have to go through your congressman or something.

❡ Markus made a video to put up here. But then someone came and told us NO VIDEOS. There was no sign anywhere saying that we could not do it. What really blew him away was that they ERASED it off of his iPhone. Wow. That was sophisticated technology.

❡ All Americans should visit Washington. It really makes you very patriotic.

More later. Sondra

❡ A poem Markus wrote about our trip to the White House today:

> *ODES TO FREEDOM #2*
> *We went to the White House today, and in the lovely Spring air that surrounded the colorful lime green shoots of new growth, we enjoyed the Glory of an ever-evolving resurrection. My gaze went down the colonnade of my recollection of newsreels—presidents and vice presidents walking toward the West Wing, the office of an oval shape, and in solemnity of national urgency and stature. The sacred walk to the West Wing where decisions are made, and the men of great positions, tête-à-tête with heads together, gather to solve the problems of current affairs and national interests, even on the stage of global dramas and important responses to events across oceans of international bonds and concerns. Yet, was the Spring more strong, and the resurrection of new life permeating the air of a newly arrived season, beautiful and resplendent, ever returning to the cool days and nights of a burgeoning observation—here at the White House. My first time so close, yet so far away behind the chains of security and watchful eyes of secret service men and women. Eagle eyed and stern, there was no joy in their faces, no Spring of resurrection in the auras that surrounded their heads of suspicion and guarded jobs to form a firewall of protection for those in the clearance of the colonnade. On a Sunday it was empty, no men of great concern headed to the Oval Office to make*

*decisions supreme. There I was, feeling the cool air
about my cheeks, looking in quiet amazement at
the flowers of the Spring, coming up from the dead
into Life Immortal—and empty was the wing in the
west, no concerns at all to be solved and
surmounted. Beauty has its own governance,
unaffected by elections and the administrations of
well-meaning men, and acts that run amuck in the
march of history, and the strife of decisions
affecting those not privy to their making. One
decision to be made in truth, and looking at this
Glory in the midst of the West Wing, I, in my destiny
of destinies would plant my feet on this sacred
ground. The Spring of resurrection so independent
and pure, ever free of time, in the liberty of an
apparent Life Immortal.*
—Markus Ray—

April 24, 2017

♪ MARTIN'S TAVERN
After we went to the White House, we went to Georgetown
to the Apple Store, and then we followed the Washington
tradition to go out for Sunday brunch. We ended up at a
very famous place called Martin's Tavern (very cool too).
Nixon used to eat at booth 2; Truman at booth 6; LBJ at
booth 25; and George Bush at table 12. Turns out Jack
Kennedy proposed to Jackie at booth 3! But it is not only
famous for that. Spies used to meet there. This is the place
where plans were created to gain intelligence that would
assist the allies in winning WW2. Even some Soviet spies
hung out there. It was a miracle to find this place and also
score a booth.
Love, Sondra

April 25, 2017

♪ RULES OF ENGAGEMENT

Reading through some books I just unpacked, I came across this book: *The Spiritual Rules of Engagement* by Yehuda Berg. See what you think:

> *"The common denominators at the heart of a soul mate relationship is that FIRST both parties have established a bond and connection with the Light within themselves. They have the common goal of connecting to the Divine Source within. Each person is secure and fulfilled in themselves—with no strings attached. Second, they are both walking the same spiritual path, nourishing themselves from the same spiritual fountainhead. Their spiritual goals are the same.*
>
> *¶ Men are channels for the Light, while women are the vessels for the Light. What men want more than anything in a relationship is the ability to make a woman happy and earn her love. The man is action orientated. Men are problem solvers. Men are doers.*
>
> *It is the job of the woman to manage and direct that influx of Light. Women are the relationship managers. Light managers.*
>
> *¶ As a woman, you are the chief executive officer of a company called Relationship. Managing it is not part of a man's skill set. Your role as a woman is to honor his desire to please you and support his role of channeling the energy of the Creator. A man wants to cherish you, and your job is to allow that to happen."*

WOW! This is very well put. We all need to think about it. Love, Sondra

April 26, 2017

¶ MORE RULES OF ENGAGEMENT
Here is some more insight from the book I started reading yesterday, *The Spiritual Rules of Engagement* by Yehuda Berg:

"The Light is the ultimate Cause of everyone's happiness. You have to recognize the powerful Light that exists in you. The only reason anyone would doubt one's worth as a human being is because one is having difficulty seeing the Light force that is inside of him or herself.

₰ According to the Law of Attraction, you must become LIKE the light to draw close to it. IF you look outside of yourself for happiness, you are becoming the effect instead of the cause. This creates disconnection and separation from the Divine Light.

So how do you connect to the Light within? You start by honoring your own interests and your passions. You start by engaging in activities that you really enjoy. Acts of sharing also connect you to the deepest levels of the sea of light. A man craves a woman who has made the Light her source of fulfillment." (p. 91)

₰ Another WOW! *"A man craves a woman who has made the Light her source of fulfillment."* That is a great line to ponder.

Love, Sondra

April 27, 2017

₰ SOMETHING I LEARNED

Something I learned this week was this: You have to keep up with the spiritual work on yourself to maintain your health. I mean, I always knew that, and do that, but I have not emphasized this enough to people. I do say that *Liberation Breathing* is a life-long spiritual path. But that is not enough to say that. People don't hear it sometimes. They have a few sessions and then quit or move on to another seminar. But I need to give an actual warning.

₰ Someone called me I have not heard from in years. She had developed all kinds of serious ailments and she was now in her later years. Now she wanted my help, BUT did not seem to have the discipline to turn things around. Had she KEPT UP with her process, she may not have ended up in such a mess.

℥ What about you? Are you keeping up? One needs to be doing a constant cleansing as a preventative measure, even if you are not sick. That is why daily spiritual practice is absolutely essential. Otherwise you end up old and sick like most people. Think about it.

Love, Sondra

April 28, 2017

℥ DAVID HAWKINS, PHD

I have mentioned David Hawkins before, especially when it comes to measuring levels of enlightenment. But I want to inspire you to read all his books if you can. There is so much in them of eternal wisdom:

> *"The mind is like a television set running its various channels for selection. Behind the screen, there is a thought-free space of JOY. This is an option that is always available—but it has to be chosen above all other tempting options. The Source of Joy is always present, always available, and not dependent on circumstances. There are only two obstacles:*
> *1) The ignorance that it is always available and present.*
> *2. Valuing something other than peace and joy because of a secret payoff.*
> *The experience of the presence of God is available and within at all times but awaits choice. That choice is made only by surrendering everything other than peace and love to God."*
> (From the David Hawkins book, *The Eye of the I*)

April 29, 2017

℥ GLASTONBURY QUEST

August 16 we are doing a special retreat on Physical Immortality and training for being a Breathworker in

Glastonbury, England. Hope you can make it. Here is what Robert Coon said about Glastonbury:

> "Many pilgrims journey to Glastonbury to examine its past. I believe that you who read these words come here to contribute to the Living Presence and Immortalist Future of Glastonbury. We have much to learn and much to share here in the Heart Chakra of the World. For Glastonbury is the heart center of this earth. It is from here that the truth of Immortality is being fully revealed to the world. This is the deepest secret of the Holy Grail. To win the Grail is to overcome death and obtain Immortal Life. To chain the Grail to a lesser, more easily obtainable goal is limitation of vision and is ignoble and unworthy of the Divine Potential of human spirit. The word is being made Flesh through Glastonbury. The Immortals of the Glastonbury Shamballic Focus bid thee welcome to Glastonbury—Ancient Avalon and New Jerusalem. I charge each of you to share this message with all beings as rapidly as Love allows. May you leave Glastonbury charged with the Spirit of Life Eternal in every atom of your being and filled to overflowing with the desire to overcome all things."

¶ When you heal your unconscious death urge, everything works. Come and join us. Glastonbury is an incredible energy vortex where you can get clear and embrace the possibilities of Physical Immortality.
Love, Sondra

April 30, 2017

¶ FROM ACIM CHAPTER FIFTEEN IN THE TEXT
Here are some more of my notes from reading the Text of *A Course in Miracles.* They are from my book, *Drinking the Divine,* I wrote to help people delve more deeply into ACIM:

> "To the ego, the goal is death, and it uses time to convince you of the inevitability of death. It craves

376

death for you but even that leaves it unsatisfied. It likes to convince you that it can pursue you after the grave. Therefore, you cannot find peace even in death. It offers you immortality in hell. Hell is its goal. The belief in hell is inescapable to those who identify with the ego.

⚶ The Holy Spirit teaches you there is no hell. Hell is only what the ego made of the present. Take this instant and think of it as all there is. Could you not give an instant to the Holy Spirit and let yourself have immortality and joy now? The Holy Instant is this instant and every instant. it is the time when you receive and give perfect communication. This means your mind is open both to receive and give. It is the recognition that all minds are in communion. It accepts everything"

(p. 81 from *Drinking the Divine* by Sondra Ray)

May 1, 2017

⚶ THE D.C. METRO
We finally ventured out needing to use the D.C. Metro. It was kind of intense. At one point we got confused when switching trains. A lady came up and told us what to do, but when we started to do it Markus realized she was wrong. Good thing he has such good intuition. A lady approached me and said she really enjoyed my scent! I honestly don't think I had any perfume on right then. The trains are very nice. We were picked up at the other end by guests at the party we were invited to.

⚶ Our hosts Alexandra and Jeff had a fabulous layout and we met some great people. She is coming for a session later this week!

⚶ Yesterday we had Lauren (the main Rebirther in this area) and her husband, Elliot, for brunch. Sunday brunch is a big thing in Washington, D.C. I served sweet potato and carrot soup, spring rolls, and apple crisp with ice cream. We had a great time. We are enjoying making contacts. Everyone we have met is so informed. We are so grateful for all the new people we are meeting in our new town!

Love, Sondra

May 2, 2017

❡ A HUMBLE PERSON
I've said this before and you may be sick of hearing it: A HUMBLE PERSON RECOGNIZES HIS ERRORS, ADMITS THEM, AND DOES SOMETHING ABOUT THEM. Let's talk about *first recognizing errors*. You can tell you are making an error if you feel stuck. You can tell when you are stuck if:

> ❖ *You feel unhappy and isolated*
> ❖ *You feel anxious or moody, rarely experiencing joy*
> ❖ *You feel helpless, can't move forward or accomplish projects and activities*
> ❖ *You are sick, in pain, and if your vital energy is blocked*
> ❖ *You feel an urge to attack someone verbally or physically*
> ❖ *You can't get your personal relationship to clear*
> ❖ *Your financial situation is shaky or faltering*

If you are experiencing any of these, you need to give yourself attention. The situation calls for you next to admit you are way off and then do some spiritual practices. You can use *Liberation Breathing, A Course in Miracles*, and prayer. If you cannot do those on the spot, at least write down all your negative thoughts on paper and reverse them to affirmations. This will at least give you some immediate relief.

Love, Sondra

May 4, 2017

❡ RESPONDING TO SYMPTOMS
If you have any symptoms or disease, you might react in
any number of ways:

> ❖ *You might go to get medical attention*
> ❖ *You might deny it is going on at all*
> ❖ *You might acknowledge it but avoid it*
> ❖ *You might be angry at the situation*
> ❖ *You might fight it and get in a battle in your mind*
> ❖ *You might resist it*
> ❖ *You might hate yourself for it*
> ❖ *You might continually complain about it or worry about it*
> ❖ *You might get depressed about it*
> ❖ *You might overdose on food, liquid, or drugs to suppress it*
> ❖ *You might get terrified of it*
> ❖ *You might mistakenly think it has more power than you do*
> ❖ *You might be mad at God for it*

It is very tempting to take one of these approaches,
especially if the symptoms stick around. The trouble is that
"what you resist persists," so any of these approaches may
only fortify the symptoms. Also, remember that "What you
think about expands," so the more you dwell on it in a
negative way, the worse it will get.
❡ So, you have to get hold of your mind. ACIM says, "The
Physician is the mind of the patient himself." You created
your symptoms and you can un-create them. Acknowledge
first that this is a blessing trying to teach you something.
Then say: "If this symptom could talk, what it would say
is_____." Then you have to process the negative thoughts
causing the condition and the resistance to giving it up.
❡ Then you can do *Liberation Breathing* to release it, or
some other spiritual practice. If you need help processing it,
we are available. Someone just now wrote for help about a
case of Bell's Palsy.   Love, Sondra

379

May 5, 2017

ɠ WHAT PRAYER IS USEFUL? (From David Hawkins)

> *"Ask to be the servant of the Lord, a vehicle of divine love, a channel of God's Will. Ask for direction and divine assistance and surrender all personal will through devotion. Dedicate one's life to the service of God. Choose love and peace above all other options. Commit to the goal of unconditional love and compassion for all life in all its expression and surrender all judgement to God."*

May 6, 2017

ɠ A MAGNIFICENT BODY
Here is an interesting quote from *Conversations with God, Book 1, by Neale Donald Walsh:*

> *"Yet those who have ears to hear, let them listen. I tell you this: You were not meant to ever die. Your physical form was created as a magnificent convenience; a wonderful tool; a glorious vehicle allowing you to experience the reality you have created with your mind, that you may know the Self you have created in your soul. I designed your magnificent body to last forever." p. 193*

ɠ So, Markus just finished editing the book on *Physical Immortality* and we sent it in to a publisher.
Love, Sondra

May 7, 2017

ɠ A GOOD HUSBAND
I want to really acknowledge my husband, Markus, for four big things he accomplished these ten days at home:

1. He spent days and days finishing the *Liberation Breathing* E-book which was messed up without an index. It was complicated to fix.
2. He spent days and nights, late into the night, editing the *Physical Immortality* book. Others we tried to get to do it could not do it. One guy actually lost it in the cloud!
3. He spent days and nights finishing *The New Loving Relationships Book,* which I had totally re-done in a second edition. Now it is perfect.
4. He put together a cabinet which I thought was going to arrive assembled. It was not. It took hours and hours and he did not complain.

❡ He is a guy who can fix anything.
Love, Sondra

May 8, 2017

❡ WATCH WHAT YOU THINK—
EVEN MORE WHAT YOU SAY
I am always telling people to watch what they think. But this obviously includes watching what you say. When you are in the middle of difficulties, what you SAY has a great impact on how long you stay in those situations. In other words, guard what you say, especially in times of trouble. Remember, THIS WILL PASS. I heard Joel Osteen once say, "Remember that there is a miracle in your mouth."
❡ I once had a student say to me over and over, "Nothing works." I kept telling him nothing worked for him because he had that thought first. He would not get it. I got frustrated with him, so I jokingly said, "I'll bet I am going to meet you in 25 years, and you are still going to say the same thing." Guess what! That happened—I ran into him literally 25 years later, and he was still saying that. As a matter of fact, he got sick from it and died, as none of the treatments he took worked. Remember this: Speak life changing words. Don't even complain about any obstacle. Call in your good.
Love, Sondra

May 9, 2017

❡ THE 99% WORLD
Ninety-nine percent of the universe is unseen, unheard, and unperceived. So, let's call our everyday physical world, the world we see, feel, hear, taste and touch—*the 1% reality. And let's call the spiritual world, the world of thoughts and consciousness and Light, the 99% world*. The 99% realm happens to be the source of all energy, consciousness, and creativity.

❡ Are you tuned in, tapped in, and turned on to the 99%? Mozart sits down and when he gets up, he dashes off the entire score of the opera Don Giovanni in one sitting.

A business student comes up with an idea for an overnight package-delivery business. It earns him only a C in class, but when he graduates, he starts the business. He calls it Federal Express.

❡ A successful filmmaker decides to turn his films into reality by creating a cross between a carnival, a world's fair, and the cartoon world. Not a single investor wants to invest a dime in his vision. But Walt Disney pursues his idea anyway and calls it Disneyland. CONNECT TO THE LIGHT OF THE CREATOR!

From the book *True Prosperity* by Yehuda Berg

May 10, 2017

❡ GO FOR SOLUTION!
I once took a course for entrepreneurs which cost several thousand dollars. The main thing I remember is the teacher writing "GO FOR SOLUTION" in very big letters over and over.

❡ I think that is important because the ego does not want a solution, it just wants to keep the conflict, the argument, the problem. We also need to trust that there is a solution to everything.

❡ We attract what we need to learn. Growth comes from always asking what you learned from a situation and why you had it. Then you have to take charge of what you are thinking to get the solution, which should be the highest spiritual thought you can come up with.

❡ Esther Hicks would say you cannot notice *what is* and complain about it, and also be a vibrational match to the solution. She would also say never wallow around in a problem more than a minute! So, if you want the solution you have to immediately get a higher thought. It is very tempting though, to wallow in the problem. This requires mind training. You can get good at this.

Love, Sondra

May 11, 2017

❡ LET GO AND MOVE ON

I was distraught over a relationship with a former friend that I could not clear. The reason we had a falling out made no sense to me. I felt it was due to her control and jealousy which she would take absolutely no responsibility for. I apologized for my end, even though I felt I did nothing wrong. I apologized anyway in case it was my karma. She still would not get off her position. It seemed hopeless and I felt so sad that I had to give myself a wet Rebirthing Session.

❡ I heard Babaji more or less tell me there is no time to fret over one person. I had already spent three days fretting, and countless hours before trying to clear, so it was obvious He did not want me to spend any more time on this. He told me she was "gone." I have to accept it. Maybe Babaji took her out. Then I remembered a speech He gave once:

- ❖ *Love and serve all humanity*
- ❖ *Assist everyone.*
- ❖ *Be cheerful. Be courteous.*
- ❖ *Be a dynamo of irrepressible happiness.*
- ❖ *There is no Saint without a past.*
- ❖ *There is no sinner without a future.*
- ❖ *If you cannot praise someone, let them pass out of your life. *(There it was.)*
- ❖ *Be original. Be inventive.*

383

❖ *Dare, dare, and then dare more.*
❖ *Do not imitate. Stand on your own ground.*
❖ *Do not lean on the borrowed staff of others.*
❖ *Think your own thoughts.*
❖ *Be yourself.*
❖ *All perfection and all virtues of the deity are hidden inside you. Reveal them.*
❖ *The Savior also is already within you. Reveal Him.*
❖ *Let His grace emancipate you.*
❖ *Let your life be that of a rose. Though silent, it speaks the language of fragrance."*

❡ I had to "let go and move on."
❡ Back to work!
Love, Sondra

May 12, 2017

❡ ARE YOU COMFORTING?
I am always trying to help people find their perfect mate. I am getting pretty good at it. But recently I said to this student who was single and looking, "What do you feel about that gal over there?" His answer was surprising but very good. He said, "No not her. I need someone who is comforting."
❡ My husband heard that and said, "He is right. That is what a man wants. That is what I love about you." (There is a way to be that without being too "mothering.")
❡ Maybe we should think about that and apply it to all relationships. It is a wonderful social skill to talk to people and make them feel comfortable—and to even make them feel comforted. And especially if we have house guests. In India they say a guest in your house is like God. They treat you that way, and they go out of their way to make you feel more than comfortable. People do not usually expect to be greeted so warmly.
❡ ACIM says every encounter is a holy encounter. People who are very successful know how to make a really warm

personal connection with every person they talk to. Are you a comforting person?
Love, Sondra

May 14, 2017

❧ COSMIC DATING SERVICE
In my many years studying relationships, I have given a lot of attention to finding the right mate. The bottom line is you have to ask God to provide you with the perfect mate. I call this the *Cosmic Dating Service*. Here is a good prayer to invoke it:

> *Beloved Divine Mother, Holy Spirit, Babaji, and all good forces necessary, I come before you this day and pray with all my heart and soul and mind to request humbly that I now receive into my life the mate to whom my love belongs, the mate of my being. Bring forth anything that I have not looked at in myself that would prevent me from receiving this now. Bring it all forward and let me release it now. I call forth all unfinished business so that I may finish it, so I will be ready to meet the mate of my being. I ask for this Divine dispensation in the name of Christ and I accept this as done as is Thy will.*

❧ My beloved subconscious mind, I hereby ask and command that you take this thought form prayer with all my mana and the vital force necessary to demonstrate this prayer to God. (Breathe three deep breaths.) Now let the rain of blessings fall. Thank you, Amen.
Best to do for thirty days, every day.
Love, Sondra

May 16, 2017

❧ LAYOVER IN RUSSIA
Hi everyone. We are stopped in the Moscow airport. I found the flight here difficult as the seats were too crammed

together, and my knees barely fit between the seats. I felt better seeing the stewardess who had her hair up in a bun with sparkling crystals. Then I saw two great movies on the plane. *Collateral Beauty*, which was very deep, and *Hidden Figures* which was so inspiring—I cried during both of these movies, and I am so glad I saw them. I am awe struck how they can create such movies!

❡ Another interesting thing was what I read on the plane in *Hello Magazine*. The new President of France has a wife who is actually 25 years older than he is. And they don't care. My husband is younger than I am, and we don't care either! Meanwhile, I am having trouble making myself understood in Russia. The waitress brought me the wrong thing twice! Still trying to get to the Canary Islands.

P.S. Announcement coming tomorrow about one of our new books!

Love, Sondra

❡ We finally made it to Tenerife. The trip from Moscow was rough. I had seen all the good movies, so I was hoping to sleep. But the plane was full of Russians with their little children. Babies were wailing, screaming, crying and it was very, very, noisy. Then someone was playing a kind of loud radio with a song in Russian. I felt like complaining to the stewardess about that, but then I figured out it was a children's rhyme and was intended to keep the babies calm. So anyway, it was a long flight. I was so happy to arrive and see our organizer, Silke, with her head still shaved from India. She is keeping it the full nine months. This was an inspiration to me and reminded me of all the times I had shaved my head, and how good I felt, and how much I got out of it. Silke is really coming into her power now and here we go. Markus and I have decided to start a fast. We will see how that goes.

Love, Sondra

May 17, 2017

❡ SITTING NEAR THE OCEAN

In India we had gotten the assignment to do the anti-death

mantra two rounds twice a day for forty days. That means 108X2 every morning and every night. It is a very, very, long mantra so this took us maybe 45 minutes each sitting. It was tough and sometimes we missed. But we did pretty well. We got quite disciplined, and that is why we thought we might be able to handle a long fast now. We shall see. We are instructed to do fruit and milk for 45 days. It is mostly for spiritual reasons but we can stand to lose some weight also. I am sharing this so I can be accountable! This also means no wine—which could be hard for me! My only problem with fasting is I wake up during the night wide awake. We have to support each other because Markus likes to eat. So, we have taken on a real challenge. I am not going to beat myself up if I cannot do it, but I would like to try. When you do something to serve the mission and Babaji it is easier.
Love, Sondra

May 20, 2017

❡ FOURTH DAY OF FASTING
Fasting always brings up stuff, which is why it is good to do. What came up for me yesterday was some suppressed rebellion against the church. I have always been a rebel which saved me, because my sister was a conformist and she died the same age as my father. However, there is a negative side to rebellion, and I felt that in my body yesterday. What was I rebelling against?
❡ Mainly, the teaching from the Lutheran church that says it is BLASPHEMY to be like God! On the other hand, the Bible says, "Be Ye Perfect, even as God is perfect." What a contradiction! I have always been afraid of my perfection, because of this, and therefore I hold myself back. This is so deep that it goes back many lifetimes of religious dogma. I prayed a lot yesterday to release this brainwashing.
❡ I was not allowed to question what was taught in church. That is why *A Course in Miracles* saved my life; it is a correction of religion.
Love, Sondra

May 21, 2017

ſ TEACHING THE LRT

I always love teaching the LRT. I never get tired of it because it is so wonderful to watch the changes people go through. I find them fascinating and learn so much.

ſ One man was falling off his chair and going into a spontaneous rebirthing during the incest section. Once I had a woman faint during this section. I don't really know of anyone else teaching this material, which is so important. Some people have had inappropriate sexual behavior in the family, but most have had what we call "emotional incest." That is where there was psychic or telepathic sexual energy flying around. Or overly confiding in a child; saying things that should have been said to the mate instead of to the child. It really complicates one's sexual life later. That is because most people set up their mate to be one of their parents.

ſ The more you do that, the less you can have sex with them, because it is taboo to have sex with one's parent. The incest pattern is suppressed at the beginning of a relationship, but when the couple moves in together or gets married, it is so intimate that one can no longer keep the pattern suppressed. So, when it comes up, sex can go out the window! We see it all the time with our clients.
Love, Sondra

May 22, 2017

ſ FASTING MIRACLES

When you do a serious fast for spiritual reasons, there are always miracles. We had two big miracles during this training:

ſ I. A TV crew came and filmed us for a documentary on Love. They also did an interview of me. Then they filmed Markus painting. That was a big surprise.

ſ 2. We got ITALY back! For many years we have not had an organizer in Italy. We really missed going there. There was an Italian Naturopath in the training who was pretty outstanding. She told us of her friend in Italy who she could

work with to organize. They want to do something in Assisi!
This is fantastic as I always wanted Markus to be able to go
there!
Love, Sondra

May 23, 2017

❡ LETTING GO OF GUILT
In the *Loving Relationships Training*, I always discuss letting
go of guilt. I have everyone write down the three things they
are most guilty about in their lives. I don't ask them to share
them, but I make the point that GUILT ALWAYS DEMANDS
PUNISHMENT. So, then I have them share how they are
punishing themselves for that guilt. (This group was mostly
Catholic, so they had a lot of guilt.) There is guilt from past
lives, guilt from hurting the mother at birth, guilt that is
religious (original sin), and guilt from things done wrong.
That is a lot of guilt. When they told me how they were
punishing themselves it was really heavy.

> ❖ *I beat up my body*
> ❖ *I have this illness*
> ❖ *I end up alone*
> ❖ *I screw up my relationships*
> ❖ *I get rid of money*
> ❖ *I get rid of love*
> ❖ *Etc.*

The problem is that the ego makes sure you keep the guilt.
It says this, "If you DARE to think you are innocent, then
you are really guilty!" ACIM is the answer. Forgiveness is
the answer. Breathing out the guilt is the answer.
Love, Sondra

May 25, 2017

❡ LITTLE MIRACLES CONTINUE
At the airport an employee of Air France came up to me
saying, "Oh, you are Sondra Ray! I have read some of your

books." We had quite a bit of overweight luggage and when Markus went to pay for that there was no charge, so she obviously fixed it for us.

¶ Then in the Madrid stopover I got an email inviting us to South Africa! This was totally out of the blue. Then our taxi driver into Paris was simply amazing. Then when we arrived at Monique's apartment, an old friend of mine, Shanti, who I have not seen for years was there waiting for me with Monique. A big surprise to see her. I LOVE IT!

¶ Today is the ascension of Jesus. We are going out to the church of Sainte-Chapelle.

Love, Sondra

May 26, 2017

¶ MESSAGES FROM BABAJI

One other miracle we have had is this: we can go under the water with our snorkel and nose plug and do a wet *Liberation Breathing* session, and we can get the answers we want from Babaji. I know it is Him replying to our requests because I would never have thought of that answer myself. Markus is especially good at doing this now. He gets the answers very fast.

¶ It is so wonderful to be tapped in like that. It is so wonderful to be in a relationship where both of us are Breathworkers. I keep telling people in seminars that this is the ideal. When I have a doubt or question or issue, Markus can give me a session and vise-versa. Therefore, we never stay stuck.

¶ If only I could convince people how great this is! If you are interested in having that kind of a relationship, we are happy to train you as Breathworkers.

Love, Sondra

May 27, 2017

¶ DON'T FORCE ANYTHING

The ability to lead a long life comes when the body is not forced to do what it does not want to do. You must clear out of yourself everything that holds you to a reality that you do not like. Then the "I" can put you in the right place, which will not have anything you do not like, because you will not have anything within you that attracts it.

₰ Karma is the old conditioning which draws the experiences to you, so that you can release them to allow for growth and change. What you hold in your energy fields draws your experiences to you. This is why forgiveness is so necessary to neutralize the memories that replay as Karma.

Love, Sondra

May 28, 2017

₰ FORGIVE AND FORGET

Lately we have had some clients who could not let go of the past. They hung on to every little grievance, and it often led to the demise of their relationship. They could not forgive. They could not forget. The ego cannot tolerate release from the past.

₰ One thing I learned along the way was this: LET ME KEEP NO RECORDS OF WRONGDOING! I also learned you have to forgive daily. That is the way to live. To be "born again" is to let the past go and to look without condemnation on the present. All healing is release from the past.

₰ ACIM says the Holy Spirit is the only true healer because He knows the past. Are you hanging on to a past grievance? Have you considered the fact that you created that grievance and you are not a victim?

Love, Sondra

May 29, 2017

₰ A TRIP TO VÉZELEY

What a great trip to Vézeley, France! In the 9th century the Benedictines were given land to build a monastery. A monk named Baudillon brought the bones of Mary Magdalene there. In 1058 the Pope confirmed the authenticity of them, leading to an influx of pilgrims that has continued until today. Many miracles have occurred at her tomb.

❡ The abbey is the main starting point for those doing the pilgrimage to Santiago de Compostela. The St. Madeleine Basilica is considered a masterpiece of Romanesque art and architecture. Keep in mind most people could not read back then, so the purpose of the sculptures on the church walls were to "tell the story" of Jesus and the Gospels. Vézeley was also the starting point for the crusades.

❡ You probably know that Mary Magdalene was one of the best followers of Jesus. She witnessed most of the events surrounding the crucifixion. She was actually the earliest witness to the resurrection. Jesus then sent her to tell the others. In the book *The Da Vinci Code,* the claim is made that she was the wife of Jesus. This could be true, yes? And in Southern France she is said to have spent the last years of her life. There is quite a Mary Magdalene presence there.

❡ At Vézeley we had a perfect experience. The weather was glorious and there was hardly anyone there but us, because it is Monday after a holiday. There was a wonderful museum in the town where Romain Rolland had done a lot of writing. He was a great French writer who was in tune with India. Afterwards, we gave Monique an LB session in our Hôtel Les Glycines (Wisteria), and it was perfect. Thank you, Monique, for this wonderful treat.
Love, Sondra

May 30, 2017

❡ LAST DAY IN PARIS
Well, it was pretty strange not to go out and have a drink and some crepes in Paris. But we are sticking with the fast. Paris is so beautiful; how could we not have a fabulous experience? It feels so great to be here. Why not consider coming to Paris for the LRT in July (14th-16th). We would love to have you. Someone from Germany enrolled yesterday.

❡ Tomorrow we go to Madrid for the LRT next weekend. Then we had a big change in our schedule. Our gig in Greece crashed because of the terrible financial situation.

The gig in Portugal crashed because of a death in the family. So Babaji told us to go back home for a few weeks, which is okay with me as this tour was scheduled for 3 months, which is too long anyway. Furthermore, He said, He has other plans for us. One has to be very flexible.
Love, Sondra

June 2, 2017

♫ EL PRADO IN MADRID
Markus and I went to visit the El Prado Museum in Madrid today. It is the main Spanish art museum in central Madrid and is one of the most visited sites in the world. It features one of the world's finest collections of European art from the 12th century to the 20th century.
♫ We could not take any photos. I have posted the one I liked the best by Goya which I got off the internet, which is a reclining nude. It was a welcome change after all the dark religious paintings. Markus has seen so many art museums in his day that he is about maxed out with that. The LRT starts tonight.   Love, Sondra

June 3, 2017

♫ BABAJI SAYS FAITH IS EVERYTHING
Be willing to offer all your problems to truth. The goal of truth requires FAITH. Had you not lacked faith that a problem could be solved, the problem would be gone. There is no problem in any situation that faith will not solve. If you lack faith, ask that it be restored where it was lost. Be not concerned with anything except your willingness to have this be accomplished. The Holy Spirit will accomplish it, not you. What you reserve for yourself, you take away from Him who would release you. You have never tried to solve anything for yourself and been truly successful. Give the Holy Spirit everything that would hurt you. Leave nothing behind. You have no problem that He cannot solve by offering you a miracle. ACIM.
Love, Sondra

June 4, 2017

❡ HOW I SOLVED A HUGE PROBLEM
After I looked at the thoughts causing it, and changed those thoughts, I wrote the following:

> ❖ *I surrender this problem to the Holy Spirit.*
> ❖ *I surrender any resentment I have that keeps me stuck in this problem to the Holy Spirit.*
> ❖ *I surrender to the Holy Spirit. the attachment I have to this problem.*
> ❖ *I surrender the separation my problem gives me to the Holy Spirit*
> ❖ *I surrender my addiction to my problem to the Holy Spirit.*
> ❖ *I surrender the way I "use" this problem to the Holy Spirit.*
> ❖ *I surrender to the Holy Spirit whatever keeps me from letting this problem go completely.*
> ❖ *I surrender my fear of healing this problem to the Holy Spirit.*
> ❖ *Oh Lord Shiva, I bow before thee in reverence. Please destroy my ignorance.*

❡ This worked! It is one thing to know your pattern, it is another thing to let go of the addiction to it. That is where we need help from a Higher Power.
Love, Sondra

June 5, 2017

❡ TALK TO THE HOLY SPIRIT
You can tell the Holy Spirit everything you like and don't like about the reality you live in, and how you want your reality to be. Then you have alignment with your *right* place and can attract it to you.
❡ When you have alignment, you have agreement about what you want. This agreement allows it to happen if you have responded to this agreement with desire, because

nothing in your energy field is in contradiction, and your desire is attracting it to you.

❡ When your desire is aligned with Spirit there is no problem. The Spirit needs to inspire and guide, and the Will needs to respond and select. The Spirit and the Will must be balanced in the heart. Summarized from ACIM
Love, Sondra

June 6, 2017

❡ DO YOU WANT MIRACLES? (Summarized from ACIM) They only arise if your mind is ready for them. They cannot be performed if you have doubt or fear. Fear prevents the Holy Spirit from giving you His control. Whenever you are afraid, it is a sure sign you have allowed your mind to mis-create. The correction of fear is your responsibility. When you ask for release from fear you are implying it is not your responsibility. Ask instead for help in the conditions that brought the fear about.

❡ Those conditions always entail a willingness to be separate. Ask for help in the correction of the separation. Fear arises from the lack of love. The only remedy for lack of love is perfect love. Perfect love is the atonement. The atonement is the correction of all your wrong thinking, and complete forgiveness.

❡ Attempting mastery of fear is useless. It only asserts the power of fear. The true resolution is mastery through love. A miracle is the reflection of the union with the Holy Spirit.
Love, Sondra

June 8, 2017

❡ GRACE OVERCOMES KARMA
Here is something interesting I read coming back on the plane to Washington:

> "Grace is a more powerful law than karma. Karma can take centuries to untangle. Grace can lift all burdens in the blink of an eye. Grace is infinitely

abundant and everywhere present. The light of Abundant Grace can instantly transmute karma. The old idea of grace as undeserved kindness is absurd! Immortals radiate Grace freely and without judgment. Grace bestows beauty. The Grace cup offers total Health to all! There is no difficulty in a Life of Grace!"

"Grace descending
Had removed the stony
From their Hearts,
And made new flesh regenerate
Grow instead."(Milton)

℈ The above is from Robert Coon's book on Physical Immortality, *The Path of the Phoenix* (p.185). I feel fortunate to know Robert Coon personally. I feel so fortunate to have Babaji's Grace. You could have it too.
Love, Sondra

June 9, 2017

℈ THERE IS NO SIN
In Spain all the students we had were raised Catholic. They were taught they were sinners, and if they had nothing to confess, the priest forced them to make something up. The interesting part was this:

They were punishing themselves for their "sins" even though they no longer practiced Catholicism.

℈ *ACIM* says that if sin were possible it would be irreversible. Instead we must realize there are *errors* and no sins. Errors can be corrected and made right. The belief in sin demands punishment. The belief that punishment is correction is insane. Punishment just reinforces the "guilt."
℈ To the ego, sin *is the truth*, and purity is seen as arrogance. ESCAPE IS THEN IMPOSSIBLE! Sin is seen as mightier than God. In *A Course in Miracles* it says:

"If sin is real, it must be forever beyond the hope of healing for there would be power greater than God's. To the ego, sin means death. You are such a sinner that you need to die." (ACIM, Text, chap. 19, sec. III; ¶8.)

❡ *ACIM* says if you have one ounce of guilt you are walking the carpet of death. You may think you have cleared your religious conditioning, but what I learned in Spain, it is very, very, deep. Ammachi says to be enlightened you have to clear the religious shadow. How do you do it? Reading *A Course in Miracles*—that is how. Breathing out your conditioning —that is how.

❡ The truth is God, who created neither sin nor death, wills not that you be bound by them. Free your mind and body from the false religious theology you laid upon it. You may also have to go through a process of forgiving the church. I did.

Love, Sondra

June 10, 2017

❡ FASTING ON ONLY LIQUIDS NOW

It is easy to get up at 6:00 AM when one is fasting. Then we do our spiritual practice. We walk along the river while doing our mantras. We recite *Om Namah Shivaya* on our mala beads while we walk, and then a secret mantra from Ammachi, and a secret mantra from Shastriji, and then we do a secret money mantra from Muniraj. Got these from our gurus. After that we write in our gratitude book. It feels really good to give the first hours of the day to God.

❡ *Om Namah Shivaya*, according to Babaji, is the highest thought in the universe. It means Infinite Spirit, Infinite Being and Infinite Manifestation. It also means, "I bow to Shiva, the part of God that destroys my ignorance or ego." It gets rid of negative thoughts while at the same time helps you manifest what you want. I highly recommend you try it. You can get mala beads at any metaphysical bookstore. Doing a spiritual practice guarantees that your day is going to be great!

ꟻ Right now, we are completing that by listening to the Aarti, which is the song we sing to Babaji. It is so holy that parts of it descended from the angelic realm in gold letters in the air to yogis sitting in Babaji's cave. Believe it or not!
Love, Sondra

June 11, 2017

ꟻ LOVE DOES NOT HURT
We have had so many clients now who are stuck on the thought "love hurts." They are afraid to get in a relationship because of this thought. ACIM says, "I can be hurt by nothing but my thoughts." If you feel you have been hurt by love, it is something else in you. Osho says that "Love," as people ordinarily use the word, "is not love; it is lust." And lust is bound to cause hurt because lust uses the other person to fulfill some desires. You cannot love with the ego. The ego becomes a barrier. There can be no effort to dominate. Most lovers are searching for their mothers, and their fathers, or the safety of the womb. That is the problem. Then the anger at the parents gets projected on the mate and causes hurt. Love however, is a spiritual phenomenon. Love is divine.
ꟻ He also talks about the difference between aloneness and loneliness. Loneliness is a state when you are ill with yourself, bored with yourself, tired of yourself and you want to go somewhere and forget yourself in being involved with somebody else. Aloneness is when you are thrilled just by your being. You are blissful just by being yourself. You need not go anywhere. You are enough unto yourself. Need has disappeared. You then have to share. You have to give. Lovers are grateful that their love has been accepted. The lonely person goes to get something. The alone person goes to give something. Think about this. Which are you?
Love, Sondra

June 12, 2017

ꟻ BIRTH TRAUMA CAUSES MISERY

Your misery is often caused by your *birth trauma*. The trouble is, you tend to heal your birth trauma the same way you had it. In other words, if your birth was slow, you might go very slow healing it. If you got stuck at birth, you might get stuck trying to heal it. Mine was all about WAITING, so I was waiting to be healed rather than getting healed. One piece of your birth could be locked in for years! Fortunately, being a skilled Rebirther, I was smart enough to finally figure this out.

¶ Also, how can you receive God's help if you have a thought from birth that "help hurts." Your delivery team tried to help you come out, but it hurt a lot (even in a normal birth). So maybe you have God set up as your delivery team. And you don't want *that kind of help*. If so, you have to be aware of that *set-up*, and change it. You might also have the thought: "My body causes pain" from birth. Then you resent your body. But it was not the body that caused the pain. It was thoughts about the way you were delivered. You need to know your pre-verbal thoughts from birth. This is incredibly helpful to clear your body. In *Liberation Breathing* we deal with this all the time. We can help you clear your birth trauma that is still causing you misery and pain.

Love, Sondra

June 13, 2017

¶ ONLY THE MIND IS SICK
The mind made sickness and employed the body to seem like the victim. But it was the mind that was sick in the first place. The body will be released when the mind acknowledges, "This is not done to me, but I am doing this to myself."

¶ ACIM says that all illness is mental illness. This does not mean "psychiatric," but rather that thoughts in the mind always precede and cause symptoms in the body. In other words, *the mind rules the body*. Healing is the effect of minds that join, as sickness comes from minds that separate. Sickness is anger taken out upon the body so that it will suffer pain. Anger is in the mind, yes? The body has no role but does what it is told. Sickness is a demand the body be a thing that it is not. In sickness it is asked to be God's enemy. (Because we are angry at God for the suffering, we imposed on ourselves.) Depression is an inevitable consequence of separation. So are anxiety, worry, or a deep sense of helplessness, misery, suffering, and intense fear of loss.

ℐ The body grows old and dies because the mind is sick within itself. The body is endangered by the mind that hurts itself. There cannot be some forms of sickness which the miracle must lack the power to heal. There is no miracle you cannot have when you desire healing. Say "I unite my will with the Holy Spirit and accept my release from Hell."
Summarized from ACIM Text
Love, Sondra

June 14, 2017

ℐ THERE IS NO DEATH
Lesson #163 in *ACIM* says, *"There is no death. The Son of God is free."* It goes on to point out the subtle ways we are killing ourselves:

> *"Death is a thought that takes on many forms, often unrecognized. It may appear as sadness, fear, anxiety, doubt, anger, faithlessness, lack of trust, concern for bodies, envy. (God did not make death)."*

ℐ I find that statement in *ACIM* quite shocking, as we don't usually see that we are killing off life with those states of mind. But we have to face all that. When your *death urge* is up, you hate what makes you live. The death urge will make you do everything wrong, and then you won't want to live even more—and things get worse.

ℐ After the death of a family member, there is a danger of hanging on to death to maintain your connection to that person. When someone dies in your family, your own death urge gets very activated. The big problem is this: The death urge keeps out the love that would heal it. In other words, you really need a lot of support and love to heal your death urge, BUT that is the very time you push away the love. The "unconscious death urge" includes the following:

❖ *The thought death is inevitable*
❖ *The thought I am separate from God*
❖ *Your personal lie*
❖ *Past life memories of dying*
❖ *Your programming from ancestors and parents*
❖ *All anti-life thoughts*
❖ *Belief systems from medicine*
❖ *Your secret wish to die if you hate your life*

✍ Probably you know that if you have read my books, but I bet you did not realize that it also includes what is in the first paragraph here. Read it again. There you have it! Love, Sondra

June 15, 2017

✍ COMMUNICATION IS EVERYTHING
We are often seeing communications problems with couples in our work. Frankly, I am shocked when I hear what some couples say to each other! Here is what a communication expert has to say:

Here are 15 categories of a form of verbal abuse. (Most of them are couched in YOUR statements with a disrespectful tone.)

1. *WITHHOLDING (Keeping to oneself in order to punish the other.)*
2. *COUNTERING, CONTRADICTING AND INTERRUPTING (Insulting a partner's intelligence.)*
3. *DISCOUNTING (Devaluing a partner's experience.)*
4. *JOKING (Teasing or sarcasm.)*
5. *BLOCKING OR DIVERTING (Changing the subject,)*
6. *ACCUSING AND BLAMING (Charging one's partner*

with inappropriate behavior.)
7. *JUDGING AND CRITICIZING*
8. *TRIVIALIZING AND DEVALUING (Saying or implying that what a partner does is insignificant.)*
9. *UNDERMINING (Attacking a partner's self-esteem.)*
10. *THREATENING (Intentionally frightening the other.)*
11. *NAME CALLING*
12. *FORGETTING (Claiming not to remember or getting foggy.)*
13. *ORDERING AND COMMANDING (Adopting an authoritative dominating or disrespectful tone.)*
14. *DENIAL (Lying about facts.)*
15. *INTERROGATING (Delivering a stream of questions in a hostile way.)*

From *The Verbally Abuse Relationship* by Patricia Evans
Love, Sondra

June 16, 2017

❡ MARKUS'S WRITINGS
There are 25 books on the shelves full of Markus's writings. He usually writes one page a day of what he feels. I opened one at random and I was moved. It is a pity no one sees these, so here is one:

"Divine Mother—you are everything to me. You are my hands and feet; the air I breathe, and the very lungs that make my breath possible. I sleep in the bed of Your Love and awake into the dawn of Your ever-present newness; always astounded at the beauty all my senses can bear to take in from Your grace. All colors come from You, all sounds and all the movements of the great winds and seas. I am but a speck of a motion You put forth as me, yet in my gratitude do I rise to larger proportions of my grandeur in You. I am this hand You provide for the actions of Your love. I am Your servant, the one who comes forth out of the void into the Light of Your Infinite Creation, to sing praises of You who are my All. I walk into the shadow of my own mistaken thoughts, committed to the healing You bestow.

Your truth corrects my error of sorrow and assures me my inheritance is only innocence and joy. I give up my past in the Presence of Your blazing benevolence and walk into a new life with the one woman who so closely resembles You. My blessings are uncountable, and the effulgence of Your Light overwhelms me. Om Haidakhandi, Om Haidakhandi."
"A Prayer of Praise" by **Markus Ray** from *Odes to the Divine Mother.*

June 18, 2017

❡ WHAT IS MANA?
Hawaiian Spiritual Masters emphasize the importance of mana. Mana is a life force which comes streaming in from another dimension. It is the Universal Divine Spiritual Power. It has a supernatural mystical quality. The amount in a person, they say, determines his or her success. It is the inherent quality of leadership. It leads to a:

- ❖ *Reservoir of strength*
- ❖ *Personal magnetism*
- ❖ *High-impact personality*
- ❖ *Charisma*
- ❖ *Genius power*
- ❖ *Inspiration of a king*

❡ (No ruler wants his mana diluted.) It is the key to manifesting results. Intention + mana = results. The most effective way of gathering mana is deep breathing and chanting. The blocks to mana are these:

- ❖ *Anger*
- ❖ *Resentment*
- ❖ *Irritation*
- ❖ *Guilt*
- ❖ *Fear*
- ❖ *Anxiety*
- ❖ *Negativity*

¶ I wrote about mana before, but it's a really important subject, like prana. Think about it. Have you had a Liberation Breathing session? This can increase your mana.
Love, Sondra

June 19, 2017

¶ FORGIVENESS PROBLEM
If there is a health problem, there is also a *forgiveness problem*. ACIM says, "Forgiveness is the key to happiness." (Lesson #121) If you have a problem, and are not happy, then there is something or someone you still need to forgive.

> "The unforgiving mind is full of fear. There is no room for love there. It is sad, with no release from pain. It suffers and abides in misery. It is torn in doubt, confused, afraid to go ahead. Afraid to stay. Afraid of sound and afraid of stillness. It is terrified of dark but especially of light. It is angry and sees only sins. It wants to live but wishes it was dead. It sees no hope of escape.
> ¶ When you have an unforgiving thought, you make a judgement and the mind is closed and will not be released. An unforgiving thought leads to distortion and smashes reality.
> ¶ Forgiveness does nothing; it merely looks and waits and judges not. Let forgiveness show you what to do through Him who is your guide, your savior and protector. He has forgiven you already."
> (ACIM; Workbook; Lesson #121)

¶ Is there anyone you have not forgiven 100%? Check it out.
Love, Sondra

June 20, 2017

¶ YOU ARE THE WRITER OF YOUR SCRIPT

People now know that their thoughts are producing their results, but they do not take this far enough. Here is another fact:

"You are the writer of the script of your life, and everyone else in the universe is playing the part you assigned to them!"

⚘ This means if you got "hurt" by someone, you actually attracted them to hurt you. Most people don't get this part. *ACIM* says, "Beware of the temptation to perceive yourself unfairly treated." So, if someone ripped you off, you wanted them to rip you off. Maybe you thought unconsciously that you deserved to be ripped off as a punishment for something.

⚘ *ACIM* says also, "I can be hurt by nothing but my thoughts." Lesson #281. So, it is still your *thoughts of* the incident doing you harm, almost more than the incident itself. Here is what you should say if you still think someone is *out there* to hurt you: "I have made a mistake in my thinking to allow you to seemingly hurt me. I recognize you are merely doing what I myself invited, and that neither you nor anyone can hurt me. I send you love from my heart— and I forgive myself and you. Knowing it is impossible for you to infringe on my perfection."

⚘ Sounds like this would be good to send to all ex-spouses, no? We have to also take responsibility for the way we are treated by all people.

Love, Sondra

June 21, 2017

⚘ CHAPTER THIRTEEN IN ACIM: (IT IS PRETTY INTENSE!)

Here are some of my notes from Chapter 13 in the Text of *ACIM*:

> *"God is thought of as cruel because we are born into this world in pain, grow up attended by suffering, and as adults learn sorrow, separation*

405

and death. IF this were the real world, God WOULD be cruel. To the ego there is no escape from guilt. Guilt hides Christ from your sight. As long as you believe the Son of God is guilty, you will walk the carpet of death! The ultimate purpose of projection, you think, is to get rid of guilt, yet you are just concealing it. The ego's destructive urge is so great that nothing short of crucifixion can ultimately satisfy it.

ℊ *The ego does want to kill you. The ego thinks it is God and guiltlessness is actually interpreted as the final guilt which fully justifies murder! Love and guilt cannot coexist. When you have accepted the Atonement for yourself, you will realize there is no guilt in you. You are not really afraid of the crucifixion. Your real terror is of redemption. Your fear of attack is nothing compared to your fear of love."*

TAKE THAT IN!
Love, Sondra

June 22, 2017

ℊ CHAPTER THIRTEEN (continued)

"The memory of God is covered over by your hostility and hatred. You do not want the separation healed. You secretly know that, by removing that dark cloud, your love for your Father would impel you to answer his call and leap into Heaven (here on earth). You want to hide your intense burning love for God. You think God's love would reduce you to ashes, make you little, make you into nothingness. Your individual death seems more valuable than your living Oneness. You are more afraid of God than the ego. Real Heaven is the greatest threat you think you could experience.

ℊ *You have two true emotions: love and fear. You react to love with fear and draw away from it. Fear attracts you. The ego cannot tolerate release from the past. You consider it natural to use your past experience as a reference point from which to judge the present. Yet this is unnatural because it is delusional. Stay in the present. Other's errors are all past. By perceiving them without sin, you are releasing them. The Holy Spirit will restore your sanity. Do not leave any spot of pain hidden from His light."*

Love, Sondra

June 23, 2017

❧ GIVE UP THE NEED FOR APPROVAL
Are you still driven by the need for approval from your family of origin? We are seeing so many clients with that issue. They are ruled by fear of disappointing the family, hurting them if they do better than parents did, or angering them if they do certain things. In this case, they have not really grown into true adulthood. It is like they have not emotionally "left the nest." Some would call this lack of "individuation."

❧ We need to "disconnect from the family mind." That does not mean you are running away from, rebelling or cutting off from the family. You can still consciously choose to accept their advice and guidance. But, Ammachi says you have to clear the family shadow. That means you get unstuck from their negative patterns and beliefs, and you are no longer run by needing their approval or disapproval. Leonard Orr, my first Rebirthing teacher, said, "The family mind is very intense." Meaning, we are very enmeshed into it, and often do not see how it is affecting our lives negatively. People are often very loyal to the family mind and it is messing up their current relationship. Are you going along with the family mind? Are you going along with their expectations?

❧ We see people doing this even after the parents have died! Maybe you are even perpetuating the roles you had in your blood family. If they are still alive, one has to set clear boundaries with the family. Start with becoming aware when you are feeling disempowered because of this. Become

aware if you are acting out of obligation, guilt, or fear. Maybe you are still unconscious about these entanglements and you need to get conscious about them. In Hawaii it is called cutting the *aka chords* or *psychic attachments*.
Get Free!
Love, Sondra

June 24, 2017

♪ ALOHA!
Today we are taking a Course in Ho'oponopono and healing. It is good to be a student of *Aloha* again.

> ❖ *"A" is the first light of dawn, the spark of God the Father and Goddess the Mother.*
> ❖ *"Lo" is the symbol and sound of eternity.*
> ❖ *"Ha" is breath, the gift, the blessing of life.*

♪ To say Aloha is to remember our gift, what we have been given. It reminds us of our inner greatness.
More later.
Love, Sondra

June 25, 2017

♪ MORRNAH SIMEONA
I am thinking about my teacher, Morrnah Simeona, who originally put out Ho'oponopono in a wonderful modern form for Westerners. I had the most amazing experience meeting her.
♪ I was invited to a luncheon in a home on Waikiki beach in Honolulu. The hostess was so grateful for the LRT that she said I could bring my organizer and my boyfriend. I did not know that there was going to be an honored guest. I had never met a Kahuna (Hawaiian spiritual master) either. When she came through the door and I looked at her, she was shape shifting from a woman to a man. Tears shot straight out of my eyes into the air toward her. I had the privilege of being seated next to her.

❡ Suddenly my head went down to my plate and I was bowing and could not raise up. Then my boyfriend's head went down, and my organizer's head went down, and everyone was prostrated. The hostess came into the dining room and blurted out, "Where is the quiche?" I said kiddingly, "Maybe the chef is on the floor in the kitchen!" still not able to raise up. Guess what, he was!

❡ So I turned my head to the side and said, "Morrnah, would you mind telling me what you are doing?" She replied, "Oh, just a little interplanetary crystal cleansing." Then we were able to sit up! Those were her first words to me, and I began a wonderful student-teacher relationship with her for the next several years. I was so blessed. She is so much on my mind during this course in Washington D.C.
Love, Sondra

June 26, 2017

❡ HO'OPONOPONO
Ho'oponopono is a Hawaiian practice of reconciliation and forgiveness. In the old days, if someone in the family was sick, they would call the Kahuna to the house. The Kahuna would have everyone in the family sit in a circle and insist that everyone would forgive everyone. It was understood that if anyone in the family was sick, it meant that there was anger between some family members. Interesting that it might not be the sick person who was angry. This would maybe take all day. My Kahuna, Morrnah Simeona, put the process in a modern form where you can do it individually, in writing, or from memory. To get the book, you need to take the course. The "short form," talked about in the book *Zero Limits* by Joe Vitale was originally given to students that had already taken and practiced the long form for many years. Ho'oponopono became "popularized" by these phrases:

- ❖ *I am sorry.*
- ❖ *Please forgive me.*
- ❖ *Thank you.*
- ❖ *I love you.*

409

But to have the book with the long form is the best. It puts things right. I love doing the long form, because it is the way I was taught. I recommend you learn this. It is done between you and Divinity. What is going on inside of you that is causing you to experience stress? This will help you release it permanently. It creates balance. It helps you clear relationships, your body, and anything in your life. I have seen so many miracles with this process.
Love, Sondra

June 27, 2017

ꞃ WHO IS CALLED A FRIEND?

> *"He who makes you turn your mind towards the Beloved, he is your best friend. But a person who diverts your thoughts away from Him and tempts you to progress in the direction of death, he is an enemy, not a friend. Try to correct yourself. The man who makes no effort to improve himself is in fact committing suicide."*

ꞃ From Teachings of Sri Anandamayi Ma
ꞃ We are flying to Poland today.
Love, Sondra

June 28, 2017

ꞃ HAPPY TO BE IN POLAND
We arrived in Berlin and were met by our organizers, Krzysztof and Aga, who drove us for two and a half hours to their town in Poland that I cannot spell! (Szczecin?) or pronounce!
ꞃ Krzysztof is a brilliant, enlightened lawyer, and he entertained us a lot with his knowledge of history and politics in Poland, Germany, and Russia. So much to know. He is a Polish lawyer working with German law, mostly for Polish people who work in Germany. I am so amazed how

these people can study law in different languages, which is hard enough in one language.

❡ Aga is a beautiful yoga teacher who works with high-end clients in their homes. They have a wonderful relationship now which has improved every year we have been here. Tomorrow we have lady's day out so I can get a pedicure, Polish style. Looking forward to the LRT. Two people from Warsaw just cancelled because they cannot find a babysitter for their dogs! Today is Aga's birthday so we are going out on the town!   Love, Sondra

June 29, 2017

❡ ESSENE GOSPEL OF PEACE
Markus is reading the books of the *Essene Gospels of Peace*, which are translated by Edmond Bordeaux Szekely from the Dead Sea Scrolls. I opened to this page which is perfect for Liberation Breathing:

> *The third communion is with*
> *The Angel of Air,*
> *Who spreads the perfume*
> *Of sweet-smelling fields,*
> *Of Spring grass after rain,*
> *Of the opening buds of the*
> *Rose of Sharon.*
> *We worship the Holy Breath*
> *Which is placed higher*
> *Than all other things created,*
> *For lo, the eternal and sovereign*
> *Luminous space,*
> *Where rule the unnumbered stars,*
> *Is the air we breathe in,*
> *And the air we breathe out.*
> *Angel of Air,*
> *Holy Messenger of the Earthly Mother*
> *Enter deep within me.*

❡ It is so wonderful to have Breathwork. If you have not tried it, I certainly hope you will. It has made my life a miracle and

411

could do the same for you. People love it in every country we visit. What is different about *Liberation Breathing* is that we first spend plenty of time helping someone unravel their preverbal sabotaging thoughts, and we figure out for them how their mind is wired that causes their problems. This makes a huge difference. Then we do Divine Mother prayers at the end of their breathing cycle and a special mantra. To my surprise, it also works really well via Skype. Why stay stuck in any problem?   Love, Sondra

June 30, 2017

❦ MY LAST ADVICE TO YOU

Even if we think or speak negatively about others, the results will be felt by us, since our subconscious is not concerned with the association of our words. Neither is it concerned with the person to whom they refer. It records them all with precise objectivity. The words, "He is not good" will be translated into "I am no good," and will backfire on the speaker in the future. So, it is like this: the only person we are speaking to is our self! Go kindly into your day and be a blessing to others. Forgive all and be a light. I have enjoyed sharing with you. Thanks go to the Divine Mother for these moments we have spent together in these passages. Through them, may you be empowered to have an awesome life!

Love,

Sondra Ray

About the Authors

SONDRA RAY, author of 22 books on the subjects of relationships, healing, and spiritual matters, was launched into international acclaim in the 1970s as one of the pioneers, along with Leonard Orr, of the Rebirthing Experience. She has trained thousands of people all over the world in this conscious connected breathing process and is considered one of the foremost experts on how the birth trauma affects one's body, relationships, career, and life. As she puts it, "This dynamic breathing process produces extraordinary healing results in all of your relationships—with your mate, with yourself, and with Life—very fast. By taking in more Life Force through the breath, limiting thoughts and memories, which are the cause of all problems and disease, come to the surface of the mind so they can be 'breathed out', forgiven, and released."

Applying over 40 years of metaphysical study, she has helped thousands of people heal their negative thought structures, birth trauma, habitual family patterns, and unconscious death urge. She encourages people to make lasting positive changes through Liberation Breathing® to be more free, happy, and productive. No matter what Sondra Ray is doing, she is always trying to bring about a higher consciousness. Recently she has written new books on the subject of *Spiritual Intimacy*© and *BABAJI: My Miraculous Meetings with a Maha Avatar*, and *Physical Immortality*, in which she envisions a shift in the current paradigm in relationships around the world to a new level of consciousness—free from anger, conflict and even death.

MARKUS RAY, artist, poet, and twin flame of Sondra Ray, received his training in the arts, holding degrees from the Cleveland Institute of Art and Tyler School of Art of Temple University in Philadelphia. He is the author of a major work, *Odes to the Divine Mother*, which contains 365 prose poems in praise of the Divine Feminine Energy. Along with the Odes are his paintings and images of the Divine Mother created around the world in his mission with Sondra Ray.

Markus is a presenter of the profound modern psychological/spiritual scripture, *A Course in Miracles*. He studied with his master, Tara Singh, for 17 years in order to experience its truth directly. His spiritual quest has taken him to India many times with Tara Singh and Sondra Ray, where Muniraj, Babaji's foremost disciple, gave him the name Man Mohan, "The Poet who steals the hearts of the people". In all of his paintings, writings, and lectures, Markus creates a quiet atmosphere of peace and clarity that is an invitation to go deeper into the realms of inner stillness, silence, and beauty. He teaches, writes. and paints along-side of Sondra Ray, and many have been touched by their demonstration of a holy relationship in action. His iconic paintings of the Masters can be viewed on markusray.com which he often creates while Sondra Ray is lecturing in seminars.

SONDRA RAY'S Author's Portal :

Bit.ly/SondraRay

MARKUS RAY'S Author's Portal :

Bit.ly/MarkusRay

Other Resources

Sondra Ray / – author, teacher, Rebirther, creator of the Loving Relationships Training®, Co-founder of Liberation Breathing® and Quests to Sacred Sites around the world.
Facebook: www.facebook.com/sondra.ray.90
Facebook Fan Page:
www.facebook.com/LiberationBreathing
Twitter: www.twitter.com/SondraRay1008
YouTube: www.youtube.com/SondraRay
Website: www.sondraray.com

Markus Ray / – poet, author, artist, Rebirther, presenter of *A Course in Miracles*, co-founder of Liberation Breathing®,
Facebook: www.facebook.com/markus.ray.169
Facebook Fan Page:
www.facebook.com/LiberationBreathing
Twitter: www.twitter.com/MarkusRay1008
Website: www.markusray.com/

Receive Markus's weekly articles on ART here:

"Art Look" – *an art lovers companion* –
www.markusray.com

301 Tingey Street, SE, #338, Washington D.C. 20003

E-mail: contact@sondraray.com
E-mail: contact@markusray.com

Babaji and The Divine Mother Resources:

Babaji's Ashram in Haidakhan (India)
E-mail: info@haidakhanbabaji.com

Haidakhandi Samaj (India)
E-mail: Info@HaidakhandiSamaj.org

See Sondra Ray & Markus Ray on these Websites:

www.sondraray.com   www.markusray.com

www.facebook.com/LiberationBreathing

We encourage you, our reader, to attend *The Loving Relationships Training* (LRT) which is produced by Immortal Ray Productions all over the world. You can see Sondra Ray & Markus Ray's worldwide teaching schedule on:

www.sondraray.com/programs-seminars/

Also, we encourage you to attend The INDIA QUEST, The BALI QUEST, or other Spiritual Quests that teach and disseminate Liberation Breathing practices, and principles of *A Course in Miracles*, as well as enhance your Divine Connection to various Spiritual Masters. These are also available on: *www.sondraray.com*

Artwork and paintings of the Spiritual Masters by Markus Ray are available on: *www.markusray.com*

Liberation Breathing® Sessions
with SONDRA RAY & MARKUS RAY

Book a Session at bit.ly/LBSession

CHANGING LIVES AROUND THE WORLD

How a Liberation Breathing Session fulfills your deepest desire.

⌘ I was thinking at the end of editing this book, "What could I say to inspire you to take up the wonderful lifestyle of Breathwork that we have devoted our lives to spreading around the world?" What could I say to you, our readers, that would get to the heart and soul of your deepest desire, and help you to fulfill that desire?

❡ What is your deepest desire, if I may ask? To be in good health? To be prosperous and affluent? To be fulfilled in your work? To have a loving family? To feel a general sense of Joy and well-being all the time?

❡ Recently I gave a talk on the redefinition of God when we were in Estonia this year. The closest actual definition of God is a Life Force that pulses and breathes through all things. It is the very atom of Creation Itself. It is the "stuff" of the Cosmos, and it is also the Energetic Force that molds and moves that stuff around into beautiful manifestations. And the true nature of this Movement is Pure Joy.

❡ Our deepest desire, then, must be to harness this Power of the Life Force in order to realize Pure Joy, to make ourselves one with an awareness of this Force of Life by which all things exist. Harnessing this Power produces good health. It surpasses most other notions of well-being. Breathwork, Liberation Breathing in our case, liberates you from problems, thoughts, memories, situations that are causing you stress and discomfort. It makes you aware of the Divine Energy that keeps you alive, in a conscious and simple form of deep continuous breathing. You link one breath with the next, in a kind of circular rhythmic flow. The results are remarkable. You take in actually more Life Force. You awaken new potentials in yourself that were previously asleep. You gain a Divine Connection.

❡ Infusing more mana, or what the Yogi's call prana, into your system of awareness, wakes up your mind and body to a new Power. This Power can then be applied to healing, to change, and to manifesting your desires. First and foremost, it can be used to manifest a quiet mind, forgiving of the past, and make you ever attuned to the beauty of new possibilities of the present.

❡ Defining God as the Life Force, Liberation Breathing gets you more in touch with God directly. And this feels tremendous. It changes everything for the better. It puts more oxygen in your cells, and expands them to release negative cellular memory. You breathe out the negative energy that has been held in the cells, and cleanse your cells with new life. You get in touch with thoughts and memories that have been lodged in your subconscious, keeping you stuck, so you can let them go. Breathwork is a matter of maintaining good health and balance in the mind and body, using the breath to make contact with the actuality of the spirit that can heal and balance, release and transmute all negative charges and vibrations in your system.

¶ Sondra Ray was a registered nurse for 14 years before becoming one of the first Breathworkers in the world. In nursing she saw a lot of people working hard to get well, but the truth is they worked even harder to get sick! Liberation Breathing is the easy path to wellness.

¶ If you have got this far and read her posts in this book, you have a good idea of the insight that Breathwork, and all the adjunct spiritual practices that go along with it, can bring into your everyday life. It is not some woo-woo etheric occult notion of calling on invisible entities in the sky to solve your problems for you. It is a practical use of the tremendous healing Powers of Breath you already possess in yourself. Breathwork awakens them to your disposal.

¶ Why don't you try it? We are available for private, one-on-one Liberation Breathing Sessions anywhere in the world. We conduct them live over a conferencing platform such as Skype, Zoom, FB Messenger, or FaceTime. Sessions last about 1.5 hours, but can go as long as 2 hours. You can book a session here: bit.ly/LBSession. Give your mind and body a chance to rest and reconnect with the essence of your Life Force, the Energy that created you and all the Cosmos. Connect with the Divine, and fulfill your one deepest desire.

Love,

Markus Ray

Come With Us on A Quest to Sacred Sites !

BALI QUEST with SONDRA RAY

♦ **JOIN SONDRA RAY** in this life changing event. Journey to **BALI,** one of the most special places on the planet. Discover your sacred Self at most holy **Besakih Mother Temple.**

♦ Pay homage to the Divine Mother of all LIFE in BALI, and usher in 2019 at one of the "Immortality Power Points". Stretch your mind and open your heart on this profound journey. Visit the sacred waters of **Pura Tirta Empul Temple.**

♦ Arrive in Bali on DEC 3rd and meet the "Mother of Rebirthing", **SONDRA RAY,** to begin this quest of spiritual awakening through **Liberation Breathing®** from the Divine Mother. Witness **Gamelan Music & Balinese Dancing.** Soak up the rich Balinese culture that for centuries has worshipped the Divine Mother in practices of unrivaled beauty and grace.

♦ Total cost of the Bali Quest is $3500 US. ($3000 for Early Reg. Before Sept 1.) This includes transfers to the beautiful **Nefatari Villas of Ubud,** double and quad villa occupancy in traditional Balinese settings, Balinese cuisine, some planned excursions, and Bali Quest training tuition.

♦ **Register Here**: https:// s o n d r a r a y . c o m / programs-quests/

♦ Only 25 Spaces available.

♦ Email <contact@sondraray.com> for info and program.

422